Dialogue and Deviance

Dialogue and Deviance ⤸

Male–Male Desire in the Dialogue Genre (Plato to Aelred, Plato to Sade, Plato to the Postmodern)

Robert S. Sturges

DIALOGUE AND DEVIANCE
© Robert S. Sturges, 2005.

First published in 2005 by
PALGRAVE MACMILLAN™
175 Fifth Avenue, New York, N.Y. 10010 and
Houndmills, Basingstoke, Hampshire, England RG21 6XS
Companies and representatives throughout the world.

PALGRAVE MACMILLAN is the global academic imprint of the Palgrave Macmillan division of St. Martin's Press, LLC and of Palgrave Macmillan Ltd. Macmillan® is a registered trademark in the United States, United Kingdom and other countries. Palgrave is a registered trademark in the European Union and other countries.

Library of Congress Cataloging-in-Publication Data

Sturges, Robert Stuart, 1953–
    Dialogue and deviance : male-male desire in the dialogue genre
(Plato to Aelred, Plato to Sade, Plato to the postmodern) / Robert
S. Sturges.
        p. cm.
    Includes bibliographical references (p.).
    ISBN 0–312–23069–9
    1. Homosexuality in literature. 2. Dialogue. I. Title.

PN56.H57S78 2005   2004053387

A catalogue record for this book is available from the British Library.

Design by Newgen Imaging Systems (P) Ltd., Chennai, India.

First edition: February 2005
10 9 8 7 6 5 4 3 2 1

Printed in the United States of America.

For my sister, Linda Ard,
and in memory of our mother, Barbara Sturges

Contents ◞

Preface ∽

Let me begin by frankly acknowledging that I have come to this project as an amateur, in all senses of the word. "Amateur," for one thing, suggests a lack of professional expertise. Many of the texts I consider in this book might properly be classified as "philosophical dialogues," and, as an English professor with a Ph.D. in Comparative Literature, I indeed lack formal training in philosophy. Furthermore, my academic specialization in medieval English and French literature has been only tangentially relevant to most of the texts considered here, linking as they do ancient Greece and Rome with early modern Italy, Enlightenment France, twentieth-century America, and several modern European cultures, as well as with the high Middle Ages. Important as professional specialization undoubtedly is in the modern academy, however, I would also argue that the academy should always make room for educated amateurs, for those willing to step outside their "areas" and try to see a bigger picture.

And "amateur" also means "lover"; it is as a lover that I come to these texts. I read Plato's *Symposium* and *Phaedrus* seriously for the first time when I encountered them on the Brown University Comparative Literature department's list of "set books" for graduate students, and it was love at first sight. Fusty and old-fashioned as it must seem to a younger generation of queer scholars, Plato helped me, like Oscar Wilde, André Gide, E. M. Forster's Maurice, and Mary Renault's Laurie, come to terms with my own sexuality. And it is as a modern gay man—all terms I use deliberately—seeking to unite my private and professional lives, my love and my work, that I first envisioned this project. My hope is that the positive qualities of the amateur may outweigh the deficiencies, and I have included throughout the following chapters references to recent professionals in these different fields for the benefit of those who wish to follow up some aspect of my argument—or argue against it—in greater detail.

A note on languages: I am a native speaker of English, and have studied several of the other languages in which these texts were originally written in a formal classroom setting: French and German as an undergraduate, Latin in graduate school. In others, Greek and Italian, I am self-taught.

In the following pages, I quote English translations of non-English texts, but in every case I have consulted editions—often more than one—in the texts' original languages as well, and I discuss specific word choices with some frequency, as is required by my primarily descriptive method, which is heavily dependent upon close readings.

Several friends and colleagues have read all or part of this book in manuscript form, and I have greatly benefited from their comments; in particular, I wish to thank in this regard Ed Johnson, Catherine Loomis, and Miriam Youngerman Miller. Marlena Corcoran first made me think I might have something to say about Plato, and her continued encouragement and enthusiasm for this project have been immeasurably important to me.

I also wish to acknowledge the important contributions that my home institution, the University of New Orleans, made to the research for this book: consistent travel funding, a sabbatical in the spring of 2002, and a University Research Professorship beginning in the fall of that year provided the mobility and the time off essential to the completion of such a project. Specifically, I thank John Cooke, Rick Barton, Shirley Laska, Bob Cashner, and Miriam Youngerman Miller. I also gratefully acknowledge the extraordinary efforts of the Earle K. Long Library's Interlibrary Loan department in tracking down obscure and far-flung research materials. Special thanks must go to my colleagues over the years in the team-taught University Honors course on ancient Greek culture, Arts and Sciences 1119, in which I first began seriously thinking about Plato: Ed Johnson, Richard Katrovas, Dana Criswell, Mike Mooney, Joyce Zonana, and Catherine Loomis.

Portions of this book in an earlier form have been presented as lectures and conference papers, and I am grateful to those who helped arrange these presentations, as well as to their audiences, whose questions and comments were most helpful in the laborious refinement of my ideas; I thank especially Robert L. A. Clark, Gina Psaki, Caroline Jewers, István Bejczy, the graduate student audience at the Catholic University of Nijmegen, John Gery, Patricia Roger, and—yet again—Catherine Loomis and Miriam Youngerman Miller.

My final and deepest thanks are reserved for my partner—and, by the time this book is published, spouse—Charles James Davidson, for his unfailing kindness and patience during my five-year obsession, and not least for his utter indifference to philosophical dialogues.

Introduction ⤳

Yesterday, around midnight, they brought us our friend Remon,
who'd been wounded in a taverna fight.
Through the windows we left wide open,
the moon cast light over his beautiful body as he lay on the bed.
We're a mixture here: Syrians, migrated Greeks, Armenians, Medes.
Remon is one of these too. But last night,
when the moon shone on his sensual face,
our thoughts went back to Plato's Charmidis.[1]

—"In a Town of Osroini"

The homosexual Greek poet C. P. Cavafy's great poem of 1917, "In a Town of Osroini," reminds us that Plato, who wrote his philosophical dialogues in the fourth century B.C., has continued to influence writers many centuries later. At first glance, however, this poem appears to be inspired less by Plato's philosophy than by the male–male desire that is the motive force behind some of those dialogues: it is the sensuality of Remon's face, illuminated by the moon, that makes his (presumptively male) friends think of Plato, and what they think of specifically is a character in one of the dialogues, Plato's uncle Charmides (as the name is usually spelled in English). Charmides was, in his youth (when the dialogue is imagined as taking place), famous for his beauty, "the handsomest young man of the day,"[2] and Plato imagines that Socrates' discussion of the virtue of *sophrosune* was inspired by the sight of Charmides' "beautiful body" and "splendid face."[3] Other translations of Cavafy's poem suggests that it is Remon's "amorous" or "erotic," rather than "sensual," face that reminds his friends of Charmides.[4] It is thus the male–male eroticism of Plato's dialogues that inspires the modern homosexual poet as Charmides inspired Socrates: "I saw inside his cloak and caught on fire and was quite beside myself."[5]

But there's more to Cavafy's poem than homoeroticism, important as male–male desire is throughout his work. The speaker of the poem is a member of a community of exiles, as is the beautiful Remon: the events recounted here are imagined as having taken place in the ancient Mesopotamian kingdom of Osroini,[6] and neither Remon nor the poem's speaker nor their friends are at home there, belonging as they do to a "mixture" of alien nationalities. Nevertheless, all these different men (and it seems to be a community of men that is imagined here) are reminded of the same thing when they look at Remon's beauty: they all differ from one another as well as from the dominant culture in which they find themselves, and yet they are also and simultaneously united, not only by their admiration for Remon, but by the recollection of Plato that Remon's beauty inspires in all of them. They are part of, and even define, the mixed culture of Osroini even as they acknowledge that they are outsiders; they are simultaneously different from and the same as one another. What unites these dissimilar men is their membership in the larger culture, their desire—and Plato.

Cavafy's poem describes a scene in which no words are spoken, but it refers to a scene of dialogue: "Plato's Charmidis" refers to the name of a character, but also to the title of the Socratic dialogue in which he appears; in recalling one, Remon's friends are necessarily also recalling the other. *Charmides* is one of Plato's early, so-called Socratic dialogues, in which Socrates and his interlocutors try out various definitions of the subject under discussion, in this case *sophrosune*, without arriving at any satisfactory conclusion; thus Cavafy's reference to "Plato's Charmidis" recalls both the virtue under discussion in it and the Socratic *elenchus*—the philosophical method involving questions and discussion rather than resolution—as well as desire between men.

This book maps the same territory explored by Cavafy's poem: the relationship between male same-sex desire and the genre of dialogue—especially as this genre is historically conditioned by some of Plato's works—in different periods of Western culture. This is a previously unexplored relationship that has nevertheless persisted throughout Western cultural history from the Greeks to the late twentieth century, as "In a Town of Osroini" suggests. The dialogue, in fact, in at least some of its manifestations, has proven to be a remarkably hospitable and attractive form for the discussion of male–male desire as it exists at all points on the homosocial–homosexual continuum, from competition to friendship to erotic passion. The relationship between desire and dialogue is not, however, an unchanging or ahistorical one; both the form of the dialogue itself and its treatment of male–male desire have been constantly reworked and modified over the centuries in a reflection of more general cultural–historical changes. This book, then, in its examination of selected dialogues from Plato to the 1990s, attempts to contribute to an understanding not only of the dialogue genre, but also of the changing, culturally specific constructions of desire between men, and the place of such desires within various Western cultural contexts.

My method is primarily descriptive, and employs close readings of the various dialogues and some related texts in order to outline the historically changing shape of these relations without losing sight of the unique specificity of each author's contribution to them. I attempt no grand overview of the history of either male–male desire in the West (an unwieldy project, which in any case has already been admirably attempted by David Greenberg[7]) or of the dialogue as a genre, nor do I make any claim to discuss every dialogue concerned with male–male desire. I limit myself instead to the examination of several distinctly observable literary–philosophical traditions in which the changing relations between dialogue and male–male desire are adumbrated with particular clarity. Neither do I intend to make any overarching theoretical claims about this relationship: obviously most dialogues are not directly concerned with male–male desire (though I argue that perhaps more dialogues share this concern, at least implicitly, than has been generally recognized), nor does a culture's interest in, or anxiety about, male–male desire always find expression in the dialogue form (though I also argue that some texts not traditionally considered dialogues nevertheless draw productively on the dialogue genre and its traditions). But the relationship between the two has been persistent enough in Western culture since Plato to deserve closer investigation and description.

Why should the dialogue genre and male–male desire be linked? One answer is that the relations between them exist in a specifically Platonic tradition: Plato is perceived throughout subsequent Western history as the first and most productive investigator of male–male desire (whether this aspect of his work is embraced or disavowed), and his investigations are carried out in dialogue form.[8] Later writers in the dialogue traditions that I examine thus usually invoke Plato, approvingly or disapprovingly, as an apologist for male–male desire. It is this explicit or, less frequently, implicit presence of Plato that makes the relationship between dialogue and this form of desire a recognizable tradition.

Or, as we shall see, several traditions. Every age constructs, and responds to, a different version of Plato, and while these versions or traditions overlap in time, changing cultural concerns bring different Platonic texts into prominence in different historical periods. While a number of Plato's dialogues (*Charmides, Laws*, etc.) deal to some extent with male–male desire, I examine the traditions initiated by three of them in particular. One line of influence, implicitly or explicitly acknowledged by each of the authors in it who follow Plato, leads from Plato's *Lysis* through Cicero's *De Amicitia* to the medieval dialogues on Christian friendship by Aelred of Rievaulx and his followers, and concerns friendship, variously defined. Another tradition moves from Plato's *Symposium* to the Italian humanist and French Enlightenment dialogues that deal with the varying relations between physical and spiritual love, a line of influence again more or less explicitly acknowledged by such authors as Marsilio Ficino, Baldassare Castiglione, Tullia d'Aragona, Antonio Vignali, Antonio Rocco, Denis Diderot, and the Marquis de Sade. A third version of Plato, implicit throughout the history of the Platonic dialogue, emerges as especially significant in modern culture: this is the Plato of the *Phaedrus*, concerned explicitly with the relationship of desire to discourse, and *Phaedrus* is the dialogue appropriated most often by modern authors from Oscar Wilde and André Gide to Thomas Mann, E. M. Forster, Mary Renault, and Robert M. Pirsig.[9] The three traditions have certain concerns in common, and I will be particularly interested in how all these texts understand the relations of sameness and difference,[10] but they also address distinct concerns of special cultural relevance in different periods. My conclusion takes up the postmodern appropriation of Plato in John Cameron Mitchell's *Hedwig and the Angry Inch* and Eve Kosofsky Sedgwick's *A Dialogue on Love*, and the interrogation of the very concept of "male–male" desire in these two texts.

Like the three Platonic dialogues, Cavafy's poem is also concerned with sameness and difference and with the possibility that the two can coexist: Remon's friends are described as being simultaneously different (from the culture in which they live and from one another) and yet united (as existing within that alien culture and as desiring, Platonic subjects). This relationship of simultaneous sameness and difference is what I call "deviance," though in doing so I emphasize difference; the term "proximity" also arises at certain points in this book to denote the same phenomenon, but with an emphasis on sameness. In both cases what interests me is a sameness that is not identity, or a difference that is not opposition.

One way of understanding deviance and deviation that I have found compelling in the context of male–male desire is Jonathan Dollimore's in his book *Sexual Dissidence*. Dollimore suggests that "deviance" does not properly suggest a binary opposition to a cultural straight and narrow path, but only a "deviation" from it. This is to say that the deviant relation to the normative is one of proximity or even inclusion rather than opposition, as Remon's friends, though aliens, are nevertheless also included in the culture of Osroini, and even give it its mixed identity. Deviance implies a sameness that includes or contains difference. The dialogues that address male–male desire, I argue, invariably understand it as deviant from (or proximate to) the dominant culture in this sense, though this deviance is differently constructed and differently valued according to the specific society and historical period in which the norm is established, and also according to the values, whether normative or oppositional, of the individual writers who respond to these cultural norms.

Writing admiringly of Oscar Wilde's erotic and discursive transgressions and their relations with the dominant discourses of his culture, Dollimore points out that

> it is because and not in spite of this shared cultural dimension that Wilde can enact one of the most disturbing of all forms of transgression, namely that by which the outlaw turns up as in-law, and the other as proximate proves more disturbing than the other as absolute difference. That which society forbids, Wilde reinstates *through and within* some of its most cherished and central cultural categories. . . . At the same time as he appropriates those categories, he also transvalues them through perversion and inversion, thus making them now signify those binary exclusions . . . by which the dominant culture knows itself. . . .[11]

"Deviance" in this definition is related to the Lacanian concept of "*extimité*," intimate otherness, that which in psychoanalytic theory questions the opposition between what is within and what is without, indeed questions the very difference between inside and outside, self and not-self.[12] This concept has recently been linked in medieval studies both to Dollimore's "deviance" and to the postmodern term "queer," "both secret inside and forbidden exterior to all that is straight and normal."[13] Far from being a phenomenon limited to late-nineteenth-century England, this deviant or resistant transvaluation of cultural categories thus has a long history, at least where the categories of gender and sexuality are concerned: "One kind of resistance, operating in terms of gender, repeatedly unsettles the very opposition between the dominant and the subordinate. I call this sexual dissidence."[14] Cavafy, too, elsewhere suggests something of this specifically homosexual deviance, the "deviate, sensual delight" that also has its place in defining the dominant culture's vigor through its poetry: "But how the life of the artist has gained. / Tomorrow, the next day, years later, the vigorous verses / will be composed that had their beginning here."[15]

This sort of deviance marks the dialogue genre whenever it addresses male–male desire, and indeed the dialogue turns out to be perhaps the genre best suited to the exploration of deviance. A dialogue is precisely not a quarrel or disagreement between opposing points of view, but a form in which deviant views are allowed a voice *in conversation* with the cultural dominant, and in which men (and sometimes women) can also explore their deviations from, as well as their proximity to, one another. The relation between Socrates and his interlocutors in Plato's dialogues is one of proximity rather than opposition, and while the dissident voices in such a dialogue may ultimately be subsumed in or contained by a dominant voice, the dominant could not exist without the deviant. The classic example would be Diotima's speech in the *Symposium*, which is presented as the one true response to the question of the nature of love that has been debated by multiple voices throughout the dialogue. Socrates condemns all the other speeches as false answers, but his recollection of Diotima's teachings nevertheless includes elements of all of these rejected deviant voices.[16] And Diotima's speech, recommending the repression of physical desire, itself deviates from the Athenian cultural norm (more tolerant of the physical expression of male–male desire), which is expressed in Phaedrus' speech in the same dialogue. The *Symposium* thus creates a new cultural ideal, from which later writers may themselves deviate.

Indeed, although Dollimore nowhere discusses the dialogue as a genre, some of his reflections on "sexual dissidence" could almost serve as definitions of it:

> this concept of the perverse dynamic denotes certain instabilities and contradictions within dominant structures which exist by virtue of exactly what those structures simultaneously contain and exclude. The displacements which constitute certain repressive discriminations are partly enabled via a proximity which, though disavowed, remains to enable a perverse return, an undoing, a transformation.[17]

The proximity of, say, Rameau's nephew to the narrator of Diderot's dialogue is indeed disavowed, but the dialogue form—conversation rather than binary opposition—makes the perverse return and transformation almost inevitable. One might say the same of Mann's Aschenbach reimagining the *Phaedrus*. It is also possible to argue that certain dialogues—Plato's *Lysis*, for example—can be understood as "pure" deviance (i.e., dialogues in which no single perspective is established as the dominant), as we shall see in chapter 1.

Dollimore is concerned with the deviance of male–male desire from a cultural norm. I also focus on the other kind of deviation suggested in Cavafy's poem, the difference-within-sameness that defines the participants in a desiring relationship themselves, as Remon's friends are united in their Platonic desire for him. The definition of same-sex desire as essentially narcissistic has not been an uncommon form of homophobia in our own period: modern conservative philosophers like Roger Scruton have suggested that homosexuality represents not only a desire for sameness, but also a fear of otherness, a narcissistic refusal to engage with what is not like oneself.[18] While, on the one hand, one might not wish to disavow the myth of Narcissus too quickly,[19] the dialogues I examine in this book also suggest just how crude a distinction it is that defines sameness and difference exclusively by genital type. Differences in age and/or status, sometimes also expressed as the difference between the insertive and receptive roles, also appear as essential components of desire—both friendly and erotic— in many of the texts discussed here, and indeed in this situation genital sex may not even be understood as the primary marker of difference: for many ancient writers, and indeed their followers in later periods, women and boys might be equally differentiated from adult men, and hence equally desirable. Within the erotic dynamic of the male–male relationship itself, as well as in the cultural relations discussed above, desire between men is thus almost always a matter of deviation, of various differences existing within an overarching similarity of (genital) type.[20] This kind of deviance, that which occurs within the dynamic of the male–male erotic relationship itself, is addressed explicitly in such humanist texts as Vignali's and Rocco's, and reappears in such modern dialogical novels as Mann's and Forster's.

Two theorists of dialogue and the dialogical also stand in the background of this book, M. M. Bakhtin and Martin Buber, as do the more recent reinterpretations of Bakhtin by Julia Kristeva and of Buber by Emmanuel Levinas. While Bakhtin is known primarily as a theorist of the novel, and his notion of dialogism as a way of understanding a novelistic author's relations with his or her characters and readers, he also regularly addresses non-novelistic genres, including the dialogue itself. Although a line of dialogue, according to Bakhtin, "may well refer to the object without any mediation," more often it is "oriented toward another speech act, one . . . which the line of dialogue reflects upon, or replies to, or anticipates."[21] In this dialogical situation,

> Every utterance, while focused on its referential object, at the same time displays an intensive reaction to another utterance, either replying to it or anticipating it. . . . Once the counterstatement (*Gegenrede*) is taken into consideration, certain specific changes in the structure of dialogic discourse come into play: dialogue becomes an arena of events within itself and its very topic of discourse is seen in a new light, disclosing new facets inaccessible to monologic discourse.[22]

Kristeva's reading of Bakhtin goes further, and understands the dialogism of the Socratic dialogue as a carnivalesque plurality of voices:

> Nietzsche accused Plato of having ignored Dionysian tragedy, but Socratic dialogue had adopted the dialogical and defiant structure of the carnivalesque scene. According to Bakhtin, Socratic dialogues are characterized by opposition to any official monologism claiming to possess a ready-made truth. Socratic truth ("meaning") is the product of a dialogical relationship among speakers; it is correlational and its relativism appears by virtue of the observers' autonomous points of view.[23]

The dialogues I consider in the remainder of this book demonstrate these qualities to different degrees: not all texts that are dialogical in form avoid monologism, and those authors who are primarily interested in expounding a particular philosophical point of view tend to eliminate the truly dialogical in Bakhtin's sense, reducing their interlocutors to mere foils. Where male–male desire is concerned, "dialogues" that support a dominant cultural norm, whatever it may be, thus tend to be less genuinely dialogical in spite of their form: Marsilio Ficino's commentary on the *Symposium*, for example, though structured as a dialogue, is entirely monological in its condemnation of male–male desire, at least in its physical expression. But dialogues that question the norm may also turn monological: the Marquis de Sade's *La Philosophie dans le boudoir* is undoubtedly set in opposition to several cultural norms, but tends toward the monological in its obsessive solipsism. It is those authors most fully committed to the genuinely dialogical possibilities of the genre as defined by Bakhtin—Plato, Aelred, Tullia d'Aragona, and others—who seem most willing to embrace deviance; it is in their works that male–male desire as a "topic of discourse" comes to be seen "in a new light."

What makes a dialogue more or less genuinely dialogical? If Bakhtin is the twentieth century's great literary theorist of the dialogical, the great modern theologian of the dialogical is Martin Buber. The radical rethinking of relationality in his *I and Thou* takes encounters with the other out of the realm of knowledge and experience, because relating to the other as an object of knowledge or experience reduces the other, Thou or You, to a possession of the self, to It. Relationality for Buber occurs in the space between I and You, in the primal encounter that does not appropriate the other to the self. This in-between space is the space of the "primal actuality of dialogue,"[24] which is initiated in uttering the basic "word pair I–You."[25] Dialogical language is for Buber the special province of life with other human beings, which is also characterized by "eros":[26]

> Here language is perfected as a sequence and becomes speech and reply. Only here does the word, formed in language, encounter its reply. Only here does the basic word go back and forth in the same shape; that of the address and that of the reply are alive in the same tongue; I and You do not only stand in a relationship but also in firm honesty. The moments of relation are joined here, and only here, through the element of language in which they are immersed.[27]

Authentic language—in which both participants are immersed, rather than possessing it, as Buber insists[28]—must be dialogical in its encounter with the other. As in the case of Bakhtin's dialogism, Buber's is reproduced to varying degrees in the dialogues I examine: those dialogues that allow for the possibility of becoming an "arena of events within itself" and thus for understanding male–male desire "in a new light," to use Bakhtin's terms, are also those that use language to stage this authentic encounter with the other—whether they represent such an encounter as taking place within the dialogical text itself or encourage the reader's own encounter with the text. It is, in fact, this relationship of "honesty" in Buber's sense, the encounter with another in his (or her) otherness, that determines how genuinely dialogical, in Bakhtin's sense, a text may be.

For Buber, Socrates as represented in Plato's dialogues is the best representative of the honest dialogical use of the first person: "It is the I of infinite conversation. . . . This I lived in that relation to man which is embodied in conversation. It believed in the actuality of men and went out toward them. Thus it stood together with them in actuality and is never severed from it."[29] As we shall see, Socrates in Plato's dialogues engages in this dialogical relation not only with his represented interlocutors, but within himself,[30] and perhaps most importantly with the readers and writers who follow him: later writers' dialogues with Plato's Socrates in the traditions that Plato initiates may be as "honestly" dialogical—or not—as the dialogues represented in their texts.

Buber's concerns were primarily theological; for him, human relationality is metaphorical: "[t]he relation to a human being is the proper metaphor for the relation to God."[31] This approach may also be helpful for readers in a secular age in understanding the importance of dialogue to earlier writers who address the divine as well as the human. "Now we may say that God carries his absoluteness into his relationship with man. Hence the man who turns toward him need not turn his back on any other I–You relationship: quite legitimately he brings them all to God and allows them to become transfigured. . . ."[32] From Socrates' invocations of the Greek gods in Plato to Aelred's Christian prayers to the humanists' neoplatonic ascent to Wilde's sense of sin to the renewed evocations of Dionysus in Mann's and Forster's fictions to Hedwig's multicultural divinities and Sedgwick's Buddhist explorations, the majority of the dialogical texts considered here situate dialogue in some religious context, and the changing nature of that religious context, too, will condition the relations between dialogue and male–male desire.

The recent reinterpretation of Buber's thought in several essays by Emmanuel Levinas stresses the same notion of "proximity"—to the divine or to the human interlocutor—that I have linked to deviance above:

> Persons who speak to one another confirm one another, unique and irreplaceable. In this there is a faithfulness on Buber's part to a tradition characteristic of Jewish mysticism itself. The mystic never speaks to himself in the second person as if he had entered into God, as if the moth that circled the fire were burned by the fire. Never coincidence, always proximity.[33]

Dialogue for Levinas here is precisely that which does not appropriate or identify itself with the other, but only approximates or allows the speaker to stand beside the other in that relationship of similarity without identity, difference without opposition, that I call deviance. "[H]uman spirituality—or religiosity—lies in the fact of the proximity of persons, neither lost in the mass nor abandoned to their solitude."[34]

As the examples above demonstrate, my working definition of "dialogue" is reasonably loose without being all-encompassing. All dialogues balance the philosophical with the fictional to some extent, and I have not hesitated to use those in which the fictional predominates, and which are generally classified as "fiction" (*Der Tod in Venedig, Zen and the Art of Motorcycle Maintenance*) or even as "musical" (*Hedwig and the Angry Inch*) as well as those conventionally labeled "philosophy" (Plato's dialogues, *De Amicitia*). Most fall into the gray area in between (Aelred's and Wilde's dialogues, *La Philosophie dans le boudoir, Corydon*). As Bakhtin suggests, dialogism—the interplay of dissident voices—is a novelistic impulse, perhaps the defining characteristic of the novel;[35] I therefore prefer not to draw excessively rigid boundaries between or among the genres.

The wide historical range also suggested in the preceding paragraphs—from Plato to the late twentieth century of *Hedwig and the Angry Inch*—is justified, of course, by the texts themselves: virtually every dialogue discussed in this book refers to some historically distant precedent. Nevertheless, I have tried to emphasize that this convenient continuity needs to be tempered by historical consciousness: what constitutes the "dominant discourse" changes radically over time. Obviously, the Platonic privileging of a certain form of male–male desire was not the dominant discourse of Ficino's period, or Wilde's (or even, exactly, of Plato's). And if, as Foucault suggests, it is the dominant discourse that constructs the minority or dissident discourses within it,[36] they too must change over time. This study seeks, in its examination of the three separate traditions, each emerging as particularly relevant in a different historical period, to understand the changing nature of deviance—the proximate relation of dominant to dissident, of same to different, of self to other—in changing historical contexts, through an exploration of those dialogical texts in which such relations appear with particular clarity.

Despite the historical distance between us and most of the dialogues to be discussed in this book, it is my hope that the reader can also experience some sense of this proximity to at least some of them as well, as I have in reading and writing about them. While we may not legitimately identify historically distant forms of desire between men with our own modern concepts of "homosexuality" or "gayness," there would be no reason, beyond antiquarianism, to interest ourselves in that aspect of these dialogues, if they did not also speak to us of male–male desire as we encounter it now. In this regard, I have found Eve Kosofsky Sedgwick's term "reparative reading" inspirational.

In the introduction to a collection of essays entitled *Novel Gazing*, Sedgwick described the theoretically unsophisticated response of a queer child encountering a literary text that appears to validate her or his queer existence: "a kind of *genius loci* for queer reading," suggests Sedgwick,

> is the interpretive absorption of the child or adolescent whose sense of personal queerness may or may not (*yet?*) have resolved into a sexual specificity of proscribed object choice, aim, site, or identification. Such a child— if she reads at all—is reading for important news about herself, without knowing what form that news will take; with only the patchiest familiarity with its codes; without, even, more than hungrily hypothesizing to what questions this news may proffer an answer. The model of such reading is hardly the state of complacent adequacy that Jonathan Culler calls "literary competence," but a much more speculative, superstitious, and methodologically adventurous state where recognitions, pleasures, and discoveries seep in only from the most stretched and ragged edges of one's competence.[37]

The image of the queer child reading hungrily for information about herself and her relation to the cultural world she inhabits must be a resonant one for any reader who has ever been such a child. Rather than critical competence, or a critical theory, or even an understanding of basic literary and historical codes, such a reader has instead her desire for recognitions and discoveries that may be pleasurable, and that may assist her in gaining knowledge of her own erotic aims, sites, identifications. It is in this spirit that at least some of the authors I examine in this book read and appropriate their predecessors, identifying with them across historical divides and inviting future readers to make similar identificatory leaps. I take up the question of past history's current relevance again in my conclusion, and I hope that my own readings are not historically naïve, but I also hope that they may provide some of the pleasures of recognition and identification for which I myself continue to read.

1. Erotics of Friendship: From Plato's *Lysis* to Aelred of Rievaulx ✏

In this chapter, I describe the intersection between one particular form of male–male desire and the philosophical-dialogue genre. It occurs in the line of influence extending from Plato's early work *Lysis* through the philosophical dialogues of Cicero—primarily *On Friendship* (*Laelius de amicitia*) and the *Tusculan Disputations* (*Tusculanae disputationes*)—to certain medieval dialogues: the *Spiritual Friendship* (*De spiritali amicitia*) of Aelred of Rievaulx and the epitomes of Aelred's work by his adaptors, Thomas of Frakaham and Peter of Blois. This line of influence is clear-cut: Cicero's debt to the *Lysis* (by way of Aristotle, Xenophon, and Theophrastus) in his own writings on friendship (and on other relations between men) is widely acknowledged,[1] and Aelred in turn discusses his own debt to Cicero directly (while Thomas and Peter essentially rewrite Aelred). These works continued to be read and to exert an influence long after the Middle Ages, but the specific tradition I am concerned with here—that which can be traced to Plato, and in which the dialogue form is used to discuss friendships between men—is most potent in this direct line from Greece to Rome to the European Middle Ages.

"Friendship" is the term most often used to describe the subject matter of these dialogues: its Latin equivalent appears in the titles of Cicero's, Aelred's, and Peter's works, and even Plato's *Lysis* is traditionally subtitled "on friendship" (*peri philias* [περί φιλίας]). In none of these cases, however, can it be assumed that such terms refer exactly to the modern notion of friendship, which is usually understood to exclude the erotic. Indeed, David Konstan demonstrates that even in classical Athens, the term *philos*, "friend," designates "a party to a voluntary bond of affection and good will, and normally excludes both close kin and more distant acquaintances"[2]— which does not sound very different from the modern understanding.

But for Plato in the *Lysis, philia*, usually translated "friendship" but also including other forms of bond or affiliation, to some extent also implies *eros*, or desire, which can include erotic desire in the modern sense, as Konstan recognizes: "[in the *Lysis*] Socrates casually collapses the difference between *philia, erōs*, and *epithumia* . . . and the discussion moves freely among cases of parental affection, erotic attraction, attachment between friends, and even the appeal of inanimate objects. . . . In this respect, the inquiry begun in the *Lysis* is completed by the investigation of *erōs* in the *Symposium*."[3] Friendship and the erotic thus coexist, in the *Lysis*, on a continuum of male–male relations. And while Cicero and Aelred both go out of their way to exclude the erotic from their accounts of friendship, in Aelred's case, at least, it reappears in only slightly disguised forms. What friendship potentially means for these writers in their different cultural contexts must be investigated separately for each, even as we simultaneously recognize their transhistorical connections. (My own continued use of "friendship" to translate *philia* should be understood to include the various other bonds described above.)

The *Lysis* is usually considered one of Plato's early dialogues:[4] in it, he shows Socrates using the *elenchus*—the famous "Socratic method" of questions and answers—to investigate the nature of friendship, or *philia*. He arrives, after trying out various approaches to the problem of friendship, at the negative conclusion (also typically associated with the *elenchus*) that neither he nor those with whom he is speaking truly can say what *philia* is. This structure is typical of Plato's "Socratic" dialogues, so called because they are often taken to represent the manner in which the historical Socrates led his real-life interlocutors to an understanding, not of a positive doctrine, but only of their own ignorance. It is because Plato does not advance any philosophical doctrine of his own in these dialogues—the famous "Theory of Forms" that he pursues in some other dialogues, for example, is notably absent from them—but rather follows closely the negative method of his predecessor Socrates that they are considered by many to be early writings. These dialogues are, however, of considerable interest in their own right, and not merely as representations of the negative Socratic *elenchus* or as forerunners of the Theory of Forms: in its specific dialogic structure, the way it constantly shifts from one approach to another, the *Lysis*, like a number of other Socratic dialogues, exemplifies a constant process of deviation, a pure deviance without any sign of a straight and narrow philosophical path that might give these deviations a center, or even an attainable goal. The various approaches to the problem of friendship, and the possible solutions to which they lead, are all different, yet related; they deviate from one another, not from a central doctrine.

In terms of this dialogue's form, then, friendly or erotic relations between men, like the topics discussed in the other Socratic dialogues, exist here as a set of propositions constantly differing from one another, none of which, in Socrates' opinion, turns out to be exactly right (or at least he claims, at the end, not to know what can be truly said about friendship or *philia*).

In content, the *Lysis* also introduces the themes of likeness and unlikeness, or sameness and opposition, along with the theme (also present in the dialogue's form, as we have seen) of what I call here deviance—difference without unlikeness, that which is neither identical nor opposite but somewhere in between—which will remain influential through the Middle Ages and, as we shall see in subsequent chapters, beyond. Relations between men are seen at certain points in the *Lysis* (i.e., in certain of the propositions on friendship that Socrates tentatively advances) to depend upon a likeness between them, at other points upon an unlikeness, and at still other points upon that which is neither one nor the other, or perhaps even upon that which includes elements of both. The ever-deviating structure of the *Lysis* is thus a reflection of the recurring themes of likeness, unlikeness, and deviation from likeness. These observations should become clearer as we proceed.

The *Lysis* tells the story of how two of Socrates' acquaintances, Hippothales and Ctesippus, draw him into a discussion of friendship with two boys, Lysis and Menexenus, who are themselves close friends. After trying out various approaches to a definition of friendship, or what it means to be a friend, in conversation with the boys, Socrates admits that he does not know what can be truly said on this subject. The boys are eventually taken home by their attendants, even though Socrates and the others try to drive these slaves away.

The story begins, literally, with a departure from the straight and narrow path. Socrates, the first-person narrator of the frame story in which the dialogue is embedded, is walking along the road that leads from the Academy to the Lyceum. (These institutions, two *gymnasia* or exercise fields outside the walls of Athens, would become the locations respectively of Plato's and Aristotle's schools, but were already school sites in Socrates' period.[5]) In his opening words, Socrates emphasizes the directness of the path he wishes to follow, and this emphasis is echoed at several points early in the dialogue. Socrates begins by stating, "I was on my way from the Academy straight [*euthu* (εὐθὺ)] to the Lyceum, along the road outside the wall and close under the wall itself" (p. 17, 203a).[6] The Greek term *euthu* (εὐθὺ), "straight," suggests a kind of single-minded determination to arrive at his goal as quickly and directly as possible, with perhaps a moral connotation of "straightforward" as well.[7] When Socrates encounters his acquaintances

Hippothales and Ctesippus and they ask him where he is going, he repeats the same formula: "I'm on my way straight [εὐθὺ] to the Lyceum" (p. 17, 203b). He is quickly diverted from his original path, however: Hippothales uses Socrates' own "straight" words to tempt him away from the straight road: " 'Come here, then,' he said, 'straight [εὐθὺ] to us' " (p. 17, 203b). After some discussion, Socrates does leave his path and accepts the young men's invitation. The repeated use of the same adverb, *euthu*, three times in a few lines, suggests a heavy emphasis on directness, rapidity, *straightness* in Socrates' original intention—as well as the abandonment of these qualities when he is led to turn aside from his literal road, a physical turning that will also lead him into discourses that are anything but straightforward, quick, or direct.

In fact, the dialogues that Socrates eventually holds with the two boys, Lysis and Menexenus, are quite different from the road he originally intended to take: just as he abandons his literal path, so he repeatedly abandons the various philosophical paths that he tries out in his attempt to discover the nature of friends and friendship. For instance, having logically eliminated "those who love" (*philountes* [φιλοῦντες], suggesting affectionate rather than passionate love), those who are loved, and those who both love and are loved as worthy of being called friends, Socrates and his young interlocutors agree to abandon this path of inquiry:

> And I said, "Lysis, in my opinion what you say is true, that if we had been examining correctly, we would never have wandered [*eplanometha* (ἐπλανώμεθα)] so. But let's not go in that direction any longer, for indeed that examination appears to me like a quite difficult path. Instead, we need to go on, in my opinion, from where we turned aside . . ." (p. 34, 213e)

The philosophical discourse is itself a path (*hodos* [ὁδὸς]), here likened to the original, literal road: in both cases Socrates is unable to stay on the straight and narrow (aimless wandering having now replaced straightness), and in neither case is he able to reach his goal, at least not within the text of the dialogue. For Socrates' attempts to return to the straight philosophical path are regularly foiled; the next approach to a definition of friendship, an attempt to show that those who are alike in goodness would properly be considered friends, also leads him to a dead end: "Consider, then Lysis, where we have gone astray [*parakrouometha* (παρακρουόμεθα)]" (p. 37, 215c). The discourse continually strays and wanders from the straight road that might lead to its goal. And since no goal is ever attained, there seems, in fact, to be no straight road at all, only multiple deviations from it.

Late in the discussion, Socrates, as he is suggesting yet another approach to the problem, declares that the entire argument has made them all drunk: " 'Do you wish, then,' I said, 'since we are drunk [*methuomen* (μεθύομεν)], as it were, from the argument, for us to grant and to declare that what is akin is something other than the like?' " (p. 51, 222c).[8] The sober straight-forwardness of Socrates' original intentions has dissolved into the intoxicating pleasures of the dialogue itself, argumentation that continually subverts its own original goal-direction in the exploration of endlessly proliferating, though attractive, byways, wrong turns, and dead ends.

At the end of the dialogue, Socrates says he had hoped to set off in a new philosophical direction with his older acquaintances: "But as I said these things, I already had in mind to set in motion [*kinein* (κινεῖν)] something else among the older fellows" (p. 52, 223a). The dialogue concludes, however, with the two boys being taken away in a physically new direction, toward home, by their attendants, even though Socrates and his interlocutors have tried to drive these slaves away; the attendants were as drunk on wine as Socrates and his interlocutors were on discourse, and could not be resisted. As they moved off (*apionton* [ἀπιόντων]) on their new road, he tells us, Socrates had to admit that they had not discovered what a friend is (p. 52, 223b). Neither the literal nor the philosophical road has yet come to an end; both remain in process.[9]

One might speculate that Socrates' willingness to continue pursuing his philosophical goal suggests that a single, true solution to the problem of friendship might eventually be found, if only the dialogue could go on long enough and include participants of the right sort.[10] But the dialogue itself emphasizes instead its own constantly diverging twists and turns, its logical byways and new directions, which are reflected in the literal paths, of Socrates and of the two boys, that begin and end the text.

The dialogue's content, as I suggested earlier, parallels (even constitutes) this constantly shifting form. In examining it, we might start by asking what exactly tempts Socrates off his straight road to begin with. How is it that Hippothales and Ctesippus are able to overcome his initial resistance and turn him away from his original goal? And what new goal does he substitute for it?

The definition of friendship eventually becomes the new philosophical goal, but it is not what originally engages Socrates' attention. When his acquaintances first hail him and suggest that he come "straight to us" rather than to the Lyceum, they are inviting him to join them in the *palaestra* or wrestling school, where, they say, Socrates will find "a great many others—good-looking ones [*kaloi* (καλοί)], too" (p. 17, 203b). The first temptation, then, is handsome young men, though Socrates responds more warmly to the promise of speeches or discourses (*logois* [λόγοις]) a few lines later (204a). He quickly returns, however, to the question of these handsome young men, asking Hippothales whom he considers the good-looking one; Hippothales' blushes reveal that he is in love with one of the boys present (204b), as Socrates recognizes, having the god-given ability "to recognize both a lover and a beloved [*eronta te kai eromenon* (ἐρῶντά τε καὶ ἐρώμενον)]" (p. 18, 204c). The dynamics of this relationship are in line with the pederastic ideals of classical Athens: the young adult male, Hippothales, is hoping to assume the role of what modern scholars, following K. J. Dover, usually call an *erastes* (though that term is not used here), or lover, while the boy he loves, Lysis, is classified as his *eromenos*, or beloved, though he has not, it appears, yet accepted Hippothales' advances.[11] If the *erastes* receives erotic gratification from such a relationship, the *eromenos* ideally receives initiation into the adult world of Greek citizenship, and must therefore choose his lover wisely for the potential benefits he may receive. Daniel H. Garrison has recently provided a convenient description of this institutionalized, and idealized, form of pederastic male–male desire in ancient Athens, one that emphasizes not only the participants' sex but, equally important, their social status and sexual roles:

> the most celebrated variety of homoeroticism was a traditional social construct long before the Classical period began. It was something men of the better class did together apart from women of the better class. As often in sexual relationships, there was an understood distinction of roles; the older partner, the initiator and aggressor, the active "lover," or *erastes*, dominated the younger, passive, modest *eromenos*. The role of the *erastes* was to comport himself with moderation and restraint, whereas the young *eromenos* was to display no sexual desire of his own, reciprocating his lover's eros with simple goodwill, *philia*. If he accepted a lover's attentions he was perceived to "gratify" (*kharizesthai*) his suitor out of gratitude (*kharis*) rather than sexual desire, but the gratitude was less for love gifts (never for money) than for the elder man's time and attention. In return for being "gratified" through intercrural sex . . . the older man would introduce the younger boy to adult society and social skills; through this means the *eromenos* would take his place in the male world of wellborn aristocrats, the "beautiful and good" *kalokagathoi*. For the adolescent boy, it was both an education in the customs of his class and a rite of passage to privileged society.[12]

Garrison, like other recent scholars, emphasizes the power relations implied in this relationship, both those that exist between the two lovers (the older partner possessing the social power accorded to an adult male citizen, the younger the power of accepting or rejecting his advances), and those disseminated more widely in Athenian society (the pedagogical aspects of the relationship ensuring the passage of social and political power from older to younger male members of the same class).[13] The issue of power and status will also play its role in Socrates' discussion of *philia*—which, as Garrison suggests, cannot be separated from *eros*, but is implicated in it as the emotion with which the younger partner responds to the elder's erotic desire.

Male–male erotic desire is thus the original topic of Socrates' discussion with Hippothales and Ctesippus, and in some sense it remains the hidden agenda of much of his following dialogues with the two boys. The discourses on friendship that Socrates initiates, first with Lysis and later with Menexenus, which will take up most of the text, are originally intended as an example of how Hippothales should approach the boy he loves in order to ensure success in his pursuit. Indeed, the rhetoric of *eros* is of considerably more interest to Plato than its physical manifestations. Not only the *Lysis*, but the other dialogues I am primarily concerned with in this book, the *Symposium* and *Phaedrus*, as well, focus on how one may most appropriately speak about *eros*, whether in defining it, analyzing its dynamics, or, as here, pursuing it.

Hippothales, it transpires, has been going about his courtship of Lysis in precisely the wrong fashion. Ctesippus complains that he has not only been speaking, but also composing poems and songs, in praise of the boy and his family (205b–d). Socrates perceives, first, that such compositions are really in praise of Hippothales himself: if his pursuit is successful, the virtues of the boy he has been praising will redound to himself (though he also runs the risk of appearing more ridiculous if it fails). Second, and more important for the rest of the dialogue, Socrates also suggests that beautiful boys "are filled full with proud thoughts and bragging whenever someone praises and exalts them" and therefore become "harder to capture" (206a). Hippothales' praise of Lysis is thus ensuring his erotic failure. But how should he proceed instead?

This is precisely the reason Hippothales diverted Socrates from his original path to begin with: " 'But it's because of these things, Socrates, that I'm consulting with you. And if you have anything else, give your advice as to what to say in conversation or what to do so that someone might become endeared to his favorite' " (p. 21, 206c). The temptation of looking at handsome young men was, as we have seen, the first inducement offered to Socrates for diverting him from his path, and the second was that of participating in discourses or speech-making. Here Hippothales combines the two: Socrates is invited to talk about how to talk to these desirable youths, an invitation Hippothales apparently believes he must find irresistible.

Hippothales phrases his request as a general one: he wants advice on how anyone might successfully proceed in his circumstances. But he is also asking how he himself might best approach one specific boy who has already been identified as exceptionally beautiful, and one whom Socrates has apparently already noticed for this reason: according to Ctesippus, " 'I know well that you're far from ignorant of the boy's looks; indeed, he's capable of being recognized just from that alone' " (p. 19, 204e). Responding to Hippothales, Socrates says that it would be difficult to offer the general advice the latter is requesting. However, he then takes this opportunity to engage the beautiful Lysis in conversation for himself: he will, he tells Hippothales, in his own discussion with Lysis, give a concrete example of how Hippothales should court his beloved: " 'But if you were willing to make him enter into discussion with me, perhaps I might be able to display for you what you need to say to him in conversation instead of the things which these fellows assert that you say and sing' " (p. 21, 206c). A. W. Nightingale points out that Socrates' elenchic method is intended to encourage self-knowledge and is therefore opposed to the empty praise of the encomium: Socrates demonstrates the pedagogical duty of a true *erastes* that Hippothales' approach ignores.[14]

But in the context of the *Lysis'* plot, Socrates is also volunteering to act as Hippothales' stand-in in the latter's erotic pursuit of the beautiful Lysis. The ensuing dialogues on friendship thus take place in a highly eroticized context, as Hippothales learns how he may successfully pay court to the boy, allowing Socrates to act as his proxy. The fact that the first dialogue will prove unflattering to Lysis' sense of his own value is presented not only as pedagogical in intent, but also as part of the strategy of seduction. But once again, the focus is on the seductive philosophical argumentation that is to lead to Lysis' acceptance of Hippothales as his lover, not on the physical relations that may eventually ensue: in order to conform to the idealized pederasty of classical Athens, Lysis must come to recognize the virtue of his prospective lover, and therefore his worthiness to be accepted, that is, the intellectual and spiritual benefits he can offer. For Socrates, at least, this understanding can come about only in conversation, that is to say, in dialogue, which Socrates explicitly contrasts with the speeches, poems, and songs that Hippothales has been offering ("the things which these fellows assert that you say and sing"). The true *eros*, that which offers something of value to the beloved, can be pursued, it appears, only through dialogue. And Lysis would seem to be the ideal partner: " 'he is exceedingly fond [*philekoos* (φιλήκοος)] of listening' " (p. 21, 206c). Lysis' "fondness" for listening is related etymologically to the topic about to be discussed, *philia* (φιλία) or friendship, and suggests a cooperativeness or willingness to follow his interlocutor's lead—a desirable quality in the *eromenos* as well.

In the course of this first dialogue, Socrates leads Lysis to an understanding that " 'if you become wise, my boy, all will be your friends and all akin to you—for you will be useful and good' " (p. 29, 210d), using terminology that will be discussed further in the following dialogue that includes Menexenus as well as Lysis. But, unlike Hippothales, whose extravagant praise of the boy threatened to make him proud and thus "harder to capture," Socrates also leads Lysis to an understanding that he lacks wisdom as yet, and still stands in need of a teacher. If praise made Lysis less susceptible to Hippothales' advances, humbling him in this way will presumably make him more receptive, especially since the terms in which he is humbled—the admission that he needs a teacher—might be understood as implying the necessity of accepting an older man's love in the ideal pedagogical sense discussed above:

> "Now is it possible, Lysis, for someone to think big in regard to those matters in which he's not yet thinking?"
> "How could it be?" he said.
> "And if you require a teacher, you're not yet thoughtful."
> "That's true."
> "Therefore, your thoughts are not [too] big, if indeed you're still thoughtless."
> "No, by Zeus, Socrates, not in my opinion." (p. 29, 210d)

If by this point we have forgotten that this first attempt at understanding friendship has been taking place in the context of Hippothales' erotic courtship of Lysis, we now receive an explicit reminder. Having led Lysis to this point, at which his need for a teacher has been admitted, Socrates feels that he has satisfied Hippothales' original request, and is on the verge of telling him so in Lysis' presence:

> And when I heard [Lysis] I looked over toward Hippothales and almost committed a blunder. For it came over me to say, "This, Hippothales, is how one needs to converse with his favorite [*paidikois* (παιδικοῖς)], by humbling him and drawing in his sails instead of puffing him up and spoiling him, as you do." But then I caught sight of him in agony and disturbed by what had been said, and I recalled that though he was standing near Lysis he wished to escape his notice. And thus I recovered myself and held back from the speech. (p. 29, 210e–211a)

We are abruptly brought back to the first dialogue's hidden agenda, that in which Socrates is acting as Hippothales' proxy in the courtship of Lysis. His point has been made: Lysis has been humbled in their conversation, and should now be more receptive to Hippothales' advances. But Hippothales does not appear to be satisfied with this outcome: he is instead "in agony" over what he has heard, for reasons that are not immediately clear. David Bolotin suggests that Hippothales is disappointed because Socrates has simply shown how a lover might encourage his beloved to become wiser, rather than directly encouraging the latter's acceptance of the former's love; Socrates has failed "to leave room in the argument for the exclusive love which he desires from Lysis," and may also seem to Hippothales to have humiliated the boy.[15] But Lysis, though humbled, does not appear to have been humiliated; he has instead enthusiastically agreed with Socrates' points about his own lack of wisdom and need for continued instruction, swearing his agreement by Zeus (literally "by the God," *Ma Dia* [Mὰ Δία]). And Socrates' encouragement of Lysis toward wisdom, as we have seen, does leave room for a pedagogical/pederastic relationship between Lysis and an *erastes*, who might well be Hippothales, though he has not been named; none of this seems like a sufficient cause for Hippothales to be "in agony" (*agonionta* [ἀγωνιῶντα]).

Socrates implies, though he does not explicitly state, a different reason for Hippothales' disturbance when he gives his reason for withholding the comment he had been about to make: Hippothales, though standing nearby with some other listeners, wished not to be noticed by Lysis; when Lysis was first introduced, we learned that "Hippothales, when he saw rather many of them standing near by, screened himself behind them and approached to where he supposed Lysis wouldn't see him, for he feared to incur his hatred. And in this way he stood near and listened" (pp. 22–23, 207b). Hippothales fears rejection, presumably if Lysis discovers his plot to use Socrates as a seducer by proxy; the plan's success, after all, depends upon Lysis being deceived. The later implication of Hippothales' agony, then, seems to be, not that his specific pursuit of Lysis has been ignored, but that the discussion might seem to be pointing too clearly toward Hippothales as its instigator (and as the pedagogue of whom Lysis stands in need), when he would prefer that its hidden agenda not be made so obvious. Socrates therefore refrains from revealing the dialogue's ulterior motive; indeed, he appears here as a conspirator with Hippothales in the (verbal) seduction of Lysis, and in the conspiracy's cover-up, as well. Menexenus, in any case, arrives at this fortuitous moment, and distracts the participants from the direction in which the first dialogue was heading, at least for the time being.

We have not, however, heard the last of this dialogue's underlying erotic motivation. Socrates continues probing into the problem of *philia*, now in conversation with Menexenus as well as with Lysis, and once again it may appear that Hippothales' courtship has been forgotten. This second dialogue is much longer than the previous one between Socrates and Lysis alone, and forms the greater part of the *Lysis* as a whole. It is in this dialogue that the question of who can be considered friends is introduced, and in which the various approaches mentioned above are tried out, one after another. We shall take a look at these different approaches shortly; but to place them in their proper context, we must first examine one further moment in the dialogue that reminds both the participants and the reader of its erotic component.

Socrates now successively introduces the possibilities that those who love (*philein* [φιλεῖν]), those who are loved, those who both love and are loved, those who are alike, those who are unlike, those who are intermediate between the good and the bad, and those who are akin as candidates for friendship, critiquing each possibility in turn. Near the end of the dialogue, in the course of their discussion on kinship, Socrates seems to spring a surprise on the two boys, and perhaps on the reader as well. First, he reintroduces erotic love into the discussion of *philia*, suggesting that desire too plays a role in friendship, and Menexenus agrees: " 'Now is it possible for one who desires and who loves passionately [*eronta* (ἐρῶντα)] not to love [as a friend, *philein* (φιλεῖν)] that which he desires and loves passionately?' 'Not in my opinion, at any rate' " (p. 49, 221b).[16] Erotic love is understood here as including friendship; the true lover (as opposed, presumably, to one whose desire is purely carnal—this distinction will be drawn more explicitly at 222a) must by definition also love his beloved as a friend, though the reverse is not necessarily the case. *Eros* and *philia* thus are not entirely separate experiences, but exist together on a kind of continuum of desire. And for Socrates, desire is always—again, by definition—for that which one lacks:

"Now surely," I said, "that which desires [*epithumoun* (ἐπιθυμοῦν)] desires whatever it is in want of. Isn't that so?"

"Yes."

"Is what is in want, therefore, a friend of that which it is in want of?"

"That's my opinion."

"And it comes to be in want of whatever it is somehow deprived of?"

"How could it not be?"

"It appears, then, Menexenus and Lysis, that passionate love, friendship, and desire happen to be for what is akin, as it seems."

They [both] assented.

"You, therefore, if you are friends to each other, are by nature in some way akin to each other."

"Just so," they [both] said.

"And therefore," I said, "if someone desires another, boys, or loves him passionately, he would never desire, nor love passionately, nor love [as a friend] [*ouk an pote epethumei oude era oude ephilei* (οὐκ ἄν ποτε ἐπεθύμει οὐδὲ ἤρα οὐδὲ ἐφίλει)] unless he happened to be akin in some way to his passionately beloved—either in his soul, or else in some character of his soul, or some of its ways, or some aspect of it."

"Very much so," said Menexenus. But Lysis was silent. (pp. 49–50, 221d–222a)

In this rich and complex passage, Socrates suggests that true, or natural, kinship is kinship of the soul, implying, as Bolotin points out, that it is not necessarily that of the family.[17] Further, the concept of "what is akin" (*oikeiou* [οἰκείου]) is derived logically from that of desire: one desires only that which one lacks. And further still, one lacks only that of which one has been deprived: desire, then, is produced—at least for the purposes of this discussion—by the lack of what one once possessed. This is why Socrates can make the leap that defines "what is akin" as the object of friendship: it is akin because it was once one's own (*hos eoiken* [ὡς ἔοικεν]). Both the term for what is akin (*oikeiou*) and that for what is one's own (*eoiken*) are etymologically related to *oikos* (οἶκος), referring to one's house, household, and possessions; the implication is that one is a friend to that which one desires as one desires lost goods or absent family members, though, as we have seen, a family relationship is not necessary to this natural kinship of the soul. And since friendship has in this instance already been included by definition within erotic desire, Socrates can also make the claim that *eros* operates in the same way, on a continuum with *philia*; we may say, following Garrison, that the erotic desire felt by the *erastes* and the friendly affection felt by the *eromenos* are to this extent similar and reciprocal.[18]

Menexenus agrees to all the steps in Socrates' speculative argument; but Lysis at this point falls silent. This is not unusual: Lysis prefers listening, as we have already been told, and he allows Menexenus to respond on his behalf throughout much of this second dialogue. What is unusual is for his silence to be emphasized as it is here. He seems to see, perhaps better than Menexenus, where Socrates' discussion is heading, and withholds his assent for that reason.[19]

For Socrates is about to spring a trap on his two young interlocutors. Following out his reasoning to its logical conclusion,

"Well," I said, "it has come to light as necessary for us to love what is akin by nature."

"It seems so," he said.

"It is necessary, therefore, for the passionate lover who is genuine, and not pretended, to be loved by his favorite(s)."

Now [both] Lysis and Menexenus, with difficulty, somehow nodded yes, but Hippothales radiated all sorts of colors as a result of his pleasure. (p. 50, 222a–b)[20]

Hippothales' reaction at this point is the opposite of his earlier response: he feels pleasure rather than agony. Even if the dialogue's ulterior, erotic motive is again in danger of being exposed at this point, the discussion has also led the boys—and Lysis in particular, who breaks his former silence to agree with Socrates, however reluctantly—to the logical necessity of accepting the kind of genuine *erastes* that Hippothales apparently considers himself to be. His goal in drafting Socrates as his proxy has seemingly been achieved: Lysis, whose very reluctance to acquiesce demonstrates the desirable qualities of modesty and good breeding, has nevertheless agreed to the logical necessity of reciprocating the love of a true *erastes* such as Hippothales presumably fancies himself to be.

My purpose in dwelling on the erotic components of this dialogue, which, after all, constitute a relatively small portion of the *Lysis* as a whole (as opposed, e.g., to the *Symposium* and *Phaedrus*, where they occupy a much more prominent position) is not to suggest that Plato (or, indeed, Socrates) is in some way endorsing or promoting the physical aspects of male–male *eros*. Such a case could, perhaps, be made: while Plato's late dialogues, notably the *Laws*, forthrightly condemn erotic activity between men,[21] others usually dated earlier—like the *Symposium* and *Phaedrus*, as we shall see—are more playful and ambiguous, even flirtatious. Dover points out that in those two works "Plato takes homosexual desire and homosexual love as the starting-point from which to develop his metaphysical theory," speculating that his social status as an aristocrat who "moved in a section of society which certainly regarded strong homosexual desire and emotion as normal," or even his own "homosexual" desire, might account for the importance he accords it.[22] Dover also focuses on the importance of the dialogue form in this respect:

it is of particular importance that he regards philosophy not as an activity to be pursued in solitary meditation and communicated in *ex cathedra* pronouncements by a master to his disciples, but as a dialectical progress which may well begin in the response of an older male to the stimulus afforded by a younger male who combines bodily beauty with "beauty of soul."[23]

This formula seems particularly applicable to the *Lysis*, in which Socrates initiates a dialogue, in an explicitly erotic context, with a boy described as "someone worth being spoken of not only for being beautiful, but because he was beautiful and good" (p. 22, 207a). Physical attraction, however, in Plato's subsequent works, must yield ultimately to a spiritual *eros* transcending individual bodies and directed at the eternal Forms, until in the *Laws* it is to be suppressed entirely, at least as in its physical manifestations between men. And we have already seen, even in the early *Lysis*, that it is the pleasure of discourse that Socrates finds intoxicating more than the boys' physical beauty, and the verbal argumentation used in erotic pursuit that interests him more than the physical outcome of that pursuit.

And yet the *Lysis* does, like the *Symposium* and *Phaedrus* in Dover's description, ground its philosophizing in the erotic desire of an older for a younger man: Plato contextualizes the dialogue in such a way as to suggest that there would be no dialogue without Hippothales' desire for Lysis, or Socrates' agreement to act as his stand-in. Furthermore, friendship, the main topic of discussion, cannot be disentangled from erotic love. And at each stage of the dialogue we are reminded that success in male–male courtship is its reason for being, from Socrates' willingness to demonstrate how Hippothales should verbally conduct his pursuit of Lysis at the beginning, to his repressed boast that he has brought Lysis to a more agreeable frame of mind at the end of the first dialogue, to Hippothales' final satisfaction near the end of the second. The erotics of dialogue itself may be temporarily obscured by the discussion of friendship, but they remain consistently in the foreground of Socrates' framing narration.

This is not to suggest that Hippothales finally reaches his erotic goal; in fact, his satisfaction at the apparent outcome of the dialogue is premature at best. Appropriately in a dialogue in which all goals, whether literal or metaphorical, are regularly deferred in favor of further byways, what may appear to be a satisfactory conclusion to the framing narrative turns out not to be the conclusion at all. While the boys' agreement that the acceptance of a true *erastes* is logically necessary may satisfy Hippothales, their agreement is reluctant at best (though Bolotin suggests that Lysis is probably "at last confessing to love [Hippothales] in return"[24]). And Socrates himself is unsatisfied with this conclusion as well: after taking note of Hippothales' pleasure, he relentlessly takes the argument in yet another new direction, suggesting that their conclusion about kinship actually falls into the logical errors they have already refuted (a point we shall return to below). In refusing to accept the former conclusion, he is also in effect retracting the logical necessity for Lysis to accept Hippothales: if Lysis has been forced into this position through argumentation, the following refutation of the argument must release him from his reluctant agreement.

It is at this point that Socrates declares, "I no longer know what to say" about friendship (p. 52, 222e). And the dialogue draws to an end, as we have seen, with Lysis and Menexenus being dragged off physically in new direction—away from Hippothales and his friends, significantly, and toward their homes and families—while Socrates considers further argumentation with the older men. It ends with an admission of defeat: ". . . what he who is a friend is we have not yet been able to discover" (p. 52, 223b). The former conclusion is taken back, as it were, and whatever triumph Hippothales felt earlier must yield to this new development. Indeed, what is suggested at the end of the dialogue is the need for further dialogue, that desire of Socrates "to set in motion [*kinein* (κινεῖν)] something else among the older fellows" (p. 52, 223a). The *Lysis* is ultimately true to its own endlessly deviating structure in its refusal to allow Hippothales erotic satisfaction. On the other hand, even that refusal is hardly definitive: Dover, using an example drawn from Socrates' contemporary Aristophanes, points out that the term *kinein* (κινεῖν), to move, was also "a slang equivalent of *binein*, 'fuck,' used in the active voice or in the passive according to whether the subject is the sexually active or the (male or female) sexually passive partner."[25] Given the homoerotic context of this dialogue, Socrates may here be jokingly imagining himself as the *erastes* of the "older fellows" themselves, as he turns his attention to them both erotically and philosophically. The pun sums up nicely the close connection between philosophical dialogue and male–male desire: here they become, if not identical, certainly inseparable.

If it endlessly deviates in its structure, as I have suggested, the *Lysis* also thematizes this deviation in what it has to say about love between men, whether friendly or erotic. I would next like to examine its philosophical terminology of likeness, unlikeness, kinship, and so on for clues about how Plato is conceptualizing these relations.

Before Socrates and his young interlocutors embark on the dialogues proper, they engage in some preliminary banter that serves to introduce the theme of friendship and to link it with the concepts of likeness and unlikeness. The passage is worth examining because we are to be reminded of it later, at several key moments in the dialogues themselves. Menexenus is the first to sit down with the older group around Hippothales and Ctesippus, and Lysis then joins his friend, along with the nameless others behind whom Hippothales conceals himself from Lysis' view. Socrates immediately engages the two boys in a series of questions about their similarities and differences, though the answers he receives don't actually provide this information:

And then I looked toward Menexenus and said, "Son of Demophon, which one of you is older?"
　"We dispute about that," he said.

"Then there would also be strife," I said, "about which one is nobler [*gennaioteros* (γενναιότερος)]."

"Very much so," he said.

"And likewise, indeed, about which one is more beautiful."

Here they both laughed.

"But I won't ask," I said, "which one of you is wealthier. For you [two] are friends [*philo* (φίλω)], aren't you?"

"Very much so," they [both] said.

"Well the things of friends are said to be in common, so you [two] won't differ in this respect, if indeed you [two] are speaking the truth about your friendship."

They [both] assented.

After that I was attempting to question them as to which one was juster and wiser. But in the middle of this, someone came up to fetch Menexenus, saying that the gymnastic master was calling him. (p. 23, 207b–d)

Socrates here introduces the issues, not only of sameness and difference, but of that difference within sameness which I have been calling deviance. For Lysis and Menexenus are assumed to be basically alike—both boys, both about the same age, both from good families of similar (upper) class backgrounds, both well-to-do in terms of wealth. (Their laughter, on the other hand, suggests perhaps that they are unlike in physical beauty: Lysis' uncommon good looks have already been established, and the boys seem to acknowledge his superiority in this area, jokingly.) Socrates also hopes perhaps to establish their similarity in justice and wisdom—that is, given what will shortly transpire with Lysis alone, he may be hoping to establish that they are similar in lacking these virtues and in needing instruction.

The boys, in other words, seem to be similar in most of the ways that count to Athenian citizens: gender, age, family, possessions, and personal virtue are all significant categories of identity, and Lysis and Menexenus are roughly the same in each case; they are similar enough to be able to dispute which of them stands higher in each of these hierarchies. However, in the very act of establishing hierarchies—in the very act of asking which is older, nobler, more beautiful, and so on—Socrates demonstrates their difference as well, a difference that is apparently most pronounced in their looks. These differences do not exactly make them unlike each other, but exist within their overall similarity; the boys do not differ so much as they deviate from each other. They are, we might say, akin without being identical.

The point may seem obvious: no two individuals are ever exactly the same, but everyone can nonetheless be situated in various categories along with others who are roughly similar. It will not, however, remain as obvious when Socrates discusses likeness and unlikeness more directly: the possibilities of absolute identity and absolute difference will arise shortly, and they should remind us of this earlier brief discussion.

In the first dialogue with Lysis alone, Socrates focuses on the acquisition of virtue and wisdom and, as we have seen, on Lysis' current inability to claim either for himself and on his continuing need for instruction. Here, too, he introduces the same categories of sameness and difference—class, age, and so on—as part of his first attempt to understand friendship. Lysis' parents are the initial examples of friendship, that is of those who "love you very much" (p. 23, 207d). The verb "love" here is *philei* (φιλεῖ), the first time this important term appears: parental love is thus covered by the same terminology as friendly love. Despite their love, or friendship, and their ensuing desire for Lysis' happiness, they do not allow their son to do as he pleases, but set various limits on his behavior: for example, despite being an upper-class male, he is subject to both a slave, the attendant who accompanies him and who will force him to go home at the end of the *Lysis*, and a woman, his mother, who will see that he gets a beating if Lysis touches her weaving (pp. 25–26, 208c–e). Lysis understands that these limitations are not really due to class or gender differences; at first he believes that it is only his age difference that makes them necessary, protesting that all these limits are imposed on him "because I'm not yet of age" (p. 26, 209a). Socrates quickly leads him to see, however, that because he is allowed to do those things he knows how to do well, it is not age, but wisdom, that really makes the difference:

> "Then will we be friends to anyone and will anyone love us in regard to those matters in which we're of no benefit?"
>
> "Surely not," he said.
>
> "Now, therefore, not even your father loves you, nor does anyone else love anyone else insofar as he is useless."
>
> "It doesn't seem so," he said.
>
> "Then if you become wise, my boy, all will be your friends and all akin to you—for you will be useful and good. But if you don't, no one else will be your friend, and neither will your father, nor your mother, nor your own kinsmen." (pp. 28–29, 210c–d)

The term "kin" (*oikeioi* [οἰκεῖοι]) is introduced here, and will, as we have seen, return toward the end of the second dialogue.[26]

Friendship is here seen to be contingent upon usefulness, and usefulness upon the acquisition of wisdom; one who is wise will be useful, and therefore everyone will be his friend (*philoi* [φίλοι]) in the sense that they will make him the object of their friendly love. Similarly, everyone will also be akin (*oikeoi* [οἰκεῖοι]) to him in the same sense. Such friendships will not necessarily be reciprocal: only those who benefit from these relationships, not the benefactors, are here considered friends. Difference is thus a condition for friendship: those in need of such benefits are by definition different from those who can supply them; but difference alone is not sufficient for friendship, since the benefactor is not, as benefactor, here considered a friend.

This approach to friendship undergoes further examination in the second, longer dialogue that includes Menexenus as well as Lysis. Lysis, who, as we have seen, considers himself not only a friend, but a friendly rival of Menexenus, wishes Socrates to "chasten" the latter as he himself has been chastened (p. 30, 211c). Socrates agrees, but he conceals the plan to humble Menexenus (pretending instead that Lysis has asked that Menexenus clarify a difficult point for him) just as he concealed Hippothales' plan from Lysis.

At this point Socrates declares that he has always wished for a friend as a desirable possession, rather than "the best quail or cock to be found among humans and indeed, by Zeus, for my part, rather than a horse or a dog" or even than "the gold of Darius, and rather than Darius himself" (p. 31, 211d–e). He also declares that he does not know how to go about acquiring such a possession, and hopes that Menexenus, who considers himself and Lysis to be friends, can enlighten him. In the previous dialogue Socrates has, of course, already arrived at the conclusion that if one becomes wise, everyone will be his friend, and the following return to the concepts introduced there suggests not that he is now rejecting that formula in itself, but rather that he is not completely satisfied with it as it stands, and that it needs some refinement or further investigation. He first addresses the problem of reciprocity, and leads Menexenus to reject approaches to the definition of friendship that are based on the distinction between those who love and those who are loved. As Bolotin points out, this line of questioning does not eliminate all those who love, who are loved, or especially who both love and are loved as friends (though Menexenus appears to think it does); however, it does not reveal any "determining principle which would include all those that are friends while excluding all those that are not. Thus, the most plausible suggestion—that friends are those who both love and are loved—has been rejected for its failure to include the entire range of friendly love."[27] For example, Socrates suggests that one may feel a friendly love for animals, or wine, or gymnastics, or wisdom itself, and therefore in some sense be a friend to that which by definition is unable to reciprocate (p. 32, 212d). Similarly, neither the definition of "friend" as one who loves nor as one who is loved without reciprocation is acceptable "because they would compel one to count as friends some who clearly are not."[28] Someone might be defined as a friend to his enemy, for example (p. 33, 213a–b). A satisfactory—that is, all-encompassing—definition of "friend," then, cannot result from this approach.

Socrates and the boys (specifically, it is now Lysis' turn) next try an approach through a different set of categories, those of like and unlike. (It is at this point that Socrates invokes the metaphorical path on which they are wandering.) Like, suggests Socrates, may necessarily be friend to like (*to homoion toi homoioi* [τὸ ὅμοιον τῷ ὁμοίῳ], p. 35, 214b). The term *homoios* (ὅμοιος) suggests resemblance or similarity, but Socrates tends to use it in an absolute sense: insofar as two individuals are like each other, they are identical. This point becomes clear when Socrates (with Lysis' agreement) suggests that in discussions of friendship, those who are alike must be alike specifically in goodness, since those who are bad are "never alike, not even themselves to themselves" (p. 35, 214c–d). Those who are alike in goodness are, insofar as they are good, also self-sufficient: " 'How then, would such things be treasured by each other, if they held out no help to each other as allies? Is that possible?' 'No it isn't.' 'And how would what was not treasured be a friend?' 'There is no way.' 'But then he who is like is not a friend to his like' " (p. 36, 215a). For Plato's Socrates, those who are alike must be identical in goodness, and therefore unable to confer, and not in need of receiving, those benefits already deemed, in the previous dialogue, necessary to the existence of friendship. In this system, love cannot arise from identity.

If this is the case, once again, as Socrates points out, "we have gone astray" (p. 37, 215c). It would seem that some difference is a necessary condition of friendship and love, and Socrates therefore moves on to a discussion of "unlikeness." As in the case of likeness, it is absolute unlikeness that concerns him: insofar as two individuals are unlike each other, likeness or unlikeness is by definition absolute, otherwise they would include their opposites, a logical impossibility. The term Socrates uses, therefore, is *enantios* (ἐναντίος), meaning not just "unlike" or "different," but "opposite," or even more extremely, "most opposite [*enantiotaton* (ἐναντιώτατον)]" (p. 38, 215e).[29] "[W]hat is opposite is most a friend to its opposite" (p. 38, 216a). This proposition, however, also leads to the same dead end as the approach through the question of reciprocity: a friend would have to be a friend to his enemy, the just a friend to the unjust, and so on. Niether those who are alike nor those who are opposite may, then, be considered friends.

Socrates and his companions now turn to another new approach, considering the possibility that "whatever is neither good nor bad" (*mete agathon mete kakon* [μήτε ἀγαθὸν μήτε κακὸν]) may "at some times become a friend of the good" (p. 39, 216c).[30] The category of "neither good nor

bad" allows for a mixture of the two that Socrates could not logically countenance when discussing the good and the bad, the like and the opposite,
in themselves. The presence of an evil might corrupt the good, but whatever has not yet been corrupted will, precisely because it recognizes the
presence of an undesirable evil, desire the good. "Then whenever it is not
yet bad, though an evil is present, this presence makes it desire [*epithumein*
(ἐπιθυμεῖν)] good" (p. 42, 217e). This formula points us for the first time
toward deviance: the individual being described in these passages deviates
from the good because of the presence of some evil; it will therefore desire
the purely good, that from which it has deviated, as long as it has not been
wholly corrupted by the presence of evil. This is neither absolute likeness
nor absolute opposition, but deviation, and it is now understood as the cir-
cumstance in which love or friendship can arise. It should also be noted
that this approach emphasizes the role of desire in friendship, though in
this case the term is *epithumia* (ἐπιθυμῖα), a longing that is not necessarily,
but may be, erotic.

This approach, as by now we might expect, also proves unsatisfactory to
Socrates. After some lengthy argumentation, it appears that the problem
lies in the very lack of absoluteness in this definition of friendship: the
desire for the good is here seen as dependent on the presence of the bad.
Evil, in this view, is necessary to friendship toward, or love and desire for,
the good. If the bad were eliminated, the need for the good would also dis-
appear, and with it the desire/love/friendship that depended upon it. The
good is therefore not, in this view, loved for itself, and the attachment to it
cannot be considered true love or friendship. "[I]f what is bad were a cause
of a thing's being a friend, and it ceased to be, nothing would be a friend
to another" (p. 49, 221c).

On the other hand, Socrates simultaneously establishes another
possibility: that some desires, neither good nor bad in themselves, are for that
reason not dependent on the presence of evil: as we have already seen, erotic
desire is the example Socrates chooses. If the bad ceases to exist, he suggests,

> "There will be, then, whatever desires are neither good nor bad, even if the
> things which are bad cease to be."
>   "It appears so."
>   "Now is it possible for one who desires [*epithumounta* (ἐπιθυμοῦντα)]
> and who loves passionately [*eronta* (ἐρῶντα)] not to love as a friend [*philein*
> (φιλεῖν)] that which he desires and loves passionately?"
>   "Not in my opinion, at any rate."
>   "There will be, then, as it seems, some [things that are] friends, even if
> evils cease to be."
>   "Yes." (p. 49, 221b–c)

Epithumia, longing, is now linked firmly to *eros*, erotic desire, and both are potential preconditions for *philia*, friendship.

Refining some of the terms and arguments rejected earlier, Socrates now returns to desire, and thus friendship, as a longing for what one does not have. This longing is no longer caused by the presence of an evil, however, that approach to the problem having just been found wanting; instead, Socrates proposes more simply that "that which desires [*epithumoun* (ἐπιθυμοῦν)] desires whatever it is in want of [*endees* (ἐνδεὲς)]" (p. 49, 221d–e). Rather than the presence of an evil, it is now proposed that an absence causes desire. And for Socrates, it appears, one must be familiar with something in order to feel its absence as desire:

> "Is what is in want, therefore, a friend of that which it is in want of?"
> "That's my opinion."
> "And it comes to be in want of whatever it is somehow deprived of [*aphairetai* (ἀφαιρῆται)]."
> "How could it not?"
> "It appears, then, Menexenus and Lysis, that passionate love, friendship, and desire happen to be for what is akin, as it seems."
> They [both] assented. (p. 50, 221e)

The adjective *endees* (ἐνδεὲς), meaning "deficient" or "lacking," is now defined further as implying *aphairetos* (ἀφαιρετός), meaning "able to be taken away" or "separable." That is to say, it now implies not merely a lack, but a lack of something formerly in one's own possession, a deprivation of something of one's own.[31] It is this subtle shift in meaning that allows Socrates to find that the three terms he has already brought together on a continuum—passionate love (*eros* [ἔρως]), friendship (*philia* [φιλία]), and desire (*epithumia* [ἐπιθυμία])—may all have as their object "what is akin" (*tou oikeiou* [τοῦ οἰκείου]), that is, belonging to one's household or oneself. It should be added that this understanding of love, including erotic desire, as springing from the loss of what was formerly one's own, which when lost becomes the object of longing, anticipates the famous speech of Aristophanes in the *Symposium*, where, however, the emphasis is placed exclusively upon the erotic: there, human beings long for, and pursue, the missing other halves of which they have been deprived, and the nature of the missing half determines the nature of the desire to which one is subject, males for males, females for females, or males and females for each other.

The notion of kinship returns, also, to that of difference within a larger similarity, or deviance. Kinship suggests a family resemblance without equivalence, a variation without opposition, individualities that deviate from a common ground without abandoning it. In the overall context of the *Lysis*, kinship in this sense must be seen as a middle ground between the absolutes of likeness and unlikeness that have been rejected as logically impossible grounds for friendship and love; it is a likeness that is not absolute, and an unlikeness that includes a degree of similarity. Socrates appears to recognize this point when he asks the boys whether they would agree that "what is akin [*oikeion* (οἰκεῖον)] is something other than the like [*homoiu* (ὁμοίου)]?" (p. 51, 222c).[32]

An element of similarity is necessary, then, to the existence of desire and hence love and friendship, as is an element of difference. We are reminded here that this point was implied when Menexenus and Lysis first sat down with Socrates, and were induced to discuss their friendship in terms of their similarities and differences; we are also reminded that the sort of kinship under discussion is of a higher, more natural form than kinship within families: "You, therefore, if you are friends to each other, are by nature in some way akin to each other" (p. 50, 221e). We are also reminded of what is at stake erotically, for if genuine erotic love is derived from kinship, the true lover, as we have already seen, must be loved in return (p. 50, 222a); this is the result that makes Hippothales rejoice.

As we have also seen, however, Socrates does not allow this apparently satisfying argument to end the dialogue.[33] Continuing his examination of what is actually akin, he eliminates the possibility that kinship between the bad can lead to friendship, on the same grounds that friendship between the bad was earlier deemed impossible (p. 51, 222d; cf. 214c–d). Kinship can thus exist only between the good, but it has also already been demonstrated that the good cannot logically be friend to the good (p. 51, 222d; cf. 215a–b). It is here that Socrates declares that he no longer knows what to say, and that the conversation is interrupted before he can engage the older youths in further argumentation.

Although the dialogue as a whole thus seems to come to a dead end, some modern philosophers find that it does indeed reach a satisfactory conclusion. David Bolotin, for instance, takes Socrates' final comments as an invitation to the reader to engage more directly with the philosophical arguments, and, pursuing their implications for himself, points out that in returning to the question of good and bad in friendship, and eliminating kinships between the bad and the good as its source, Socrates neglects the intermediate beings, those who are neither good nor bad—the very beings who have just previously provided the most productive approach to friendship. Of such intermediate beings, Bolotin suggests that, following Socrates'/Plato's own logic, "[t]he being who is good, we can say, insofar as he is deficient, is a friend who loves the good that is his own, and insofar as it is good, it is a friend which "accepts the friendship" (cf. 219a4) of itself as a living and needy being."[34] This solution, that intermediate beings can be friends only in some sense to themselves, leaves no room for the reciprocity that we normally expect of friendship, and indeed can hardly be termed "friendship" in any ordinary sense. Accordingly, Bolotin also asks how these self-sufficient beings might be related:

> Might not some of them, at least, be one another's friends, if only in a limited sense? For even without needing one another, and without longing for one another in order to become whole (cf. 215b4), they might still, being kindred, desire and enjoy one another's company. And if this were so, their friendly feeling for one another might be in a sense exemplary. For their affection would be free of the illusions which deceive the most generous or erotic of human friends. And it would also be free of the selfishness at the root of all human desire for useful friends. Therefore, some of the self-sufficiently good might enjoy with each other among the purest, if not the deepest, of "friendships." Moreover, if any of them have become good in the course of time, they might also be akin to others of their kind who are still becoming so. And their affection toward these "youths," though conditional upon the others' desire and ability to improve, would be similarly pure.[35]

Bolotin's solution, even here, radically devalues not only friendship, but all forms of relationality. In fact, the quotation marks around the word "friendship" indicate that, pure as his examples may be, their admitted lack of depth may not really qualify them for this term as it is normally understood. Bolotin also devalues its erotic component, as indeed he tends to do throughout his commentary: in his discussion of the intermediate as friend of the good, for instance, he elides Plato's use of the terms derived from *eros* in favor of phrases like "friendly desire."[36] Here, he rejects the longing for wholeness that characterizes Socrates' discussion of kinship, and thus the similarity between this section of *Lysis* and Aristophanes' speech in the *Symposium* noted above, in suggesting that these friends will not experience any such longing. He also is concerned to assert the "purity" of true friendship between older and younger men or boys, though Socrates himself never rejects the physical expression of eros in this dialogue. In engaging with Plato's dialogue, Bolotin goes perhaps too far beyond what it actually says.

More helpful for our purposes here is Hans-Georg Gadamer's essay, "*Logos* and *Ergon* in Plato's *Lysis*."[37] Gadamer, too, finds that Plato does supply a true doctrine of friendship, or at least that the engaged reader can discern such a doctrine. In his reading, Socrates' interlocutors are simply too young and inexperienced to understand the nature of friendship, and can only be pointed in the right direction (this, according to Gadamer, is why Socrates is preparing to shift his attention to the older youths at the end of the dialogue).[38] For Gadamer, reciprocity—de-emphasized by Bolotin—is the key to friendship, not the utility that is emphasized earlier in the *Lysis*. The concept of that which is akin, *oikeion*, provides the model of this reciprocity:

> Socrates uses oikeion and its semantic field to say that there is a need in me of das Zugehörige, a need of that which pertains to me. And that is a need which does not cease when it is met, and that in which the need finds fulfillment does not cease to be dear to me. That which pertains to me and to which I belong, is as reliable and constant for me as everything in my household. Socrates concludes that when someone loves another as a friend, his longing is directed to the other person in such a way that the former fulfills himself in his longing. Ultimately what he seeks is that quality in the other which pertains to him and which gives his longing legitimacy.[39]

Gadamer's reading does not devalue friendship as Bolotin's does, and remains considerably closer to what Plato's text actually says, though it too requires that the reader look beyond Socrates' own claim that this approach is inadequate. Gadamer does, however, like Bolotin, tend to undervalue the erotic component in the relationships under discussion here. Elsewhere he places the term "friendship" in quotation marks, not, like Bolotin, to indicate a lack of depth, but rather as a reminder that there is more to this friendship than modern usage normally allows;[40] however, he quickly assimilates the erotic to "friendship," and does shy away from its more physical implications (he declares that Hippothales' pursuit of Lysis "was the custom then," placing friendship's erotic aspect in a historical margin[41]).

Nevertheless, Gadamer's belief that reciprocal kinship is the correct definition of friendship remains useful for our purposes, because it leaves room for simultaneous similarity and difference: "he who feels friendship for someone sees in the other something which he himself is not, but the thing which he sees, which he is not, is more like something which has not yet been achieved in himself, something more like a potential in himself, which leads him to look for a model in another."[42] From this perspective, desire, friendly or passionate, is derived from the recognition of one's own deviance, deviance not only from the good one perceives in another but also, once that good has been perceived, deviance even from one's own potential self. The desire for the good in oneself and that for the good in another are not truly separable, as Bolotin would have it; and, as the previous quotation suggests, if the good in another is also *oikeion*, one's relation to it will remain "reliable and constant."

Gadamer's position shifts somewhat by the end of his essay, where he seems to be interested in eliminating difference and thereby deviance:

> The *reader* might notice that the answer, "to oikeion," contains the deeper meaning of what was meant by "the same" at an earlier stage in the discussion, and very likely it will not be lost on him that what is called "oikieion" and "the same" can also be called "good". . . . sameness and difference, longing and fulfillment, growing intimacy with others and with oneself, are all one and the same thing.[43]

Whereas earlier, difference, that "which he is not," was essential, here difference has been assimilated to sameness, a move that Socrates claims logically invalidates this whole approach to friendship, as we have seen. I prefer, with the earlier passage, to preserve both sameness and difference in a relationship of deviance, both from others and from oneself. I also prefer Socrates' own open ending, which allows the dialogue its own continual deviation, to the tidier and more conclusive solutions proposed by Plato's modern readers.

Certainly Socrates demonstrates this internal self-deviation throughout the *Lysis*, producing a kind of internal carnivalesque, to use Bakhtin's and Kristeva's terminology, in which multiple perspectives clash. It is what leads him constantly to re-evaluate the directions in which his discussion is leading both him and the boys. There are a number of points at which Socrates believes he has arrived at the truth concerning friendship, and just as regularly he finds himself questioning his own inner conviction, especially after the questions concerning likeness and unlikeness have been introduced into the discussion. When he has reached the conclusion that those who are alike in goodness must be friends, for instance, he declares to Lysis that "we've gotten hold of who are friends" (p. 36, 214d–e). Immediately, however, he also finds that he is "uneasy about something" in this opinion, necessitating further investigation (p. 36, 214e). Socrates does not merely pretend self-doubt as a way of leading the boys into a deeper analysis: the same sequence of belief and doubt recur at a later point, this time clearly indicated as an internal division not immediately enunciated to his interlocutors. When they have agreed that "whatever is neither bad nor good is itself, because of the presence of an evil, a friend of the good," Socrates says that "I rejoiced greatly myself, as if I were a hunter and had, to my satisfaction, what I had been hunting [for myself]. But then some most strange suspicion came over me—from where, I don't know—that the things we had agreed to were not true" (p. 43, 218c), and again further investigation is called for. Finally, after finding that the doctrine of kinship makes it necessary for an *eromenos* to love a true *erastes*, and witnessing both Hippothales' delight in, and the boys' reluctant acceptance of, this conclusion, Socrates still, he tells us, found himself "wishing to examine the argument [for myself]" (p. 50, 222b).

This continual self-doubt, the constant internal movement away from every apparent conclusion or goal, is entirely consistent with other aspects of the *Lysis*. Like the original, physical walk "straight to the Lyceum" that opens the dialogue and never reaches its goal, the path of argument as Socrates and the boys pursue it continually turns aside, and this refusal to conclude the conversation comes about because of Socrates' own inner self-deviations. The pattern of pure deviance—the process of constant differentiation without any central doctrine—is thus characteristic of nearly all aspects of this dialogue, from the philosophical argumentation to the narrative structure to the characterization of Socrates himself. It is deviance as *différance* (to adopt Derrida's term[44]), a differentiation that is also a deferral of the goal or conclusion. This *différance* is most significantly for our purposes here a characteristic of male–male desire itself, whether friendly or passionate, *philia* or *eros*: while the last definition of the source of such desires leaves us with deviance, a differing of the self from another that is also akin or similar, that definition like the others remains subject to further, open-ended scrutiny. A true definition or doctrine of male–male desire is indefinitely deferred.

One area in which this process of constant differentiation or deviance may seem incomplete is the relationship between Socrates and his interlocutors. While Lysis and especially Menexenus sometimes resist or question Socrates' approaches to the issues at hand or offer definitions of their own, they, like many of Socrates' interlocutors in other Platonic dialogues, are consistently led to ultimate agreement with him: each time Socrates believes he has solved the problem, the boys think so too, until he leads them off in a different direction. In the long run of the dialogue as a whole, Plato does not allow their views to differ from his. Socrates, internal self-deviation and all, remains in control, and leads the boys to an understanding of his and their own ignorance. The entire dialogue, then, may also be seen as a demonstration of what Lysis learns in its first movement, that he is not yet wise and remains in need of a teacher—in this case Socrates himself. (From this perspective, the *Lysis* appears to be an example of Buber's category of pedagogical dialogue, which, though dialogical, "is incompatible with complete mutuality."[45]) As we have seen, Socrates himself understands this lesson at least partly in erotic terms, and must restrain himself from explaining that it should serve Hippothales' desire to make Lysis his *eromenos*. But in the ensuing dialogue, it is not Hippothales who instructs Lysis, but rather Socrates himself who continues to do so: Socrates thus becomes the true figure of the *erastes*, his philosophical argumentation being perhaps as seductive to Lysis as it will later be to Alcibiades in the *Symposium*. It should be remembered that, although Hippothales apparently believes he will do so, Lysis never accepts Hippothales as his *erastes*, but merely falls silent (p. 50, 222a) before Socrates' argument.

Socrates, of course, is an *erastes* with a difference, seeking the betterment of Lysis without the typical accompaniment of physical pleasure. And even the betterment he seeks for the boy is atypical: rather than initiating Lysis into his proper place in Athenian society and showing him his role in appropriate power relations within Athenian society, Socrates stages a little rebellion at the end of the dialogue and encourages Lysis to defy the authority of his father's representative, the slave who, it has already been established (pp. 25–26, 208c–209a), is exercising appropriate power *in loco parentis*: when the slaves insist that Lysis and Menexenus come home, "at first, we and those standing around tried to drive them away," but, the slaves having been made belligerent by drink, "we were therefore defeated by them, and we broke up our group" (p. 52, 223a–b). The form of the dialogue both demonstrates the boys' need for an instructor/*erastes* in Socrates himself, and also suggests that Socrates, as a new kind of *erastes*, will locate the betterment of his charges not within traditional power relations, but in the development of their own power of thought, specifically in the recognition of what they do not know. (We might also recall how the use of the verb *kinein* suggests Socrates' role as philosophical *erastes* to Hippothales himself and his older companions.) And this recognition may well, as Socrates' accusers ultimately decided, lead finally to a criminal deviation from what Athenian society would deem proper treatment of its youth.[46]

One author upon whom the *Lysis* exerted a noticeable influence is Cicero, whose own dialogues on friendship and desire between men allow considerably less room for any sort of deviation than does the *Lysis*. The particular dialogue form adopted by Cicero, indeed, all but eliminates the truly dialogic: in both the *Tusculan Disputations* and *Laelius: On Friendship*, the main speaker dominates the discussion to the near-elimination of his interlocutors, and even of the dramatic setting. Even if Socrates' interlocutors in the *Lysis* generally follow his lead, they are nevertheless necessary to his thought: Plato represents their responses to Socrates' questions and their requests for clarification as that which allows Socrates to develop and refine his arguments. It is also worth remembering that the boys' agreement is at times reluctant, or assumed from their silence, which is to say that the dramatic situation, the interplay of characters, is never forgotten, and plays its part in the dialogue's overall refusal of resolution.[47] Even beyond his relations with Lysis and Menexenus, Socrates is also, as we have seen, in a dialogical relationship with himself: his own internal reflections suggest an unresolved inner division in which his own voice regularly deviates from itself. The very fact that no doctrine of friendship is ultimately offered as true, itself implies the possibility of further dialogue, whether with the older youths, as Socrates himself suggests, or with the reader, as critics like Bolotin and Gadamer recommend.

Cicero, however, while introducing the dialogue form and the dramatic setting much more deliberately and self-consciously than Plato does, also eliminates precisely those dramatic elements of disagreement and deviation that Plato emphasizes, and this elimination of the truly dialogical in terms of form reflects a similarly single-minded doctrinal content as well as a more authoritarian and hierarchical society than the Athenian *polis*, as Pierre Grimal has argued: Plato's dialogues are often conversations brought about by chance encounters in the street, while Cicero's are carefully composed, patrician gatherings; Socrates chooses his interlocutors according to their characters, Cicero's speakers according to their social status.[48] This social setting is conducive to the more monological, authoritarian form. The *Tusculan Disputations* provides a good example. Its five books are represented as dialogues between two speakers called "A" and "M" (possibly "Auditor" and "Magister," though their exact referents are unknown). These dialogues are imagined as having recently taken place in Cicero's villa at Tusculum; they were composed in 45 B.C., that is, during the last years of the Roman Republic, after Julius Caesar's ascension to the dictatorship had forced Cicero's retirement from politics. They are, in fact, dedicated to the Brutus who was about to assassinate Caesar. Cicero also makes reference to the recent death of his daughter Tullia, and these dialogues function as a kind of philosophical consolation in his troubles, as Cicero demonstrates to his younger companion that death is not an evil, but a deliverance (Book I), that pain is only an insignificant evil (Book II), that the right attitude, achieved through philosophical reflection, can alleviate distress (Book III) and other disorders (Book IV), and that virtue leads to happiness (Book V).

Clearly, these books are dialogical in only the most nominal way: Cicero, or M, has specific conclusions in mind and they are clearly stated with almost no input of any kind from A. Nor does M himself deviate in any way from his foreordained conclusions. The dramatic setting, too, is quickly forgotten as the brief initial discussions between M and A turn almost immediately into M's lengthy disquisitions.

The introductory sections of each book prepare us for the authoritative, monologic nature of the ensuing texts, as in the opening of Book I. Like the other books, it begins not with the dramatic situation of the dialogue itself, but with a long address to their dedicatee, Brutus, in which Cicero explains his choice of the dialogue form. Having decided to dedicate his retirement to philosophy, he tells Brutus (referring to his famous former career as an orator) that

> just as in my youth I used to be constantly declaiming speeches for the courts—and no one ever did so longer—so this is now a declamation [*declamatio*] of my old age. I called upon my friends to put forward any subject which any of them wished to hear discussed, and this I debated either as I sat or walked about. The result is that I have put together into five books the dissertations [*scholas*], as the Greeks term them, of as many days. The procedure was that, after the would-be listener had expressed his view, I opposed it. This, as you know, is the old Socratic method [*vetus et Socratica ratio*] of arguing against your adversary's position; for Socrates thought that in this way the probable truth was most readily discovered; but in order that the course of our discussions may be more conveniently followed I shall put them before you in the form of a debate and not in narrative form. (pp. 10–11, I.iv.7–8)[49]

It is significant that Cicero refers to this text as a *declamatio*, that is, as a speech like those given by students of rhetoric as part of their training. It is, by implication, not really a dialogue with interlocutors at all, but a speech meant to persuade an audience of the correctness of his opinions. While he declares that he will put this speech into the form of a debate or discussion (*agatur res*), it also seems that it could just as easily have taken the form of a monologic narrative (*narretur*), and indeed he also uses the term *scholas*, with the implication of a lecture delivered to students. Whether imagining himself as a student or a master, Cicero will be showing off his own oratorical skill in persuading his listeners of the truth of his views.

He takes this kind of rhetorical persuasion to have been the method or system (*ratio*, suggesting a plan thought out in advance) of Socrates as well, but despite his respect for Socrates and Plato, Cicero is generally unwilling to represent the same sort of wayward, inconclusive, constantly deviating thought process that we have observed in the Socratic dialogues such as *Lysis*. His own method or *ratio* more closely resembles certain of Plato's late dialogues (e.g., *Sophist, Statesman, Laws*), in which one speaker (often someone other than Socrates) takes he lead and appears to be expounding some positive doctrine of Plato's. In the *Tusculan Disputations* too, A's few disagreements—and with them, the dialogue form itself—are immediately eliminated, allowing M (i.e., Cicero himself) to monopolize the remainder of the text in arguing for his own dogmas, not only against A's former objection, but against other philosophers' doctrines as well. The opening dialogue of Book II is exemplary in this regard: "A. I consider pain the greatest of all evils. M. Greater even than disgrace? A. I do not venture to go so far as that and I am ashamed of having been dislodged so speedily from my position" (pp. 160–161, II.v.14). No "dialogue" could be more *pro forma*. Even when invited to comment, A declines: "A. Are you asking me to interrupt you? I could not even entertain the wish to do so: so conducive to belief do I find your words" (pp. 194–195, II.xviii.42). Arguing his foreordained doctrine from the very first, Cicero leaves no more room for internal than for external deviation; there is no encounter here, in Buber's sense, or dialogue, in Bakhtin's.

Cicero's editor suggests that his discussion of male–male erotic desire in the *Tusculan Disputations* is a response to Plato's *Symposium* and *Phaedrus*,[50] but it reads much more like a rebuke to the homoerotic elements of the *Lysis*, with which Cicero was also familiar. It occurs in Book IV of the *Tusculans*, which is dedicated to demonstrating that all disorders of the soul can be eliminated through correct philosophical reflection. Among these disorders are distress (*aegritudo*), or excessive concern with present evils (discussed in Book III), fear (*metus*), or excessive apprehension of future evils, delight (*laetitia*), or excessive pleasure in present goods, and lust (*libido*), or excessive desire for future goods. Among the subdivisions of *laetitia* is love, including, but apparently not limited to, excessive sexual pleasure: "In fact the whole passion ordinarily termed love [*amor*] (and heaven help me if I can think of any other term to apply to it) is of such exceeding triviality that I see nothing that I think comparable with it" (pp. 406–407, IV.xxxii.68). (Cicero seems to be emphasizing both that Latin lacks the multiple terms for this state found in the Greek language, and that Latin's lack of nuance is in fact appropriate and correct.[51]) A further subdivision is "so-called love of friendship [*iste amor amicitiae*]" (pp. 408–409, IV.xxxiii.70), the topic of the *Lysis*. Though he does not mention the Platonic dialogue by name, the context suggests that it may well be the one Cicero has in mind:

> For what is the so-called love of friendship? Why is it no one is in love with either an ugly youngster or a beautiful old man? For my part I think this practice had its origin in the Greek gymnasia where that kind of love-making was free and permitted. Well then did Ennius say: "Shame's beginning is the stripping of men's bodies openly." And though such loves be, as I see is

possible, within the bounds of modesty, yet they bring anxiety and trouble and all the more because they are a law to themselves and have no other restraint. (pp. 408–409, IV.xxxiii.70)

This passage may be understood as a rebuke to the homoerotic elements of the *Lysis*. The overall context of "love of friendship," in particular, suggests a connection with Plato's dialogue "on friendship," and in that context the reference to exercising naked in the gymnasia as the origin of homoerotic desire is reminiscent of that dialogue's dramatic setting in a wrestling school.[52] Similar sentiments linking Greek culture to homoeroticism can be found in other Roman writers, and Craig A. Williams notes that they "imply a certain distance between Roman and Greek customs."[53]

Cicero does not condemn male–male desire as in itself inferior to the male–female variety; indeed, his remarks occur within a larger condemnation of any excessive delight in sexual pleasure, and he admits that male–male love may exist "within the bounds of modesty." This suggestion is in line with recent scholarly analysis of Roman representations of male–male eroticism, for example that of John R. Clarke:

> The Greek artists focused their romantic notions in scenes of courting; when they depicted intercourse it was almost invariably . . . intercrural coitus. . . . the Roman artists infused images of anal intercourse between men with the same tender intimacy that pervades the images of male–female lovemaking on the Arretine ware and the House of the Menander cups. The artists went to great pains to make the male who is in the receptive position as dignified and attractive as the insertive partner. Whereas representations of rear-entry penetration of boys and women by males on Greek vases emphasize male domination and power over his (unwilling) and often unattractive partner, these Roman depictions make *both* males as attractive as possible and show them mutually attracted to each other, even though in most cases one is a man and the other a boy.[54]

Cicero does, however, simultaneously imply that erotics between men may more often be even more excessive than those occurring within a legal marriage, precisely because such male–male relations are not recognized as a legal category, but "are a law to themselves and have no other restraint."[55] He suggests, in fact, that "nature has granted wider tolerance" to "the love of women" (pp. 408–409, IV.xxxiii.71)—wider though not, as Williams points out, exclusive tolerance.[56] Cicero also rhetorically deconstructs "friendship," assumed here to take place exclusively between men, as no more than a category of sexual pleasure, itself—when excessive—a subdivision of the psychic disorder *laetitia*. Only modest loves or friendships—presumably those that do not include a component of physical expression—are recognized as possibly suitable for the virtuous man, and even those only marginally; the Platonic link between male–male erotics and philosophy is rejected as part of Cicero's overall response to the *Lysis*.

While the evidence from the visual arts may imply an idealized view of male–male eroticism among the Roman elite similar to the Athenian idealization of *paiderastia*, Cicero's apparent rejection of any physical expression of such desire also finds support in another Roman construction of male–male erotics, one found more frequently in written texts. As Marilyn B. Skinner has pointed out, in Rome, unlike Athens, the seduction of a youth of the citizen class, far from being idealized, was classified as the crime of *stuprum*. Indeed, erotic relations with boys were, "in law, all but restricted to slave concubines" because of the Roman cult of virility "that precluded a prospective soldier or statesman acceding to the demands of another."[57] Romans constructed male–male desire in various ways, and Cicero, while drawing on more than one of them, is primarily condemnatory.

This kind of condemnation leaves little or no room for the genuinely questioning attitude of Socrates—either for the speaker's self-questioning or for the ongoing interrogation of the subject at hand.[58] The *Tusculan Disputations*, in their concern with the pursuit of Stoic resistance to excess, do not pursue the possibility of even the more positive, "modest" emotional relations between men, but eliminate discussion as well as debate and disagreement: A has disappeared entirely from Book IV by it conclusion, leaving only the monologic voice of Cicero's M. In the same way, erotic relations between men are now regarded as a deviation from the more "natural" love of women (a question not addressed in the *Lysis*)—but such deviations are no longer valued as they were for Plato.[59]

Laelius: On Friendship takes up the question of emotional bonds between men at considerably greater length and in a more positive light, though here too the erotic bond is undervalued, if less directly than in the *Tusculans*. *On Friendship* for the most part simply eliminates any mention of the erotic component of friendship or of the possibility that a continuum connects friendly and erotic love, which, as we have seen, was so important to Plato. Cicero does indeed include vague references to the misuse of friendship that might be taken as another condemnation of male–male erotics in the context of friendship, similar to that found in the *Tusculan Disputations*: "People who believe friendship gives a good opportunity for all sorts of laxity and crime [*libidinum peccatorumque*] are making a dangerous mistake. That is not why nature gave us this blessing; she did not give it in order to pander to our vices, but to help us behave decently" (p. 217, xxii.83).[60] The discourses of *libido* and of nature are reminiscent of the slightly earlier *Tusculans* (*On Friendship* is dated to 44 B.C.), but if Cicero does have male–male erotics in mind here as an abuse of friendship, his concern is expressed so indirectly as to be nearly undetectable; this is typical of his elimination of the erotic from his discussion of friendship, which indeed virtually rules out desire of any sort.

On Friendship resembles Plato's Socratic dialogues, at least superficially, more closely than do the *Tusculan Disputations*. Its fictional framework is placed, like many of Plato's dialogues, in the past, specifically in 129 B.C., and like Plato, Cicero (who was not born until 106 B.C.) does not represent himself as a participant in the dialogue, but claims instead to have heard about the discussion from one who was there, Q. Mucius Scaevola the Augur. The dramatic situation is similar to that in Plato's *Symposium*, for example, which is remembered and recounted long after it is supposed to have taken place, though this structure does not play the crucial philosophical role that it does (as we shall see) in the *Symposium*. Scaevola and another participant, C. Fannius Strabo, convince their father-in-law, the distinguished orator C. Laelius Sapiens, to tell them about friendship, on the occasion of the death of Laelius' friend, Scipio Africanus the younger. Like many of the characters in Plato's dialogues, these are historical figures, but Laelius' speech is an exposition of Cicero's own doctrine of friendship.

Cicero's view of friendship is based on that sameness between two individuals that Plato causes Socrates to declare logically incompatible with friendship. Friends, for Cicero, are similar to the point of identity: "Friendship may be defined as a complete identity of feeling [*consensio*] about all things in heaven and earth: an identity which is strengthened by mutual goodwill and affection" (p. 187, vi.20). *Consensio* implies not just agreement or consent (*consentio*), but a feeling-together or unanimity, and Cicero shortly strengthens this identity of feeling even further, suggesting that "[w]hen a man thinks of a true friend, he is looking at himself in the mirror [*exemplar aliquod intuetur sui*]" (p. 189, vii.23). *Exemplar* actually suggests not so much a mirror image as an exact copy or transcript; still, the mutual similarity of friends is so close as to suggest identity—friends cannot be differentiated.

Friendship, in fact, is for Cicero a form of self-love, and is therefore natural in the same way; it is a much simpler thing for Cicero's Laelius than for Plato's Socrates precisely because love of what is like oneself—or indeed of what is identical with oneself—is natural, and thus in need of no further explanation.

> Birds and fishes and the beasts of the field, tame and wild—every living being loves itself! The feeling is inborn in every creature. And inborn, too, is

the need to find other creatures of the same species on to which they can fasten themselves. The urge that impels them to do so bears some resemblance to human love. And indeed human nature engenders the same pair of feelings [*quanto id magis in homine fit natura*]—with a special degree of intensity. For they, too, love themselves; and they, too, search for a partner whose personality they can unite so utterly with their own that the two are almost transformed into one. (pp. 216–217, xxi.81)

Love of friends is the equivalent of love of self, and a friendship for Cicero resembles the conventional modern view of marriage as a natural union in which two become as one.

If friendship is this sort of natural union or identity, there can be no question of the sort of longing for that which one lacks that Plato discusses in the *Lysis*. Given that a friend in another self, "[e]ven when a friend is absent, he is present [*adsunt*] all the same"; even in death, "he is still alive. He is alive because his friends still cherish him, and remember him, and long for him" (p. 189, vii.23). Note that longing here, unlike Platonic longing, does not presuppose absence, but is actually a sign of the dead friend's continued presence in his survivors' minds.[61]

Nor does the existence of friendship presuppose any sort of lack or deficiency, as is assumed in the *Lysis*. Here again, in fact, Cicero seems to be rebuking that assumption on Plato's part. Laelius gives the example of his own attachment to Scipio Africanus: "Did he *need* me? Of course he did not. Nor, for that matter, did I need him. I was attached to him because I admired his fine qualities; and he returned my feeling because he also, on his side, appeared not to have formed too bad an opinion of my own character" (p. 193 [translator's emphasis], ix.30). It is the presence of admirable qualities, not the need for them, that brings friendship into being, and these admirable qualities are the same in each of the two friends; again the emphasis is on the naturalness of affection between similar beings, "a wholly natural phenomenon" (p. 194, ix.32).

Because these feelings are stimulated by mutual admiration, only those who are similar in goodness can truly be friends—another argument that Socrates rejected early in the *Lysis*. This goodness, in fact, is what obviates need: "the most generous and liberal friends are those who have the very least need of anyone else, because they themselves already possess wealth and power and, above all, goodness, which is the strongest resource a man can command" (p. 204, xiv.51). In many ways, then, *Laelius: On Friendship* seems like Cicero's point for point refutation of the *Lysis*, and the result is a monologic doctrine of friendship, represented as unerringly true, and thus also opposed to the very errancy or deviance of Socrates' discourse in the earlier dialogue. (Near the beginning of the dialogue, C. Fannius Strabo directly compares Laelius to Socrates—"that one individual at Athens who was specifically declared to be the wisest of men by the oracle of Apollo himself" [pp. 178–179, ii.7]—in wisdom.)

It is true that Cicero occasionally introduces the possibility of difference into his doctrine of friendship, and along with difference the reader might also expect a consideration of absence, need, desire, and so on. Laelius/ Cicero's response to difference, however, is usually to attempt to erase it, as in his strategy for dealing with the Roman social hierarchy:

> A particularly important point between one friend and another is this. The superior must place himself on an equality with his inferior. It often happens that one man stands out among the others, as Scipio stood out in what you might call our group. All the same, he never had the slightest desire to place himself above Philus or Rupilius or Mummius, or even his other friends of lower rank. (p. 211, xix.69)

Unlike Plato's Socrates, who tries to situate Lysis and Menexenus in their proper places on the social hierarchy, thereby emphasizing both their larger similarity and their differences within it, Cicero's Laelius here is caught in the contradiction between, on the one hand, his major doctrine of identity between friends and, on the other, the reality of differences in social rank. It is a real difficulty for Cicero, who tries to resolve it with the superior's voluntary acceptance of the role of equal. Such social realities cannot, of course, be so easily eliminated, and Cicero has Laelius propose a second, and somewhat contradictory, resolution: "If an individual happens to be superior in character or intellectual qualities or worldly wealth, it is his duty to pass on this advantage to his kinsmen and friends, thus making sure that the people who are closest to him have their share" (p. 212, xix.70). It is thus up to the superior both to lower himself to his friend's level and to "lift the friend to his own level" (p. 213, xx.72)—which of course requires the initial recognition of difference, need, and the absence of certain goods in the inferior friend (and therefore of desire), problems that, as we have seen, Cicero is generally unwilling to admit into his doctrine of friendship. A bit later, therefore, the issue of advising friends provides another opportunity for the resolution of difference: while the very nature of advice implies that one friend needs something from the other, and thus that the other must be in some way superior, Cicero understands advice as a way of bringing the friends back into unity, once again eliminating the difference. While "it is an essential feature of genuine friendship both to offer advice and to receive it" (p. 221, xxiv.91), it also "unites human hearts. But this cannot happen if one of the personalities involved fails to remain consistently the same [*unus animus erit idemque semper*] . . ." (pp. 221–222, xxv.92). Difference in this case can be satisfyingly resolved into sameness, internal as well as external—and Laelius does not return to the more intractable problem of social rank.

It is at least possible that Cicero's discomfort with difference within friendship, especially with hierarchical differences, is linked to the erotic. Ellen Oliensis has suggested that "any asymmetrical relation between two Roman men is conceivably also a sexual relation," and that therefore "the *obsequium* of a freeborn client can always be maliciously misconstrued as a readiness to perform any service, including sexual service."[62] Cicero's rejection of the asymmetrical patron/client model of friendship may also mask a rejection of the homoerotic possibilities of friendship.

Age difference, too, at the end of *On Friendship*, is eliminated (and with it any hint of Plato's pederastic eroticism): friendship "shines brightest when it is shared by persons of the same age," and "the most satisfying thing of all really is to reach the end of the race with the same companions who were with you at the starting post" (p. 226, xvii.101).

It is tempting to interpret Cicero's insistence on the necessity of sameness or identity to friendship in political terms, especially since so many of his examples and metaphors of friendship are drawn from the political sphere and indeed from Cicero's own situation in 44 B.C. Konstan, in fact, argues that Cicero's view of friendship is shaped by politics: ". . . in the crisis leading up to and following Caesar's assassination, Cicero seems to have been especially preoccupied with the relationship between friendship and political allegiance."[63] A former Consul who had been proclaimed *Pater patriae*, "Father of His Country" after violently suppressing the Catilinarian conspiracy, Cicero was living in retirement by the time he composed *On Friendship*, an unwilling retirement from public life made necessary by Julius Caesar's election as Dictator and the subsequent suspension of the normal workings of the Republican government, with which Cicero had been closely identified. (At this point, Cicero's political "last hurrah"—his *Philippics* in the Senate, directed against Mark Antony—was still in the future.) It is likely, therefore, that his allusions to the difficulty of maintaining both friendships and political power have a personal application. If friendship requires the elimination of hierarchy, for example, "no one can love the person he fears—or the person he believes himself to be *feared* by. Tyrants are courted, naturally: but the courting is insincere, and it only lasts for a time" (p. 204, xv.53). It is difficult not to find a lament over the breakdown of the Republican governmental forms and the ascension of Caesar in lines like these.[64]

Nevertheless, there is also something imperial—even imperialist—in Cicero's own language about friendship: ". . . a good man is attracted by other good men; he wants to annex [*trahat*] them for themselves. This is almost like an ordinance of nature, as if the two of them were bound together by ties of blood. For nature has a greedy [*rapacius*] urge towards everything that is in conformity with itself [*similium sui*]" (p. 203, xiv.50). The verb *traho* carries a suggestion of violence that Grant's "annex" captures well: it means to draw after oneself or in one's train, to take to oneself, and in Cicero's period could be used of plundering or despoiling. Indeed, Cicero himself elsewhere uses it in precisely this latter fashion.[65] This choice of terms, then, situates friendship within the Roman tradition of empire-building, seen here as greedy or rapacious, but also as entirely natural. This greed, like the longing for a deceased friend, is not really desire, because it is directed only at that which one already naturally possesses, that which one recognizes as one's own and self-same. The friend, like Rome's conquered Italian neighbors being made citizens in the Republican period, is annexed because of likeness—because he naturally belongs to oneself. Despite the language of blood relationship, this is not the kinship we encountered in the *Lysis*, which allowed room for both sameness and difference, but rather a kind of conquest, the arrogation to the self (by violence if necessary) of what is naturally self-identical. This sort of friendship expands the self not qualitatively, through the addition of qualities that it did not previously possess, but rather quantitatively, through the incorporation of more of what one already has.

Friends can thus become possessions for Cicero's Laelius as they never were for Plato's Socrates: Socrates would *rather* have a friend than possessions like quails, cocks, horses, dogs, or gold (p. 31, 211e), but for Laelius friends are qualitatively similar, though finer, possessions:

> When a man is overflowing with wealth and goods and all kinds of abundance, and has got hold of everything that money can buy—horses, slaves, splendid clothes, expensive plate—he will be very foolish if he fails to add friends to that list, since *they* are the finest equipment [*supellectilem*] that life can offer. . . . Friendship, on the other hand, remains a firm and durable asset [*possessio*]. (p. 205 [translator's emphasis], xv.55)

Supellex literally means household furniture, while *possessio* suggests the exclusive use or enjoyment of an object, sometimes of an estate. Laelius is being ironic here—obviously friends are not possessions in the same sense that slaves are—but the language is suggestive nonetheless, and what it suggests is the same theme of appropriation of that which is naturally one's own.

An old friend is later compared to one's own familiar horse (p. 211, xix.68).[66]

The dialogue form, here as in the *Tusculan Disputations*, reflects this imperialist doctrine of friendship. Rather than the dialogue-as-seduction that we found in the *Lysis*, Cicero's *On Friendship* presents dialogue-as-coercion. Like the *Tusculans*, this "dialogue" is not truly dialogical; though the term used is *sermonem*, discussion, the other discussants contribute nothing beyond their deference to Laelius, whom the reader is clearly intended to perceive as authoritative: "Somehow expositions of this kind seem to carry special conviction when they are placed in the mouths of personages of an earlier generation, especially when these were eminent men" (p. 177, i.4). His interlocutors, indeed, compete with each other to defer to Laelius' wisdom; when Fannius requests that Laelius speak about friendship, Scaevola quickly adds his own plea: "If you will, I shall be quite as delighted as Fannius. Indeed, when he asked you, I was just about to make the same request myself" (p. 185, iv.16). Later, this language takes on a more violent tone than is ever found in the *Tusculans*. When the other two insist that Laelius continue speaking, he jokingly responds that "[t]his is really coercion! Your tactful choice of weapons does not change the situation at all—whatever may be said about your methods, they are violent [*cogitis*]" (p. 191, viii.26). *Cogitis* suggests that his discourse is forced or compelled; ironically, his listeners are so eager to defer to him that they force him to take the lead.

The single-minded, monologic nature of the "dialogue" in *On Friendship* thus reflects the unified, preordained doctrine of friendship that it enunciates. In a discourse on friendship as self-identity, there can be no disagreement, and in a doctrine that annexes others to the imperial self, there can be no deviation from that self-sameness, neither external discussion nor internal self-questioning. As Laelius himself says, "friendship is something which inspires the same opinion in everybody" (p. 219, xxiii.86). No dialogue, in short, is possible.[67]

And neither is erotic desire: in a doctrine of male–male relations based on this notion of the self-same and the appropriation of what is naturally one's own, there is no room for the deviant, which, as we saw in the *Tusculan Disputations*, is now to be condemned as merely unnatural.[68] The refusal of dialogue goes hand-in-hand with the refusal of same-sex desire.

Cicero's *Laelius: On Friendship*, like his other works, was widely read and admired in the Middle Ages. Pope Gregory I the Great, indeed, condemned Cicero's writings because their rhetorical charm distracted young men from the study of scripture;[69] ironically, Cicero, who condemned male–male erotics as unnatural, becomes in this formulation himself a seducer of

young men. At any rate, *On Friendship*'s influence on later medieval literature, including such authors as Jean de Meun, is considerable. Most significant for our purposes here is the influence it exerted on the twelfth-century
Cistercian theologian Aelred of Rievaulx, particularly in his dialogue on
Spiritual Friendship (*De spiritali amicitia*).

This influence is directly acknowledged at several points in Aelred's text,
and *On Friendship* is cited throughout it. Far from being the seducer imagined by Gregory the Great, in fact, Cicero is here imagined as having had
the potential to save Aelred from a life of sinful loves:

> When I was still just a lad at school, and the charm of my companions
> pleased me very much, I gave my whole soul to affection and devoted myself
> to love amid the ways and vices [*inter mores et uitia*] with which that age is
> wont to be threatened, so that nothing seemed to me more sweet, nothing
> more agreeable, nothing more practical, than to love. And so, torn between
> conflicting loves and friendships [*amores et amicitias*], I was drawn now here,
> now there, and not knowing the law of true friendship, I was often deceived
> by its mere semblance. At length there came into my hands the treatise
> which Tullius wrote on friendship, and it immediately appealed to me as
> being serviceable because of the depth of his ideas, and fascination [*sic*]
> because of the charm of his eloquence. And though I saw myself unfitted for
> that type of friendship, still I was gratified that I had discovered a formula
> for friendship whereby I might check the vacillations [*discursus*] of my loves
> and affections. (pp. 45–46, Prologue 1–3)[70]

Aelred presents himself here as a schoolboy—that is, in the all-male environment of a school—participating in loves that were also "vices" [*uitia*].
Commentators such as John Boswell have understood this and similar passages in Aelred's writings as indicating that "[t]here can be little question
that Aelred was gay and that his erotic attraction to men was a dominant
force in his life."[71] Most scholars would now reject Boswell's essentializing
terminology along with his arguments that the medieval Christian church
was, before the thirteenth century, relatively tolerant of same-sex erotics,
and that a "gay" urban subculture flourished in the twelfth century.
Nevertheless, the evidence from Aelred's writings does suggest a heavy emotional investment in same-sex desire, even when the physical aspects of this
desire are sublimated into a purely "spiritual" friendship.[72] (It is worth noting that in describing his youthful infatuations, he distinguishes between
those he calls "friendships" [*amicitias*] and those he calls "loves" [*amores*].)
Cicero's *On Friendship* appears in this passage precisely as the book that
allowed the young Aelred to imagine another kind of male–male relationship than those in which he was then engaged. These youthful loves seemed

to him, on the one hand, sweet and agreeable, but were also, on the other, a source of conflict and vacillation [*discursus*]; Cicero's text thus held out at least the potential for stability in human relations, though Aelred apparently was unable to give up the sweetness of his loves and apply Cicero's "formula" to his own life until he joined the Cistercian monastery. There he found another source of "sweetness" in the Christian scriptures, and decided to write his own treatise combining Cicero's stability with the sweetness of the Christian religion and specifically Cistercian monasticism (p. 46, Prologue 4–5). The result is the *Spiritual Friendship*, a dialogue begun around the time he became abbot of Rievaulx in 1147, but not completed until shortly before his death in 1167.[73]

Cicero's dialogue is mentioned early in the first of the three books that (along with the Prologue cited above) comprise the *Spiritual Friendship*, in a conversation between Aelred and a monk named Ivo, a dialogue imagined as taking place on one of Aelred's visits to another monastic house dependent on Rievaulx. Ivo seeks to learn about friendship from Aelred, who suggests that the "laws and precepts" set forth by Cicero might suffice (p. 52, I.5–6). Ivo, however, repeating Aelred's own experience recounted in the Prologue, finds, as a monk, that pagan writings lack the "sweetness" and "authority" of Christian scripture, and requests instruction in friendship in a specifically Christian context (pp. 52–53, I.7). Nevertheless, Aelred still proposes that they accept Cicero's definition of friendship: "Friendship is mutual harmony in affairs human and divine coupled with benevolence and charity" (p. 53, I.11; cf. Cicero, *Laelius de amicitia* V.20).

Despite his paganism, Cicero and the high medieval Christian church were in agreement in at least one area, the condemnation of erotic relations between men; historians and critics since Boswell (notably Mark D. Jordan and Elizabeth Keiser) have paid considerably more attention to manifestations of the Christian hostility to nonprocreative sex, or "sodomy," that appeared in the eleventh and twelfth centuries.[74] As we might expect both from Aelred's initial adoption of Cicero's formula and from his position within the church, Aelred too refuses to countenance the erotic within the realm of true friendship[75]—though in a less direct manner than Cicero in the *Tusculans*. One way of conceptualizing same-sex desire in the Middle Ages is as the "unspeakable sin" or "unspeakable vice," not to be discussed directly (by a priest in the confessional, for instance) for fear of introducing the innocent to a hitherto unfamiliar sin.[76] Aelred's indirect references to same-sex desire may be seen as part of this reticent tradition, but they may be discerned nonetheless.

When in the first book, for example, Ivo asks Aelred to distinguish true spiritual friendship from other sorts, he characterizes the other sorts by asking rhetorically "[h]ow many persons leading a worldly existence and acting as partners in some form of vice [*uitiis*], are united [*copulantur*] by a similar pact and find the bond of even that sort of friendship to be more pleasant [*deliciis*] and sweet [*dulcis*] than all the delights of this world!" (p. 58, I.33). The language of "vice," "sweetness," "delight," and so on implies once again that Aelred as author is using the figure of Ivo to recall his own sinful youth and same-sex loves, as recounted in the Prologue. Aelred initially rejects the relationships described by Ivo, as he has rejected his own earlier loves, as one form of false friendship, because, as Cicero and Plato also suggest, true friendship can exist only between those who are good; in Judeo-Christian terms (quoting Psalm 10:6), "he does not love his fellow-man who loves iniquity" (p. 58, I.35).[77] This type of false friendship, in fact, defined as "carnal friendship [*amicitia carnalis*]" (p. 59, I.38–39) looms large throughout the remainder of Aelred's dialogue: carnal friendship, he claims, "is undertaken without deliberation, is tested by no act of judgment, is in no wise governed by reason; but through the violence of affection is carried away through divers paths [*sed secundum impetum affectionis per diuersa raptatur*]" (p. 60, I.41). Again, we find here language that combines violent affection with instability, as in the sinful loves of Aelred's youth. In rejecting such loves, Aelred is also rejecting same-sex erotics— though, as we shall see, this rejection is ultimately more ambivalent than appears at first glance. True friendship allows for a sense of security and stability that for Aelred was missing in his youthful carnal loves, for "how can there be any security in the love of him who is tossed about by every wind, who consents to every counsel?" (p. 98, III.28).

If Aelred is similar to Cicero in his refusal to countenance male–male erotic desire as a component of friendship, he derives much of his positive doctrine of friendship from Cicero as well. Like Cicero in *On Friendship*, Aelred finds in sameness—including, though not limited to, sameness in virtue—the essential condition for true friendship, accepting Cicero's doctrine without considering any other possibilities (such as those raised by Plato). The "harmony" cited above in Aelred's adoption of Cicero's definition, in fact, is quickly reified as identity or sameness in Book I: ". . . those who have the same [*eadem*] opinion, the same will, in matters human and divine, along with mutual benevolence and charity, have, we shall admit, reached the perfection of friendship" (p. 54, I.13). Identity of opinion and will are necessary to friendship's "perfection," though this very formula also implies the existence of lower degrees of friendship, in which this identity is not complete, but which may deserve the name of friendship nonetheless. "Perfect" friendship, however, requires an identity of feeling now justified not by the political or historical examples that Cicero cites, but by scripture; citing Romans 12:15, for example, Aelred declares, "let him rejoice with his friend in his joys, and weep with him in his sorrows, and feel as his own all [*omnia sua esse sentiat*] that his friend experiences" (p. 55, I.20). This sameness of will and desire, in fact, also characterizes the angels' existence, making human friendship an image of an eternal, divine relationality: "Among them pleasant companionship and delightful love created the same will, the same desire [*affectum*]" (p. 63, I.56).

The theme of sameness as a specifically Christian value linking earthly friendship with eternal life is developed further in Book III, composed along with Book II some twenty years after the *Spiritual Friendship* was begun. As Douglas Roby points out, the last two books are even more clearly Ciceronian than the first: in terms of dramatic setting, for instance, they reproduce the situation of *On Friendship*, with two interlocutors, now the monks Walter and Gratian, asking a more venerable colleague (Aelred) to discuss his views on friendship (Ivo is only a memory in Books II and III).[78] As one might expect, the doctrine of sameness remains intact: though Walter has experienced only lower forms of friendship, he agrees that the goal is "out of many to make but one [*ex pluribus unum facere*]" (p. 113, III.86), while Aelred himself echoes Laelius in finding in the friend an image of oneself: "For friends ought to be so alike that immediately upon seeing one another a likeness [*similitudo*] of expression is reflected from the first to the second, whether he be cast down with sorrow or serene with joy" (p. 130, III.131).

At the same time, however, the more specifically Christian reinterpretation of Cicero's doctrine is also more fully developed, by means of references both to Scripture and to the Fathers of the Church: " 'Indeed, among dissimilar characters,' as blessed Ambrose remarks, 'friendship cannot exist' " (p. 99, III.30); the Ciceronian sentiment is now justified as a Christian rather than a pagan one. Similarly, Cicero's doctrine of the friend as an image of the self is also set into a Christian context: "Our Lord and Savior himself has written for us the formula of true friendship when he said: 'You shall love your neighbor as yourself.' Behold the mirror. You love yourself" (p. 107, III.69).

If Cicero's doctrine of sameness among friends is rooted in an imperialist discourse of annexation and possession, Aelred's is thus rooted in a Christian ideology of monotheism—and of eternal life: "your friend is the companion of your soul, to whose spirit you join and attach yours, and so associate yourself that you wish to become one instead of two, since he is one to whom you entrust yourself as to another self. . . . For friendship should be stable and manifest a certain likeness to eternity [*quamdam aeternitatis speciem praeferre*], persevering always in affection" (p. 93, III.6): as for Buber, proximity to the human other figures proximity to the divine. References to the Christian afterlife as the source and fulfillment of human friendship—like the reference in Book I to the angels' mode of existence— suggest something of the stability Aelred found in giving up his conflicting and vacillating loves in favor of "spiritual friendship."[79]

Indeed, friendship from this perspective is an image of the divine unity itself, an idea anticipated in Book I:

> He has willed, moreover, for so his eternal reason has directed, that peace encompass all his creatures and society unite them; and thus all creatures obtain from him, who is supremely and purely one, some trace of that unity [*unitatis*]. For that reason he has left no type of beings alone, but out of many has drawn them together by means of a certain society [*societate*]. (p. 62, I.53)

This is as close as Aelred comes to enunciating a social theory in the *Spiritual Friendship*: human society as a whole is a reflection of the divine unity itself, and friendship provides the bonds on which society is based; it is therefore a divinely sanctioned and natural bond (like Cicero, Aelred sets human social bonds in the context of animal societies, pp. 62–63, I.54–55; cf. *On Friendship* xxi.81) in which human beings to some extent can even participate in the divine mode of existence. This relationship is further elaborated, in an even more specifically Christian context, in Book II.

> And so in friendship are joined honor and charm, truth and joy, sweetness and good-will, affection and action. And these take their beginning from Christ, advance through Christ, and are perfected in Christ. Therefore, not too steep or unnatural does the ascent appear from Christ, as the inspiration of the love by which we love our friend, to Christ giving himself to us as our Friend for us to love, so that charm may follow upon charm, sweetness upon sweetness and affection upon affection. And thus, friend cleaving to friend in the spirit of Christ, is made with Christ but one heart and one soul, and so mounting aloft through degrees of love to friendship with Christ, he is made one spirit with him in one kiss. Aspiring to this kiss the saintly soul cries out: "Let him kiss me with the kiss of his mouth." (pp. 74–75, II.20–21)

This remarkable passage, with its Christian neoplatonic ladder of love and friendship, may remind the modern reader (coincidentally) of Diotima's speech in Plato's *Symposium*, to be considered in the next chapter. Here its interest lies in the way it relates human friendship to the Christian doctrine of Christ's divine love of humanity: if the exact identity between friend and friend is an idea derived directly from Cicero, here it is understood as a product of the friends' identity in Christian belief. It is cleaving together precisely as Christian believers that is rewarded with the union of the friends' hearts and souls in that belief, a belief that ultimately brings them into union with Christ as well. The language of this essential unification of hearts and souls is derived from Scripture (Acts 4:32), as is, even more strikingly, the language of unification with Christ: the quotation from the beginning of the Song of Songs (1:1) referring to the kiss was commonly understood in Cistercian thought as a metaphor for the union of the soul with Christ.[80] As Ivo suggested in Book I, only Christian doctrine— ultimately Christ himself—can provide certain authorization for friendship (p. 53, I.8); friendship may be, as Cicero claims, natural, but it also requires regulation by Christian law (p. 64, I.61). The sweetness of Aelred's unstable youthful loves has therefore by Book II been transformed into a spiritual sweetness—but a sweetness that also retains, in Aelred's quotation of the passionate love song's desire, some of the eroticism of those earlier loves.

Aelred's Christian context, in fact, allows him to deviate considerably from the pure Ciceronian doctrine of friendship; despite his respect for Cicero's text, which he cites (often without attribution) on nearly every page of the *Spiritual Friendship*, Aelred also suggests, by the final book, that Cicero in some cases does require correction by means of Christian revelation. (His eventual deviation from Cicero is foreshadowed even in Book I, when Aelred suggests that Cicero's definition of friendship may contain "too much or too little" and could be rejected [p. 54, I.17].) Nature, for example, is no longer the primary source of value that it was for Cicero, because Christian revelation exhorts human beings to transcend their natures. Aelred can thus take a somewhat chiding tone toward his pagan source, as in his discussion of the friendship between David and Jonathan recorded in I Samuel. Whereas Cicero, according to Aelred, declares it impossible that anyone would choose friendship over power because "nature is too weak to despise power" (p. 117, III.95), Jonathan in I Samuel 23:17 provides an inspiring example of one who went beyond nature, indeed "was found a victor over nature [*uictor naturae*], a despiser of glory and of power, one who preferred the honor of his friend to his own, saying: 'You shall be king, and I will be next after you' " (p. 117, III.95). Aelred is here being unfair to Cicero, who claims that those who value friendship over power are rare, not nonexistent (*Laelius de amicitia* 17.63–64), but the unfairness is itself instructive: Cicero, whose definition in Book I provided the starting point for a discussion of friendship, by Book III can in certain instances be repudiated, as Aelred uses the Bible to distance himself from his pagan source. Aelred thus represents Christian "spiritual friendship" as a deviation from, and perfection of, pagan friendships.

This Christian deviance from the norm that was established in Book I also allows room for desire, which, as we have seen, was largely absent from Cicero's conception of friendship. The goal of a union in friendship that cannot achieve its perfection until it also includes union in Christ is by definition a goal that is always deferred in the course of human life, and which is therefore also always desired; desire, far from being eliminated, is thus actually instituted as a condition of friendship. The "aspiring" saintly soul is in a state of desire for the kiss. This particular deviation from Ciceronian doctrine is evident throughout the *Spiritual Friendship*. In fact, it is built into the structure of the dialogue itself. Whereas Cicero emphasizes the violent coercion that leads to Laelius' speeches, Aelred represents himself as being led into dialogue as a response to desire. In Book I, he initiates the conversation because he has perceived Ivo's desire for himself: during a discussion with the other monks, Aelred noticed that

> you would raise your head and make ready to say something, but just as quickly, as though your voice had been trapped in your throat, you would drop your head again and continue your silence. Then you would leave us for a while, and later return looking rather disheartened. I concluded from all this that you wanted to talk to me, but that you dreaded the crowd, and hoped to be alone with me. (p. 51, I.2)

Aelred has read these signs correctly; Ivo identifies his situation precisely as a form of desire directed at Aelred himself:

> That's it exactly, and I deeply appreciate your solicitude for your son. His state of mind and his desire [*mentisque*] have been disclosed to you by none other than the Spirit of Love. And would that your Lordship would grant me this favor, that, as often as you visit your sons here, I may be permitted, at least once, to have you all to myself and to disclose to you the deep feelings of my heart without disturbance. (pp. 51–52, I.3)

The very opening of the dialogue, then, suggests in its dramatic situation the kind of spiritual friendship that will be formulated in more abstract terms in the succeeding books: Christ inspires Aelred to respond to a potential friend's desire for intimacy, the sharing of feelings that characterizes true friendship. Ivo wishes to be distinguished from the other monks by Aelred's friendship; as Aelred later points out, Christian love is to be directed toward all, but intimate friendship is reserved for the few (see pp. 112–113, III.83–84). Aelred responds to Ivo's desire by providing the opportunity for it to be fulfilled: his very first words to Ivo place this desire in a Christian context, and suggest that they are already situated with regard to each other in such a way as to allow spiritual friendship to develop: "Here we are, you and I, and I hope a third, Christ, is in our midst. . . . Come now, beloved [*carissime*], open your heart, and pour into these friendly ears whatsoever you will . . ." (p. 51, I.1). A very similar scene opens Book II and introduces the new interlocutors Walter and Gratian: once again Aelred has observed the signs that a monk, Walter, desires him in the same friendly way that Ivo desired him earlier. Walter too is distressed at the presence of other people, in this case from outside the monastery (p. 69, II.1). And once again Aelred responds by fulfilling his desire: "You know, 'the best appetizer is hunger'; and neither honey nor any other spice gives such relish to wine as a strong thirst does to water. And so perhaps this conference of ours, like spiritual food and drink, will be more enjoyable to you because of the intense longing preceding it [*quo aestus praecessit ardentior*]" (p. 70, II.3). Desire, then, even desire of the particularly seething or surging type suggested by *aestus*, is a precondition not only for the relations between human beings and Christ, but for friendship between men as well.

Cicero eliminated desire by eliminating difference, or tried to; despite Aelred's emphasis on the sameness of friends, his reintroduction of desire suggests the reintroduction of difference as well. Friends, for instance, may be united to each other, but still desire a higher good from which both friends differ, and which therefore both friends lack. Friendship, in fact, is imagined as that which unites friends in their shared difference from this higher good, even among the angels, who are united, as we have seen, in "the same will, the same desire" (p. 63, I. 56). The angels, as members of the familiar celestial hierarchy of seraphim, cherubim, and so on, also differ among themselves, and friendship for them is that which harmonizes this difference: "Assuredly, since one seemed to be superior, the other inferior, there would have been occasion for envy, had not the charity of friendship prevented it" (p. 63, I.56). Hierarchy here is not eliminated through the pretense of equality that Cicero suggested as a way to overcome difference in social rank; rather, it is accepted and harmonized in the shared desire that defines the angels' friendship. Since Christian spiritual friends share the same desire as well, their differences too can be harmonized without being eliminated.

Once again the contexts of Christian doctrine and monastic life allow Aelred a perspective that subtly deviates from the context of Roman political experience found in Cicero's *On Friendship*, and that allows room for deviation within the identity of desire that constitutes spiritual friendship. The kind of difference that is not eliminated, but accepted as part of the friendship, would be foreign to Cicero's Laelius, but can be tolerated and harmonized within the context of Christian monasticism—the more easily, perhaps, because within the monastery there is relatively little at stake in terms of the honors, riches, and power that for Laelius made friendship such a rare (or, for Aelred, impossible) experience in the world of Roman politics. Monastic poverty eliminates the competition for such prizes; without such competition, difference is less problematic. Walter points out that monks "are permitted to receive nothing and to bestow nothing" (p. 119, III.100), though they do, as Aelred responds, have other resources: "to be solicitous for one another, to pray for one another, to blush for one another, to rejoice for one another, to grieve for one another's fall as one's own, to regard another's progress as one's own" (p. 119, III.101).

The best examples of friendship that can include difference are those drawn from Aelred's accounts of his own friendships in Book III. Aelred, discussing how one should select friends, suggests that certain vices may be curable, and that persons subject to them, once "healed," may become eligible for friendship; among these curable vices are irascibility, fickleness, suspicion, and garrulity (p. 94, III.14). Walter, however, immediately objects that Aelred himself had a close friend who was never cured of his irascibility, and even implies that Aelred chose not to chastise him for his vice: "he was never hurt by you even to the end of his life, though he often offended you" (p. 95, III.16). Aelred admits that some people are naturally prone to such vices, which in that case may never be entirely cured; in fact,

> they may occasionally offend a friend by a thoughtless word or act or by a zeal that fails in discretion. If it happens that we have received such men into our friendship, we must bear with them patiently. And since their affection toward us is established with certainty, if then there is any excess in word or action, this ought to be put up with as being in a friend, or at least our admonition of his fault ought to be administered painlessly and even pleasantly. (p. 95, III.17)

The possibility of an ongoing difference within a friendship is at least tacitly acknowledged here; in other words, there is at least some room in Aelred's theory of friendship for relationships that are not based entirely on the self-identity recommended by Cicero. It is friendship itself—the offending friend's acknowledged affection—that allows such differences to continue, with or without an admonition. Friendship among men, as among the angels, is that which harmonizes difference, not that which eliminates it. Friendship in life, then, may be seen as a matter of deviance within sameness, rather than as the perfect sameness recommended in the more abstract discussions.

This point is made even clearer in the ensuing discussion of a current friend of Aelred's described by Gratian as one whom "you prefer to all of us" even though "you will not neglect anything that pleases him no matter how trivial it may be, yet he cannot bear even trifles for your sake" (p. 95, III.18). Once more Aelred admits that "since the wills of both did not fuse into one, it was easier for me to yield my will than his" (p. 95, III.20); later he continues, "[i]f, indeed, as is sometimes the case, my feeling differs [*dissentiat*] from his, we give in to each other so that sometimes he yields to me, but generally I yield to him" (p. 100, III.38). Ideally, such differences may be outgrown as the friendship progresses, as Aelred suggests happened with his own closest friend, who began by pointing out their differences— "what in me pleased him but little" (p. 128, III.123)—but with whom Aelred eventually "attained that stage at which we had but one mind and one soul" (p. 128, III.124). This resolution of difference into identity may be the ideal spiritual friendship, mirroring the attainment of union with Christ, but that fact does not prevent other kinds of friendship from having their own genuine value, like Aelred's friendships with the irascible man or the one to whom he must yield. The friends' wills in such cases do not become one; this is not identity, but difference maintained and harmonized, and this too produces a true spiritual friendship, even if not the ideal one. There is for Aelred, in other words, room for deviance even within the concept of true spiritual friendship itself.

The yielding of one's own will to that of a friend also suggests the possibility of an internal deviation, one within the self: one may "yield" in practice without giving up one's own opinion internally. Aelred discusses this problem explicitly in Book III by distinguishing the vice of "[s]imulation [*simulatio*] . . . a kind of deceptive agreement, opposed to the judgment of reason" (p.123, III.111) from "dissimulation [*dissimulatio*]," which "is in a sense a dispensing with, or a putting off of punishment or correction, without interior approval, in consideration of place, time, or person" (p. 123, III.112). This kind of self-division, a deviation in action from one's own internal disapproval, is a necessary component in friendships when the friends are unequal or dissimilar, again suggesting that Aelred's concept of friendship leaves considerable room for difference despite the underlying theory of sameness, and deviates from its own original Ciceronian definition of friendship. This yielding is necessary in friendships that have not, or not yet, attained the ideal sameness of will and desire that characterizes perfect friendship; as we have seen, such relationships are still genuine and valuable spiritual friendships in their own right. In fact, Aelred develops a rather neoplatonic hierarchy, or "ladder" of friendships that may not attain the ideal unity but that may nonetheless prove to be productive stages leading toward it. If difference and desire imply each other, the lower forms of friendship, characterized by difference, may also be where we might expect to find desire, and indeed it is on the lower rungs of the ladder of friendship that male–male desire returns to play its part in Aelred's theory of friendship. This idea is introduced indirectly in Book I, in the course of rejecting "carnal" friendships in favor of the true "spiritual" ones:

> Yet, since such great joy [*dulcedo*] is experienced in friendship which either lust [*libido*] defiles, avarice [*auaritia*] dishonors, or luxury [*luxuria*] pollutes, we may infer how much sweetness [*suauitatis*] that friendship possesses which, in proportion as it is nobler, is the more secure; purer, it is the more pleasing; freer, it is the more happy. Let us allow that, because of some similarity in feelings, those friendships which are not true be, nevertheless, called friendships, provided, however, they are judiciously distinguished from that friendship which is spiritual and therefore true. Hence let one kind of friendship be called carnal, another worldly, and another spiritual. The carnal springs from mutual harmony in vice; the worldly is enkindled by the hope of gain; and the spiritual is cemented by similarity of life, morals, and pursuits among the just. (p. 59, I.36–38)

It should be noted, first, that Aelred allows that these inferior, false friendships are also the source of the experience of a great and presumably genuine "joy," sullied as they may be by "lust" and "luxury" as well as by "avarice." This passage may remind the reader that Aelred's own youthful loves, discussed in the Prologue, were themselves "sweet," though unstable and ultimately less satisfying than the sweetness of the monastery. The pleasure of male–male "lust" (like that of another form of desire, avarice), while it may be condemned, is not denied its own place in the hierarchy of friendship. Indeed, these carnal relations are not denied the name of friendship, though they, along with the avaricious worldly relations, are to be carefully distinguished from the higher form of spiritual friendship; the similarity of feelings in such friendships is thus acknowledged at the same time that Aelred insists on their ultimate difference from the feelings involved in the truest kind of friendship. Carnal friendships are thus a form of deviance from spiritual ones: differing within similarity, or similar despite difference. Even the friendship polluted by luxury or defiled by lust is recognized as joyous; Aelred provides a particularly clear example of the deviant as proximate, of the outlaw turning up as in-law, to use Dollimore's phrase.

A comparable hierarchy is reintroduced in Book II, in the discussion of the kiss of Christ cited above. Here Aelred introduces another three-part hierarchy. To begin with, all kisses are similar in that "in a kiss two breaths meet, and are mingled, and are united. As a result, a certain sweetness of mind is born, which rouses and binds together the affection of those who embrace" (p. 75, II.23). The language here is physical and even erotic, with its union of two breaths, followed by arousal and embrace; the physical— or carnal—thus provides the overall framework within which the three different types of kiss are to be understood. "There is, then, a corporeal kiss, a spiritual kiss, and an intellectual kiss. The corporeal kiss [*osculum corporale*] is made by the impression of the lips; the spiritual kiss by the union of spirits; the intellectual kiss through the Spirit of God, by the infusion of grace" (p. 76, II.24). While the corporeal kiss may be misused in lust (p. 76, II.25), it also has its legitimate place in the hierarchy, as a sign of reconciliation, peace, or unity, "or as a symbol of love [*dilectionis*], such as is permitted between bride and bridegroom or as is extended to and received from friends after a long absence" (p. 76, II.24). (The understanding of friendship as the equivalent of marriage is further developed in Books II and III, as we shall see below.) The spiritual kiss (*osculum spiritale*), "made not by contact of the mouth but by the affection of the heart," is "characteristically the kiss of friends who are bound by one law of friendship" (p. 76, II.26). It leads, as we have seen, to the highest kiss, the intellectual "kiss of Christ alone" (p. 77, II.27). The latter two kisses, spiritual and intellectual, are thus arranged not in a static hierarchy, but as rungs on a ladder, the lower leading to the higher. Aelred does not explicitly suggest a similar relationship between the corporeal and the spiritual kisses, and indeed remains wary of physical desire throughout Book II (as in the denunciation of carnal friendships, "rising like a mist from the concupiscence of the flesh" [p. 84, II.58], that shortly follows; nevertheless, he leaves the reader sufficient room to understand the corporeal kiss itself as one that might also lead up the ladder.[81]

This implication becomes more concrete in Book III, when Walter fears that true spiritual friendship is beyond his capacity, and proposes instead a harmless, pleasing, companionate friendship based on mutual goodwill and tolerant of difference and disagreement (p. 113, III.85–86). For Aelred, returning to the categories of friendship established in Book I, this kind clearly "belongs to the carnal" [*carnalium est*] (p. 113, III.87)—but now the carnal friendship can explicitly serve as an introduction to the spiritual (which, as we have seen in Book II, leads to the ultimate kiss of Christ):

> And yet this friendship except for trifles and deceptions, if nothing dishonorable enters into it, is to be tolerated in the hope of more abundant grace, as the beginnings [*principia*], so to say, of a holier friendship. By these beginnings, with a growth in piety and in constant zeal for things of the spirit,

with the growing seriousness of maturer years and the illumination of the spiritual senses, they may, with purer affections, mount to loftier heights [*ad altiora*] from, as it were, a region close by [*quasi e uicino conscendant*], just as yesterday we said that the friendship of man could easily be translated into a friendship for God himself because of the similarity existing between both. (pp. 113–114, III.87)

By the end of the dialogue, then, Aelred is acknowledging that the carnal friendship of Book I may indeed be a rung on the ladder leading to spiritual friendship, and from thence to spiritual union with Christ.[82] Once again the relation is one of deviance: the lofty heights of spiritual love may be reached from the lowlands of carnal friendship because the latter is "a region close by": not identical with the goal, but similar enough to provide access to it under the right conditions. Those conditions include, undoubtedly, a rejection of the lustful, physical aspects of male–male desire; but the desire that arises from human difference can still play its part in the human desire, or friendship, "for God himself." Aelred's own friendships again provide a model: one boyhood friend in particular—presumably from the days of Aelred's carnal loves—"devoted to me from boyhood [*a puero*] even to middle age, and loved by me, mounted with me through all the stages of friendship [*per omnes amicitie gradus*], as far as human imperfection permitted" (p. 127, III.120) until "I deemed my heart in a fashion his, and his mine, and he felt in like manner towards me. And so, as we were progressing in friendship without deviation, neither's correction evoked the indignation of the other, neither's yielding produced blame" (p. 129, III.125). Deviation is ultimately to be eliminated; but the unstable, deviating loves of youth are the first step toward that perfect stability of eternity, "a foretaste [*portio*] of blessedness thus to love and thus to be loved" (p. 129, III.127).

This passage also suggests another manner in which Aelred deals with difference, including difference in social status within the monastery. At certain points, it should be noted, Aelred encounters the same difficulties that Cicero did when discussing social hierarchies. Whereas "a superior must be on a plane of equality with the inferior" (p. 115, III.90), hierarchy is no more easily eliminated in the medieval Christian world, or even in the monastery itself, than in Roman society. Thus Aelred, as abbot, finds himself in a position of authority when it comes to the promotion of other monks, despite his desire for equality (see pp. 124–125, III.115–118). Aelred is forced to acknowledge the reality of difference in friendship, sometimes seemingly against his will.[83] At other points, however, Aelred invokes a more flexible means of dealing with hierarchy, one that emphasizes the exchange of roles. From the beginning, Aelred expresses a certain discomfort with the very concept of hierarchy. In Book I, for instance, Ivo both requests Aelred's instruction and refers to himself as Aelred's spiritual son, suggesting the deference that might be expected from a younger monk toward the older abbot. Aelred himself, however, encouraging Ivo's friendship, suggests a more interactive relationship: "Speak freely, therefore, and entrust to your friend all your cares and thoughts, that you may both learn and teach, give and receive, pour out and drink in [*profundas et haurias*]" (p. 52, I.4). The two are imagined here as exchanging the roles of preceptor and student, benefactor and beneficiary; given the context of Aelred's youthful loves just established in the Prologue, in fact, it seems fair to characterize the relationship with the more loaded modern terms "active" and "passive"; certainly the language of emitting and receiving fluids does nothing to counteract this impression. (Ivo replies that his role as the inferior partner in this friendship is only "to drink in, not to pour out" [p. 52, I.5].) Hierarchy is not exactly denied here: the roles remain in place. But by imagining friendship as a situation in which the occupants of those roles are constantly shifting, Aelred rethinks the social hierarchy in a potentially carnivalesque way, to use Bakhtin's and Kristeva's terminology, that suggests a greater overall equality.[84]

Walter, at the beginning of Book II, adopts a similar procedure: on the one hand, though Aelred refers to him as "brother [*frater*]" (p. 69, II.1) while he, like Ivo, thinks of himself as "your son [*puero tuo*]" (p. 70, II.6), Walter also phrases their hierarchical relationship in such a way as to suggest another exchange of roles. Complaining that Aelred had, that day, neglected the monks in favor of outsiders, he asks "who could preserve his patience through a whole day seeing those agents of Pharaoh getting your full attention, while we, to whom you are particularly indebted [*quibus specialiter debitor es*], were not able to gain even so much as a word with you?" (p. 69, II.2). Aelred as abbot in some sense "owes" his inferiors his attention, but the language of indebtedness places him in the position of beneficiary in the monastery's emotional economy. The same is true of Aelred's friendship with the irascible man of Book III: on the one hand, Aelred must take the active role and can "restrain an outburst at any time by a mere nod, even when it is already breaking forth into speech" (p. 100, III.37). But on the other hand, it is apparently just as often that the unnamed friend must take on this active role, and reprove or restrain his monastic superior's own anger or other inappropriate outburst:

> How often has the nod of my friend restrained or extinguished the flame of
> anger aroused within me and already bursting forth into public gaze! How

frequently his rather severe demeanor has repressed the unbecoming word already on my lips! How often when carelessly breaking into laughter, or lapsing into idleness, I have recovered a proper dignity at his approach! (p. 120, III.103)[85]

While the social hierarchy cannot really be eliminated, Aelred imaginatively performs, in the dramatic course of the dialogue itself, the repositioning of friends on different social levels recommended by Cicero's *Laelius*. This performative trying-out of active and passive roles allows that recommendation to be embodied in a way that never occurs in Cicero's text. While hierarchical difference is acknowledged, it is used to play out the possibility of differences within the self—active/passive, benefactor/beneficiary, and so on—as well. Cicero's dialogues never allow for the kind of internal self-deviation that we find in Aelred, as we do in Plato's Socrates.

The modern reader is apt to find an element of gender in these performative exchanges of role: an active superiority that takes authority, in the Middle Ages as in Greco-Roman civilization, is likely to be gendered masculine, while the passive partner who accepts his superior's orders is lower on the social hierarchy and is likely to be gendered feminine, a division of roles justified medically and legally in the Middle Ages, as well as in popular opinion.[86] From that perspective, the sequential performance of dominance and submission by both Aelred and his monks in these passages suggests as well a certain fluidity in gender identity. Certainly the tradition of allegorical interpretation of the Song of Songs cited above allows Aelred to identify himself with the Song's bride, longing for "the kiss of his mouth" (p. 77, II.27).

Both Plato and Cicero exclude the feminine from their discussions of male–male desire, sameness, and difference: not only are no women actually present in these debates, but, perhaps surprisingly to a modern reader, the very language in which their discussions are couched refuses femininity in its examination of sameness and difference: the metaphors are of master and slave, hunter and hunted, political opponents, and so on but never of male and female or masculine and feminine. What for the modern reader are the primary categories of difference—male/female—are excluded. Aelred's figurative language, referring though it does to the all-male world of the monastery, brings gender to the discussion of sameness and difference, and it is the Judeo-Christian scriptures that allow him to do so, not only the Song of Songs but Genesis and the Gospels as well.[87]

In a sense, the church's literal condemnation of same-sex eroticism is transformed by Aelred's references to Genesis (and later biblical texts' reinterpretations of Genesis), in which the monastery is reimagined as an all-male Garden of Eden, with masculine friends taking on the roles of so many Adams and Eves. The theme is introduced in Book I, with a reference to the Gospel of John's citation of Genesis (John 15:16):

> For spiritual friendship, which we call true, should be desired, not for consideration of any worldly advantage or for any extrinsic cause, but from the dignity of its own nature and the feelings of the human heart, so that its fruition and reward is [*sic*] nothing other than itself. Whence the Lord in the Gospel says: "I have appointed you that you should go, and should bring forth fruit," that is, that you should love one another. For true friendship advances by perfecting itself, and the fruit [*fructus*] is derived from feeling the sweetness of that perfection. (pp. 60–61, I.45–46)

The references to fruit, whether desirable, as here, or forbidden, as in Genesis, will recur throughout the dialogue, and serve as one of its unifying images.[88] Here Aelred cites, and reinterprets, the gospel's previous reinterpretation of the divine command in Genesis to "be fruitful and multiply" (Gen. 1:28), but the fruitfulness in this case refers to spiritual friendships among Aelred's monks, rather than the original injunction to sexual reproduction.[89] In this move from Genesis to John to Aelred's own text, male–female sex thus becomes the sign of male–male friendships, the spiritual sweetness taking the place of the fruits of physical reproduction, that is, offspring. Monastic friends become the spiritual equivalents of Adam and Eve in the Garden.[90]

The Genesis theme is continued more explicitly as Book I proceeds. Speaking of the Creation (Gen. 2:18–22), Aelred again uses it to demonstrate the divine origin of male friendship:

> Finally, when God created man, in order to commend more highly the good of society, he said: "it is not good for man to be alone: let us make him a helper like unto himself." It was from no similar, nor even from the same, material that divine Might formed this help mate, but as a clearer inspiration to charity and friendship he produced the woman from the very substance of the man. How beautiful it is that the second human being was taken from the side of the first, so that nature might teach that human beings are equal and, as it were, collateral, and that there is in human affairs neither a superior nor an inferior, a characteristic of true friendship. (p. 63, I.57)

The function of human sexual difference[91] here is not reproduction, but rather to provide a model of friendship. For Aelred, this difference does not rule out similarity or even identity; indeed, that which scripture presents as sex differences are to be decoded as symbols of spiritual sameness. It might seem as if difference is simply being erased in passages like this, but the very fact that Aelred chooses to use the moment of primal sex/gender differentiation as his model of friendship is itself suggestive: the sameness of friends is similar to, and in some sense based on, the difference between the sexes. This passage also suggests the extent to which Aelred presents social hierarchies as cultural constructs rather than as inherent givens: the monastery may have to live within conventional hierarchies, but they are not to be mistaken for nature. This may, indeed, be precisely what allows Aelred and his monks their performative exchange of roles.

For Aelred, the meaning of the passage just quoted is thus that "nature from the very beginning implanted the desire for friendship and charity in the heart of a man" (p. 63, I.58). Friendship and sex difference are here imagined as, not exactly identical, but mutually productive of meaning. Aelred returns to the Edenic imagery in Book III, when he asks Walter whether, if he were in Adam's position, his dominion over the creatures could be enjoyed without a friend:

> Let us imagine that the whole human race has been taken out of the world leaving you as the sole survivor. . . . And consider yourself also as transformed to that ancient state, having all creatures under your dominion, "all sheep and oxen; moreover, the beasts of the fields, the birds of the air, and the fishes of the sea that pass through the paths of the sea." Tell me now, whether without a companion [*socio*] you could enjoy all these possessions? (p. 110, III.77)

The quotation is drawn from Psalm 8:8–9, but the reference to having dominion over the other creatures places it once more in the context of Genesis, and specifically of Adam's situation before the creation of Eve (Gen. 1:26). Once again the relationship of Adam and Eve is transmuted into an image of monastic male–male companionship, the literal, sexual level of the male–female reproductive function again being used as a figure for affectionate relations between men. This point is immediately made explicit. Describing the monastery, Aelred again employs Edenic or paradisal imagery:

> The day before yesterday, as I was walking the round of the cloister of the monastery, the brethren were sitting around forming as it were a most loving crown. In the midst, as it were, of the delights of paradise with the leaves, flowers, and fruits of each single tree, I marveled. In that multitude of brethren I found no one whom I did not love, and no one by whom, I felt sure, I was not loved. (p. 112, III.82)

Eden has now explicitly become identified with the all-male world of the monastery, its fruits, as suggested in Book I, taking not the forbidden form, but the ideal one imagined in Book I: they are the delights of monastic friendship. This is Eden as it should be, the earthly paradise—a foretaste of heaven, not the Eden corrupted by temptation and sin. This is perhaps the dialogue's ultimate example of the exchange of roles: the brethren have become so many Adams and Eves, all equally loving and beloved. The constant evocation of Adam and Eve as the model of friendship for men accommodates both difference and similarity; indeed, they come to seem mutually dependent, as even gender roles are constantly exchanged and performatively tried out, rather than being rigidly policed. As each of Aelred's monastic friends, and Aelred himself, take on the roles of Adam and Eve, dominant and submissive, masculine and feminine, the monastery also comes to be seen as a refuge from the outside world's hierarchical norm. Aelred's dialogue, in fact, is remarkable in its attempt to include the feminine without introducing hierarchy (an attempt doomed to failure, of course, in the dominant discourse of his medieval Christian environment). Friendship is again established as a relation of equals, though this equality is more complex for Aelred than for either Plato or Cicero. For Aelred it is a matter of performatively trying out these different roles in different relationships rather than of assuming the equality of rigidly unchanging social identities, and dialogue is the genre suitable to such a performance: the Judeo-Christian scriptures allow Aelred a certain fluidity in masculine status that a Roman writer like Cicero could not countenance. It is also a fluidity that allows him to imagine himself and his fellow monks as partners in the prototypical marriage of Adam and Eve,[92] and that thus allows a certain male–male erotics back into his theory of friendship.

Aelred's best-known image of male–male marriage is drawn from his earlier treatise entitled *The Mirror of Charity* (*Speculum caritatis*). While the relationship of Jesus and the apostle John is invoked as the justification of spiritual friendship, that relationship is itself characterized, in highly erotic language, as a marriage:

> Lest someone think that this very holy sort of charity should seem reproachable [*improbandum*], our Jesus himself, lowering (Himself) to our condition in every way, suffering all things for us and being compassionate towards us, transformed it by manifesting his love. To one person, not to all, did he grant a resting-place on his most sacred breast in token of his special love, so that the virginal head might be supported by the flowers of his virginal breast, and the fragrant secrets of the heavenly bridal-chamber [*thalami*] might instill the sweet scents of spiritual perfumes on his virginal attachments more abundantly because more closely.[93]

Boswell points out that *thalamus* must refer to marriage in twelfth-century Latin,[94] and suggests that "Aelred's idealization of love between men was a dramatic break with the traditions of monasticism, which had urged since the time of Basil and Benedict that particular friendships of any sort—especially passionate ones—were a threat to monastic harmony and asceticism," but that in Jesus, "he could invoke an authority higher than that of Benedict, Basil, or even his hero Augustine."[95] To be sure, the chastity of this male–male marriage is emphasized throughout; nevertheless, it is a marriage—or spiritual friendship—based on passionate love. In Dollimore's terms, the dominant society's most valued icon is here subject to a perverse transvaluation suggesting that the deviant—the "reproachable," as Aelred calls it—is already contained within the dominant.

In a similar fashion, the *Spiritual Friendship* likens the corporeal kiss between friends to that which unites bride and bridegroom, as we have already seen, and uses the language of union usually reserved for marriage as a way of discussing friendship throughout (e.g., p. 103, III.48). The monastic life, and this eroticized male–male friendship, are thus represented as a highly desirable deviation from the external world's dominant male–female norm, while the condition of friendship itself, as in Plato, is also construed as deviance: the loved one is neither identical nor opposite, but can take on a variety of roles, including gender roles, and may therefore best be understood as another "region close by," proximate, a deviation from the self, which is also fluid in its own self-deviation.

The dramatic form of Aelred's dialogue itself reflects this notion of friendship as deviance. Unlike Laelius' or even Socrates' interlocutors, Aelred's play a genuinely dialogic role in his text; in Books II and III Walter and Gratian even have their own relationship independent of Aelred, one that is more fully developed even than that between Lysis and Menexenus. Whereas the latter friendship is mentioned from time to time in Plato's dialogue, it is not dramatically developed throughout the text as Walter's and Gratian's is: joking, teasing, competing for Aelred's attention—the modern reader is tempted to say flirting—with each other, their friendship has a mimetic plausibility that is of literary interest in its own right, regardless of the dialogue's philosophical component. They seem to be on one of the lower rungs of friendship, in fact, in that they are not of one mind, and yet perhaps also to be developing the higher form of friendship Aelred recommends.

Thus Gratian's first appearance in Book II immediately follows Walter's enthusiastic response to his reading of Book I; he also invokes the ladder of friendship:

> *Walter*: . . . But what you said last, the statement which aroused me so completely and almost carried me away from all earthly things, I desire to hear developed more fully, namely that among the stages leading to perfection friendship is the highest.
>
> But see, here comes our friend Gratian, and quite opportunely. I might rightly call him friendship's child for he spends all his energy in seeking to be loved and to love. It is opportune he came along, since he might be too eager for friendship and be deceived by its mere semblance, mistake the counterfeit for the true, the imaginary for the real, the carnal for the spiritual.
>
> *Gratian*: I thank you for your courtesy, brother. One not invited but rather boldly imposing himself, you grant a place at the spiritual banquet. But if you thought that I should be called friendship's child in earnest and not in jest, I should have been sent for at the beginning of this talk, and then I would not have had to lay aside due modesty and make a display of my eagerness. Nevertheless, Father, continue where you began, and for my sake set something on the table, so that, if I cannot be satisfied as he is (for after consuming I know not how many courses, he summons me now to the remnants of the banquet of which he has grown disdainful), I may at least be able to be refreshed a little. (pp. 73–74, II.15–17)

The encounter's joking tone, as Gratian points out, is also more than slightly bitchy: Walter suggests that Gratian, as is implied by his name (derived from *gratia*, charm or the quality of being pleasing), is somewhat promiscuous in his pursuit of friendship among the monks, and may be too satisfied with the carnal variety to be able to distinguish it from the spiritual. Indeed, from this perspective Gratian (similar to Ivo in Book I) seems like the young Aelred, in constant pursuit of unstable loves among the other young men with whom he is associated. Gratian's form of desire, if Water is correct, may be of the sort Aelred must reject; but as we have seen, this carnal love may also be a rung on the ladder leading to spiritual friendship. Certainly Gratian is eager to participate in Walter's conversation with Aelred, in part, perhaps, because of jealousy (his references to being fed the leftovers from Walter's banquet suggest hurt feelings beneath their jesting tone even as the metaphor suggests a literally carnal understanding of the spiritual conversation), but also because of genuine eagerness for instruction in friendship. The two monks are on friendly terms at the same time that they are rivals; it is, in other words, an example of the friendship that includes deviance, which we also find illustrated elsewhere in the text. Nevertheless, as is also suggested elsewhere, this kind of friendship seems to be included in the dialogue at this point precisely as an answer to Walter's desire, aroused by Aelred's Book I: Gratian's entrance is a dramatically meaningful one, suggesting a future for their relationship despite, or even because of, their differences.

Gratian, indeed, believes that there are no limits to friendship, and Walter's better-informed disagreement leads to their next friendly argument:

> *Walter*: . . . I should like you to set up a definite limit for friendship, particularly on account of Gratian here, that he may not, in accordance with his name, be so eager to be gracious that he recklessly becomes vicious.
>
> *Gratian*: I sincerely appreciate your thoughtful concern for me; and if I were not hampered by my eagerness to hear, I should, perhaps, take my revenge on you now. (p. 78, II.31–32)

The (joking) accusation, again, is one of carnality and even vice: it is difficult for the modern reader not to find in Gratian the representation of a man who is overeager in his carnal affection for other men—and one whose desires are treated with considerable indulgence, not only by Walter's teasing, but by the image of him recorded in Aelred's text as well. It is Walter's difference from him—his further progress up the ladder of friendship—as well as Gratian's own eagerness for instruction from Aelred that may lead Gratian himself to a higher understanding of friendship.[96] This is to say that the dialogue form itself is crucial: its representation of difference and of the productive interaction of a variety of voices (not just the voice of Aelred the master) produces the possibility of change, as opposed to the static, nondialogic self-identity of Cicero's *Laelius*. Thus Gratian himself is eventually drawn to an appreciation of spiritual friendship, though his teasing rivalry with Walter never disappears.[97]

This is not to suggest that difference is eliminated. Indeed, as Walter and Gratian draw closer together in their views, they start challenging Aelred's own argumentation, for example in pointing out his inconsistency as regards the doctrine of sameness. As we have seen, the theory of friendship as identity gives way before Aelred's concrete examples of difference within friendship, and Walter does not hesitate to point out the contradiction: "your former friend has passed away, and this other has satisfied you, although we do not see how [*licet nos non uiderimus*] . . ." (pp. 95–96, III.21). Unlike Cicero's *On Friendship*, and even unlike Plato's *Lysis*, the *Spiritual Friendship* does not insist on the interlocutors' complete agreement with the main speaker, or, therefore, on an ultimate univocality.

Indeed, Aelred stresses this point from the beginning: when Ivo in Book I requests a specifically Christian theory of friendship to supplement or replace Cicero's, Aelred declares "I confess I have been won over, but, not knowing myself or the extent of my own ability, I am not going to teach you anything about these matters but rather to discuss [*conferam*] them with you. For you yourself have opened the way for both of us . . ." (p. 53, I.9). Rather than Cicero's *declamatio*, Aelred offers to "discuss" the issues, and allows Ivo to set the agenda. In fact, this passage suggests that, as for Plato, the pursuit of friendship requires by its very nature a multiplicity of voices. It also implies a rebuke to Cicero: rather than the language of coercion that Laelius employs in his agreement to discuss friendship, Aelred prefers the language of persuasion or winning over. He also prefers the language of desire, as we have seen: "this conference of ours, like spiritual food and drink, will be more enjoyable to you because of the intense longing preceding it." Dialogue, like friendship itself, is a matter of desire. Aelred's own text, then, is itself in dialogue with Cicero's, from whose supposed truth it constantly, dialogically, deviates.

Perhaps it is not surprising that Aelred's followers—those like Thomas of Frakaham and Peter of Blois who in subsequent decades created imitations and epitomes of the *Spiritual Friendship*—both removed the dialogues from Aelred's text and, in McGuire's words, "castrated it,"[98] leaving out "individual and personal examples" and attempting "to make a theoretical treatise out of what had been an artistic and spiritual whole."[99] In the period of Peter Damian and Thomas Aquinas, the discussion of desiring relations among the members of a monastic community may have seemed more palatable the less it was personalized through dialogue, and the more monological its authority became.

2. Spiritual Erotics: From Plato's *Symposium* to Sade's *La Philosophie dans le boudoir* ⌒

Philosophers and other writers obviously continued to address the question of friendship after the twelfth century, and often did so with particular reference to Plato and Socrates; Montaigne is a prime example. However, after the important work of Aelred and his adaptors, they did so less frequently, and less influentially, in the dialogue form.[1] The specific tradition examined in the preceding chapter—the dialogue tradition initiated by Plato's *Lysis*—was thus most influential in Roman and medieval culture. Western European intellectuals of the early modern period, as classical Greek became a more important focus of their education, and as ancient Greek texts became more widely available in printed editions, regained direct access to Plato's works (as distinct from the indirect transmission of his ideas by Latin authors such as Cicero), and their preference for those Platonic works most amenable to neoplatonic Christianization established certain of the dialogues—notably the *Symposium* and the *Republic*—as Plato's masterpieces, a valuation still widely accepted.

The *Symposium* in particular, especially as interpreted by Marsilio Ficino, had a profound influence on Renaissance thought, and its *nachleben*, as a recent commentator has suggested, "is very nearly as broad as the breadth of humane letters in the West."[2] In this chapter I cannot attempt an overview of this vast *nachleben*, nor shall I even attempt a "reading" of the *Symposium* as a whole.[3] But a number of Renaissance dialogues (especially those composed in sixteenth-century Italy), taking their cue from Diotima's speech in the *Symposium*, rethink the Platonic body/soul hierarchy, and especially the question of the physicality or spirituality of male–male erotic desire, in terms appropriate to their own cultural circumstances. In this chapter, therefore, I examine these questions as they are raised in the *Symposium* itself and subsequently reinterpreted in the Italian Renaissance—and, later, in the French Enlightenment. I consider a larger number of texts in this chapter than in the preceding one, and for that reason I am unable to provide such close readings as I attempted there. But the terms in which male–male desire was considered in the *Lysis* and the dialogues derived from it—sameness and difference, body and soul, deviation—remain to a large extent in place in the dialogues I examine here, so that close reading may now profitably give way to a broader view appropriate to the *Symposium*'s greater influence.

The *Symposium*, in some ways the most "literary" of Plato's dialogues, takes place at a drinking party held in the home of the tragic poet Agathon, in celebration of his victory in the annual dramatists' competition at the festival of Dionysus.[4] The dialogue consists, for the most part, of the various guests' speeches in praise of Love (or Eros, the god of love), and their responses to one another's speeches. Unlike the early *Lysis*, with its constantly deviating structure of thought, which never alights on a final true doctrine, the *Symposium*, probably written in the mature middle period of Plato's philosophical career,[5] does propose, in Socrates' speech, a single doctrine of love that Socrates declares to be the truth, while the other speeches are deemed false, or at least incomplete. Furthermore, in adumbrating this true doctrine of love, Socrates—or Diotima, the woman whose teachings on this subject Socrates claims to be quoting in his speech—also outlines the more general Platonic Theory of Forms, making the *Symposium* a cornerstone in our understanding of Plato's middle-period philosophy more generally. For the *Symposium*, like other dialogues composed in this period, and unlike the earlier "Socratic" dialogues such as the *Lysis*, enunciates Plato's own theories rather than Socrates', and turns Socrates into a spokesman for his follower's ideas.

The dialogue's structure is even more complex than I have suggested so far, because the dialogue presents the symposium, or drinking party, itself to the reader at several removes: it is supposed to have taken place at some point in the dialogue's "past," and in the dialogue's "present" is being described for the benefit of someone who wasn't there. This point is important for the establishment of the singular truth of Diotima's doctrine.

Briefly, we are first introduced to a certain Apollodorus and his anonymous friend; the friend has asked Apollodorus for a description of Agathon's symposium. Apollodorus responds, not with a flashback to the symposium itself, but rather by recalling a similar encounter he had a few days earlier with another friend, Glaucon, who also asked for information about the famous party, because his previous sources were unable to give a clear description (172a–b). Apollodorus notes that the symposium in question took place years earlier, when Apollodorus and his friends were still children, and that Apollodorus himself had therefore not been present at it; he has heard the story of the symposium from yet another, older acquaintance, Aristodemus of Cydathenaeum, who was present at the symposium, and whose version of the events was later corroborated by Socrates himself (172b–173b). Apollodorus agrees to tell his friend what he told Glaucon, which is what Aristodemus told him (173c–174a); the remainder of the text recounts what Aristodemus remembered of the actual symposium: some of the speeches he remembered clearly, others less clearly (like that of Phaedrus [178a]), still others not at all (like those given between the speeches of Phaedrus and of Pausanias [180c]). Most importantly, there is no indication that Aristodemus has forgotten anything of Socrates' speech, in which the latter invoked Diotima's doctrine of love (201d–212c).

Structurally, then, the situation is as follows: (1) Diotima's speech (2) is remembered and recounted by Socrates in his speech, which (3) is remembered and recounted in the account Aristodemus gives to Apollodorus, which (4) Apollodorus remembers and recounts in the account he gives to Glaucon, which (5) Apollodorus again remembers and repeats to the anonymous friend and hence to the reader. Diotima's teachings, in this somewhat diagrammatic view of the dialogue's structure, thus appear as the central and originary moment for the doctrine being presented here as true, a doctrine that—unlike the ideas contained in the other speeches—has been passed on *unchanged* through the years, from speaker to speaker to speaker. As I suggested above, this strategy is important in establishing the truth of Diotima's teachings: if, as she says, *eros* is the desire for immortality through "the procreation and begetting of children in the beautiful" (p. 151, 206e),[6] then Diotima's teachings are, unlike the other speeches that Aristodemus has in whole or in part forgotten, demonstrably—precisely by their survival through many years and in the memory of many different speakers—among the progeny she describes as "more immortal [ἀθανατωτέρων]" (p. 154, 209c) than physical children. The very structure of this dialogue thus demonstrates the truth of one of its central doctrines, *eros* as a path to immortality through the begetting of immortal "children," and the eternal truth of this doctrine, as proven by the dialogue's structure, is quite different from the *Lysis'* constant deviations, both structural and doctrinal.[7] We shall return to Diotima's speech shortly.

Despite the various other opinions expressed, then, the *Symposium* demonstrates that there is a single, true doctrine of Love or *eros*; retrospectively, the other speeches must therefore be understood as deviations from this truth. They are not, certainly, opposed to it, and yet they are not identical with it either; as many commentators have noted, each of the earlier speeches contains some portion of the final, true doctrine of love, which will be transformed when placed in the context of Diotima's teachings and contribute to the final whole.[8] (Ironically, one of these speeches—Aristophanes'—has achieved greater immortality, at least in popular culture, than Diotima's.[9]) Before returning to Socrates and Diotima, I examine, briefly, the preceding speeches in terms of what they may have to contribute to our understanding of the place of male–male desire, deviance, and dialogue itself, in Plato's doctrine and in the dialogues written under Plato's influence. I then return to Socrates and Diotima to examine how these preceding ideas deviate from Plato's "true" doctrine.

As in the *Lysis*, Socrates, as Aristodemus recalls their encounter, is on his way somewhere, namely to Agathon's party, and as in the *Lysis*, he is initially distracted from his goal. In some ways, however, the situation is now reversed: whereas in that dialogue, Socrates was distracted from pursuing his way toward the Lyceum by the promise of beautiful boys, and never did reach either his geographical or his philosophical goal, in the *Symposium* he is distracted from the symposium's pleasures of the flesh by those of the intellect: he pauses in thought on the porch, a distraction his host perceives as the pursuit of wisdom (175d). In both cases, however, the physical pursuit of erotic desire comes to be understood as a lesser goal than the pursuit of philosophical truth, a goal that, as I have suggested, Socrates does claim to reach in the *Symposium*. Nevertheless, the speeches, including Socrates', that make up the greater part of the dialogue do, like the *Lysis*, take *eros* as their starting point.

One of the guests, Eryximachus, proposes that they should drink only moderately and send away the flute-girl in favor of a more philosophical form of entertainment, the aforementioned speeches in praise of the god Eros, and also suggests that he originally got the idea for such speeches from Phaedrus. This is an important moment, as R. E. Allen points out: the speeches are not to be merely descriptive, but must be encomia to Eros, a god who also had a dark and even destructive side in ancient Greek culture.[10] It seems possible that Eryximachus proposes this limit on the speeches because he is himself in love with Phaedrus—he flatters Phaedrus by calling him the "father of the discourse" (p. 117, 177d), and admits that he wishes to "gratify him" (p. 117, 177c; the verb is *charisasthai* [χαρίσασθαι], which will shortly be used by Pausanias to describe physical gratification). As in the *Lysis*, discourse on the relations between men (for the *eros* praised in these speeches is usually, though not always, of the type that occurs between males) is initially understood as a mode of male–male seduction. In any case, the other guests agree to Eryximachus' proposal.

Phaedrus himself makes the first speech, or at least the first that Aristodemus remembered, and it introduces the very concern with sameness and difference that played such an important role in the *Lysis*. Phaedrus suggests that Eros, being the oldest of the gods (according to Hesiod and others), is also "cause to us of greatest goods. For I cannot say what good is greater, from youth on, than a worthy lover [*erastes* (ἐραστὴς)], and for a lover, a worthy beloved [*paidika* (παιδικά)]" (p. 118, 178c). The syntax, though not necessarily the content, of this sentence suggests a kind of mutuality or reciprocity that was not part of the typical Athenian social doctrine of pederasty, in which only the elder party experienced erotic desire. This impression is quickly confirmed: Phaedrus at first tends to emphasize the likeness of *erastes* and *eromenos* rather than their differences, despite using the term *paidika*, which emphasizes the beloved's youthfulness: they tend to respond to each other in the same way. Thus, in a famous passage,

> I say then that a man in love, if discovered doing something shameful, or suffering it from another and failing through cowardice to defend himself, would not be so pained at being seen by his father or friends or anyone else as by his beloved [*paidikon* (παιδικῶν)]. We see this same thing too in the beloved [*eromenon* (ἐρώμενον)], that it is especially before his lovers [*tous erastas* (τοὺς ἐραστὰς)] that he feels shame when seen in something shameful. If then there were some device so that a city or an army might be made up of lovers and their beloveds [*eraston te kai paidikon* (ἐραστῶν τε καὶ παιδικῶν)], it is not possible that they could govern their own affairs better than by abstaining from all things shameful and vying for honor among themselves; fighting side by side, men of this sort [*hoi toioutoi* (οἱ τοιοῦτοι)] would be victorious even if they were but few among nearly all mankind. (p. 118, 178d–179a)

While Phaedrus does go on to discuss lovers alone, in this passage he seems deliberately to refrain from distinguishing between the behavior of the *erastes* and the *eromenos* or *paidika*. What would be true of the lover—his feelings of pain if his beloved were to observe him either doing something shameful or allowing it to be done to him—would also, we are told, be equally true of the beloved, whose behavior in this sense is therefore indistinguishable from that of the lover. Even more intriguingly, their imagined behavior in a hypothetical army of lovers is also the same, and although these imagined soldier-lovers are initially described according to their traditional roles of *erastes* and *paidika*, they are eventually assimilated to one another in the collective term *hoi toioutoi*, translated here as "men of this sort." Love here seems to have the same effect on both parties; rather than maintaining the strict division of *erastes* and *eromenos* so important to aristocratic Athenian pederastic culture, they are made the same.

While Phaedrus does also discuss what lovers (*erontes* [ἐρῶντες]) alone will do—die for the one they love—he does so in such a way as again to confuse the categories. His first example, oddly enough, is Alcestis, who dies for her husband; for women as well as men can apparently be lovers in this sense. The gods honored Alcestis for her "zeal and virtue concerning Eros" (p. 119, 179c). Orpheus provides a negative counterexample, because he went in pursuit of Eurydice while still alive, rather than dying for her, and was duly punished. The third case considered is that of Achilles, like Alcestis explicitly contrasted with Orpheus because he "dared choose to help his lover [*erastei* (ἐραςτῇ)] Patroclus and avenge him, not only dying in behalf of but also in addition to the slain" (p. 120, 179e).

However, whereas Alcestis was imagined as the lover, Achilles is now the beloved; Phaedrus has moved from praise of the lover's self-sacrifice for the beloved's sake to praise of the beloved's identical self-sacrifice for the lover's sake, again deliberately confusing the two roles, as he emphasizes at the end of his speech:

> Aeschylus talks nonsense in claiming that Achilles was the lover of Patroclus [*Achillea Patroklou eran* (Ἀχιλλέα Πατρόκλου ἐρᾶν)], when he was not only more beautiful than Patroclus but doubtless than all the other heroes too, and still beardless, since he was very much younger, as Homer tells. For though the gods really do honor this virtue of Eros in the highest degree, they marvel and admire and reward it still more when the beloved [*eromenos* (ἐρώμενος)] cherishes the lover [*erasten* (ἐραστὴν)] than when the lover cherishes the beloved. For lover is more divine than beloved: the god is in him and he is inspired. That is also why they honored Achilles more than Alcestis, and sent him to the Isles of the Blest. (p. 120, 180a–b)

Whereas Phaedrus initially claimed that only the lover would die for the beloved, by the end of his speech he has reversed his position, and now suggests that the beloved may die for the lover as well, and even that the gods find this kind of self-sacrifice more worthy than the other: because the lover is actually possessed by the god Eros himself, he is less responsible for his own worthy actions than is the beloved. But, unaffected by the god's dictates, the worthy actions of the *eromenos* are entirely his own doing, and therefore more deserving of the gods' rewards in the afterlife. The roles of *erastes* and *eromenos* are, thus, first distinguished from each other, with greater favor going to the lover, who alone is capable of self-sacrifice for love; the roles are then confused, as the lover Alcestis and the beloved Achilles are equated, both in their self-sacrifice and in their difference from the counterexample of Orpheus; finally, they are distinguished again: both are capable of similar self-sacrifices, but now greater favor goes to the beloved. The overall effect of the speech as a whole, then, is to blur and confuse the boundaries between erotic roles. After Phaedrus' speech, they seem harder to tell apart—that is, more alike—than at any other point in the dialogue.

Phaedrus may simply be a logically confused character, as many commentators claim;[11] his speech may also be his, or even Plato's, deliberate attempt, at least for the sake of argument, to reduce the unlikeness of lover and beloved, and thus to suggest that love, as is also suggested of friendship early in the *Lysis*, requires—or in this case even produces—likeness. If the themes of likeness and unlikeness were being explored in the *Symposium* as they were in the *Lysis*, we might expect the following speeches to take up the issue from other perspectives, and that is indeed what happens in the next speech that Aristodemus remembers, that of Pausanias. Pausanias emphasizes difference rather than sameness, drawing distinctions where Phaedrus blurred boundaries.

For Pausanias, in fact, difference is built into the very nature of Eros, for there are two Aphrodites, the Common (*Pandemon* [Πάνδημον]) and the Heavenly (*Ouranian* [Οὐράνιαν]), and thus two Erotes. (The god Eros is sometimes understood as merely the agent of the goddess of sex, Aphrodite, that is, as the one who carries out her general will in specific cases; but *eros* may also refer to desire more generally, "something more than sex and perhaps other than sex," as Allen puts it.[12]) The Common Aphrodite governs the desires of most men, who pursue both women and boys, desire the body more than the soul, and therefore choose stupid partners who are willing simply to provide physical pleasure. Their erotic lives are random, good or bad according to chance (p. 121, 181a–c). Heavenly Aphrodite, on the other hand, governs something like the idealized Athenian pederasty: her followers are concerned exclusively with boys, and then only with those of an appropriate age—"on the verge of getting a beard" (p. 121, 181d)—and these relationships endure, in some unspecified form, throughout the partners' lives (pp. 121–122, 181c–d). Pausanias praises this form of *eros*, perhaps because he is involved in a similar longstanding relationship with Aristophanes. (Ongoing physical eroticism between adult males was frowned upon, as one of them would have been imagined as necessarily playing a subordinate role;[13] it is, perhaps, for this reason that the precise nature of this ideal lifelong relationship is not specified.)

Pausanias also draws a distinction among the practice of this form of *eros* in various city-states: some consider that the "gratification of lovers is beautiful" (*kalon to charizesthai erastais* [καλὸν τὸ χαρίζεσθαι ἐραςταῖς]), others that it is shameful (*aischron* [αἰσχρὸν]), while in Athens such judgments are based on yet further discriminations (182a–b). The lover's behavior is encouraged if it is noble, that is, if the object of his pursuit is noble of soul, regardless of looks; and while the beloved's parents may discourage him from gratifying a lover, this reluctance may be understood as a test of the lover's own nobility of soul (182b–184e): if he can contribute intelligence and virtue to the beloved's education, "it is beautiful for the beloved [*paidika* (παιδικὰ)] to gratify the lover [*erastei* (ἐραστῇ)]" (p. 125, 184e).

The partners in a love relationship, then, may be similar in terms of their shared nobility of soul, but here, in opposition to Phaedrus' speech, the traditional distinction between the roles of lover and beloved is carefully preserved, and further distinctions are added: those among the love customs of various peoples, those between the two Aphrodites and Erotes, and most importantly the spiritual distinctions between their followers. Thus the experience of love does not alter the nature of the soul, as it seems to do for Phaedrus, but rather reveals the true nature of the soul as it already exists. For Pausanias, the Heavenly Aphrodite includes pederasty and excludes male–female desire and procreation, but not the physical expression of male–male desire, as long as the latter includes spiritual love. The Common Aphrodite may include the physical expression of male–male desire, but it also includes male–female sex and procreation, and excludes spiritual love. It is thus a deviation from the norm established by the Heavenly Aphrodite: it is in some sense like the Heavenly Aphrodite—both inspire forms of erotic desire because both are, in fact, Aphrodite—but it is also unlike the Heavenly Aphrodite in the crucial ways just discussed. Pausanias, in sum, chooses to emphasize difference and deviance in his encomium on love, where Phaedrus chose to emphasize sameness. As in the *Lysis,* the problem of likeness and unlikeness remains at the heart of the question of male–male desire. It is the desire between men and women that is deviant for Pausanias, and, for the traditional Athenian, idealized pederasty that provides the norm from which it deviates.

It ought to be Aristophanes' turn to speak next, but he has the hiccups,[14] and Eryximachus agrees to take his turn, with a speech that emphasizes *eros* as universal harmony. He starts by invoking the notion of difference in terms reminiscent of the speech of Pausanias:

> For the nature of bodies has this twofold Eros; the health and sickness of the body are admittedly different and unlike [*heteron te kai anomoion* (ἕτερόν τε καὶ ἀνόμοιόν)], and what is unlike desires and loves unlike things. So the Eros in the healthy body is one thing, that in the diseased body another. As Pausanias just now said, it is beautiful to gratify what is good for men but shameful to gratify the intemperate; so also among bodies themselves it is beautiful to gratify what is good and healthy for each body, and it must be

done, and this has the name of medicine, but it is shameful to gratify what
is bad and diseased, and it must not be gratified if one intends to be a real
practitioner. (p. 126, 186b–c)

One might understand Eryximachus' speech as erasing human desire from
the discussion; here he turns instead to medical practice as a means of establishing likeness in the human body, and the rest of his speech suggests that
similar forms of harmony are the province of agriculture, music, astronomy,
and so on. But given his direct references to, and agreement with,
Pausanias' speech, it seems more likely that his speech actually is an attempt
to establish the male–male desire praised by Pausanias as a model of universal harmony. For Eryximachus, though, it is not so much a question of
a hierarchy of norm and deviant as it is one of eliminating the deviant
entirely: health and sickness are presented as absolutes of good and bad,
and the function of medicine is to restore the good and get rid of the bad.
Sickness and evil are also associated with difference or unlikeness
(*anomoion* [ἀνόμοιόν]), which must thus also be purged in favor of the
harmony of like and like. Where Pausanias emphasizes difference and, as
we have seen, deviance at all levels as the nature of *eros,* Eryximachus
emphasizes the likeness and harmony of soul between partners as the model
of his definition of *eros,* universal harmony.[15]

Eryximachus also places the doctor in the role of *eromenos,* that is, of the
one who must choose between gratifying the "good and healthy" or the
"bad and diseased" as Pausanias suggested the *eromenos* might choose
between a spiritually worthy and an unworthy *erastes.* The job of the physi-
cian (or musician, or astronomer, or farmer) as *eromenos* is thus also to
eliminate the discordant elements and promote likeness; presumably the
same could be said of a literal *eromenos.* Where Eryximachus begins with
difference, then, he ends with *eros* as likeness.[16]

In all these discussions of likeness and unlikeness—both in the *Lysis*
and the later dialogues derived from it, and thus far in the *Symposium*—
what is for us in the modern West the primary category of difference,
anatomical sex, is for the most part left out of the discussion: for Plato
and for Cicero, and even to a great extent for Aelred (in spite of his
use of the metaphors of sex and gender difference), the assumption is
normally that the male sex is under discussion. Differences of class, age,
wealth, social status, personality, spiritual worth, and so on are always
assumed to be differences among men. The speech of Aristophanes introduces sex differences into the discussion; however, even here they do not
prove to be the all-important categories that they have become in modern
culture.

Aristophanes, having recovered from his hiccups, says that he will praise the power of Eros by recounting a myth about "human nature and its condition" (p. 130, 189d). His well-known story declares that human beings were originally divided into three sexes, the male (children of the Sun), the female (children of the Earth), and the androgyne (children of the Moon). They were spherical beings, with two sets of genitalia (male for the males, female for the females, and one of each for the androgynes), two faces, four arms, four legs, and so on, apiece. They were such powerful beings that they tried to displace the gods; therefore, in order to weaken them, Zeus cut them all in two and eventually had Apollo rearrange the separate halves into the form humans now take (pp. 130–131, 189d–191a). Zeus also, out of pity, rearranged the genitals so that humans descended from the androgynous sex may reproduce, and those descended from the males may find erotic relief from their solitude, thus allowing them to "look after the other concerns of life" (p. 132, 191c). Eros thus undertakes "to make one from two, and to heal human nature."

> Each of us then is but the token [*symbolon* (σύμβολον)] of a human being, sliced like a flatfish, two from one; each then ever seeks his matching token [*to hautou hekastos symbolon* (τὸ αὑτοῦ ἕκαστος σύμβολον)]. Men sectioned from the common sex, then called androgynous, are woman-lovers; the majority of adulterers are from this sex, while on the other hand women from this sex are man-lovers and adulteresses. Women sectioned from a woman pay scant heed to men, but are turned rather toward women, and lesbians [*hetairistriai* (ἐταιρίοτριαι)] come from this sex. Those sectioned from a male pursue the masculine; because they are slices of the male, they like men while still boys, delighting to lie with men and be embraced by them. These are the most noble boys and youths because they are by nature most manly. Some say they're most shameless, but they're wrong: they don't do it out of shamelessness but out of boldness and courage and masculinity, cleaving to what is like themselves [*to homoion autois* (τὸ ὅμοιον αὐτοῖς)]. A great proof: actually, it is only men of this sort who, when they grow up, enter on political affairs. When they reach manhood they love boys, and by nature [*physei* (φύσει)] pay no heed to marriage and the getting of children except as compelled to it by custom and law [*nomou* (νόμου)]; it suffices them to live out their lives unmarried, with one another. So this sort becomes wholly a lover of boys or a boy who loves having lovers, ever cleaving to what is akin [*suggenes* (συγγενὲς)]. (pp. 132–133, 191d–192b)

On the one hand, humans are here defined in part by their unique relation to sexual differentiation: apparently unlike other creatures, humans are in origin not sexually dimorphic, but trimorphic, and entirely self-contained; Aristophanes does not discuss the *Ur*-humans' capacity for reproduction, but apparently it is not sexual in nature, since sexual reproduction is introduced only after they are split. Sex differences thus existed originally in a wider variety, but less importance was attached to them, as they were unnecessary to the propagation of the species. *Eros*, in fact, even after the split, subsumes sexual difference within a larger sexual sameness: desire is for the "matching token," that is, the other half of the broken *symbolon* (an object such as a knucklebone broken in half to make a contract, each party keeping one of the halves), even in the case of the formerly androgynous male–female couples; they, too, like the male–male and female–female couples, are seeking "what is akin" (*suggenes*, suggesting both a congenital similarity and a kinship), according to their original natures. As we saw in the *Lysis*, kinship includes both sameness and difference: for male–female couples, the sameness is in their androgynous origin, which insures that they "match," while their genital difference allows for reproduction; for male–male couples, the sameness lies both in their origin and in their genital sex (which, given the conventions of ancient Greek society, allows them to focus on the nonreproductive aspects of existence, such as politics), difference apparently being confined to age, as in traditional Athenian pederasty. (The existence of "*hetairistriai*," usually translated as "lesbians" but perhaps more accurately as "female lovers of women," is noted, but their social role goes unexamined.) Difference or unlikeness thus has its role to play—the two halves of the *symbolon* need not be identical, as long as they fit together—but Aristophanes' emphasis on "the desire and pursuit of wholeness" (p. 133, 193a)—his definition of *eros*—inevitably values the similarity of what "matches," the fact that the halves of the *symbolon* are halves of the same thing, over the elements of unlikeness within it. Deviance—difference within similarity—for Aristophanes as for Socrates at one moment in the *Lysis*, is essential to *eros*.

Aristophanes also introduces the idea of "nature" (*physis*) into the discussion, as the various forms this pursuit may take are ascribed to the originary natures of individuals. In addition, he agrees with Phaedrus and Pausanias on the crucial spiritual component of true *eros*: "No one can think that it is for the sake of sexual intercourse that the one so eagerly delights in being with the other. Instead, the soul [*psyche* (ψυχὴ)] of each clearly wishes for something else it can't put into words" (p. 133, 192c–d). Both of these ideas will prove important in Diotima's climactic speech.

However, one further speech remains before Socrates speaks of her. Agathon's encomium of Eros is preceded by his brief exchange with Socrates, who tries to engage him in dialogue, but is prevented from doing so by Phaedrus: "My dear Agathon, if you answer Socrates it will no longer make the slightest difference to him how anything else turns out here, if

only he has someone to converse with, especially someone handsome"
(pp. 135–136, 194d). The scene is reminiscent of the *Lysis*: here as there,
logical argument is linked to erotic desire through sublimation. Socrates
delights in Agathon's looks, but responds to them intellectually rather than
physically, once more, by implication, taking on the role of the true *erastes*.
While the *Symposium's* speeches respond to one another, as we have seen,
true dialogue has been deferred, and is now deferred once more, though it
will reappear in Socrates' response to Agathon's speech, as will Socrates' status as the true lover.

In the meantime, Agathon is set up through his encomium as, in some
ways, a straw man for Socrates to demolish in the succeeding dialogue and
speech, though in other ways his speech, like the others, has something to
contribute to Diotima's doctrine. Most commentators place it among the
weakest—as literature and as moral philosophy—of the *Symposium's*
encomia.[17] It is, rhetorically, a traditional encomium, filled with praise that
emphasizes corporeal beauty and youthfulness in "a singing heap of flattering adjectives."[18] For our purposes, it is most important to note that Agathon
defines the effects of Eros in terms of kinship, here opposed to "estrangement": "He empties us of estrangement [*allotriotetos* (ἀλλοτριότητος)] but
fills us with kinship [*oikeiotetos* (οἰκειότητος)], causing us to come together
in all such gatherings as these . . ." (p. 139, 197d). Here kinship is contrasted explicitly with *allotriotes* (ἀλλοτριότης), estrangement, foreignness,
or alienation, rather than the *enantiotes* (ἐναντιότης) or *anomoiotes*
(ἀνομοιότης)—difference or unlikeness—that we have encountered in
Lysis and in the speech of Eryximachus. *Allotriotes* has a more specific
nuance of human relationality: whereas the other terms may be used of any
kind of difference, *allotriotes* is used of people's relations with one another
(or with themselves). In this sense—although Agathon recognizes other
functions of *eros* similar to those raised by Eryximachus (197a–b)—when
it comes to our central concepts of like and unlike, he, like Aristophanes,
makes *eros* a matter of specifically human similarity and difference.
Whereas for Aristophanes, however, *eros is* that ancient identity that longs
to be reinstated, for Agathon *eros creates* new kinship in place of former
strangeness. Eros, that is, is itself—or himself—external to human beings
rather than an essential part of their makeup, a god rather than the universal impulse toward which both Eryximachus' and Aristophanes' speeches
tended to orient the discussion.

Socrates quickly dismantles Agathon's "heap of flattering adjectives."
Where Agathon praised the god as beautiful and good, Socrates returns to
the theme of *eros* or desire as lack familiar from the *Lysis*: "what desires,
desires what it lacks" (p. 142, 200b). Therefore, if Eros is the love of the

beautiful and the good, it is precisely the beautiful and the good that it must lack: "So if Eros is lack of beautiful things, and good things are beautiful, he would also lack good things" (p. 143, 201c).

So much is quickly established in the dialogue following Agathon's speech; but the positive doctrine of love emerges not in the dialogue, but only in the lessons of Diotima, remembered and recounted by Socrates in his own speech. As I have suggested, and as many commentators have noted, this speech draws on each of the former ones in formulating this doctrine; indeed, this retrospective structure, in which Socrates speaks with Diotima's voice, which in turn "prophetically" includes the preceding speeches, is perhaps the best example in Plato's dialogues of Kristeva's polyphonic, carnivalesque dialogism.[19] As we have seen, the *Symposium*'s literary structure of memories within memories encourages a retrospective reading, in which Diotima's true doctrine is to be compared with the others—now revealed as faulty or incomplete—that came before it. Such a retrospective comparison, revealing as it does the partial truths as well as the flaws in the preceding speeches, shows them to be deviations in the sense I have been using this term: different from the singular truth revealed by Socrates and Diotima, but also to some extent contained within it. The different is also, and simultaneously, the same; the unlike is also like. In this sense, the philosophical structure of the *Symposium* as a whole is precisely one of kinship, of differences that do not preclude a family resemblance, similar to the kinship that often defines friendship and *eros* in the *Lysis* as well as the *Symposium*'s earlier encomia.

Deviance also governs Diotima's own doctrine of *eros*. Eros himself is a deviant figure of the intermediate sort that helped define *philia* in the *Lysis*: neither good nor beautiful, as we have seen, but, as Socrates remembers Diotima telling him, "since you yourself agree that he is neither good nor beautiful, do not any the more for that reason suppose he must be ugly and bad, she said, but rather something between these two" (p. 145, 202b). Eros at this point in the dialogue is an indeterminate figure, one that deviates from all clear-cut definitions without occupying a clearly defined space of his own: he differs from good and beautiful, bad and ugly, but he does not differ absolutely. (This point is developed further in the myth of Poros and Penia, 203a–e.) In fact, it transpires that Eros is also neither god nor mortal, but intermediate between the two: "being in between both, it fills the region between both so that the All [*to pan* (τὸ πᾶν)] is bound together [*sundedesthai* (συνδεδέσθαι)] with itself" (p. 146, 202e). The "All" or "whole" (*to pan*) suggests a universal unity or harmony like that proposed by Eryximachus, but it is a harmony composed of differences, in need of *eros* to bind them: *sundedesthai* is a passive form of the verb *sundeo* (συνδέω), to bind or tie different things together. Whereas Eryximachus emphasizes the resulting harmony or unity itself, Diotima places the emphasis on the necessary act of binding, allowing the deviations that comprise the whole their continued existence along with the whole itself. Eros is related to philosophy in the same way: not possessing wisdom, but not so ignorant as to be unaware of his lack, he is thus a philosopher, a lover of wisdom (203e–204c) and therefore of happiness and hence the good (204c–205d). Here Diotima shows Aristophanes' speech, too, to be a deviation from her doctrine:

> Yes, and a certain story is told, she said, that those in love are seeking the other half of themselves. But my account is that love is of neither half nor whole, my friend, unless it happens to be actually good, since people are willing to cut off their own hands and feet if they think these possessions of theirs are bad. For they each refuse, I think, to cleave even to what is their own, unless one calls what is good kindred [*oikeion* (οἰκεῖον)] and his own, and what is bad alien [*allotrion* (ἀλλότριον)]; because there is nothing else that men love than the good. (p. 149, 205d–e)

Once again we should be reminded of *Lysis*: only the good may be considered lovers, as only the good may be considered eligible for friendship. The kindred, *oikeion* (here opposed, as in Agathon's speech, to the human alien, *allotrion*), is what one cleaves to only if it is also the good; in fact, goodness is an essential element of the truly kindred, since, as was suggested in the *Lysis*, the bad cannot be akin even to themselves. Even so, the kindred is not identical to the self, or it would not excite desire: it is what one lacks, but not so completely that one cannot recognize it as that which one lacks. Aristophanes' speech, then, is itself lacking in this essential element; in retrospect, it deviates from Diotima's doctrine because it does not specify love of the good. But again, this deviation does not suggest complete difference, either: Diotima does not exactly reject Aristophanes' speech, but implies that it may contain a partial truth, if the object of love is also defined as good. Aristophanes' speech is included in Diotima's doctrine even as it differs from it.[20]

Diotima's metaphor for the "work" (*ergon* [ἔργον]) of *eros*, the behavior it actually incites, is drawn from conception and childbirth or begetting (*tokos* [τόκος]) (p. 150, 206b), an image of women's experience here applied primarily to men. If eros is desire to possess the good, it must also be desire to possess the good forever, since a noneternal possession would be by definition less good (206a). Therefore, "Eros necessarily desires immortality with the good . . . since its object is to possess the good for itself forever. It necessarily follows from this account, then, that Eros is also love of immortality" (p. 151, 207a). Here "in the animal world," as Diotima says (p. 151, 207d), immortality can be achieved only through begetting, "by giving birth, ever leaving behind a different new thing in place of the old" (p. 152, 207d). Change is a characteristic of this world (as distinct from the divine):

> even in the time in which each single living creature is said to live and to be the same—for example, as a man is said to be the same from youth to old age—though he never has the same things in himself, he nevertheless is called the same, but he is ever becoming new while otherwise perishing, in respect to hair and flesh and bone and blood and the entire body.
>
> And not only in respect to the body but also in respect to the soul [*ten psychen* (τὴν ψυχὴν)], its characters and habits, opinions, desires, pleasures, pains, fears are each never present in each man as the same, but some are coming to be, others perishing. (p. 152, 207d–e)

The assumption of self-sameness "in the animal world" is replaced with a radical self-difference not only of body, but even of soul: not merely the fact of difference itself, but the continual process of differentiation rules this world. Even here, this differentiation is imagined not as thoroughgoing unlikeness or opposition, but rather as a deviation from an assumed norm of sameness—"a man is said to be the same from youth to age"—but in this case, it is the real difference within merely apparent sameness that is emphasized. The longing for immortality—that is, the eternal continuation of the same—is thus faced with the brute animal fact of change. *Eros* is what counters change and allows for some kind of immortality.

But the immortality available to human beings is itself a form of deviance. If giving birth is "leaving behind a different new thing in place of the old," mortals achieve immortality only through another process of differentiation: "For it is in this way that all that is mortal is preserved: not by being ever completely the same, like the divine, but by leaving behind, as it departs and becomes older, a different new thing of the same sort as it was" (p. 152, 208a–b). If the regular course of an individual human (or animal) life is one of constant differentiation from an assumed sameness, giving birth shifts the emphasis: it, too, produces something different, but now it is the preserved element of sameness that is emphasized. In both cases neither absolute likeness nor absolute unlikeness is at issue, but deviation, sameness within difference or difference within sameness.

There are, of course, different sorts of immortality appropriate to different individuals, though what they have in common is desire "of procreation and begetting of children in the beautiful" (p. 151, 206c). Plato has Diotima "prophetically" refer to the speech of Phaedrus by citing his examples of Alcestis and Achilles, whose immortality depends upon their having begotten not human children but glory, "the fame of their own virtue [*athanaton mnemen aretes peri* (ἀθάνατον μνήμην ἀρετῆς πέρι)]" (p. 153, 208d). (Again, a previous speech contributes to the true doctrine, but its vision of *eros* is incomplete: here Alcestis and Achilles die not for love, but for honor, as Allen points out.[21]) Diotima also "prophetically" draws upon the speech of Pausanias in making this distinction between the *eros* involved in pregnancy of the body and that of the soul, a distinction anticipated in his differentiation of the two Aphrodites and Erotes. "Some men are pregnant in respect to their bodies, she said, and turn more to women and are lovers in that way, providing in all future time, as they suppose, immortality and happiness for themselves through getting children" (p. 153, 208e). Although the noun "men" is not specified in the text, the fact that they turn to women in order to have children demonstrates that it is indeed the—pregnant—male sex to whom Diotima is referring here, and the confusion of biological functions is interesting: as we have seen before, sex and gender are not necessarily the primary cases of difference for ancient writers as they are for moderns (perhaps because the power differential is so great that the male sex is always the default position, as it were, even in cases of pregnancy—though the recurring example of Alcestis would seem to suggest otherwise[22]). In any case, this assumption of maleness also argues that the following discussion refers to male–male *eros* in particular, which would also follow from Pausanias' distinction, though again men are not initially specified. Those who achieve immortality by begetting "practical wisdom," including temperance and justice in particular, rather than human children, are pregnant in soul rather than in body (208e–209a):

> Others are pregnant in respect to their soul—for there are those, she said, who are still more fertile in their souls than in their bodies with what it pertains to soul to conceive and bear. . . . whenever one of them is pregnant of soul from youth, being divine, and reaches the age when he then desires to bear and beget, he too then, I think, goes about seeking the beautiful in which he might beget; for he will never beget in the ugly. Now, because he is fertile, he welcomes beautiful rather than ugly bodies, and should he meet with a beautiful and noble and naturally gifted soul, he welcomes the conjunction of both even more, and to this person he is straightway resourceful in speaking about virtue, and what sort of thing the good man [*ton andra ton agathon* (τὸν ἄνδρα τὸν ἀγαθὸν)] must be concerned with and his pursuits; and he undertakes to educate him. (p. 153, 209a–c)

By the end, this passage is referring specifically to the male sex, *andra* meaning "man" as opposed to "woman." And the erotic relations under discussion bear some resemblance to the traditional Athenian pederastic ideal described earlier by Pausanias, though once more the earlier speaker's (and the Athenian tradition's) understanding of *eros* is shown to have been only partial. Whereas Pausanias allows erotic "gratification for the sake of virtue" (p. 125, 185b), such physical relations are purely metaphorical for Diotima: the "conjunction" that takes place here is between beautiful souls. The *eromenos* metaphorically acts, not as a sexual partner in begetting the lover's educational discourses, but rather as the one who makes the delivery possible. The soul of the *erastes* becomes pregnant on its own, because of its own "divine" nature; the *eromenos* is simply the stimulus for the metaphorical birth of the *erastes'* discourses.

The process described here is reminiscent of the one we observed being played out in the *Lysis*. There, as here, the initial stimulus is "beautiful rather than ugly" male bodies—the youthful bodies of potential *eromenoi*. And the process we observed in the *Lysis*, by which this initial physical stimulus is transmuted into discourse, occurs even more quickly here in the passage from beautiful bodies to "speaking about virtue" in conjunction with a beautiful soul.

The conjunction described here, in fact, is one of dialogue: it is the exchange of words that will produce these immortal children of practical wisdom, children who will be "more beautiful and more immortal" (p. 154, 209c) than human children. It also, it should be noted, assumes a spark of the divine in the soul of the *erastes*, for it is the divine that causes the soul's pregnancy. The move from a physical desire to a conjunction that is verbal and spiritual rather than physical is an example of the Socratic *askēsis* analyzed so productively by recent historians of philosophy from Foucault to David Halperin and Alexander Nehamas. *Askēsis*, for Foucault, is the practice of self-discipline necessary to make "an ethical subject" of oneself, and to make of one's life a work of art.[23] It does not, however, necessarily include abstention, as the modern understanding of the term "ascetic" might imply: for Foucault

> [t]he moral reflections of the Greeks on sexual behavior did not seek to justify interdictions, but to stylize a freedom—that freedom which the "free" man exercised in his activity. This produced a state of affairs that might well seem paradoxical at first glance: the Greeks practiced, accepted, and valued relations between men and boys; and yet their philosophers dealt with the subject by conceiving and elaborating an ethics of abstention.[24]

The tension between *askēsis* as freedom and *askēsis* as abstention is explored more fully in Diotima's discussion of the ideal spiritual love that nevertheless has its roots in the physical. She further explores the relations among beautiful bodies, beautiful souls, and divinity with the famous image of "the ladder of love," itself the exemplar of yet another form of difference within sameness: it is based on a hierarchy composed of *different* rungs on the *same* ladder of love. Famously, Diotima (through Socrates) presents *eros* as a series of stages, beginning with physical desire for a beautiful, and, as usual, presumptively male, body. It is also a series of stages leading to the brief perception of a divine unity from which difference is ultimately eliminated.

The physical, however, is a necessary first step toward this goal, and the physical is initially linked to difference: "It is necessary [*dei* (δεῖ)], she said, for him who proceeds rightly [*orthos* (ὀρθῶς)] to this thing to begin while still young by going to beautiful bodies; and first, if his guide guides rightly [*orthos* (ὀρθῶς)], to love one single body [*eros auton somatos eran* (ἑνὸς αὐτὸν σώματος ἐρᾶν)] and beget there beautiful discourses" (pp. 154–155, 210a). The love of bodies is crucial to the process under discussion: the repetition of *dei* (necessary) and *orthos* (rightly) make it clear that this stage cannot be skipped. Equally important is to love—or desire (*eran*)—one particular body. This is to say that the initial stage on the ladder is constituted by the discrimination among bodies, by recognizing difference. As usual in Plato, however, the interaction between the two bodies in question is not genital contact, but discourse: the *erastes* is led by "his guide" (identified as "Love" by some commentators[25]) to become himself the spiritual guide for an *eromenos*.

On the next rung, the process of ascending from difference to unity begins with the recognition that all beautiful bodies are the same insofar as they are beautiful. "Realizing this, he is constituted a lover of all beautiful bodies and relaxes this vehemence for one, looking down on it and believing it of small importance" (p. 155, 210b). The identity of beauty in all beautiful bodies is now recognized; sameness replaces difference. The physical itself, however, remains essential—it is still the beauty of bodies being recognized. And one might note also that, while the lover is not longer as "vehement" in his love for the particular body, that love is not necessarily eliminated: it may be a small thing, but not necessarily nonexistent.

Only in the following stages does the lover ascend from love of bodies to love of souls. After this he must come to believe that beauty in souls [*psychais* (ψυχαῖς)] is more to be valued than that in the body, so that even if someone good of soul has but a slight bloom, it suffices for him, and he loves and cares and begets and seeks those sorts of discourses that will make the young better, in order that he may be constrained in turn to contemplate what is beautiful in practices and laws and to see that it is in itself all akin to itself [*pan auto hautoi suggenes* (πᾶν αὐτὸ αὑτῷ συγγενές)], in order that he may believe bodily beauty a small thing. (p. 155, 210b–c)

The process of discovering the sameness or self-identity of all beauty continues: beauty of souls is "more to be valued," and, as Diotima has already suggested, begets the lover's discourses. The "souls" in this passage are plural, suggesting again the self-identity of beauty in all beautiful souls. Interestingly, however, at this stage the physical has still not been abandoned: like the singularity of the desired body in the previous passage, here physical beauty is "a small thing," but it has not been erased. Indeed, at least "a slight bloom" of physical beauty seems to be for the lover a necessary adjunct of beautiful souls. The emphasis, of course, is not on these small distinctions, but on the larger unity of beauty itself—all beauty, whether in bodies, souls, or, in the next stage, of the "practices and laws" that are apparently to be the subject of the lover's discourses, is akin to itself, unified and self-same.

This unity finally becomes the soul's object of love in the next-to-last stage, as the guide (or Love) leads the lover to a contemplation of the beauty of various sorts of knowledge. "[L]ooking now to the beautiful in its multitude [*poly ede to kalon* (πολὺ ἤδη τὸ καλὸν)]," the lover may

no longer delight like a slave, a worthless, petty-minded servant, in the beauty of one single thing, whether beauty of a young child or man or of one practice; but rather, having been turned toward the multitudinous ocean [*poly pelagos* (πολὺ πέλαγος)] of the beautiful and contemplating it, he begets many beautiful and imposing discourses and thoughts in ungrudging love of wisdom, until, having at this point grown and waxed strong, he beholds a certain kind of knowledge which is one, and such that it is the following kind of beauty. (p. 155, 210c–d)

At this point, the love of singular bodies—and souls, practices, and so on—is finally transcended, and in that transcendence is freedom: only slaves and servants remain bound to love of the singular. (We might recall here Socrates' famous claim, in Xenophon's *Memorabilia*, that even one kiss can cause instant enslavement to desire.[26]) Further discourses, themselves beautiful, result, until he is ready for the final vision of beauty itself. Even at this point, that final vision has not been achieved: beauty remains multiple, many-sided, as the repetition of *poly* suggests; it is still characterized by difference.

It is only in the lover's ultimate, fleeting vision—one that in its very fleeting nature reminds the modern reader of Buber's encounter with the divine Other—that beauty achieves complete self-identity, though, paradoxically, it is also at this stage that Diotima reminds Socrates, and he reminds his audience, of its basis in the love of boys: again as for Buber and Levinas, proximity to the divine is figured in human proximity:

> First, it ever is and neither comes to be nor perishes, nor has it growth nor diminution.
>
> Again, it is not in one respect beautiful but in another ugly, nor beautiful at one time but not another, nor beautiful relative to this but ugly relative to that, nor beautiful here but ugly there, as being beautiful to some but not to others.
>
> . . . [I]t exists in itself alone by itself, single in nature forever [*auto kath' auto meth' autou monoeides aei on* (αὐτὸ καθ' αὑτὸ μεθ' αὑτοῦ μονοειδὲς ἀεὶ ὄν)], while all other things are beautiful by sharing in *that* in such manner that though the rest come to be and perish, *that* comes to be neither in greater degree nor less and is not at all affected.
>
> But when someone, ascending from things here through the right love of boys [*orthos paiderastein* (ὀρθῶς παιδεραστεῖν)], begins clearly to see *that*, the Beautiful, he would pretty well touch the end. (pp. 155–156, 211a–b)

The vision of the Beautiful is thus also a vision of self-sameness, of that which is eternally only itself, "single in nature." The play of otherness that has tempted the other speakers is here seen clearly as only one or another of the stages that lead to this eternal vision, which, Socrates has declared, alone can constitute true happiness, fleeting though it may be. Desire is ultimately for the contemplation of this transcendent unity, a contemplation with the potential to unite the lover with the divine ("If any other among men is immortal, he is too" [p. 157, 212a]). But just as, rhetorically, various aspects of the preceding speeches have been combined with Diotima's own wisdom to produce this climactic speech, which thus transcends them without, paradoxically, leaving them behind, so even in this final vision the audience is reminded of the earlier stages in Diotima's own speech (in 211c), and is specifically reminded that the original basis for achieving this vision is *orthos paiderastein*, to love boys in the right way. Even the true doctrine of *eros* thus contains what it might seem to transcend or disavow, and male–male desire—though only of the right sort, that is, physical desire sublimated into discourse—returns as the necessary foundation on which the ladder of *eros* is built. "Small thing" though it may be, it is also a thing that cannot be eliminated even in its disavowal:

> It is there, if anywhere, dear Socrates, said the Mantinean Stranger, that human life is to be lived: in contemplating the Beautiful itself. If ever you see it, it will not seem to you as gold or raiment or beautiful boys and youths, which now you look upon dumbstruck; you and many another are ready to gaze on those you love and dwell with them forever, if somehow it were possible, not to eat or drink but only to watch and be with them.
>
> What then do we suppose it would be like, she said, if it were possible for someone to see the beautiful itself, pure, unalloyed, unmixed, not full of human flesh and colors, and the many other kinds of nonsense that attach to mortality, but could behold the divine beauty itself, single in nature? (p. 156, 211d–e)

This is a powerful disavowal of the human attachment to individuals and to bodies: Plato's famous distaste for the body and preference for the invisible world of the Forms seems to stand exposed here in full force. In fact, the truly human is now located precisely in the contemplation of the Form of Beauty, which also turns out to be "the truth" (p. 157, 212a), and in a contemplative transcendence of the flesh's "nonsense." But this transcendence is more in the nature of a sublimation—in its literal sense, a making-sublime—of male–male desire than it is an elimination of it; indeed, the desire to "gaze on those you love" is apparently the best comparison Diotima can think of to convince Socrates that gazing on the Beautiful is preferable.[27] It's only a comparison, to be sure, not to be confused with the real thing; but neither Diotima nor Socrates—nor Plato—can ever quite leave it behind (at least in the *Symposium*), nonsensical though it may be. This little thing, the nonsense of male–male desire, is still the only possible basis for the true doctrine of *eros*: once again that which has, in Dollimore's terms, been outlawed, returns perversely as that which defines the law itself.[28]

One might well ask, at this point, why Plato feels it necessary to include male–male physical desire in his philosophical scheme at all, even as an early stage to be sublimated. The question might be considered along with that of why the true doctrine of *eros* is put into a woman's mouth, or more precisely into the mouth of a man quoting a woman. The two questions together raise the issue of difference and sameness from yet another perspective: David Halperin suggests, in answer to the second, that Diotima is made a woman precisely in order to eliminate sex differences as they were understood in classical Athenian society.[29] Having made Diotima a woman, however, also raises the question of heterosexual reproduction, a question that appears to render difference itself necessary to human life, in opposition to Plato's own valorization of an ideal of self-sameness achieved in the contemplation of an ideal Beauty and Truth. Pederasty, then, in some form, however sublimated, must remain an idealized alternative to male–female reproduction precisely in order to promote this supposedly higher ideal of sameness, even of sexual sameness, as the first step toward the contemplation of higher forms of sameness.[30]

It is perhaps for this reason also that the *Symposium* does not end with this climactic speech. Socrates concludes his recitation of Diotima's doctrine with a dramatic peroration (212b–c), and it seems like a fitting conclusion—but, of course, it isn't the conclusion at all. The drunken and beautiful Alcibiades famously crashes the party at this point in order to crown the day's dramatic victor, Agathon (212e–213b), and then delivers one final, and even more carnivalesque, encomium, the "satyr play," as Socrates calls it (222d), to the evening's dramatic speeches. Alcibiades brings physical desire back to the table, as it were, and his participation allows a final consideration of the relationship between the desires of the body and of the spirit.

Alcibiades, having crowned Agathon, realizes that Socrates is present, and immediately begins a flirtation that is simultaneously funny and serious: he notes that Socrates has contrived to lie next to the beautiful Agathon (213c), and Socrates wittily responds by casting himself in the role of *erastes* to Alcibiades' *eromenos*. Alcibiades appears, however, not as the ideal, chaste *eromenos*, but as one who has been seized by madness: "I very much tremble at his madness and his love for having lovers" (p. 159, 213d). In their topsy–turvy relationship, it is the supposed *erastes* who is chaste, and the *eromenos* who is pursuing him, which is to say that the strict erotic roles are deliberately broken down. Alcibiades also, in a sense, breaks down the rules of the symposium itself, first by being a gate-crasher, and then by the nature of his speech. Invited to join the others by making a speech in praise of *eros*, he declares that he can praise no one but Socrates—the supposed reason being Socrates' own jealousy, which flirtatiously recasts Socrates in the role of *erastes*; as in Aelred of Rievaulx, the sequential trying-out of different erotic roles suggests a degree of sameness between Socrates and Alcibiades, though in this case it is their differences that will be emphasized. Eryximachus, as master of ceremonies, agrees that Alcibiades may speak about Socrates instead of *eros* (214c–d), and Alcibiades insists that what he (unlike the ironic Socrates) says will be "the truth"—with Socrates himself as the guarantor of his truthfulness:

> I'll tell the truth [*talethe ero* (τἀληθῆ ἐρῶ)]. Just see if you allow it.
> Why certainly I allow the truth, he said, and I insist you tell it.

> I can hardly wait to start, said Alcibiades. But you must do this: if I say anything untrue, interrupt me right in the middle, if you wish, and say that I said it falsely; for I won't willingly say anything false. (p. 160, 214e)

This interesting exchange has two different effects. First, it suggests that a discussion of Socrates can fulfill Eryximachus' condition that Alcibiades should, like the symposium's other attendees, deliver an encomium of love. This is not to say that Socrates is Eros, but that he can, at least structurally, hold the same place in Alcibiades' encomium that Eros held in the other speeches; praise of Socrates must in some way involve praise of *eros*. Second, this speech—like that of Socrates himself—will be "the truth" (*aletheia* [ἀλήθεια]): because Socrates never does accuse Alcibiades of lying (he eventually accuses him of having ulterior motives [222c–d], not of falsehood), and hence vouches for his accuracy, what Alcibiades proposes in his speech may be regarded as true in the same sense that Diotima's doctrine is true, and even as a kind of supplement to it.

When Alcibiades delivers his speech, he gives himself rather than Socrates the role of Eros—it is he who, like Eros in Diotima's doctrine, desires what he lacks, and who declares that at one point in his pursuit of Socrates he even, like Eros, "loosed my arrows, as it were, and I thought I'd wounded him" (p. 165, 219b). Socrates represents that which Alcibiades, again like Eros the philosopher, knows he lacks.

What Eros lacks and desires, however, is wisdom, and wisdom is not exactly what Alcibiades pursues, because his desire is mediated by the desire for a human being, Socrates himself. His desire, in other words, is for that which Socrates desires, rather than for wisdom itself. For this reason his desire takes the form of a physical poison like snake's venom, or of a Dionysian frenzy, rather than the form of rational discourse: in hearing Socrates' philosophizing,

> I'd been bitten by something more painful, and in the most painful place one can be bitten—in the heart or soul or whatever one should name it, struck and bitten by arguments in philosophy that hold more fiercely than a serpent, when they take hold of a young and not ill-endowed soul and make him do and say anything whatever—but again, I see here people like Phaedrus and Agathon, Eryximachus and Pausanias and Aristodemus and Aristophanes; and what should be said about Socrates himself and the rest of you? For you have all shared in philosophical madness and Bacchic frenzy [*baccheias* (βακχείας)]. (p. 164, 218a–b)

Alcibiades' imagery suggests that, for him, philosophy is precisely irrational and a physical rather than a spiritual experience: the term *baccheias* in the plural can signify not merely "frenzy," but "Bacchic orgies."[31] Socrates appears here as a figure not of Eros but of Dionysus, as earlier in the speech he was compared a statue of Silenus, which contains figures of the gods (215a–b), or to the satyr Marsyas, whose music "causes possession" (p. 161, 215c). For Alcibiades, then, philosophy is erotic madness because it is mediated by his physical desire for Socrates.

This is not, of course, Socrates' understanding of philosophy, as Alcibiades' speech also makes clear when he recounts his own attempts at convincing Socrates to become his *erastes*. He offered, he says, the physical pleasures of his beautiful body in return for Socrates' help in becoming good (218c–d). While the relationship he proposes resembles the Athenian pederastic ideal, it is unusual in that the prospective *eromenos* is here engaged in courtship of an *erastes*, rather than the other way around, which suggests both the excessively physical nature of Alcibiades' desire and the exchange of erotic roles we have already witnessed between these two.[32] And Socrates refused, as in the *Lysis*, to become the typical *erastes*:

> [Y]ou intend to take no slight advantage of me: on the contrary, you are trying to get possession of what is truly beautiful instead of what merely seems so, and really, you intend to trade bronze for gold. But please, dear friend, give it more thought, lest it escape your notice that I am nothing. (p. 165, 218e–219a)

In refusing the typical *erastes*' physical pleasure, Socrates emphasizes, as we might expect, the difference between the merely physical pleasure Alcibiades offers and the genuine value of the goodness Alcibiades thinks he perceives in Socrates, but he also emphasizes his own true nothingness— a reminder that Alcibiades' desire is for precisely the wrong sort of thing, not for wisdom and goodness themselves, which Socrates does not claim to possess, but for Socrates' desire for these goods. For this reason, Alcibiades finds that he cannot separate himself from "the animal world"—in his case, as a political leader and general, from the world of Athenian public life— except when he is in Socrates' physical presence: "Before him alone I feel ashamed. For I am conscious that I cannot contradict him and say it isn't necessary to do what he bids, but when I leave him, I am worsted by the honors of the multitude. So I desert him and flee, and when I see him I am ashamed by my own agreements" (p. 162, 216b).

If Diotima's doctrine emphasized the links among the rungs on her ladder of *eros*, the manner in which the love of individual physical beauty can, properly understood, lead ultimately to a vision of nonindividuated beauty itself, Alcibiades' speech suggests what may happen when those links are severed, when the lover cannot transcend or sublimate his love for an individual. Alcibiades loves the beauty of Socrates' soul rather than his body, and the philosophical discourses produced there; he also loves the beauty of the public practices that Diotima places on the third rung of her ladder (210b–c) along with this disdain for bodily beauty. But Alcibiades can progress no further: he cannot transcend his love for the "one single thing" that is Socrates. The other attendees understand this, and regard Alcibiades' speech as a self-deprecating confession: "After Alcibiades said this, they laughed at his frankness, because he seemed still in love with Socrates" (p. 168, 222c). As Foucault suggests, "[t]he Socrates of the *Symposium* was . . . the one everybody wanted to be near, everybody was enamored of; the one whose wisdom everybody sought to appropriate—a wisdom that manifested and proved itself precisely in the fact that he was himself able to keep from laying hands on the provocative beauty of Alcibiades."[33] *Askēsis* is necessary only because the body is so insistent in its desires.

Socrates, too, laughs off Alcibiades' confession as a comic "satyr play— or rather your Silenus play" (p. 1679, 222d), and responds with further flirtation, pretending to think that Alcibiades' motive was to drive a wedge between himself and the supposed object of his own affection, Agathon, whom he invites to take Alcibiades' place next to him with the promise that he will next deliver an encomium to Agathon (222e–223a).

But the *Symposium* concludes before he can make good on this promise, with the entrance of more Dionysian revelers, leading to further drinking until Aristodemus passes out. On awakening, he finds Socrates still engaged in discussion with the tragic poet Agathon and the comic poet Aristophanes (223b–c); he is arguing the claim that "he who is a tragic poet by art is a comic poet too" (p. 170, 223d). Following so closely on Alcibiades' speech, this scene suggests that what the symposium's partiers saw as comical in it might from another perspective look tragic: the inability to transcend love of the particular is also Alcibiades' tragic truth, and the reason Socrates does not contradict his speech. If Socrates and Diotima speak for the ideal of unified, undifferentiated love, Alcibiades speaks for the more common human experience of love for what is different and particular, a love both comic and tragic for deviance itself.

Eros in the *Symposium*, then, is a matter of both sameness and difference, a lower "animal" difference that may, ideally, guide the lover to an ideal sameness, or, tragicomically, remain fixed at a lower love of individual difference. Even in this lower form of love, individual differences are also subsumed within male–male sexual sameness, as Diotima's speech suggests. This is to say that human love as experienced by Alcibiades is a matter of deviation, of difference within sameness even at the level of the individual love relationship. It is also a deviation from the true, idealized love of beauty in its self-identity. Only at that highest level of contemplation is difference finally eliminated altogether—but since, for Socrates, *eros* is by definition desire for what one lacks, that highest stage of contemplation comes close to eliminating *eros* itself as well, or rather, it remains erotic only insofar as the lover does not fully identify himself with the object of his contemplation.[34] (Socrates seems to recognize this point when he admits that his discourse might not in the long run really be concerned with *eros* as it is normally understood: "Consider this speech, then, Phaedrus, if you will, an encomium to Eros, or if you prefer, name it what you please" [p. 157, 212c].) Properly speaking, then, *eros*, even for Socrates, must always be a matter of deviance—and for that very reason must be valued less highly than the undesiring self-identity of the beautiful.

Each of the alternate doctrines of *eros* proposed earlier individually values various forms of deviance, various balances between sameness and difference, as we have seen. As a group, too, they represent an overarching, carnivalesque deviance, a likeness within unlikeness, that structures the dialogue as a whole, each of them contributing to Diotima's speech even as they all differ radically from it. In some sense, the *Symposium* is more truly dialogic than the *Lysis*, despite the relative dearth of actual dialogue to be found in it as compared with the earlier text. The other speakers rarely serve, as they so often do in the *Lysis*, simply to confirm Socrates' intellectual explorations of a problem. Instead, each of them is given an opportunity to develop his own conception of *eros* fully, without rebuttal from Socrates (except in the case of Agathon— and even there, the question of how thorough his rebuttal really is remains a matter of debate[35]). While it is undoubtedly true that, as most commentators agree, Plato intends Socrates' speech to be understood as true,[36] merely agreeing with him to the exclusion of the other views expressed here would be a poor response to the dialogical complexities of the *Symposium*.

As I suggested earlier, the *Symposium*'s influence on subsequent Western culture has been incalculable. In the remainder of this chapter, I limit myself to brief discussions of a number of texts that directly discuss male–male desire, that use the dialogue form to do so, and that are demonstrably indebted to Plato's *Symposium*. Perhaps the earliest such response is another *Symposium* composed by Plato's approximate contemporary, Xenophon, after Plato wrote his.[37] Xenophon also wrote other Socratic dialogues, often taken to reflect the real Socrates better than Plato's, that discuss male–male desire, in particular the *Memorabilia*, as we have seen.[38] But his *Symposium* in particular seems to refer directly to Plato's, and provides a revealing alternative perspective on Socrates' views of *eros*.

The setting is, as in Plato, a party given in honor of the victor in a competition, in this case a "boy [*paidos* (παιδὸς)]" (p. 227, I.2)[39] named Autolycus, who has won the boys' pancration in the Great Panathenaea festival. The party is given by Callias, a young man in love with Autolycus, as we are informed at the outset (I.2). The atmosphere is, then, one conducive to expressions of male–male erotic desire—though, since Autolycus' father is also a guest, Callias' expressions of his desire are to remain within modest boundaries. While the guests discuss many different topics (the subject of their conversation is not erotics, but rather what each participant is "most proud of" [p. 236, III.4]), the text both begins and ends with *eros*. The beginning, in fact, suggests a positive view of *eros* on Xenophon's (or the narrator's) part: in discussing the guests' response to the beauty of Autolycus, he suggests that

> There was not a man there whose feelings were not moved at the sight of him. Some became more silent, and the behaviour of others underwent a sort of transformation. Possession by a god always seems to have a remarkable effect. Those who are influenced by other gods tend to become more intimidating in their appearance, more truculent in their speech and more aggressive in their conduct; but those who are inspired by discreet Love [*tou sophronos Erotos* (τοῦ σώφρονος Ἔρωτος)] wear a kindlier expression, speak in a gentler tone and behave in a way more befitting a free man. (p. 228, I.10)

"Discreet" love—*sophronos*, suggesting temperance and moderation—of the modest type being practiced here by Callias is presumably to be distinguished from the kind of erotic madness described by Alcibiades, and perhaps has more in common with the spiritual and philosophical *eros* promoted by Socrates, which also tends toward moral improvement; still, it is a kind of possession, and Eros is a god, not the Platonic "daimon" of Diotima's doctrine—a god whose influence need not result in the violent suffering often depicted in Greek culture,[40] and indeed one whose influence is gentler than that of the other gods. Nevertheless, physical eroticism remains, for Xenophon's Socrates as for Plato's, a temptation whose very pleasureableness is a moral danger. In IV.10–18, another guest, Critobulus, boasts that he is most proud of his good looks, also taking the opportunity to praise the beauty of his own beloved Clinias, invoking the same image of a temperate love inspired by male beauty as a rationale for the pride he takes in it (IV.15). Socrates, however, critiques his infatuation with Clinias, and disclaims responsibility for it (IV.24). Kissing, the physical expression of *eros*, presents a moral danger: "It's an insatiable thing, and it produces a kind of delicious anticipation. That's why I say that anyone who wants to be able to behave responsibly ought to refrain from kissing the young and attractive" (p. 244, IV.26). Strict *askēsis*, here meaning self-control to the point of abstention, is the only ethical response to physical erotic pleasure—precisely because it is such a delicious, even addictive pleasure (as in the passage from the *Memorabilia* cited above). Indeed, physical contact is a pleasure to which even Socrates is not immune, as Charmides points out:

> "I've seen you yourself, I swear, with my own eyes, when you were both in the school-room searching for something in the same book, touching Critobulus' head with your head and his bare arm with yours[.]"
> "Dear me!" said Socrates. "So that's why I had a sore arm for more than five days, as if some wild beast had bitten me, and felt a sort of ache in my heart. . . ."
> In this way they combined joking with seriousness. (p. 244, IV.27–29)

Xenophon regularly points out the joking tone of this symposium, though it is often, as here, unclear exactly which aspects of the conversation are intended as jokes and which are serious.[41] Presumably Socrates' warning against physical expressions of *eros* is serious, while his claim of physical injury is a joke—but is Charmides' accusation itself only a joke, or are we to understand Socrates as truly susceptible to the beauty of which Critobulus has been boasting? It should be noted that when in the following chapter Critobulus and Socrates engage in their mock beauty contest, it is Socrates who decides that the judges—the beautiful boy and girl who have provided the evening's entertainment—reward the victor not with garlands, but precisely with kisses (V.9): Socrates here leads himself into temptation. In either case, Xenophon's portrait of Socrates is even more flirtatious than Plato's, and tends humorously to subvert the austerity of his doctrines.

Indeed, the metaphor Socrates chooses to express the characteristic on which he prides himself is the profession of "pimp [*mastropou* (μαστροποῦ)]" (p. 249, IV.57). It is certainly no more than a clever metaphor for "a man who is able to recognize people who are likely to benefit each other, and who can make them desire each other" (p. 251, IV.64), as Socrates does philosophically—but here again, Xenophon's Socrates remains in touch with physical reality to a degree that Plato's does not. Xenophon and his Socrates are, that is to say, more representative of typical Athenian attitudes toward male–male erotics than is the somewhat eccentric Plato.

Even so, when Socrates finally comes to discourse on love directly (VIII), he defends a view of *eros* in accord with that which he enunciates in Plato's *Symposium*, at least in its broad outlines if not in every particular. He praises

Callias for the good qualities of his love-object, including "self-discipline [*sophrosunen* (σωφροσύνην)]" (p. 258, VIII.8); he speculates about the double nature of Aphrodite familiar from Pausanias' speech in Plato's dialogue—but now the distinction is the more Socratic one between "physical love" and "love of the mind" (p. 259, VIII.10); he rebukes the notion, derived from the same speech of Pausanias, of an army of lovers united by physical passion (VIII.32–34); and so on, all in service of the idea that "love for the mind [*psyches* (ψυχῆς)]" is much better than physical love [*tou somatos eros* (τοῦ σώματος ἔρος)]" (p. 259, VIII.12–13). Xenophon's Socrates may find physical pleasure irresistible, but like Plato's he suggests that it must ideally be transcended. Like Plato's, too, he idealizes male–male desire—but only as the basis of spiritual love, physical love being consigned to the female: "All the mortal women whom Zeus loved for their physical beauty he left mortal after he had had sex with them, but all those men who won his regard by their nobility of mind he made immortal" (p. 262, VIII.29).

Xenophon's Socrates also discusses likeness and unlikeness in his discourse on love, and finds that likeness characterizes the true "love for the mind," while physical love is characterized by unlikeness. Love of the mind, for Xenophon's Socrates, is at variance from traditional aristocratic Athenian pederasty not only in that it eschews the physical, but also in that it is reciprocal: the *eromenos* can return the *erastes'* love precisely because it is of the mind and not of the body:

> In the first place, who could hate a person by whom, he knows, he is considered truly good, and secondly who, he can see, is more concerned about what is good for his favourite [*paidos* (παιδὸς)] than what is pleasant for himself, and moreover whose affection, he trusts, could not be diminished even by the calamity of a disfiguring disease? Must not those whose affection is mutual look at each other and converse in amity; must they not trust and be trusted, be considerate to each other, share pleasure in their successes and sorrow if anything goes wrong . . . ? Aren't all these characteristics filled with Aphrodite's charm? (p. 260, VIII.17–18)

Having already established that the *erastes* himself has a comparably noble nature (VIII.16), Socrates now describes an *eromenos* who is equally good; this noble identity of character in turn allows the kind of mutuality or reciprocity of "affection" (*ten philian* [(τὴν φιλίαν)]) in which the active and passive roles are shared—both lovers must "trust and be trusted" (*pisteuein de kai pisteuesthai* [πιστεύειν δὲ καὶ πιστεύεσθαι]). Furthermore, this kind of love, despite the deliberate use of the term *philia*, is not just friendship: it is characterized by "Aphrodite's charm" (*epaphrodita* [ἐπαφρόδιτα]) as well—presumably that of the Heavenly Aphrodite, invoked elsewhere in the speech, whom Socrates associates with nonphysical desire.

Love of the body, on the other hand, is plagued by unlikeness, and therefore cannot be reciprocal. The lover "whose attachment is physical" (p. 260, VIII.19) cannot expect his *eromenos* to return his affection, and indeed an *eromenos* motivated by the physical is quickly assimilated to the figure of the prostitute, "one who sells his youthful beauty for money" (p. 260, VIII.21). In the absence of likeness of mind, the unlikeness of body between the partners can lead only to contempt:

> Certainly, the fact that he is young and his partner is not, or that he is beautiful and his partner is so no longer, or that he is not in love and his partner is—this will not stir his affection. A boy does not even share the man's enjoyment of sexual intercourse as a woman does: he is a sober person watching one drunk with sexual excitement. (pp. 260–261, VIII.21)

Here, too, Xenophon's Socrates departs from the idealized view of Athenian pederasty: the *eromenos* is imagined as a prostitute, and one who is motivated only by material benefits is both contemptible and contemptuous of the older man. In itself, this attitude is similar to the one that idealized male–male desire as primarily a pedagogical relationship. But in the context of the rest of Socrates' remarks, which condemn physical contact outright, his own ideal appears to eliminate all physical expression of *eros*, a step which does differ from the traditional point of view. Difference is assigned to the realm of the physical—and at this point male–male differences in age and beauty even outweigh male–female sex differences.[42]

Xenophon is not a Platonic philosopher, and never addresses the primary problem that Plato associates with love between those who are the same, namely, how can one desire what one already possesses? For him, likeness is unproblematically of the mind or spirit, and the primary characteristic of his ideal *eros*, whereas difference characterizes the physical, which must be transcended. Nevertheless, Xenophon's Socrates, more than Plato's, also recognizes and even participates in the physical aspects of eroticism, which remains the deviant outlaw in his attempt to sublimate physical desire, too. It is the dialogue form rather than the content of Socrates' speeches that illustrates this aspect of Socratic male–male desire: as we have seen, the flirtatious teasing among the participants in Xenophon's symposium to some extent offsets the Socratic doctrine itself. It should also be noted that while Socrates is declared a "truly good [*kalos ge kagathos* (καλός γε κἀγαθὸς)] man" (p. 265, IX.1) near the end of the dialogue, his doctrine does not claim the same kind of truth-status here that Diotima's does in

Plato's text: Xenophon's Socrates is more tentative, using such phrases as "[o]ne might guess" (p. 259, VIII.10), "it seems to me" (p. 263, VIII.35), and "I imagine" (p. 264, VIII.36) to approach an understanding of *eros*. Certainly, Socrates' views are given pride of place, but the Socratic refusal of true knowledge also allows more room for other, deviating ones such as those of Critobulus and Charmides; in this sense Xenophon's dialogue is more truly "dialogic," at least in Bakhtin's sense, than Plato's—and since dialogue requires more direct interaction among the participants than does the Platonic lecture series, it is also perhaps more erotic.[43]

If Plato is, as I and others have suggested,[44] eccentric, for fourth century B.C. Athens, in his desire to sublimate male–male physical desire to such an extreme extent, he may also be said to anticipate the tendency that Foucault discerned in certain Greek writers of the Roman era,[45] and specifically in a pair of dialogues, one, the *Dialogue on Love*, by Plutarch (A.D. 45–120) and the other, the *Affairs of the Heart* (early fourth century) falsely attributed to Lucian.[46] Both refer to Plato, and specifically to the *Symposium*. Both debate the respective merits of male–female love and pederasty, Plutarch's deciding in favor of the former, Pseudo-Lucian's—ironically, as Foucault points out[47]—in favor of the latter. Nevertheless, both signal, in Foucault's view,

> the effort to constitute a unitary erotics, very clearly organized on the model of the man–woman, and even husband–wife, relationship. In comparison with this single love (it is supposed to be the same, whether it is directed to women or to boys), the pederastic attachment will in fact be disqualified, but without a rigid line of demarcation being drawn, as it will be later, between "homo-" and "heterosexual" acts.[48]

This "unitary erotics" is developed in terms of the reciprocity of erotic pleasure: because the idealized Athenian model of pederasty precluded the possibility of a respectable younger partner experiencing such pleasure, it can be devalued when and if mutuality and reciprocity—that is, the qualities that came to be associated with heterosexual marriage—become more highly valued. Foucault argues that marriage was, in fact, for a variety of reasons, reevaluated in the Roman period, as one aspect of the emphasis on self-discipline whose growth he describes in the second and third volumes of *The History of Sexuality*: "A stylistics of living as a couple emerges from the traditional precepts of matrimonial management: it can be observed rather clearly in an art of conjugal relationship, in a doctrine of sexual monopoly, and in an aesthetics of shared pleasures."[49] The dialogues—or perhaps more properly, the debates—on *eros* dating from the Roman period, then, frame their topic in terms of the differences between boy-love and, specifically, conjugal love.[50]

Framed by the story of an older woman's desire to marry a younger man, the debate in Plutarch's *Dialogue on Love* takes place in two stages: in the first, the young man, Bacchon, asks the advice of two of his male admirers, Anthemion, who favors marriage, and Pisias, who believes Bacchon should remain unmarried and devoted to male love; Anthemion's position is argued primarily by his "advocate" Daphnaeus, Pisias' by Protogenes. Plutarch himself is to judge (the story is ostensibly being recounted by his son Autobulus). In the second, the lady having decided the matter for herself by abducting Bacchon, Plutarch renders his judgment in favor of marriage. In the first segment, Protogenes draws on Plato in defense of male–male love, notably in a section (p. 375, 760d) devoted to the mutual inspiration of lovers on the battlefield, a section comparable to Phaedrus' speech about the army of lovers in the *Symposium*. Protogenes also makes several arguments against the love of women, most importantly that it is a merely natural urge to procreation (which thus links humans with beasts) and that because it cannot be detached from pleasure it also fails to achieve the philosophical detachment necessary to virtue (pp. 314–319, 750b–751b). Daphnaeus turns these arguments back against him, claiming that behavior in accordance with nature is itself a virtue, and that boy-lovers are hypocrites: however much they may claim to exalt philosophy and virtue, in fact their desire is for physical pleasure as well (pp. 320–325, 751b–752b); in addition, boys who allow themselves to be possessed in this way are guilty of "weakness and effeminacy [*malakiai kai theluteti* (μαλακίᾳ καὶ θηλύτητι)]" (p. 23, 751d).

As Foucault points out, Plutarch's decision in this case—couched in the form of an encomium on Eros similar to those that make up Plato's *Symposium*—draws its arguments from "the traditional erotics of pederasty,"[51] but they are applied, at first, equally to the love of boys and to married love: female beauty is as conducive to love of the soul as male (pp. 412–415, 766d–f), and a man can feel friendship for his wife as well as for another male (pp. 426–427, 769a–b). In fact, while it is never denied that spiritual love can properly exist between males, the exclusive conjugal union is ultimately judged to be the only true friendship, on the basis of reciprocal sexual pleasure: "There can be no greater pleasures [*hedonai* (ἡδοναὶ)] derived from others nor more continuous services conferred on others than those found in marriage, nor can the beauty of another friendship [*philias* (φιλίας)] be so highly esteemed or so enviable" (pp. 432–433, 770a). This is true precisely because its exclusivity demands a virtuous self-restraint, while its conjugality allows sexual pleasure to both parties: only marriage can conjoin friendship and physical pleasure.[52]

Heterosexual marriage is emerging here as the straight and narrow path from which male–male desire is an inferior deviant: it is no longer a question of whether or not a man should take physical pleasure in his relationship with a boy, but whether he should engage in a relationship in which pleasure is mutual—which is to say marriage—or one-sided.

Man and woman are not by any means treated here as social equals, but within the erotic bond, "each partner is, from the standpoint of *Eros*, always an active subject."[53] Sexually, husband and wife can mirror each other in a way that is not available to male couples, at least as long as one partner in such a relationship is imagined as necessarily taking a subjected position that precludes pleasure. From this perspective, the difference in social status between husband and wife is what allows an erotic sameness or mirroring in sexual pleasure, while the social sameness of two freeborn men supposedly disallows this erotic reciprocity. Erotic sameness or reciprocity requires a gendered difference in social standing. In other words, the gender identity of two men also creates a social identity which makes the deviance necessary to desire impossible; gender difference is now essential to desire precisely in its linkage with a difference in status. And if gender difference becomes the essential form of difference in erotic relations, male–male desire will necessarily be relegated to a position not only of deviance, but abjection. This has not yet happened in Plutarch's dialogue, but as Foucault suggests, "one sees, in Plutarch, a new stylistics of love being formed."[54]

The potential for the abjection of male–male desire, at least in its physical expression, is reflected also in the debate form that Plutarch adopts. Rather than the easy give-and-take of Xenophon's *Symposium* or even the more informal sections of Plato's, Plutarch's debaters exhibit an irascibility that cannot really be harmonized: "During [Daphnaeus's] speech, it was obvious that Pisias was full of anger and indignation against Daphnaeus; hardly had the latter ceased when Pisias exclaimed, 'Good lord, what coarseness, what insolence!'. . ." (p. 325, 752b). This is not the kind of "proximity" imagined by Levinas in his commentary on Buber, but rather a clear-cut opposition (perhaps more easily assimilated to Bakhtinian theory). Only a decision declaring one the winner and the other the loser could bring this debate to an end: Plutarch's decision in favor of male–female marriage, in fact, silences the advocates of pederasty as no one else is silenced in the dialogues we have examined previously. Despite his advocacy of reciprocity between men and women, no real reciprocity between men is visible in Plutarch's text; his manipulation of the dialogue form as well as its content leaves little room for alternative erotics.

Pseudo-Lucian's later dialogue *Erotes*, usually translated as *Affairs of the Heart*, is a similar debate: Theomnestus, a man widely experienced in the love of both boys and women, asks Lycinus to judge between the two; Lycinus in turn recounts an earlier debate between Charicles, a lover of women, and Callicratidas, an Athenian boy-lover, in which Lycinus himself was the judge. Charicles and Callicratidas in their remembered debate use many of the same arguments already familiar from Plutarch: male–female procreation is natural (whether this is regarded as good or bad), boy-love is more spiritual and conducive to virtue, and so on Once again, the two men serve primarily as reifications of their erotic tastes, here seen even more clearly not as complements but as opposites (*dieireto* [(διῄρητο]) (pp. 158–159, ch. 5): Charicles loves women exclusively, Callicratidas loves only boys, and their argument is pursued with passionate commitment, despite Lycinus' own attempts to see it as mere amusement; he says that he has agreed to Theomnestus' request for a decision "because I've known it to be far from a laughing matter ever since the time I heard two men arguing heatedly with each other about these two types of love" (pp. 157–159, ch. 5). As in Plutarch, it would seem that there is no possible harmony or even coexistence of these views, but, while Lycinus does declare a winner, he does so without suggesting abjection for the loser: ". . . all men should marry, but let only the wise be permitted to love boys, for perfect virtue grows least of all among women. And you must not be angry, Charicles, if Corinth yields to Athens" (p. 229, ch. 51). Here marriage is still the norm, and the love of boys—understood as exclusively spiritual—a deviation. In this case, however, it is the winner of the debate: not an abjected deviation, but one included in the norm and superior to it because of the superior virtue and spirituality of the male. The decision is not so clear-cut as in Plutarch, and, appropriately in this more ambiguous situation, the dialogue form is more flexible as well: rather than ending with Lycinus' decision, the debate continues in the dialogue's "present," when Theomnestus argues, similarly to a position we have already observed in Plutarch, that the spiritual understanding of boy-love is mere hypocrisy: rather than being truly spiritual, boy-lovers engage in it for the physical pleasure it provides (ch. 53–54).

There is thus no sense of real resolution at the end of the *Affairs of the Heart*, and Foucault suggests that it should be read not as a triumph for boy-love, but as "a fundamental objection to the very old line of argument of Greek pederasty, which, in order to conceptualize, formulate, and discourse about the latter and to supply it with reason, was obliged to evade the manifest presence of physical pleasure."[55] The spokesman for this evasion in the classical period, is, of course, Plato's (and Xenophon's) Socrates, and Pseudo-Lucian addresses his relationship with Alcibiades, as depicted in Plato's *Symposium*, directly. Callicratidas first invokes them as a model of his virtuous pederasty: "One should love youths as Alcibiades was loved by Socrates who slept like a father with him under the same cloak"

(p. 227, ch. 49); this reference comes at the end of Callicratidas' speech, and Lycinus' decision in favor of this virtuous boy-love follows immediately. Theomnestus' coda to the debate, however, invokes Socrates in the opposite sense, as one of his philosophical hypocrites: "Socrates was as devoted to love [*erotikos* (ἐρωτικὸς)] as anyone and Alcibiades, once he had lain down beneath the same mantle with him, did not rise unassailed" (pp. 234–235, ch. 54). Socrates here becomes as ambiguous as the dialogue form itself; no longer necessarily or exclusively the spokesman for "virtuous" boy-love, he now appears also and equally as a representative of its physical expression, a role in which he will resurface in the Renaissance. As Foucault notes, Pseudo-Lucian "demonstrates the essential weakness of a discourse on love that makes no allowance for the *aphrodisia* and for the relations they engage."[56]

Gender difference plays a greater role in Pseudo-Lucian's dialogue than in Plutarch's. Charicles, in fact, characterizes male–male desire as effeminacy, and even as castration. The traditional Athenian assumption that allowing oneself to be penetrated outside the socially controlled upper-class pederastic relationship was a sign of lower status or effeminacy is here brought even within that relationship in an image of shocking violence. Originally, says Charicles, men obeyed the natural laws of procreation.

> But gradually the passing years degenerated from such nobility to the lowest depths of hedonism and cut out strange and extraordinary paths to enjoyment. The luxury, daring all, transgressed the laws of nature [*physin* (φύσιν)] herself. And who ever was the first to look at the male [*to arren* (τὸ ἄρρεν)] as though at a female [*hos thely* (ὡς θῆλυ)] after using violence like a tyrant [*tyrannikos* (τυραννικῶς)] or else shameless persuasion? The same sex [*physis* (φύσις)] entered the same bed. Though they saw themselves embracing each other, they were ashamed neither at what they did nor at what they had done to them, and, sowing their seed, to quote the proverb, on barren rocks they bought a little pleasure at the cost of great disgrace.
>
> The daring of some men has advanced so far in tyrannical violence as even to wreak sacrilege [*hierosulesai* (ἱεροσυλῆςαι)] upon nature with the knife. By depriving males of their masculinity they have found wider ranges of pleasure. But those who become wretched and luckless in order to be boys for longer remain male no longer, being a perplexing riddle of dual gender [*physeos* (φύσεως)] . . . (pp. 182–183, ch. 20–21)

This passage combines a number of discourses against male–male desire in a way that, as we shall see, will also be invoked by other, later authors. Such desires are, to begin with, against nature: *physis*, which suggests both the natural order of things and a particular being's own natural kind, gender, or sex. They are also tyrannical (*tyrannikos*): the political as well as the natural order is invoked to suggest that male–male desire is always a matter of unjust, and undemocratic, domination. The religious order is invoked as well with the term *hierosulesai*, referring specifically to violence against the gods—nature, or the order of gender, is here given divine status. Most importantly, the order of sex and gender is made to march alongside these other orders of authority: not only are slaves and enemies feminized by penetration, feminization is now a function of any male–male physical eroticism. Physical expressions of desire between males are always and invariably identical with gender confusion, and thus with the loss of social status. Sex-sameness is now inscribed as the primary characteristic of male–male desire, a sex-sameness which is intolerable because it confuses gender roles. This form of deviance—this sex-sameness that contains the potential for gender difference—is, for Charicles, a violation of all legitimate forms of authority. Callicratidas may argue that male–male desire is truly spiritual, but Theomnestus' coda to the debate reminds us that what Callicratidas and Lycinus are defending can now also be understood in a new, and purely physical, light. We have come a long way from the Platonic assumption that spiritual love may be assumed to exist only between males: with the promotion of faithful marriage, male–female relations take on an element of spirituality, those between men an element of carnality. Plato, indeed, now appears as the cultural dominant for both Plutarch and the Pseudo-Lucian, and as such is himself subject to Dollimore's perversion and inversion, as that which he disavows returns as supposedly the true basis of his thought.

This vision of male–male desire as an unauthorized and unnatural gender confusion is replayed throughout the Middle Ages in debate poems such as "Ganymede and Helen"[57] and in Alan of Lille's influential twelfth-century dialogue *De Planctu naturae*, or *The Complaint of Nature*. While the latter does not mention Socrates or refer to Plato directly, and therefore falls outside the scope of this chapter, it is a dialogue (between the narrator and the allegorical figure of Nature) representative of the medieval Christian condemnation of same-sex desire, and specifically of the confusion of gender roles, here expressed in terms of grammatical gender. The narrator's opening salvo is reminiscent of the constellation of discourses just observed in Pseudo-Lucian:

> Nature weeps, moral laws get no hearing, modesty, totally dispossessed of her ancient high estate, is sent into exile. The active sex [*actiui generis*] shudders in disgrace as it sees itself degenerate into the passive [*passiuum*] sex. A man turned woman blackens the fair name of his sex. The witchcraft of Venus

turns him into a hermaphrodite. He is subject and predicate: one and the same term is given a double application. Man here extends too far the laws [*leges*] of grammar.[58]

Men like these, who refuse Genius his tithes and rites, deserve to be excommunicated [*anathema merentur*] from the temple of Genius.[59]

Here, some eight centuries after Pseudo-Lucian, we may find the same set of authoritative discourses employed there to condemn male–male physical eroticism: the language of nature, of law (here grammatical law) [*leges*], of religion (excommunication, *anathema*, here from the allegorical temple of another natural, procreation-related figure, Genius), and most importantly of gender (here metaphorically grammatical as well as sexual), still figure as parts of the same nexus of condemnation. The context, of course, is now Christian: despite Alan's allegorical use of pagan figures (and a certain anti-clericalism), he was at some point in his career a monk and wrote on Christian theology, pastoral care, and scriptural interpretation;[60] the language of excommunication itself places him in the twelfth-century Christian tradition. Nevertheless, the concerns are the same as Pseudo-Lucian's: male–male erotic desire leads to gender confusion, and thus a confusion in social status, and is also a form of rebellion against authority.[61] The difference is that the Christian Alan can offer no alternative praise of this form of desire, but can only attempt to eliminate it.[62] In this Christian context male–male desire can no longer have even an element of spiritual-ity (though we might compare Aelred's creation of a somewhat different Christian context), but is thoroughly carnal.

In early modern Italy, as Virginia Cox has demonstrated, the dialogue became in some ways the preeminent form for the philosophical discussion of all manner of topics, love included. Cox draws formal distinctions among the Renaissance Italian dialogues along different axes. One is the monological/dialogical or open/closed axis, classical models for which Cox finds in Plato and Cicero, respectively. As we have seen, in such works of Plato as the *Lysis* and the *Symposium*, the endlessly deviating dramatic form of the dialogue itself is essential to its meaning, as is the dialogical relation-ship it sets up with the reader, while Cicero's *Tusculans* and *De amicitia* for the most part dispense with dialogue in favor of a master's monological lec-ture. Cox finds both types of dialogue in the Italian Renaissance, but points out that in the late Cinquecento, "the concept of authority carried great prestige," that "didacticism had no negative connotations," and that the authoritative, Ciceronian model dominated at certain points;[63] Jon R. Snyder, indeed, finds in Italian Renaissance theories of dialogue a steady development away from a dialectical model and toward one in which "the art of questioning, doubting, exploring the lateral paths and possibilities of thought . . . is definitely banished from the scene of speaking and is at last lost to sight."[64]

The reason for this reverential attitude toward authority may be found in Italy's unique political circumstances in the sixteenth century. In contrast to Tudor England, for example, with its centralized court and system of patronage, in Italy, according to Cox,

> where no such real political nucleus existed, this same cultural role was performed by a far more fluid and intangible ideal "court" or "academy," united across political boundaries by a shared language and literary heritage. . . . This was an entity which existed, of course, only as a generous figment of the collective imagination, and it is hardly surprising under the circumstances that the Italian cultural elite showed such an anxiety for self-definition.[65]

This anxiety about self-definition is expressed in the reverence for authority—political or religious—that provides the agenda for many humanist dialogues. And this reverence for authority is sometimes expressed specifically as the suppression or denunciation of male–male desire; while drawing on Plato, many humanist thinkers also draw on the medieval Christian tradition in obscuring or disavowing classical Athenian pederastic culture: rather than a means of initiating young men into their society's power structures, male–male desire, at least in its physical expression, is now regarded by mainstream thinkers as a subversion of political and religious authority. And as we might expect, following Dollimore's model, other thinkers outside the mainstream reveal this disavowed desire to be the basis of the very culture that prohibits it.

Cox also distinguishes among Italian Renaissance dialogues along the axis history/invention. Authority is at issue in this distinction as in the dialogical/monological one, and again Cicero and Plato provide Cox's models: ". . . if the vital persuasive mechanism of *auctoritas* is to work, it is necessary for the reader at least to suspend disbelief in the documentary character of the dialogue."[66] While Plato set his dialogues among historical figures, the casualness—and indeed the homoeroticism—of their *mise-en-scène* made them seem less suitable as models for dialogues set in Renaissance courts than Cicero's sobriety.[67]

Humanist thinkers such as Marsilio Ficino had, or themselves made possible (with printed editions and translations), more direct access to the classical Greek authors than was available to most readers in the medieval Latin West. Ficino, in fact, was an early translator (for his patrons from

1462 to 1473, the Medici family) of Plato's works into Latin, and later into Italian. He was also an early interpreter of Plato from a Christian perspective, in his *Platonic Theology* (1482) and in his *Commentary on Plato's Symposium on Love* (*De amore*, 1484),[68] itself a dialogue—at least technically—in which several speakers expound the hidden meanings of the various speeches in the *Symposium*. This new access to classical writers, in particular Plato, had its effect on early modern attitudes toward male–male desire—as did the continuing Christian tradition in which these writers were conducting their investigations.[69] But in Ficino's Latin text we may also observe the reverence for authority—the Church's in particular—that Cox discerns (in a more secular context) in later vernacular dialogues.

Ficino, for example, in his *Commentary*, attempts a neoplatonic reading of the *Symposium* that will not be offensive to the Church ("as if to test the religious orthodoxy of his work, he sent copies of it to two members of the clergy: a Hungarian bishop named Joannes Pannonius [1434–1473] and Cardinal Francesco Piccolomini of Siena [1439–1503]"[70]). What he finds attractive in Plato's *Symposium* is, then, its account of the soul's ascent to a divine unity—that is, one important but small portion of one speech, Socrates'/Diotima's—rather than the dialogue's literary drama, the dialogic contrasts among the doctrines of its various speakers, or, in particular, the desire between men that informs and structures those doctrines, including Diotima's.[71] Sears Jayne summarizes Ficino's argument as follows:

> [T]he cosmos consists of a hierarchy of being extending from God (unity) to the physical world (multiplicity). In this hierarchy every level evolves from the level above it in a descending emanation from God and desires to rise to the level above it in an ascending return to God. This desire to return to one's source is called love, and the quality in the source which attracts this desire is called beauty. The human soul, as a part of the hierarchy of being, is involved in this same process of descent from God and return to God; in human beings the desire to procreate inferior beings is called earthly love, and the desire to rise to higher levels of being is called heavenly love.[72]

We are here clearly in the realm of Plato's commentators rather than of Plato himself, and in fact relatively little of Ficino's "commentary" addresses Plato's *Symposium* at all. Instead, Ficino uses the *Symposium* as a pretext for working out his own mystical theology/philosophy, more heavily influenced by the neoplatonic philosophers Pseudo-Dionysius, Proclus, and Plotinus than it is by Plato's text: while the doctrine of emanations, for instance, may ultimately be derived from other Platonic dialogues, it plays little or no part in the *Symposium* itself. Nevertheless, the basis of Ficino's doctrine in the relationship of unity to multiplicity is relevant to the themes I have been pursuing: the two terms are neither opposed to each other nor likened; instead, multiplicity is understood as a derivation of unity, that is, as a deviation or difference contained by sameness. Human love—spiritual, not physical—in the world of multiplicity is therefore understood in a positive light because "in both of its phases, descending and ascending, it is part of a natural cosmic process in which all creatures share."[73] Human love in its multiple desires is itself a matter of deviation from the divine unity.

However, although Jayne emphasizes the positive valuation of human love, in fact Ficino devotes considerably more attention to the desire for, and achievement of, unity with God; the deviation of human love must ultimately be absorbed into the complete self-identity of the divine: "Certainly above every multiplicity of a composite thing [*super omnem rei composite multitudinem*] must be the one itself, simple by nature [*unum ipsum simplex debet esse natura*]. . . . But above the One, that is, God Himself, we cannot place anything because the true One is devoid of all multiplicity, of all compositeness" (VI.15, pp. 137–138; pp. 231–232). Multiplicity must in the long run be sacrificed for unity as human love, however good it may be on its own level, must give way to heavenly love. Physical expressions of eros, in particular, are understood as hatred, illness, and destruction.[74]

The nature of correct human love itself, in its very refusal of the physical, suggests the same movement away from multiplicity:

> Therefore those who, as we have said, are born under the same star are so constituted that the image of the more beautiful of them, penetrating through the eyes into the soul of the other, matches and corresponds completely with a certain identical image [*consimili cuidam simulacro*] which was formed in the astral body of that soul as well as in its inner nature from its creation. The soul thus stricken recognizes the image before it as something which is its own. It is in fact almost exactly like the image which this soul has long possessed within itself, and which it tried to imprint on its own body, but was not able to do. The soul then puts the visual image beside its own interior image, and if anything is lacking in the former as a perfect copy of the Jovial body, the soul restores it by reforming it. (p. 114, VI.6; p. 206)

This is one of several instances in which Ficino explains physical erotic attraction—or explains it away—by decorporealizing it, rendering erotics a matter of images within the soul rather than of bodies themselves.[75] To be sure, the continued existence of these images requires the continued presence of their source, "a beautiful body"—but this requirement is only proof of the "poverty" of the physical eye (p. 115, VI.6; p. 207). The love of such bodies is, significantly, a matter of deviance: the soul's image of the body of the beloved is "almost exactly"—but not exactly—like its own internal image. This deviance, however, is quickly erased as the soul refashions the beloved's image to conform with the divine image it carries within itself: even in the correct form of human love, decorporealization allows unity to replace multiplicity. Likeness, in fact, is regularly assumed to be a require- ment for love throughout the *Commentary*;[76] this passage merely serves to explain how that likeness comes to be.

Since this likeness is most significantly a likeness of souls and images rather than of bodies, sex and gender differences are of relatively little con- cern to Ficino.[77] Spiritual human affection can exist between men as well as between men and women (as we might expect, love between women does not arise as an issue): the first speech, a commentary on Phaedrus' speech in the *Symposium*, thus illustrates virtuous, that is, nonphysical, love with Phaedrus' three couples, Alcestis and Admetus, Orpheus and Euridice, and Patroclus and Achilles (p. 42, I.4). Such an allowance for male–male desire is virtually unavoidable in a commentary at least purportedly on Plato's *Symposium*—but Speech I merely mentions these relationships, eschewing Phaedrus' discussion of their precise nature.[78] Indeed, all physi- cal expressions of male–male desire are condemned as violently as in Alan of Lille, perhaps as part of Ficino's effort to satisfy his clerical critics that pagan philosophy may indeed be adapted to Christian ends without a corol- lary adaptation of pagan erotic practices. Thus Speech II, the commentary on Pausanias' encomium, turns the latter's enthusiasm for Athenian ped- erasty into a purely spiritual eros, and condemns, among other condemna- tions of the physical expression of eros, that which goes "against the order of nature with men" (p. 54, II.7; p. 155).[79] More violently, Speech VI, the commentary on Diotima's doctrine, cites Plato's later dialogue the *Laws* to associate the physical expression of male–male erotics with murder:

> But it should have been noticed that the purpose of erections of the genital part is not the useless act of ejaculation, but the function of fertilizing and procreating; the part should have been redirected from males to females.
>
> We think that it was by some error of this kind that that wicked crime arose which Plato in his *Laws* roundly curses as a form of murder [*homocidii spetiem*]. Certainly a man who snatches away a man about to be born must be considered a murderer no less than one who takes from our midst a man already born. He who destroys a present life may be bolder, but he who begrudges light to the unborn and kills his own unborn sons is more cruel. (pp. 135–136, VI.14; pp. 229–230)[80]

We may find several purposes being served in such passages. Nature is once again invoked, explicitly in Speech II and, in the form of reproductive physiology, implicitly in Speech VI, with the effect of legitimating sexual intercourse between men and women at the same time that it removes legitimacy from the physical expression of male–male erotics. By invoking (not quite correctly) the *Laws* as well as the legal category of murder, the second passage also identifies men who engage in such expressions as criminals, and in particular as "bold" rebels against civic authority, as well as against the intellectual authority of Plato himself. The constellation of effects is similar to those we observed in Pseudo-Lucian and Alan of Lille, and serves the same purpose of policing erotic expression, here as in Alan to a far greater extent than in their ancient predecessors.

Most importantly, Ficino's *Commentary* essentially eliminates Alcibiades altogether: In Speech VII, which we might expect to be a commentary on Alcibiades' speech, including his attempt to seduce Socrates, these aspects of Plato's text are simply ignored, except for a defense of Socrates from having "polluted himself with a stain so filthy" (p. 155, VII.2; p. 242). The Christian language of sin is also invoked specifically in this speech, with regard to what sounds like a neoplatonic understanding of Athenian pederasty ("an older man who is inclined toward the likeness of a younger"): "Hence they are driven to do many sinful things together" (p. 163, VII.6; p. 251). We are not allowed to forget that Ficino's Neo-Platonism is also Christian in its emphasis, and that references to pederasty or other forms of male–male desire—except the most purely spiritual—also require the invocation of the discourse of sin as an automatic response.

The dialogue form used by Ficino is perhaps—along with Cicero's—the least truly dialogical we have observed; though comparatively early, Ficino's Latin dialogue thus shares the authoritative quality of the later vernacular dialogues and theories discussed by Cox and Snyder. Since Ficino is primarily interested in developing his own singular vision of divine unity and how it may be achieved, the speeches that comprise his *Commentary* are similarly unitary. The speakers are virtually indistinguishable from one another, and the dramatic setting is almost nonexistent: the speakers are brought together by Lorenzo de' Medici because he wished to "renew the Platonic banquet"; Plato's *Symposium* is read aloud, its various speeches are divvied up for commentary among the participants, and the dramatic frame disappears.[81] Instead, Ficino provides a steady working-out of his own theories, in which the speeches agree with, and build upon, one another. This is neither Buber's moment of contact nor Bakhtin's dialogism. A very superficial difference thus produces a profound likeness; as in the theory itself, deviation is ultimately to be absorbed into unity of effect, as physical desire between men—though less necessarily between men and women—is to be sublimated into spirituality.

Subsequent humanist authors writing in the Italian vernacular(s) used the dialogue form more flexibly, whether reproducing Ficino's attitudes or questioning them. Numerous such dialogues were produced throughout the sixteenth century, far more than can be discussed here. Vernacular dialogues on love written in Ficino's wake, not surprisingly, were dismissive of male–male desire, the most influential being Leone Ebreo's *Dialoghi d'amore* (1501), Pietro Bembo's *Gli Asolani* (1505), Baldassare Castiglione's *Il Cortegiano* (1518), and Sperone Speroni's *Dialogo d'amore* (1542).[82] But even as these dialogues rejected the physical expression of male–male desire, some of them, notably Ebreo's and Speroni's, influenced as much by Aristotle as by Plato, were less hostile to the body and its pleasures than Ficino had been.[83] Meanwhile, humanism itself came to be associated in the cultural imagination with homoeroticism, as Leonard Barkan has demonstrated in a discussion of Ariosto's early "proper usage" of the term "humanist," *umanista*: in a verse epistle addressed to Bembo, the "absolute human embodiment" of humanism, Ariosto declares that "few humanists are without that vice which did not so much persuade, as force, God to render Gomorrah and her neighbor wretched!"[84] For Barkan, "Ariosto is designating in a new way a term for scholar-and-poet. And the defining context for this new man is homoerotic."[85]

Barkan finds in Renaissance representations of the myth of Ganymede a coded expression of this relationship between humanism and the "homoerotic."[86] Some humanist writers, however, perhaps more Aristotelian than purely neoplatonic in their critical attitudes, provide a more direct, and more sympathetic, consideration of male–male erotics in their dialogues, and are thus more pertinent to the concerns of the present study. These dialogues include Gian Paolo Lomazzo's *Il libro dei sogni* (ca. 1568), Antonio Vignali's *La cazzaria* (1520s), and Tullia d'Aragona's *Dialogo della infinità d'amore* (1547), as well as Antonio Rocco's seventeenth-century *L'Alcibiade fanciullo a scola* (1651).[87]

The different city-states of sixteenth-century Italy each constructed its own version of male–male desire that is reflected in that city-state's dialogues, but certain overall patterns may nevertheless be discerned. In some ways the ancient pederastic construction was renewed, with men primarily in their twenties pursuing adolescents, and with sodomy regarded primarily as the fruit of youthful ardor: age difference thus was understood as a typical, if not necessary, aspect of male–male desire.[88] The ancient Athenian class similarity of *erastes* and *eromenos*, however, was less typical: sodomitical relations crossed class as well as age boundaries, another signal that the power structure of sodomy was quite different in the Italian Renaissance than in classical Athens (one that may suggest a further reason for the attempts at suppressing it in all the Italian city-states).[89] Not being officially sanctioned in any form, sodomy for that very reason may have been less restricted in its expression than it had been in ancient Greece, where its social relations were more carefully defined. Perhaps most important for our purposes is this very aspect of male–male sodomy: it was harshly regulated,[90] yet widely practiced. As Michael Rocke suggests, "[s]odomy was an integral facet of male homosocial culture."[91] The paradox of this official disavowal of what was nonetheless an important social practice is evident in the vernacular texts to which I shall now turn.

I would like to examine a few representative dialogues that place themselves in the Socratic/Platonic tradition and that deal with male–male desire, both those that agree and those that disagree with Ficino. Representative of, and perhaps best known in, the first category is Castiglione's *Book of the Courtier* (*Il Cortegiano*), first published in 1518 and immensely popular. It purports to record several conversations at the court of the Duke of Urbino in 1506, in which a group of real-life notables discuss their ideas of the ideal courtier and court lady.

Like Ficino's, Castiglione's interest in male–male desire—indeed, in love generally—is merely incidental to this primary concern. Nevertheless, Castiglione's debt to Plato's *Symposium* is clearly acknowledged, and is of interest for our purposes as much for what it does not say as for what it says. Certainly Castiglione acknowledges the existence of male–male erotic desire, and his tone in referring to it is not particularly condemnatory, as in the pun recounted in Book II (which is largely concerned with the ideal courtier's wit) concerning a certain Beroaldo's attraction to good-looking young men. As Beroaldo starts to enumerate the "three counts" on which he is obliged to travel to Bologna, his friend jokes that the three counts are " 'first, Count Ludovico da San Bonifacio; second, Count Ercole Rangone; third, the Count of Pepoli.' Whereupon everyone laughed, because these three counts had been pupils of Beroaldo and were handsome youths who were then studying at Bologna" (p. 119, II.63; p. 207).[92] The joke seems a reasonably good-natured one, and is far in tone from the vituperation with which Ficino treats similar desires. Perhaps less good-natured, but still a joke, is the example, given in the same book, of jokes made by changing a word in a line of verse:

> And messer Geronimo Donato, while visiting the stations at Rome in Lent [*la Quadragesima*] along with many other gentlemen, met up with a company of beautiful Roman ladies; and when one of the gentlemen said: "*Quot*

coelum stellas, tot habet tua Roma puellas," he replied at once: "*Pascua quoque haedos, tot habet tua Roma cinaedos,*" pointing to a company of young men coming from the other direction. (p. 116, II.61; pp. 202–203)

The first Latin quotation, from Ovid's *Ars amatoria* (I.59), says that "as many stars as has the sky does your Rome have girls"; the second, altering it, means that "as many lambs as have the meadows does your Rome have *cinaedos.*" The exact connotations of the term *cinaedus* have been discussed at length by classical scholars; generally speaking, it suggests a man who plays the receptive role in anal intercourse, and was used as an insulting term in both Greek and Latin.[93] Here again, the insult is a comical one: while both of these jokes may well be understood as an informal way of policing physical expressions of male–male desire, they also recognize its existence with a certain degree of sophistication.[94] Thus the discussion of sexual continence in Book III cites, along with various examples of men who mastered their desire for women, "Pericles, who on merely hearing someone praise a boy's beauty too emphatically upbraided him sharply" (p. 178, III.39; p. 307) without drawing a distinction between them. The combination of a sophisticated recognition of sodomy with a simultaneous disapproving oversight of it is not unusual in the early modern Italian city-states, as we have seen.

It might seem that male–male desire in Periclean Athens is too distant to pose much of a threat, and that male–male desire can be safely acknowledged there. However, when it comes to dealing directly with Plato's philosophically authoritative *Symposium* itself, Castiglione's more typical response to its implications of homoeroticism is—like Ficino's response to the implications of Alcibiades' speech—to erase them from his text and to substitute male–female relations for them. An interesting example arises in Book III, which is concerned with describing the ideal court lady and the ideal courtier's relations with her. Referring to Phaedrus' speech in the *Symposium*, Cesare Gonzaga suggests that "if one could assemble an army of lovers that would fight in the presence of the ladies they love, that army would conquer the whole world, unless similarly another army of lovers were to oppose it" (p. 188, III.51; p. 324). It is a close paraphrase of the *Symposium* 178e, but Phaedrus' army of male–male pairs of lovers fighting side by side has been replaced by one of single warriors fighting to impress their watching ladies. Male–male desire has simply been processed out of the Christian humanist understanding of love.

This point is even clearer in Book IV, when Pietro Bembo concludes the proceedings with a discourse on the true nature of love, a version of Diotima's ladder of love that differs significantly from its model in terms of the stages that the lover undergoes and especially in terms of the object that inspires it. (Another of Castiglione's models is to be found in Book Three of the real Bembo's *Gli Asolani*.[95]) As usual (and as is true of Socrates'/ Diotima's speech), he assumes that the desiring subject is male, but where Diotima bases her ladder on the love of boys, Bembo at every opportunity substitutes the love of women. For one example, even when the lover is learning to reach beyond the love of bodies toward the love of souls, "the Lady may in reason and without blame go even so far as to kiss" because "a kiss may be said to be a joining of souls rather than of bodies" (p. 253, IV.64; p. 430). Throughout, it is the lady who inspires the lover—in spiritual as well as in physical desire.

Like Ficino's speakers, Castiglione's neoplatonic Bembo moves up the ladder of love toward a divine unity, and that unity is achieved not, as for Socrates and Diotima, through the contemplation of a beauty or beauties external to the mind, but rather through the soul's contemplation of itself: "facing toward the contemplation of its own substance," the soul "rises to its noblest part, which is the intellect; and there, no longer darkened by the obscure night of earthly things, it beholds divine beauty," and in the highest stage, "beauty guides it from the particular intellect to the universal intellect" (p. 256, IV.68; p. 435). Castiglione's Bembo makes more explicit the inward turn already visible in Ficino's neoplatonism: the solitary self leads itself to the vision of universal intellect. The complex Platonic unity, briefly glimpsed after passing through the love of the universe's beauty, which is never quite left behind, is reduced to a neoplatonic solipsism. Indeed, Bembo warns that it would be better not to desire human beauty at all: at the first hint of desire (for a woman), the lover "ought to administer a quick remedy and arouse his reason, and therewith arm the fortress of his heart, and so shut out sense and appetite that they cannot enter there by force or deception" (p. 251, IV.62; p. 427). Ideally, the physical senses are not to serve as they do in Plato as a necessary first step on the ladder of love; instead, they are to be shut down completely. The ladder of love, for Bembo, is only the second-best choice: "if the flame is extinguished, the danger is also extinguished; but if it continues to live and grow, then the Courtier, feeling himself caught, must firmly resolve to avoid all ugliness of vulgar love, and must enter into the divine path of love, with reason as his guide" (p. 251, IV.62; pp. 427–428). Either at the beginning or at the end of the process, the senses must be closed down in favor of the inward turn toward intellect alone. Plato's distrust of the body is transformed into a wholesale rejection, his complex deviations of body and soul, multiplicity and unity, into a simple set of binary oppositions.[96]

It is, perhaps, no accident that Castiglione's Christianity is, at least in Book IV, more explicit that either Alan of Lillie's or Ficino's: the discussion concludes with a disagreement about whether the divine vision is equally accessible to men and to women. Gasparo Pallavicino, asserting that it is not, brings an explicitly Christian orientation to Bembo's vision:

> Thus, we do not read that any woman has had this grace, but that many men have had it, like Plato, Socrates, Plotinus, and many others; and likewise many of our holy Fathers, like St. Francis, upon whom an ardent spirit of love impressed the most holy seal of the five wounds: not could anything except the power of love lift St. Paul [*san Paulo apostolo*] to the vision of those secret things whereof no man is allowed to speak; nor show St. Stephen the opened heavens. (p. 259, IV.72; p. 440)

Gasparo here explicitly reorients the dialogue away from the classical tradition, concerned with the contemplation of beauty, with which he briefly begins (Plato, Socrates, Plotinus), and toward a more extended consideration of an explicitly Christian experience, not of abstract beauty, but of divine grace as represented by the Christian saints and martyrs (St. Francis of Assisi, St. Paul, St. Stephen protomartyr). It is a reorientation followed by Giuliano de' Medici, in his defense of women's spiritual abilities: he begins with Diotima, but quickly turns to St. Mary Magdalene and the other female martyrs (pp. 259–260, IV.72; p. 440). Gasparo and Giuliano have only made the Christianity implicit throughout Bembo's discourse more explicit, and the nuances of Plato's thought give way before a monolithic Christian value system. While alternatives to orthodox Christianity were in plentiful supply in Renaissance Italy, none of Castiglione's courtiers gives them voice: Bembo's discourse has the effect of shutting down all dialogue even as he recommends shutting down the senses: "everyone seemed almost to feel in his mind a certain spark of the divine love that had inspired the speaker, and all wished to hear more" (p. 259, IV.71; p. 439).

Up until this point, Castiglione's is one of the most dialogical, even carnivalesque, of the dialogues, in Bakhtin's and Kristeva's sense, that we have encountered: on all other subjects, the disagreements are wide-ranging and pursued with a good-humored intensity.[97] Each participant has his or her own clearly delineated personality (quite unlike those in Ficino's *Commentary*)—Gasparo Pallavicino, for example, can be counted on to enunciate the antifeminist position with some regularity—and the conversation among them has an easy give-and-take that allows a positively Bakhtinian multiplicity of perspectives on every issue raised: the relative importance of the courtier's various talents, his proper relationship to his prince, the forms his wit should take, the relative merits of men and women, and so on. But the doctrine of love itself, precisely because it cannot be disentangled from Christian orthodoxy, wins universal assent. As a subject of Christian orthodoxy, male–male desire cannot be allowed a voice in this dialogue: Bembo's discourse becomes an object of knowledge rather than the opportunity for a dialogical encounter, to use Buber's terminology; proximity (to other humans as to the divine) is eliminated in favor of identity of thought.[98] Where desire is concerned, Castiglione thus reproduces within his own text the same movement from the dialogical to the monological traced by Snyder in the wider history of Renaissance theories of the dialogue genre.

The association of Christianity with a refusal of male–male desire is thus more subtle in Castiglione's urbane work than in Alan of Lille's diatribes or Ficino's vituperation, but it is perhaps more insidious: rather than argue with the ancient tradition of male–male desire, Castiglione—outside the realm of the joke—simply silences it by ignoring it. No longer even a deviant or abjected alternative, male–male desire is, elegantly, erased, along with the value of the body in Bembo's discourse and the dialogic nature of the dialogue itself when its subject matter turns to the doctrine of (Christian) love.

The Venetian Tullia d'Aragona, on the other hand, in her *Dialogue on the Infinity of Love* (*Dialogo della infinità d'amore*, 1547) illustrates the link between humanism and "homoeroticism" explored by Barkan. She follows Leone Ebreo (here called "Filone" after the main speaker in his *Dialoghi d'amore*) and Sperone Speroni (in whose *Dialogo d'amore* she had appeared as a speaker) in restoring an element of the physical to neoplatonic doctrines of love. She also uses a woman's voice to introduce the question of sex and gender in love, and pays quite explicit attention to the physical expression of male–male desire.[99] Throughout her dialogue—primarily between herself and the humanist scholar Benedetto Varchi—Tullia d'Aragona seems less committed to preserving ideas of unity either in her doctrine or in her use of the dialogue form itself, and more interested in the real and irreducible differences among embodied humans. Indeed, the split between the Christian neoplatonism of, on the one hand, Ficino, Bembo, and Castiglione, and of, on the other, Ebreo, Speroni, and Tullia d'Aragona, can be described in terms of the latter group's Aristotelian deviation from the neoplatonic norm: whereas for the former group, the knowledge of universal beauty is retrieved from within the soul, for the latter, knowledge requires physical sense perceptions of the external world. The split may also be associated with the difference between representations, based on the concept of authority, of the world of the aristocratic courts (like the court of Urbino eulogized in Castiglione's *Courtier*) and those of the bourgeois cities, with their universities—and their "honest courtesans" such as Tullia d'Aragona.[100] It is significant that her text praises the theories of Ebreo and Speroni, but not those of Ficino and Bembo (though she admires the latter's eloquence).

The characters Tullia and Varchi, in fact, do not accept even Plato's own authority, and this text at times is in dialogue with Plato's *Symposium* itself, for instance on the question of whether the lover or the beloved is nobler. Whereas Plato's Phaedrus defends the nobility of the lover (*Symposium* 179b), Tullia and Varchi work their way to a different conclusion; as Varchi suggests, "the loved one is doubtless the agent, and consequently more noble, while the lover is the passive recipient (*il paziente*), and therefore less noble, despite the contrary view which the divine Plato appears to hold on this distinction" (p. 70; pp. 202–203). The dialogue thus regularly questions all authorities, finding some more satisfactory than others. Tullia, in fact, regularly claims to be speaking from her own life experiences rather than on the basis of authority, despite her ability to cite other philosophers, for instance in her initial claim—the main topic of discussion—that love is not infinite:

> *Varchi*: . . . Anyway, what reasons can you adduce to prove that love has an
> end?
> *Tullia*: No particular reason, but it is as I say.
> *Varchi*: So you want me to bow [*creda*] to authority!
> *Tullia*: No, Sir. I want you to bow to experience, which I trust by itself far
> more than all the reasons produced by the whole class of philoso-
> phers. (p. 71; p. 204)

The experience of a courtesan may be deemed as reliable as the theories of the philosophers in a discussion of the nature of love: here, too, Tullia's arguments are based on observations of actual human behavior in all its changeableness and multiplicity. Such passages are also of interest in that they demonstrate a genuinely dialogical style of argumentation: multiple positions may be expounded without necessarily being resolved, and Tullia does not serve merely as a pretext for Varchi's discourses. Even when she agrees with Varchi, he reminds her that "[i]t is not enough to say 'Yes, Sir' like that" (p. 60; p. 193)—unlike Socrates' interlocutors in a typical Socratic dialogue (e.g., *Lysis*). In fact, Tullia and Varchi exchange the roles of Socrates and his interlocutor, sometimes one, sometimes the other taking the philosophical lead—a point that is even made explicit with a reference to the *Symposium*:

> *Tullia*: . . . To tell you the truth, I don't seem to know anything, except that
> I know nothing.

Varchi: That itself would be no mean feat. You could compare yourself to
           Socrates, who was the wisest and most virtuous man in the whole of
           Greece.
Tullia: I didn't mean that mine was the Socratic ignorance [*in cotesto senso*].
           You are putting excessively subtle interpretations on what I say.
           However, if Socrates was so wise and virtuous, why don't you make
           a practice of imitating him? For as you know, he discussed every-
           thing with his friend Diotima and learned all manner of wonderful
           things from her, especially concerning the mysteries of love.
Varchi: And what do you think I'm doing?
Tullia: Quite the opposite of everything that Socrates [*egli*] did. Since he
           adopted a learning stance, whereas you're imparting lessons.
Varchi: No, you've got it wrong. Where do you think I derive my modest
           utterances, if not . . .
Tullia: Come, come. Tone things down. Go back to the main subject. . . .
           (p. 66; p. 198)

Both speakers in this passage are simultaneously identified and disidentified
with Socrates. Tullia lays claim to Socrates' famous dictum that he knew
nothing except his own ignorance, but then disingenuously refuses to be
identified with Socrates when Varchi jokingly does so—only to identify
herself instead with Socrates' own authority, Diotima. Varchi is told to be
more Socratic, and in turn indirectly lays claim to the Socratic identity in
response ("what do you think I'm doing?"); accused of being the opposite
of Socrates, he tries to reclaim the identification, only to be redirected to
the original discussion. And Socrates himself is here represented the one
who is both wise and ignorant: for Varchi he is the master, "wisest and most
virtuous," and Tullia to be identified with him only in a joke, whereas for
Tullia Socrates is the student learning of love, whose "learning stance" they
should both emulate. In fact, she is scolding Varchi for being excessively
authoritative—even as she herself takes the reins of the dialogue and turns
it back from its deviant path into the original argument. Such complex
identifications and disidentifications simultaneously claim and disavow
authority, and thus allow for a genuine dialogism. The model here is the
discussion, not the lecture, and Tullia insists that the true dialogic, conversational mode be followed—even if that insistence is itself, for the moment,
excessively authoritative: the roles of master and student remain dialogical
if they are constantly being exchanged.

   Tullia's opinions deviate not only from those of various authorities,
including Varchi, but also from her own: like the Socrates of *Lysis*, she
changes her mind about the nature of love by the time the discussion is
finished. Her initial opinion is that love "is nothing other than a desire to
enjoy with union what is truly beautiful or seems beautiful to the lover"

(p. 69; p. 202), and that, as we have seen, "love has an end." The notion of union is, of course, neoplatonic insofar as it concerns what is truly beautiful, though adding "seems beautiful" leaves room for a considerable divergence from the truly neoplatonic spiritual love. Varchi initially suggests that, as Tullia puts it, "while one loves, one does not love within limits. But when one no longer loves, the issue simply doesn't arrive. This logic is truly manna from heaven!" (p. 74; p. 207). Tullia's last comment seems sarcastic, given that she is not satisfied with Varchi's solution: reversing roles again ("[n]ow let me do the talking for a while" [p. 75; p. 208]), she pursues the question through several permutations until she reaches a conclusion that includes both body and soul. "Honest love"

> [h]as as its main goal the transformation of oneself into the object of one's love, with a desire that the loved one be converted into oneself, so that the two may become one or four [*un solo o quattro*]. . . . And as this transformation can only take place on a spiritual plane, so in this kind of love, the principal part is played by the "spiritual" senses, those of sight and hearing and, above all, because it is closest to the spiritual, the imagination. But, in truth, as it is the lover's wish to achieve a corporeal union besides the spiritual one, in order to effect a total identification with the beloved, and since this corporeal unity can never be attained, because it is not possible for human bodies to be physically merged into one another, the lover can never achieve this longing of his, and so will never satisfy his desire. Thus, he cannot love with a limit. . . . (p. 90; pp. 222–223)[101]

Tullia's language at the beginning of this passage surprisingly suggests that the movement toward greater unity may alternatively, and equally, be a movement toward greater multiplicity: the two lovers aim to lose their "twoness," but what they achieve instead is just as likely, and less laudably, to be "fourness" rather than "oneness": if each lover transforms himself or herself into the other, there may, spiritually, be only one being once that process is complete, but there may also be four, if each partner is both self and other. And while she agrees with the earlier neoplatonists that the love in question is primarily spiritual—the physical senses of sight and hearing being considered in most neoplatonic dialogues to be more spiritual than the others—Tullia also stresses the corporeality of the lovers' desire, which is for physical as well as spiritual merging—a merger that can, as Tullia points out, never literally take place on the physical level. It is thus, at least by implication, physical desire that is infinite rather than spiritual. Tullia's theory of love is heavily invested in the world of physicality as well as of multiplicity, and takes us far from the neoplatonic rejection of the body in favor of spiritual unity. It should be noted that Tullia does not necessarily approve of the physical element—but experience teaches her that it must be taken into account.

This passage, which contradicts Tullia's earlier statement that love does have an end, also demonstrates her own internal dialogism, the self-deviation that we have also observed in the Socrates of *Lysis*. Varchi, too, manifests this kind of dialogic self-deviation in his scholastic strategy of counterargumentation, briefly demonstrating the ways in which both propositions—love is infinite, and it is not—can be logically argued; to which Tullia replies that she must now consider both propositions as true (pp. 87–89; pp. 219–221), before going on to offer her own solution, quoted above. The dialogue form's potential is thus exploited here to its fullest extent, with a variety of opinions being offered, and none accepted without further discussion, a use of the form consonant with the world of multiple, irreducible selves that Tullia, perhaps disapprovingly, imagines.

Even her proposed solution, though praised by Varchi, raises further issues for discussion. He suggests that the physical desire for procreation, which Tullia has not discussed, is an acceptable form of love; and asks, if physical desire is acceptable, what Tullia thinks of pederasty. The point seems to be that Tullia's theory has not mentioned the procreative function of sex. Therefore, first, she might not consider it to have any place in true love; and, second, if physical desire can legitimately be nonprocreative, why should male–male desire not be allowable? "I wonder what you would say about those men who love boys [*gioveni*], whose urge cannot obviously be a desire to generate something similar to themselves" (pp. 93–94; p. 226).

The resulting discussion is complex and fascinating. Tullia agrees that procreative love is natural and not to be blamed unless it becomes "unbridled and overpowering" (p. 94; p. 226), suggesting again that her recognition of physical desire requires self-control and, though not its elimination, at least its subordination to the spiritual. In fact, the very absence of the possibility of procreation also causes her to condemn male–male erotics:

> I consider that those men who entertain a lascivious love for youths are not following the true dictates of nature, so they fully deserve the punishments that canon and divine law have imposed on them, as well as the penalties set up by man-made and civil justice. What is more, I can scarcely believe that people who practice such an ugly, wicked, and hideous vice, whether an artificial or habitual form of behavior, are real human beings. I shall be glad if later on you could give me your own view on this, for I know full well that in classical Greece [*appresso i greci*] the opposite notion was common and that Lucian wrote a dialogue in which he praised this vice, as did Plato. (p. 95; p. 228)

Tullia cites the conventional constellation of discourses on male sodomy that we have observed before: it is unnatural (here because it is nonprocreative), it is sinful in a Christian context and goes against civil authority, it is an "artificial" or "habitual" action, which also suggests a deliberate rebellion against authority. In addition, she adds an aesthetic component (sodomy is ugly and hideous). She does not, however, cite the expected argument that sodomy is a form of gender inversion, typically the main reason given for its "unnaturalness" in the Middle Ages and Renaissance; instead, she suggests that the sodomites' transgression is even more fundamental: they trespass beyond the boundaries of the human itself. This is all virulent enough for anyone; but then Tullia also adds that she might be wrong, which is to say that the entire tradition on which she has based her critique of sodomy might be wrong. In asking Varchi's guidance she is again inviting him to play the Socratic role, which in this case means to undertake a defense of sodomy.

She could not be asking a more qualified individual. Benedetto Varchi was widely believed in Florence to be a pederast himself, and had been arrested for the rape of a male adolescent in 1545; he pled guilty. Varchi was also beaten by Piero Strozzi's followers for having allegedly seduced Strozzi's younger brother, an episode to which Tullia alludes near the end of the dialogue.[102] According to Rinaldina Russell, Varchi actually used arguments derived from Plato's *Symposium* to justify his "amorous pursuit of young pupils."[103] He takes a similar tack in the *Dialogue*, carefully distinguishing between Pseudo-Lucian's defense of sodomy and Plato's own spiritual form of male–male desire. He defends the latter by citing Diotima's doctrine that pederastic lovers ideally do generate "something similar to themselves," though in spirit rather than in body (p. 96; p. 229)—and adds that Tullia should not be deceived by the behavior of modern sodomites (p. 97; p. 229).

Tullia is skeptical of Varchi's spiritual defense of classical pederasty, and inquires why, if such love was purely spiritual, "Socratic lovers [*questi socratici*] tend not to love those who are unprepossessing, or simply too old?" (p. 97; p. 229).[104] Varchi, in a long philosophical argument, defends the typical neoplatonic notion that the beautiful are also predisposed to goodness (pp. 97–100; pp. 229–232), but Tullia accepts his reasoning only with her own qualification: "The followers of Plato also turn their love toward those who are most beautiful, because they judge them to be the best and most intelligent individuals, *although they are enticed by their beauty as well*" (p. 100; my emphasis; pp. 232–233). This may well be Tullia's most radical statement: she accepts Varchi's explanation of virtuous male–male desire—it is a love of the morally good, and of the intellectually superior—but she insists on retaining its element of physical desire, the enticements offered by beautiful bodies, as well. For Tullia, love always deviates from the purely spiritual neoplatonic ideal, and this may be especially true of male–male erotics: no longer abjected, it is now allotted its place in Tullia's theory of love; but it is also, with its element of nonreproductive physicality, a deviation from the theory that requires its own separate discussion and justification.

Tullia pursues the physicality of male–male desire by inquiring why the classical pederasts preferred not only the physically beautiful, but the youthful as well. Varchi responds by suggesting that such was not really their preference: the spiritual "love" of youths "in time becomes friendship. Once its name is changed, it no longer seems to be the same feeling, but only then does love become truly perfect" (p. 100; p. 233). Tullia remains justifiably skeptical, and after a lengthy argument gives in, not because she is convinced, but only on the basis of Varchi's authority:

> *Varchi*: . . . When I say that this kind of love is far more complete, and, consequently, far rarer than perhaps you think, you must believe me.
> *Tullia*: Unfortunately [*pur troppo*], I do believe it, and more wholeheartedly [*più*] than you can imagine: perhaps even more than you do. Indeed, I do not deny that such love may exist. I admit it on your authority, for I know you would hardly assert it if you did not at least believe it to be true—I do not say "if it were true"—and also because I see no reason to dissuade me that it is so. (pp. 101–102; p. 234)

Tullia's agreement is interestingly equivocal. She accepts Varchi's authority, and agrees, not that such a spiritual male–male love actually exists, but that it *may* exist. In fact, she will not even admit that Varchi's declaration of its existence is true, only that he is sincere in believing it to be true. From this perspective—that of her third sentence in the passage just quoted—the more positive first sentence of her response takes on a different cast: her belief is, perhaps, in the rarity of this form of love rather than in its existence—which is why her agreement is "unfortunate." (Her implied questioning of just how much Varchi really believes what he has just said may also remind us of his own reputation for pederastic sodomy.) Again, Tullia seems willing to accept the value of such a love, but unwilling to separate it from the physical—which, as we have seen, is for her an essential component of all love. Christian dogma makes it impossible to admit male–male desire into the mainstream, but Tullia also represents a certain kind of humanist free-thinking that carves out its own deviant niche within Christian orthodoxy, never denying its truth but also exploring the possibility of alternate perspectives.

The dialogue as a whole, as I have suggested, is remarkably open to such alternatives: Tullia and Varchi are both willing to change their minds, and Tullia, herself bringing an explicitly female voice to these debates (as in her defense of women's intellectual and spiritual capabilities), also shows herself willing to be guided by Varchi's sodomitical voice. Despite her neoplatonic sympathies, Tullia d'Aragona continually implies the possibility— even the necessity—of multiple perspectives in the world of irreducible physical difference that she inhabits, perspectives that remain in dialogical tension with one another to the end. She thus provides a resistant alternative to the authoritative, Ciceronian mainstream of the Cinquecento dialogue form.

Even more resistant are the dialogues that praise sodomy, Antonio Vignali's earlier *La cazzaria*, composed in Siena in the 1520s, and Gian Paolo Lomazzo's later *Il libro dei sogni*, a Florentine text from 1568. Best known for the allegory of recent Sienese politics that occupies its second half—in which the city is symbolized by a body politic both highly sexualized and in disarray, the various parties represented by the Cunts, Assholes, Big Cocks, Little Cocks, and Balls[105]—*La cazzaria* also includes, in its first half, a spirited defense of sodomy. Not surprisingly in the city of Bernardino of Siena, the fifteenth-century Franciscan who in the 1420s had preached a series of vitriolic antisodomy sermons in Florence,[106] *La cazzaria* was originally composed for private circulation among Vignali's humanist friends in the Accademia degli Intronati,[107] though it had been published by the 1530s.

A dialogue of seduction between the older Arsiccio (Vignali's own Academic pseudonym, and the name under which *La cazzaria* was eventually published) and his younger colleague Sodo, *La cazzaria* also places itself directly in the Platonic tradition initiated by the *Symposium*, as Arsiccio offers two different glosses on the speech given by Aristophanes in that text. First, he rejects one that he claims was offered by Bembo:

Rejecting the opinion of Plato in the *Symposium*, Pietro Bembo holds that the cock and the cunt [*il cazzo e la potta*] were created together in the following manner: When God had created man and woman from clay, to measure whether or not they were the same size, He placed the man on top of the woman, and—being freshly made—they stuck together. Seeing this, the Master wanted to repair them quickly, and without realizing it, in His haste he left the woman upright on her feet, which—because she was still fresh and soft—caused her weight to slide downward. And so it is that most women are fat and disproportioned below the waist, because the matter that made up her widest part slipped and created this disproportion. (pp. 110–111; p. 79)[108]

Vignali's reference is not to the speech of Socrates/Diotima, but to that of Aristophanes, which has regularly appealed to the popular imagination more than the other, and which is here taken to represent Plato's own opinion. In a parody of Christian neoplatonism, the contemporary neoplatonist Bembo is understood as rejecting Aristophanes' account of creation in favor of one that conflates the biblical accounts in Genesis 1–2 (man and woman are made of clay, as in Gen. 2:7, but are created simultaneously, as in Gen. 1:26–28); indeed, the mythological, nonbiblical additions—the measurement, the slippage of clay—come close to parodying the Bible itself as well as Christian attempts to assimilate Plato. (Needless to say, Bembo nowhere makes the claim attributed to him here, though he does give the Aristophanic myth a purely heterosexual interpretation in *Gli Asolani*.[109]) And whereas Aristophanes' myth posits three originary types of human (male, female, hermaphrodite), which are used to explain erotic preferences after Zeus splits these originary creatures (men who desire men, women who desire women, women and men who desire each other), Bembo is here represented as explaining the origins of only two sexes and their external sex characteristics.

Bembo's gloss having been rejected because "if it were true, it would naturally follow that the pussy would be no bigger than the cock," Arsiccio tries out various other myths, all more or less comically misogynous, to explain the origins of genital difference: when the first humans were divided, "all the earth that now is the cock remained stuck to the man's crotch; and as it leaped from the woman, it left behind the hole that today is the cunt"; or, a bent stick was mixed into the original clay, and "in the pulling it tore a little, as can be seen from the largeness of the cunt"; or, "the balls would have been torn out along with the cock, and if they went into the pussy too the hole would not seem so big"; and so on (pp. 111–112; pp. 79–81). One ancient book supposedly even concludes that "all these accounts are fairy tales and foolishness" (p. 112; p. 81). All the explanations offered suggest that the sexes were originally one sex, an observation that supports Thomas Laqueur's view that a "one-sex" physiological theory dominated Western medical thought before the seventeenth century.[110] This view implies, of course, that desire is in some sense always same-sex desire, since sex differences are accidental rather than essential. Nevertheless, Arsiccio does discriminate between same-sex and other-sex desire, declaring in a passage full of double entendres that his own contribution will focus on anal sex: he will in future "give my attention to the asshole [*culo*]. Having some experience of that subject, I will go to great lengths [*mi distenderei*] to demonstrate how much more I can bring to it" (p. 113; p. 82). And this form of pleasure is one he takes with boys: he has begun writing his work in Latin "to protect the virtue of women, which I have always valued so highly that, if the greatest necessity had not confounded me, I would never have wanted to fuck around with them at all. And thus I've acquired the reputation of a buggerer who prefers boys and follows them around [*e andar loro dietro*]" (p. 114; p. 83). This self-description may also hark back to Aristophanes' speech in the *Symposium*, in which the men split off from women "run after women," though here it is transposed to a homoerotic context. In any case, glossing Plato eventually leads Vignali's spokesman to male–male desire, a process that itself parodies Renaissance neoplatonism and its association with male–male erotics. In fact, *La cazzaria* itself in some ways turns out to be the book in praise of anal penetration that Arsiccio promises to write; thus, Arsiccio cannot believe "that the nectar and ambrosia in Paradise is so sweet as the sweetness that a cock feels in a tender, white young asshole" (p. 93; pp. 60–61). And this is by definition a male–male activity, because women's assholes "cannot strictly be called assholes, but belong to the cuntish species" (p. 91; p. 58).

In addition to parodying Christian neoplatonism, *La cazzaria* attacks the Church itself, and the fraternal orders in particular, as the source of hypocrisy with regard to male–male anal pleasure (perhaps Vignali has the friar Bernardino of Siena himself in mind here):

> they want us to give up buggery [*il bugerare*], so that it may belong entirely to them, and make us take up again the cunts they have rejected and disdained. And they go on arguing that it is better to fuck your mother, your sisters, your nieces, and daughters—and fuck them in the most vicious way possible—as long as it is a cunt you are fucking and you are not buggering anyone. And they justify this by saying it is because when you fuck someone up the ass you waste human seed, and thus human generation may be diminished, in contradiction of the commandment, "Be fruitful and multiply." Stupid cows! They can't see that they themselves contradict it completely. . . . in choosing to be friars and fleeing the inconvenience of wives and the annoyance of children, they have chosen the way and the method to end and annul the human race. . . . why do they not prohibit fucking women up the ass? For no other reason than because women's assholes are not assholes. . . . (pp. 89–90; pp. 56–58)

Arsiccio's furious denunciation of Christian, fraternal doctrines concerning sodomy is, of course, inaccurate, but it does suggest a cultural–critical way of thinking about the religious prohibition, here comically understood as a specific and limited social construction resulting from the friars' own sacrilegious scorn for the biblical injunction. If the association of male–male sodomy with pleasure can be taken as a defense of its naturalness, a position that will be argued explicitly by Antonio Rocco in the next century, Vignali appears to be attempting a refutation of the typical constellation of complaints against sodomy, that it goes against both religion and nature. The third term in this constellation, law, is also taken up in *La cazzaria*:

> If you want to see just how much dignity the asshole has, take care to read the civil law code. . . . For no other type of assault does it prescribe a greater penalty than for assault on the asshole: it commands that whoever violates an asshole should immediately be burned at the stake, believing that such a person is not worthy of remaining in the world, dead or alive. (p. 95; p. 63)

Perhaps more accurate than his description of fraternal doctrine, Vignali's understanding of the civil laws regulating it is even more comically inverted.[111] Laws against anal sex are here understood as guaranteeing respect for the anus; since the context is a defense of male–male anal sodomy, and since the asshole is a metonym for male–male sodomy throughout the text, the laws against sodomy are understood, to comic effect, as actually guaranteeing its protection. It is not too much of a stretch to see in such texts as Vignali's, and later Rocco's, a transgression comparable to that which Dollimore ascribes to Wilde:[112] they not only reinstate that which their culture disavows, they transvalue cultural law itself through a process of inversion. The outlaw turns up as in-law.

Nature, religion, and law are thus all reinterpreted in support of male–male sodomy in a cultural critique that anticipates Rocco's and Sade's more sophisticated ones—though in this case the object of parody may be as much the neoplatonists' association with homoeroticism as it is the cultural prohibitions on sodomy. Sodo, though he initially mounts a vigorous dialogical objection to Arsiccio's praise of the asshole, is eventually converted—or seduced—to Arsiccio's way of thinking: in a successful dialogue of seduction, the seducer's "philosophy" is ultimately assimilated and, in Buber's terms, becomes an object of knowledge rather than truly Other; Levinas' "proximity" is reduced to sameness. But the dialogical relationship between the text and its dominant culture remains in place, subverting prohibition from within.

One further sixteenth-century dialogue that should be mentioned in this context is Lomazzo's *Il libro dei sogni*, in which Leonardo da Vinci himself is questioned about his well-known preference for boys: asking about Leonardo's apprentice Salai, the questioner inquires, "did you play the game from behind [*di dretto*], which the Florentines love so much?"[113] Rocke argues that love between men, "*l'amore masculino*," is defined in this text as not only sodomitical, but "one of the threads that helped to create and reinforce bonds between males and to fashion the texture of their collective life."[114] Sodomy here is not merely natural, but a positively useful social virtue; as in *La cazzaria*, the outlaw is an in-law, and the deviant is made proximate.

Another link between the free-thinking humanist dialogues of the sixteenth century and the French Enlightenment of the eighteenth is provided by Antonio Rocco's scandalous satirical dialogue *L'Alcibiade fanciullo a scola*, published in Venice in 1651.[115] Exactly what Rocco is satirizing, however, is open to question. The dialogue concerns the erotic education of an adolescent Alcibiades at the hands, not of Socrates, but of one Filotimo, his schoolmaster and, in the course of the dialogue, seducer. Rocco takes for granted the truth of what Pseudo-Lucian's Theomnestus says, and what Tullia d'Aragona implies, of male–male desire: that it is not exclusively or even primarily spiritual, but that it is, most importantly, physically pleasurable. Expressed as anal sex between an adult man and an adolescent boy, in fact, male–male desire is, at least according to Filotimo (and he is supported in this by the narrator) physically pleasurable for both parties. One might perhaps, then, understand the *Alcibiade* as a satire of pederasty's classical claims to a spiritual and pedagogical function, represented by Filotimo's sometimes sophistical arguments, his misogyny, and his own physical interest in seducing Alcibiades. But his arguments also provide in many instances a cogent response to the Christian and neoplatonic abjection of the physical in male–male desire, such that the dialogue as a whole may be read equally well as a critique of neoplatonic, and even Christian, ideology, a critique that revalues pleasure—which is what makes the *Alcibiade* scandalous.

The beautiful and desirable Alcibiades, in the first half of the dialogue, raises the traditional objections to Filotimo's desire, which "offends honor, and repudiates both law and nature" (p. 48):[116]

> it's an infamous vice, abominated by nature and called the vice against nature. Our laws prohibit it. Athena, the great patroness of Athens, abhors it; and they say that the gods punished certain cities, soiled by this crime, with fire, sulfur, and brimstone, and that they destroyed and submerged them. . . . And remember that the punishment doesn't stop at temporal pains, but that the soul itself, when separated from the body, is subjected [*nell'animo separate si essercitino*] to incomprehensible, eternal torments. Wouldn't you wish me to abhor it? And that it should terrify and repel me? (p. 50)

Alcibiades' constellation of objections to sodomy includes the familiar ones: it goes against nature, it is against the law, and it is, of all sins, the one most repugnant to God—or, in ancient Athens where the dialogue is ostensibly set, to the gods. That the setting is only ostensible is of considerable importance in this dialogue: despite the pseudo-Athenian décor, Rocco's, and hence Filotimo's, real argument is with the Christian ideology here expressed. It is seventeenth-century Venice's laws, not those of ancient Athens, that forbid sodomy, it is Judeo-Christian culture that perceives it as unnatural, and it is the Judeo-Christian scriptures that, at least in the medieval and Renaissance ideological reading, describe the destruction of Sodom and Gomorrah as a punishment for this sin.[117]

Filotimo, in a remarkable passage, is quick to point out the ideological underpinnings of this set of beliefs regarding sodomy, and does so in a way that also parodies neoplatonic thought. Sodomy, to begin with, is an esoteric exercise, for initiates only, like neoplatonic philosophy itself:

> if your mind were capable of such important mysteries, I would seriously discuss them with you, and would have you understand that those of elite intelligence [*giudiziosi*] have spread a veil of horror over these celestial pleasures in order to render them inaccessible to the vulgar, in order not to confer these treasures upon everyone. Precious things are prized because they are rare; sacred things are venerated because they are mysterious. (p. 50)

Sears Jayne has demonstrated that some of the difficulties of Ficino's *Commentary*, for example, are derived from this esoteric intention, the desire to keep the philosophical mysteries of neoplatonism hidden from the vulgar majority incapable of understanding them.[118] Here, however, sodomitical pleasure itself is the philosophical mystery. Rather than sublimating pederasty into philosophical pedagogy as earlier authors might have done, Rocco (or Filotimo), to an even greater extent than Tullia d'Aragona, embraces Theomnestus' accusation that pederastic philosophers express their desires physically, and indeed makes physical pleasure itself a central esoteric doctrine. His seductive education of Alcibiades, too, parodies the Platonic/neoplatonic ascent up the ladder of understanding: "But in order not to neglect my duty, I am going to open and habilitate your mind as much as possible, and, proceeding in an orderly fashion, to make you able and cognizant of all things" (pp. 50–51). The truth in this case is sodomitical truth, and the Platonic understanding is not an understanding of Beauty, but a true view of sodomy.

Anal sex, to start with, is "against nature" only because the anus (*il fiore*) is, anatomically, positioned over against the "cunt" (*la fica*) (p. 51), which is conventionally called "nature" because human beings are born from it; this arbitrary linguistic convention, however, says nothing about the genuine naturalness or unnaturalness of a given act, precisely because of its arbitrariness. In fact, "those acts to which nature inclines one are natural" (p. 51):

> If, therefore, it is a natural inclination to look at handsome boys, how could it be against nature? And if nature makes nothing vain or useless, if she doesn't begin anything she doesn't plan to finish, having created in boys this beauty that excites hearts to love and adore them, would she leave their lovers up in the air? Do these beauties exist for nothing? Are they vain, useless? No, no, they are delightful objects made to satisfy desire, which, tending always toward its own good, has pleasure as its goal. (p. 51)

Nature, then, underwrites men's desire for boys: simply by making boys desirable to men, she implicitly legitimizes the goal of the desire they excite. The implied teleological view of nature allows no sublimation, either: the single goal of physical desire is its natural conclusion in physical pleasure, not the sublimated philosophical or pedagogical motive promoted by earlier authors. Beauty exists to excite desire: thus handsome boys are "charming objects," with the emphasis on their status as objects of desire as well as on their charm. Erotic desire in turn exists to be satisfied. "Nature," a cultural ideal in this context at least since Alan of Lille, is here subjected to the inversion/perversion familiar from Dollimore: it is defined by the very activities it was alleged to disallow.

The governing assumption is that such desire is natural in the first place, and the following paragraph justifies this assumption in the familiar terms of likeness and unlikeness that continue to govern the discussion of homoerotic desire.

> Has not this same nature established love between the most similar beings? Now, is there not a greater resemblance of masculinity between man and boy than between male and woman? By giving to boys the characteristics of girls, does she not imply the conversion of one enjoyment to the other? (p. 51)

This is an odd and seemingly contradictory passage: On the one hand, love exists between those who are more similar in preference to those who are less similar (presumably why love tends to exist within rather than between species), and the anatomical genital similarity of boys and men is now taken to be the one that counts. But on the other hand, it is equally the likeness of boys to girls that signals their desirability: gender difference is a simultaneous component of erotic desire, alongside anatomical similarity. Rocco seems not to notice what looks to the modern reader like a glaring self-contradiction—perhaps because the concept of deviance is familiar to him from earlier philosophical accounts. Boys and men are both, and simultaneously, same and not-same; it is precisely the simultaneity of genital similarity and gender difference, likeness without identity, that creates desire. Furthermore, the androgyny of boys is itself deviant: boys possess the gender traits of girls (including breasts—"small ones, it's true, but more beautiful and precious for that very reason" [p. 69]) without being identical to them, either.[119]

For Filotimo, indeed, excessive similarity precludes love. He recognizes the existence of erotic activity between adult men, for instance, but rejects it, both as a matter of his own personal (and classical) taste in positions and penises (p. 67), and as a more general rule: " 'Age modifies the form and nature of amorous experience,' said the master: 'a kid's meat is delicate; that of a buck is most fetid; but those who go for billygoats are renegades of love, wild beasts, corrupt creatures. Male love is youthful' " (p. 75). Love between adult men implies a hypermasculine savagery or wildness; again, true love is for that which deviates, neither for the self-same nor for the completely different. By the same token, the love of adult women is also condemned in a number of unattractively misogynous passages, such as this one following a description of the pleasures of male–female intercourse:

> I would give credit to women for everything, if I did not find superior advantages in boys. If this nest of love, the unique and singular charm of boys in love, lacks the heat of that of women, it has a temperate warmth, a refreshing attraction for the flames of passion: this fire is mitigated and made gentle by coolness rather than more intense heat. (p. 66)

Adult women, too, unexpectedly enough, are in some sense too much like adult men to provide the partial unlikeness necessary to love. Their heat recapitulates the heat of adult male passion, and therefore intensifies desire uncomfortably, when what is really required is a dissimilar, and satisfying, coolness (and note the manner in which the boy's original similar "warmth" is transmuted into a dissimilar "coolness" by the end of the sentence).

Boys, however, are not so dissimilar that they cannot share the man's erotic pleasure. If, as Foucault suggests, the late antique reevaluation of marriage and abjection of pederasty, illustrated in the dialogues of Plutarch and Pseudo-Lucian, was connected to the potential reciprocal pleasure between husband and wife, Rocco, unlike most classical authors, suggests that boys, too, can legitimately participate in such reciprocity. Alcibiades himself, perhaps, as an allegedly Athenian youth, familiar with the traditional disbelief in a respectable boy's ability to experience erotic pleasure, raises the question of the boy's pleasure directly, near the end of the dialogue: ". . . tell me sincerely what pleasure we may have, when we lend ourselves [*condescendere*] to your wishes?" (p. 79). Filotimo's long response is an encomium to the mutual enjoyment of anal sex:

> [The boys'] organs, watered with the seed's sweetest warmth, experience an incomparably sweet pleasure in this act; not counting the other pleasures that they experience in their softer, venereal parts. This is the reason for the pleasure they universally enjoy, which depends to a great extent on the lover's experience and skill . . . (p. 81)

Boys may experience, it appears, a double pleasure in sodomy, the incomparable pleasure of orgasm coupled with the pleasures experienced in the anus itself. Both pleasures are made possible in part by the adult lover's erotic technique: his pleasure produces a reciprocal pleasure in the boy. It also seems, however, that these pleasures are more accessible to some boys than to others, according to their individual physiological natures:

> As for why certain boys have more enjoyment than others, this come from the fact that the parts of their "gardens" are linked more closely by nerves to those of their "birds," which facilitates the animal spirits' communication, and the immature excitement of the "little bird" leads, as it were, to that of the "little garden," so that some of them feel such a pleasure in being pinned [*nel farsi chiavar*] that it makes them mad with desire, begging, even forcing their lovers to satisfy them. These are the youths who are lively above all others, because the abundance of these animal spirits [*spiriti chiavarelli*] gives agility to their movements and ardor to their actions . . . (p. 82)

Even the erotic pleasure of boys deviates from that of men: they experience a similar orgasmic enjoyment, as well as the pleasure of passivity, of "being pinned," that is theirs alone. They are, once again, both like and unlike their adult lovers, whose pleasure is (or at least should be, in Filotimo's view) limited to the penetrative: their anatomical similarity also includes a physiological difference. The scientific tone of such passages, in which the effects of certain practices are objectively (in style, at least) observed and recorded, may also remind us that, in the second half of the seventeenth century, Rocco is, in his own odd way, participating in the positivist scientific revolution of his period as well as looking backward to medieval understandings of Aristotle.[120] Rocco's tone suggests that boys' erotic pleasure is an observable fact, regardless of what the classical—or the Christian—tradition has to say about it.

For both these traditions are, as I suggested above, subjected to a rigorous cultural critique in the *Alcibiade*, and are revealed as ideologies in a very modern sense: as mystifications of material realities designed for the benefit of a particular social grouping. If sodomy is not, as Filotimo has demonstrated, against nature, it may well be against law and religion, as Alcibiades also claimed earlier. But in that case, the prohibitive civic and religious laws are themselves against nature, which remains Filotimo's standard of judgment. As for Athenian law, Filotimo, or Rocco, claims, as we have seen, that it prohibits sodomy—perhaps drawing on Plato's prohibition in the *Laws* rather than on the historical record; or, more likely, using ancient Athens to comment on contemporary Venetian laws against sodomy.

> That the laws of certain peoples, and in particular those of the Athenians, as you have said, prohibit it, is not bad in itself. They adjust their laws to their own interests; but they do not submit their interests to justice; this prohibition favors women, and it must please them, because it keeps them from being left neglected and abandoned. . . . they have ordained this law with care for the interests of the State and of politics rather than for the dictates of reason or the inclinations of nature. (p. 56)

Procreation, in Filotimo's view, must be rigorously enforced: men would not freely choose to mate with women unless constrained to do so by the force of law. If, as Filotimo suggests in the passage quoted earlier, "nature has established love" between those who are more similar in preference to those who are less similar, and boys are more similar to men than women are, women, and hence the procreative function necessary to the continued existence of the state, must be kept from falling into disuse. (This argument and similar ones are not uncommon in the libertine literature of the seventeenth and eighteenth centuries.[121]) Ideologically, the state must prohibit sodomy, and can most effectively do so with the pretense that it is against nature—when in fact, as we have seen, nature vigorously promotes sodomy—and against religion—when religion itself may properly be regarded as an ideological construct. Procreative heterosexuality may thus be understood as an Ideological State Apparatus in Althusser's sense.[122]

Religion functions in this way as well, in support of state interests, and Filotimo's ideological critique of the Christian understanding of the story of Sodom and Gomorrah is the *Alcibiade*'s centerpiece. (Greek religion is dealt with in the observation that the gods themselves are sodomites: Jupiter with Ganymede, Apollo with Hyacinthus, Hercules with Hylas, and so on [p. 57].) He suggests of political legislators that "in explaining by the will of God that which is motivated by their own caprices, they have lent credence to their decrees and their prompt execution. . . . making us, habitually from our cradles, imbibe their doctrines with our mothers' milk, so that our souls are inseparable from them" (p. 58). As modern theorists of ideology like Althusser and Gramsci suggest, ideology falsely naturalizes the value system most beneficial to the ruling class and to the self-perpetuation of the state: the formation of the subject is precisely its subjection to this ideological system from infancy.[123]

The Sodom and Gomorrah story is Filotimo's prime example. The supposed remains of the cities—the sulfurous lake beneath which they were submerged, according to Alcibiades (p. 50)—is explained purely in terms of natural science (pp. 59–60), while the story attached to it is explained as Moses' ideological fiction. Passing by this lake was for him a "happy opportunity to weave a fable both entertaining and useful for his purposes":

> There were more women in his band, all become ugly and noxious because of their journey, more suited to the preservation of continence than to inflaming desire; the soldiers, meanwhile, turned ardently to the convenient enjoyment of boys, and completely abandoned that of women. The wise leader, understanding this, and considering that in a short time his empire would become extinct, or at least that it would not increase in the hands of his successors, if procreation did not replenish the gaps, therefore prohibited the enjoyment of boys, adding that this was the express order of God, and that it was to punish it that the He had submerged five cities in sulfur and fire, and that this was the vestige of divine vengeance. Under the urgent pressure of circumstances, by means of this vague allusion, the discreet legislator made laws against the delights of boys. (p. 60)

Filotimo does not blame Moses for having recourse to this fiction: it was both expedient and politically necessary in his specific circumstances as leader of a state that was still under construction. But the invocation of God's will to police his soldiers' procreative sexual intercourse had drastic and unforeseen consequences: in itself against nature because it prohibited one natural outlet for the male sexual drive, it also, taking the form of divine scripture, caused the subsequent unnatural deformation of sexual behavior that Alcibiades himself has wrongly been raised to believe natural. A political fiction designed to address a circumscribed social need got out of hand and became naturalized as a governing ideology. That Filotimo finds the story almost comically bizarre reinforces his status as defender of objective scientific observation: implicit in his tone is the assumption that modern rationalism can and should refuse such fantasies in favor of the truly natural pleasures of sodomy. The final sentence of the passage just quoted also suggests that his observations on the development of erotic ideologies may be generalized to include all laws: human law itself, including most importantly religious prohibitions, must be regarded as more or less unnatural expressions of ideology. Here as elsewhere, one of the dominant culture's most sacred icons—the Bible itself in this case rather than the book of Nature—is subjected to the process of inversion, as that which it outlaws returns as an essential in-law.[124]

With Rocco's dialogue we thus return to the use of the dialogue genre itself as a form of seduction, a use familiar from Plato's *Lysis*. Here, however, as in *La cazzaria*, the philosopher employs dialogue on his own behalf. Indeed, he invites Alcibiades to enter into the discussion precisely as a way of overcoming his resistance: "It is the act of a reasonable person, my dear Alcibiades, to do or refrain from doing, in accordance with reason, that which pleases him. If you are such a one, as can clearly be seen in all your actions, tell me, I pray you, what reason causes you to be so inexorable and cruel against your very amorous master's most ardent desire" (p. 49).[125] Like Socrates', Filotimo's discussion will be based on reason, and he insists that his interlocutor produce equally logical reasoning as a basis for his behavior. Having shown that Alcibiades' supposed reasons are in fact merely ideological prejudices, Filotimo's discussion seduces his student with surprising rapidity. Only halfway through the text, Alcibiades admits that he has "received complete satisfaction from your arguments" (p. 65)—but, as is also true of Vignali's *La cazzaria*, the dialogue continues for the sheer pleasure that the student takes in hearing the master's reasoning:

> "Let's give it a try, then, my dearest boy," said the tumescent [*incazzito*] master, "experience will teach you the truth better than discourses and glossing."
>
>   "I wish noting else," responded the boy, "but once the need to convince me has passed, you may become more sober and unwilling to speak; therefore, continue with your argument, and don't worry about the rest." (p. 80)

As in the *Lysis*, erotic satisfaction is sublimated in discourse; but for Rocco, the sublimation is only temporary: the seductive nature of the dialogue is such that it must ultimately give way to physical pleasure—which itself, as we have seen, is now understood as the philosophical goal, "the apparition of these supreme wonders" (p. 85) to speak neoplatonically, or indeed Platonically. "[T]he impassioned master, with the gentlest thrusts, continued to enjoy his charming student, so that in the end, when the latter did not have his master's cock up his ass, he did not know what pleasure was, and did not believe that it would be possible for him to become as perfect as his master by any other route" (pp. 86–87).

And yet the seductive philosophical dialogue is not abandoned until the last possible moment: "You will be the earthly paradise, where living men find their happiness. And if man is more perfect than a soul alone, you will be even more glorious paradise, because in the first, only the souls are happy, while with you the bodies are, too" (p. 86). It would appear that physical pleasure is incomplete without its verbal commentary, a libertine tendency that, along with the education of the senses, we may also observe in Sade. As in Vignali, the Other is in some sense converted into an object of knowledge, yet here the sensuous encounter continues: hardly the kind of encounter Buber envisioned, this dialogue nonetheless posits an ongoing dialogical relationship between master and pupil. Sade will give this relationship its most extreme form.[126]

Sade should, in fact, be placed within the scientific/libertine tradition to which Rocco also belongs, and, as a figure of the French Enlightenment, is anticipated in some of his views by such figures as Denis Diderot. Diderot's brilliant scientific dialogues collected as *Le Rêve de d'Alembert* (*Entretien entre Diderot et d'Alembert, Le Rêve de D'Alembert*, and *Suite de l'entretien*) follow a train of scientific reasoning to reach conclusions about a number of moral issues, among them same-sex erotic desires and acts. Diderot's scientific dialogues do not refer to Plato and therefore, strictly speaking, lie outside the scope of this study, but the final one is, for the reasons just mentioned, worth discussing here briefly. So is the more celebrated literary/philosophical dialogue *Le Neveu de Rameau,* or *Rameau's Nephew*.

While this text does not, like the *Suite de l'Entretien*, discuss male–male desire itself, it does refer obliquely to the *Symposium* in such a way as to raise the issue without directly confronting it. Near the beginning of this dialogue, between a narrator, "I" ("Moi") and his interlocutor, the nephew of the famous composer Rameau, "He" ("Lui"), the former uses Alcibiades' description of Socrates to characterize the nephew:

I: Are you still in good health?
HE: Yes, usually, but not all that good today.
I: What? And you with a paunch like Silenus and a face—
HE: A face you would take for his behind [*son antagoniste*] . . . (p. 37; p. 399)[127]

This exchange immediately follows a brief direct reference to Socrates and is itself followed by another a few pages later (pp. 37, 39; pp. 399, 401),[128] suggesting that the reader is meant to understand this Silenus citation as a comic inversion of the *Symposium*:[129] whereas Alcibiades refers to Socrates as a Silenus in order to discuss the spiritual goods concealed behind his ugly exterior, the narrator and the nephew here refer to the latter's body exclusively. The nephew thus becomes a kind of anti-Socrates, an impression confirmed by his anti-Socratic attitudes throughout the dialogue: he favors imitative art and is an expert mimic (thus opposed to Socrates' and Plato's rejection of mimesis), and believes in multiple truths rather than a singular, ultimate reality (and thus opposes the Platonic Theory of Forms).[130]

Toward the end of the dialogue the comparison (or contrast) is tacitly renewed: when the narrator encourages the nephew to try and produce a genuine work of art, the nephew comes close to doing so and uses the childbirth metaphor familiar from the *Symposium* to express this experience: he thinks "there is something" in his head, declares "I feel something, yes, I do indeed," and "extemporize[s] speeches of anger, sympathy, hatred and love"; "[t]hen he said: 'That's about it, I think. It's coming. It shows you what it means to find an *accoucheur* who knows how to stimulate and induce labour pains and deliver the baby'" (p. 115; p. 481). The nephew thus places himself in the position of the lover in Diotima's speech, pregnant with discourses of which he can be delivered only in the presence of the midwife/beloved: he is a sort of *erastes* to the narrator's *eromenos*, though now in the *Symposium*'s spiritual rather than any physical sense.

Diderot's original inversion of the *Symposium* is itself to some extent now reversed: the nephew, it appears, might really be able to produce spiritual offspring, literary or musical, in the narrator's presence; the nephew's Silenus countenance thus does, ironically, conceal spiritual goods, though the people he usually consorts with are not of the sort to encourage their delivery (and though they are of the mimetic sort that Diderot favored but that Plato would not have approved). The narrator and the nephew are thus linked (only) implicitly in a spiritual–erotic relation similar to, though not identical with, that privileged by Diotima. The physical aspect of male–male desire is itself explored in the *Suite de l'entretien*.

The *Suite de l'entretien*, or *Sequel to the Conversation*, is a brief coda to the preceding dialogues *Entretien entre Diderot et d'Alembert* and *Le Rêve de d'Alembert*, in the first of which Diderot represents himself arguing with the mathematician d'Alembert for a thoroughgoing materialist view of reality, and in the second of which he depicts d'Alembert's subsequent troubled sleep, attended by his friend Mlle. de l'Espinasse and his doctor Bordeu, who continues arguing for Diderot's materialist viewpoint. In the short final dialogue, Bordeu pushes his views even further, into moral territory, somewhat to the consternation of his interlocutor, Mlle. de l'Espinasse. It is here that Diderot, through Bordeu, broaches the subject of sexual ethics.[131]

It is axiomatic for Bordeu that pleasure is a good in itself: quoting Horace, he declares that "supreme merit is to have combined the agreeable with the useful. Perfection comes from reconciling these two things. An action which is both agreeable and useful must be the summit of aesthetic achievement. We cannot deny the second place to the useful alone, and the third place will be for the agreeable alone" (p. 226; p. 197).[132] Although

Bordeu relegates pleasure without usefulness to a lower category than usefulness with or without pleasure, it is pleasure that the subsequent conversation confronts most fully: using this standard of judgment, Bordeu brings Mlle. de l'Espinasse to consider the possibility that premarital sex, masturbation, and so on may be greater goods than the qualities of chastity and continence. Nothing, he asserts, is "so puerile, ridiculous, absurd, harmful, contemptible and bad as these two rare qualities," despite "the magnificent paeans of praise sung by fanatics, and in spite of civil laws which protect them" (p. 227; pp. 197–198). Like Rocco's Filotimo, Diderot's Bordeu links religious prohibition (or its celebration of sexual "purity") to civil law, though he seems to give religious ideology pride of place as the origin of these values, rather than the political considerations that Rocco put first. But also like Filotimo, Bordeu considers such prohibitions to be truly against nature, specifically as they apply to same-sex erotic desires and acts:

> So this is the question I will put to you: take two acts, both of which are con-
> cerned with pleasure alone, both of which can only give pleasure without
> usefulness, but one of which only gives pleasure to the person performing it
> while the other shares the pleasure with a fellow creature, male or female (for
> in this matter the sex makes no difference, nor even who does what with
> what), and tell me what the verdict of common sense will be between the
> two. (p. 230; p. 202)

There are a number of ways to understand this passage: mutual pleasure may be preferable to masturbation, or to any relations in which one party does not experience pleasure. In any case, however, mutual pleasure is not understood to exclude erotic relations between members of the same sex: we are far from the classical claim that only one partner experiences pleasure in male–male erotic relations, and equally far from the Christian and neoplatonic prohibition on them.[133] Like Rocco, Diderot presents his spokesman as a dispassionate scientific observer; when Mlle. de l'Espinasse, like Alcibiades, protests that such unions "strike me as being against nature," Bordeu, like Filotimo, declares that "[n]othing that exists can be against nature or outside nature" (p. 230; p. 202).

This is the line of reasoning that Sade pushes to a certain limit in his works.[134] Margaret C. Jacob has argued that in the scientific revolution of the seventeenth and eighteenth centuries, "nature was mechanized. Its bodies . . . became simply, unrelentingly, matter in motion,"[135] and that this philosophical development was reflected in two different kinds of pornographic writing: the "naturalist," which generally dominated the earlier period, and the "materialist," which became more "pronounced in the 1690s," though "it would never entirely obliterate naturalism."[136] Although she does not discuss Sade directly, in Jacob's scheme Sade, writing at the end of the eighteenth century, would seem to be influenced by both the naturalist and the materialist modes. The naturalist mode offers "a vision of the sexual as natural":[137]

> For the naturalist, passions and desires are inherently good and hence useful. He could prescribe the joys of flogging, and could even proclaim that women enjoy it. These arguments did not, however, lead the naturalist to proclaim the equality of male and female desire. . . . Naturalists, operating within an essentially Aristotelian framework, could glory in sexuality and create completely private worlds; they could even seek to arouse. Their artifice, though, was limited by their assumption of male activity and female passivity. . . . In this model, the naturalist simply presumed the transparently natural and unnatural in sexual matters.[138]

In these respects Jacob's materialist would go further than the naturalist, shifting the focus from this transparent nature itself to the laws of nature and inspired by Hobbes and Descartes rather than Aristotle, and more or less equalizing male and female: "the virile engines have lost their exclusive hold on motion and force: they have been joined by activated, energized female participants."[139] While Sade, like other materialist pornographers cited by Jacob, certainly created active female narrators, such as Juliette,[140] and energetic female participants in his pornographic fantasies, such as Mme. de Saint-Ange in *La Philosophie dans le boudoir*, it is true as well that his spokesman in the latter text, Dolmancé, also naturalistically declares, as a foundational tenet of his libertine philosophy, that nature created woman solely for man's pleasure:

> Had it not been Nature's intent that man possess this feeling of superiority, she would not have created him stronger than the beings she destines to belong to him at those moments. The debility to which Nature condemned woman incontestably proves that her design is for man, who then more than ever enjoys his strength, to exercise it in all the violent forms that suit him best, by means of tortures, if he be so inclined, or worse. (p. 345; p. 159)[141]

As critics have often noted, however, Sade seems more interested in power relations than in gender relations:[142] the weak naturally serve the pleasure of the strong, and it is only insofar as women are weaker than men that they are to be judged to be subservient. Women in his system can become powerful if they take on characteristics traditionally considered masculine. Indeed, *La Philosophie dans le boudoir* is an orgiastic philosophical dialogue—one that refers, if only obliquely, to the *Symposium*—in which Sade explores the nature of gender more consistently than in any other work. Most of the characters in this text explicitly cross gender boundaries, and among its female characters only Mme. de Mistival, the dialogue's sole "weak" figure, brutally victimized at the orgy's conclusion, fails to exhibit the traits traditionally considered "masculine," which Sade associates with power.

This constant regendering of both the male and female participants renders any discussion of "male–male" desire in *La Philosophie dans le boudoir* problematic. Not only do its libertine women, Mme. de Saint-Ange and her protégée Eugénie de Mistival (Mme. de Mistival's daughter), take on an active, "masculine" role, the sodomite Dolmancé claims, if only by implication, a "feminine" passivity at certain points in the dialogue. The shifts in gender positions and sexual roles may suggest that erotic desire between men—or between "masculine subjects"—is only one aspect of a more fluid and polymorphous eroticism that Sade truly privileges. Nevertheless, and even for this very reason, Sade's dialogue can suggest something about materialist/naturalist libertine attitudes toward male–male desire in the late eighteenth century, and something as well about the manner in which such attitudes were conditioned by Plato's *Symposium*.[143]

Sade's hero in *La Philosophie dans le boudoir*, Dolmancé, is a confirmed sodomite whose erotic interest, it appears, is exclusively in other men, with whom he takes both the insertive and receptive roles in anal intercourse, as his friend the libertine Chevalier de Mirvel (Mme. de Saint-Ange's brother) points out in the first of *La Philosophie*'s seven dialogues, before Dolmancé himself even appears (pp. 189–190; p. 8). Indeed, the Chevalier is astonished that his sister is bringing a girl, Eugénie, to Dolmancé for her education in libertinism: "What! With Dolmancé . . . you're bringing a woman here?" (p. 190; p. 9 [ellipsis in text]); and Mme. de Saint-Ange notes enviously that women are excluded by their anatomies from the pleasures her brother has recently experienced in a three-way with Dolmancé and another man ("You must have known the most extreme pleasure, to find yourself thus between two; they say it is charming" [p. 190; p. 8]). Male–male desire and erotic enjoyment are thus initially understood as qualitatively different from those experienced between men and women; indeed, they are perceived here as separate, though not exclusive, tastes or preferences: Dolmancé himself prefers men, but while the Chevalier may enjoy male–male sodomitical pleasures, they are to his taste "extravagances which I should never prefer to the pleasure of women" (p. 190; p. 9). For a brief moment in the third dialogue, Mme. de Saint-Ange even implies—perhaps ironically—that erotic taste may constitute the self: "EUGÉNIE— . . . But, my dear, your husband is strictly bound by *his tastes*? Does he never ask anything else of you? MADAME DE SAINT-ANGE—Never in a dozen years has he been *untrue to himself* [*ne s'est pas démenti*] a single day" (p. 228; p. 44; emphasis added). But more often, as Barthes points out, "sexual preference never serves to identify a subject."[144]

Dolmancé himself aphoristically confirms these views of erotic taste: a man's preference for other men, for example, may well, as Mme. de Saint-Ange suspects, exclude women: "The libertine details of masculine passions, Madame, have little therein to provide suitable stuff for the instruction of a girl who, like Eugénie, is not destined for the whoring profession" (p. 247; p. 62); that is, these pleasures are, *as pleasures* rather than commerce, exclusively male. "When 'tis a question of a man's pollution, he would infinitely prefer to entrust the business to another man, not to a woman. As a man knows what suits himself, so he knows how to manage for another" (p. 260; p. 75); Dolmancé expresses no equivalent sentiments regarding female–female mutual masturbation. And yet, such tastes are only that, tastes or tendencies: Dolmancé may refuse to deflower Eugénie, but even his preference for men is not, he declares in the fifth dialogue, absolute:

> *MADAME DE SAINT-ANGE*: Refuse a maidenhead . . . as fresh, as pretty as this—for I defy anyone to say my Eugénie is not the loveliest girl in France—oh, Monsieur! Monsieur, indeed, that's what I call holding too closely to one's principles!
>
> *DOLMANCÉ*: You say I am too scrupulous, Madame? 'Tis unkind. For there are multitudes of my colleagues, stricter in their worship than I, who most assuredly would not bugger you. . . . I, I've done it, and would do it again: it is not, thus, as you suspect, a question of carrying my worship to the point of fanaticism. (pp. 291–292; p. 107; ellipsis in text)

La Philosophie dans le boudoir was completed in 1795. Among the Marquis de Sade's real-life alleged crimes was that of having engaged in sodomy with his male servant Latour in the course of their notorious 1772 Marseilles orgy with several female prostitutes, male–male sodomy being the specific crime for which he and Latour were sentenced to death and burned in effigy, leading, as a recent biographer notes, to Sade's legal, though not his actual, death.[145] Such incidents, both in his life and throughout his works, as well as Dolmancé's function as Sade's spokesman, have led critics to speculate on Sade's own "sexual orientation," to use a perhaps anachronistically modern term. Simone de Beauvoir suggests a degree of transsexuality in

Sade's psychic makeup;[146] Neil Schaeffer refers to "Sade's bisexuality."[147] Certainly Sade's interest in male–male desire—and in men for whom such desire excludes the desire for women—surfaces throughout his fiction, from the Comte de Bressac in *Justine* to the Bishop in *Les Cent Vingt Journées de Sodome*. But Sade's works exhibit at least as obsessive a concern with women's sexuality, and *La Philosophie dans le boudoir* in particular, with its pornographic delight in depicting all possible permutations of sexual roles and positions, explores the relations between the two.

Dolmancé, for example, regularly re-genders young Eugénie as masculine, contentedly gazing at her buttocks next to Mme. de Saint-Ange's: "Ah, 'tis lovely, my angel, 'tis delicious too! Let me compare them both. . . . I'd see them one next to the other—Ganymede beside Venus!" (p. 203; p. 20; ellipsis in text). Eugénie thus begins her education as Zeus' catamite, a figure drawn from Greek mythology and one familiar, from medieval to Enlightenment culture, as a sign of male–male desire, specifically of the ancient Athenian variety that depends upon age difference—appropriately to Eugénie's status as Dolmancé's pupil.[148] As she develops, however, she is equipped with a dildo and takes on the more active role of an adult male; Dolmancé exclaims, "Truly, the little rascal buggers me mannishly! [*comme un homme*]" and even, "This matchless girl has fucked me like a god [*comme un Dieu*]" (p. 263; p. 79). Eugénie not only functions sexually as an adult man; in Dolmancé's image, she also takes on the godlike role of Zeus himself, reversing their original roles and thus turning Dolmancé into the Ganymede figure. Dolmancé goes even further, and does not hesitate to re-gender the male as female: early on, the Chevalier recalls Dolmancé's request to him during their previous encounter: "deign, O my love, deign to serve me as a woman [*de femme*] after having been my lover, and enable me to say that in your divine arms I have tasted all the delights of the fancy I cherish supremely" (p. 190; p. 8). The implication seems to be that, if the Chevalier is now reciprocally to play the woman, Dolmancé has himself just played the woman to the Chevalier's penetrative man. Dolmancé's re-gendering of himself is more explicit in the third dialogue:

> The question has often been raised, which of the two fashions of sodomistic behavior is the more voluptuous? Assuredly, 'tis the passive, since one enjoys at a single stroke the sensations of before and behind; it is so sweet to change sex, so delicious to counterfeit the whore, to give oneself to a man who treats us as if we were a woman, to call that man one's paramour, to avow oneself his mistress! Ah! my friends, what voluptuousness! (p. 247; pp. 62–63)

The further implication of all these encounters would seem to be that where erotic relations are concerned, gender is entirely performative, that anyone, regardless of sex, can take on either role, as Jacob suggests is true in "materialist" pornography. As in Aelred's *Spiritual Friendship*—oddly enough!—the trying-on of various gender roles, masculine and feminine, active and passive, by various characters overcomes differences, in this case differences of sex and, in Eugénie's case, of age, rather than of social status (since the characters discussed so far are all of the aristocratic class[149]).

And yet, these pleasures are so voluptuous precisely because they are transgressive: to "counterfeit" the woman while secure in the knowledge that one is a man, to be treated "as if" one were a woman [*comme une femme*] rather than to *be* a woman, is what defines this form of enjoyment. It may involve a change of *gender* role, but genital *sex* remains the same. As several critics have noted, Sade tends to understand male and female biology as comparable in at least one important respect, that of orgasm: the female orgasm is understood as a "discharge" similar to the male ejaculation.[150] Note, for example, Dolmancé's demonstration of the female orgasm on Eugénie's body: ". . . the seminal glands swell, enlarge, and finally exhale a liquid whose release hurls the woman into the most intense rapture. This is known as *discharging* [*Cela s'appelle* décharger]" (p. 205; p. 22). This may be a reminiscence of the older "one-sex" model of male and female anatomy familiar from the historical work of Thomas Laqueur; but as Laqueur suggests, this model implied not equality between the sexes but a universal hierarchy based on male superiority. This model was not replaced by a model of absolute difference until the eighteenth century, according to Laqueur. "Sometime in the eighteenth century, sex as we know it was invented. The reproductive organs went from being paradigmatic sites for displaying hierarchy, resonant throughout the cosmos, to being the foundation of incommensurable difference."[151] Sade thus harks back to the earlier model, and with it to Jacob's "naturalist" rather than "materialist" philosophy.

In the passage on orgasm just cited, for instance, Dolmancé continues: "when it pleases your friend here, I'll show you, but in a more energetic and more imperious manner, how the same operation occurs in a man" (p. 205; p. 22). The "operation" is the same, but its male version has a greater force that women can only envy. Sex differences are thus primarily based in degrees of power rather than in anatomy—but female physiology is nevertheless a contributing factor in women's relative powerlessness.

For Sade, it also limits her pleasures. A male body can provide the "imperious" pleasure of male orgasm at the same time as the "voluptuous" pleasure of transgressing gender roles, and of being penetrated, "at a single stroke the sensations of before and behind"; women may take transgressive pleasure in wielding the false phallus, but it provides no comparable physiological sensation. Male–male sodomy thus takes a privileged position (as it were) in Sade's system, as the source of the greatest possible erotic pleasure. A woman may be comparable to Ganymede, as a receptive man may be comparable to a woman; but for Dolmancé the comparison is never complete. Speaking of his preference for anal sex, he declares that "I worship it in either sex; but I'll confess a young lad's [*d'un jeune garçon*] ass gives me yet more pleasure than a girl's. . . . To fuck women in the rear is but the first part of buggery; 'tis with men [*dans l'homme*] Nature wishes men to practice this oddity, and it is especially for men she has given us an inclination" (p. 230; p. 47). He also assures the Chevalier, "I take far more pleasure with you than with Eugénie; there is an immense difference between a boy's and a girl's ass" (pp. 290–291; p. 106). Again it appears to be physiology that makes the difference: Dolmancé eliminates age differences by conflating "men" and "boys" (and the Chevalier, at age twenty, is biologically an adult [p. 188; p. 7]), while he and the Chevalier appear to be roughly equivalent in social status. It is the male body itself that is to be understood as naturally preferable. Thus all Dolmancé's erotic encounters involve male–male sodomy or at least, and less satisfactorily, its counterfeit.

In fact, in this pornographic dialogue that seems to delight in revealing everything, in verbally (and, in illustrated editions, visually[152]) unveiling all forms of erotic experience for the reader's edification, male–male desire remains the single ultimate erotic mystery. At the heart of *La Philosophie dans le boudoir*, shortly after Dolmancé reads aloud the long treatise linking libertinism with revolutionary politics in the sixth dialogue, Dolmancé, in a telling exchange, proposes to retire, with Augustin, Mme. de Saint-Ange's gardener (who, because of his youth and working-class stamina, has been previously summoned to assist in Eugénie's education), to a separate room invisible both to the dialogue's other characters and to the reader:

DOLMANCÉ:	Mesdames, I am going to ask your permission to spend a few moments in a nearby room with this young man.
MADAME DE SAINT-ANGE:	But can't you do here all you wish to do with him?
DOLMANCÉ, in a low and mysterious tone:	No; there are certain things which strictly require to be veiled.
EUGÉNIE:	Ah, by God, tell us what you'd be about!
MADAME DE SAINT-ANGE:	I'll not allow him to leave if he does not.
DOLMANCÉ:	You then wish to know?
EUGÉNIE:	Absolutely.
DOLMANCÉ, dragging Augustin:	Very well, Mesdames, I am going . . . but, indeed, it cannot be said.
MADAME DE SAINT-ANGE:	Is there, do you think any conceivable infamy we are not worthy to hear of and execute?

LE CHEVALIER:	Wait, sister. I'll tell you. (*He whispers to the two women.*)
EUGÉNIE, *with a look of revulsion*:	You are right, 'tis hideous.
MADAME DE SAINT-ANGE:	Why, I suspected as much.
DOLMANCÉ:	You see very well I had to be silent upon this caprice; and you grasp now that one must be alone and in the deepest shadow in order to give oneself over to such turpitudes.
EUGÉNIE:	Do you want me to accompany you? I'll frig you while you amuse yourself with Augustin.
DOLMANCÉ:	No, no, this is an *affaire d'honneur* and should take place between men only [*entre hommes*]; a woman would only disturb us. . . . (pp. 347–348; pp. 160–162)

Since the reader never does find out what Dolmancé and Augustin are up to in the next room, Sade's biographer Neil Schaeffer refers to this scene as "Sade's joke about a mystery perversion,"[153] and correctly suggests that "we are shown more than we want to know, and yet teased into wanting to see something even worse."[154] But the scene is also more than just a joke; it firmly establishes Dolmancé's, and Sade's, philosophical/erotic system as one that ultimately excludes women. Drawing on the medieval tradition (discussed in chapter 1) that regarded sodomy as the sin that may not be spoken, Dolmancé, who speaks at length about sodomy, now assigns its former unspeakability to this new unnamable "turpitude" that can occur only between men. The male Chevalier knows what it is, and the masculinized Mme. de Saint-Ange may "suspect" it—but she cannot participate. Indeed, the language of honor—this encounter is to be an "*affaire d'honneur*"— suggests a duel or male–male competition, which may also be understood as a form of male homosociality precisely in its exclusion of women. This ultimate perversion, then, so extreme that it alone cannot be shown even in Sade's extreme text, places male–male desire at the heart of Sade's erotic philosophy.

The invocation of "Nature" above (p. 230; p. 47) and throughout *La Philosophie dans le boudoir* links Sade's to other Enlightenment defenses of sodomy like Diderot's and to their predecessors', such as Rocco's. For Sade, too, nothing that exists can be outside nature: "Absurd to say the mania offends Nature; can it be so, when 'tis she who puts it into our head?" (p. 230; p. 47). Sade, indeed, goes further than Diderot in suggesting, as in the passage cited above, that Nature, for whom the destruction of the human species is actually more desirable than its propagation, prefers the union of those who are similar to that of those who are different. In fact, sodomy resembles murder, which is also transvalued in Dolmancé's system: ". . . the whole extirpation of the breed would, by returning to Nature the creative faculty she has entrusted to us, reinvigorate her, she would have again that energy we deprive her of by propagating our own selves" (p. 238; p. 54). Nature is also the basis of Dolmancé's defense of cruelty—that aspect of Sade's thought for which he is most widely known—as Nature "always urges us to delight in ourselves" regardless of our pleasure's effect on others (p. 253; p. 68).[155]

Male–male desire, then, is here both natural and based on biological similarity rather than on difference; women's less powerful biological dispositions render them less erotically desirable, while men who display the signs of phallic power are objects of desire regardless of other differences. Thus the dialogue's one lower-class character, Augustin the gardener, in spite of his class, shares an all-important characteristic with the Chevalier: the latter is provided with a "superb member" (p. 189; p. 8), while Augustin's, measured by Dolmancé, proves to be "fourteen long, eight and a half around . . . a superb prick" (p. 268; p. 84). (How class differences might affect the secret encounter between Augustin and Dolmancé is, of course, never investigated, but it should be recalled that the aristocratic Chevalier is in on the secret too.)

Sade's take on the "naturalistic" stance thus tends to locate the source of desire in similarity, indeed phallic similarity, rather than difference; indeed, in his defense of incest Dolmancé assumes that the greater the similarity, the greater the desire: "If, in a word, love is born of resemblance [*ressemblance*], where may it be more perfect than between brother and sister, between father and daughter?" (p. 236; p. 53).[156] Male–male sodomy may be Dolmancé's preferred form of desire between similar beings, but incest can thus provide a model of such relations as well, suggesting that similarity itself is what is truly desired. From this perspective, self-sameness may logically be understood as the most desirable of all forms of relationality. To answer Dolmancé's question, in Sade's system "love" between male relatives, brother and brother or father and son, might logically be the most perfect of all.

Or, to follow Sade's reasoning even further, one might say that the love of the self-same—indeed, of the self—would be the most desirable. Sade's universe is indeed ultimately a solipsistic one; Schaeffer even suggests that "[i]t is not too much to say that his primary relationship was with himself."[157] Sade's celebrated sadism derives from this solipsistic perspective; as Dolmancé himself puts it,

> Nature has endowed each of us with a capacity for kindly feelings: let us not squander them on others . . . May our sensibility's hearth warm naught but

our own pleasures! Let us feel when it is to their advantage; and when it is not, let us be absolutely unbending. From this exact economy of feeling, from this judicious use of sensibility, there results a kind of cruelty which is sometimes not without its delights. (p. 217; p. 34)

The most perfect pleasure, then, will be that which denies any relationality other than the exertion of the self's power. Even between two libertines, as Barthes suggests, "[t]he Sadian relationship . . . is not one of reciprocity but of revenge. . . ."[158] The sovereignty of the self is the ultimate goal of desire. In this sense Sade is perhaps more thoroughgoing than any other writer of dialogues in his rejection of difference in favor of self-sameness: erotic pleasures derived from the similarity of man to man or of family members, while superior to those derived from difference, are in the long run only substitutes for the masturbatory pleasures derived from the exercise of the sovereign, powerful, male self.[159]

As one might expect from such a writer, Sade's dialogues can hardly be called "dialogical"; in fact, they are less so than his novels, notably *Justine*, in which the hapless but principled heroine consistently contradicts the libertine voices that throughout the novel attempt to convince her of the pointlessness and self-destructiveness of her invincible virtue. The libertines all try to deliver quite similar lectures on the same themes that Dolmancé constantly elaborates (the naturalness of all desires, the necessity of sacrificing everyone else to the self's sovereign pleasures, etc.), but Justine insists to the end of the lengthy narrative on arguing the opposite moral and philosophical positions, thus allowing for the possibility of an alternate perspective that rarely arises in *La Philosophie dans le boudoir*. Sade's earlier dialogue, the *Dialogue entre un prêtre et un moribond* (1782) follows a similar pattern—except that unlike Justine, the priest, in the end, is won over to the dying libertine's point of view.[160] In these fictions Sade demonstrates a questioning attitude typical of the Enlightenment, an era in which resistance to authority became in some sense the intellectual norm: the authoritative voice found in the Italian Ciceronian tradition itself "would have seemed in some sense barbarous."[161]

But in *La Philosophie dans le boudoir* no one needs to be won over. Young Eugénie is conventionally shocked at Dolmancé's first advances, but the pleasure he and the other libertines teach her convert her immediately to their point of view. Eugénie enthusiastically participates in the violent degradation directed against her repressive mother at the end of the seventh dialogue, but even within a few pages of the beginning of the third dialogue—the first in which Eugénie appears—she has been found a willing pupil. The Chevalier initially resists Dolmancé's cruel plans for

Mme. de Mistival ("'tis horrible, what you have us do" [p. 360; p. 172]) but Dolmancé quickly secures his equally enthusiastic participation; within a few pages, the Chevalier is proposing his own punishment for Mme. de Mistival, that she be "[c]ut into eighty thousand pieces" (p. 362; p. 174).[162] No moral or philosophical objection to Dolmancé's system is allowed to stand even briefly, or, indeed, to be discussed: his lessons are immediately accepted by all. (Mme. de Mistival, of course, objects to the libertines' treatment of her, but her indignation is allowed no moral or philosophical resonance; Barthes points out that Sadeian victims "are merely mechanical voices . . . accomplices in filling out libertine speech."[163]) Sade's dialogue, then, resembles Cicero's or Ficino's in its relentless promotion of a single-minded philosophical project, without the dialogism of, say, a Tullia d'Aragona.

Indeed, the tendency of Sade's libertine characters, Dolmancé included, to deliver lectures rather than engaging in real dialogue reaches its most extreme limit in *La Philosophie dans le boudoir*, when Dolmancé, in the course of the fifth dialogue, has the Chevalier simply read aloud from a pamphlet—over forty pages long—linking libertine philosophy with revolutionary politics: "Yet Another Effort, Frenchmen, If You Would Become Republicans" (pp. 296–339; pp. 110–153). While Dolmancé claims to have bought the pamphlet, Eugénie suspects that he is actually its author, and Dolmancé agrees that it repeats his own "discourses" (p. 339; p. 154). It is here that we find almost all of *La Philosophie*'s references to Plato, the *Symposium*, and ancient Athens, and it is thus here also that Sade places himself within the tradition of the *Symposium* and of the subsequent dialogues influenced by it. Like the Pseudo-Lucian and Antonio Rocco, Sade invokes Alcibiades as a figure for the physical expression of male–male erotic desire: claiming that in ancient Athens "no species of lechery was forbidden" to citizens, Dolmancé's pamphlet declares that "Socrates, whom the oracle described as the wisest philosopher of the land, passing indifferently from Aspasia's arms into those of Alcibiades, was not on that account less the glory of Greece" (pp. 317–318; pp. 131–132). As in Plutarch, the Pseudo-Lucian, and Rocco, male–female desire, here represented by the courtesan Aspasia, is contrasted with male–male desire, here represented by Alcibiades. And although the comparison ostensibly suggests the "indifference" of the two loves, it must also be seen as a defense of male–male sodomy, which of the two is the only "species of lechery" "forbidden" by the post-Revolutionary but still Church-influenced system of government that the pamphlet critiques. We are far removed here from the chaste Socrates of many classical and humanist dialogues; indeed, Sade's regular use of the term "socratize" to describe a particular erotic activity (digital stimulation of the anus) playfully brings the philosopher into the orgy: "Eugénie, let me kiss your beautiful behind while I bugger mamma, and you Madame, bring yours near, so that I can handle it . . . socratize it [*que je le socratise*]" (p. 358; p. 170).

Sade's use of the Platonic tradition to defend—or promote—male–male sodomy continues with a reference to Plutarch's appropriation of the *Symposium*. Speaking now explicitly of sodomy between men, the pamphlet declares that

> it is not dangerous. Would the Greek legislators have introduced it into their republics had they thought it so? Quite the contrary; they deemed it neces-sary to a warlike race. Plutarch speaks with enthusiasm of the battalion of lovers: for many a year they alone defended Greece's freedom. The vice reigned amongst comrades-in-arms, and cemented their unity. (pp. 326–327; p. 141)

Although Plutarch, as we have seen, draws on Plato's description of an army of male–male lovers, the reference there is not as explicit as Sade makes it; instead, Sade is placing himself more directly in the tradition initiated by Plato himself. And unlike Castiglione, who heterosexualized the army of lovers that Phaedrus describes in the *Symposium*, Sade insists that the "battalion" is entirely male, and that it leads to unified agreement; if Phaedrus, in his original speech in the *Symposium*, confuses the traditional Athenian distinction between *erastes* and *eromenos*, in Sade it is eliminated altogether in favor of an undifferentiated "unity."[164]

The solipsism noted above with regard to Dolmancé is played out in this pamphlet as well. Alcibiades here stands not only for the physical expres-sion of male–male desire; he is also a sign of impiety—another positive value in Sade's system and in the pamphlet, which urges its post-Revolutionary audience to abolish religion and all moral codes derived from religion. Claiming that "no god meddles in our affairs" and that there-fore all supposed duties to a divinity must vanish, the pamphlet goes on to suggest that "with them vanish all religious crimes, all those comprehended under the indefinite names of *impiety, sacrilege, blasphemy, atheism*, etc., all those, in brief, which Athens so unjustly punished in Alcibiades" (p. 308; p. 122). Alcibiades thus links sodomy and impiety. We may discern in the references to him and to Socrates the usual constellation of objections to the sodomite: he is unnatural, he threatens gender distinctions, he violates the laws of God and man. As in Rocco's dialogue, however, these accusa-tions are disputed: current legal restrictions on sodomy are based not on nature, but on social and religious conventions, as is demonstrated by the different attitudes toward it in different cultures such as ancient Greece (and Sade is as much a comparative cultural critic as Rocco) and are therefore unjust; sodomy does not violate divine law because there is no god; sodomy does not violate gender distinctions, but reinforces the military ideal of masculinity. In Sade, the *Symposium* thus emerges as a source of defenses for the physical expression of male–male desire, and a single-minded one at that: gone are the *Symposium*'s multiplicity of contrasting voices—not to mention Socrates' climactic speech in which the body is transcended. Plato's dialogue becomes simply one part of the puzzle that Sade's pamphlet assembles in his monologic defense of libertinism. As in Castiglione, the Bakhtinian dialogical is in some sense eliminated, though here in the name of an oppositional libertinism rather than of a conservative Christianity.

Indeed, this pamphlet, in arguing for the abolition of religion, also argues for the abolition of any limits on the exercise of power: the strong individual must no longer be restricted from imposing his will as he sees fit, whether in theft, rape, murder, and so on. Sade's solipsism, one aspect of which is his defense of desire based on sameness, is at its most extreme in this pamphlet: in its refusal of the dialogue form, not only does it introduce a thoroughly monologic form at the heart of the dialogue, it also, in content, insists that society as a whole must conform to the desires of the libertine, not vice versa. As Gilles Deleuze points out,

> [w]ith Sade we witness an astonishing development of the demonstrative use of language. . . . The libertine may put on an act of trying to convince and persuade. . . . But the intention to convince is merely apparent, for nothing is in fact more alien to the sadist than the wish to convince, to persuade, in short to educate. He is interested in something quite different, namely to demonstrate that reasoning itself is a form of violence, and that he is on the side of violence, however calm and logical he may be. He is not even attempting to prove anything to anyone, but to perform a demonstration related essentially to the solitude and omnipotence of its author. The point of the exercise is to show that the demonstration is identical to violence.[165]

Nowhere is this essential point demonstrated more clearly than in *La Philosophie dans le boudoir*'s shift from dialogue to treatise.[166] The pamphlet's "republicanism" is thus reducible to the unitary good of the isolated individual, searching, in his pursuit of sameness, for the destruction of all that does not resemble himself:[167] once again the dominant culture's icon, this time republicanism, is revealed as logically committed to that which it disavows. We are now a long way from Plato's and some of his successors' interest in deviations. With Sade, the potentials for male–male desire opened up in the *Symposium* and in the tradition it instigates ironically become a new and unyielding orthodoxy; Foucault suggests that Sadeian sexuality "is no longer anything but a unique and naked sovereignty: an unlimited right of all-powerful monstrosity"[168] and that, after Sade's dead end, "[i]t is the agency of sex that we must break away from."[169] As the Enlightenment ushers in the modern world, however, along with the modern "homosexual," another of Plato's dialogues, the *Phaedrus*, opens up some new possibilities.[170]

3. Erotic Style: From Plato's *Phaedrus* to the Modern Novel ⤴

The relationship of male–male desire to language has been an implicit theme of many, if not most, of the dialogues discussed so far, especially Plato's: in both the *Lysis* and the *Symposium*, dialogical discourse and oratory stand in for erotic intercourse between males, whether as seductive go-betweens leading to the physical expression of love, or as themselves love's truest expression, transcending the physical. The *Phaedrus*, a dialogue probably roughly contemporary with the *Symposium* and often associated with it, makes this concern explicit: while it includes many of the Platonic doctrines on male–male desire familiar from the *Lysis* and the *Symposium*, it also, in a juxtaposition that can seem startling, discusses language, rhetoric, and writing. Discourses on love occupy the first half of the dialogue, while the second half, in an apparently abrupt change of subject, takes up these questions of language.

Exactly how and why the subject does and does not change is the topic of the first part of this chapter, which examines how the *Phaedrus* presents male–male desire and its relation to language. In the second part, this chapter also investigates the afterlife of this relationship in modern dialogues and other dialogical texts. In the nineteenth and twentieth centuries, several Western European cultural developments intersected in ways of interest to this book's thesis: problems of language came to dominate philosophy; the novel became the dominant literary form (even as the dialogue itself became an increasingly marginal form); and the modern concept of homosexuality was invented.[1] The *Symposium* and other Platonic dialogues have continued to exert a profound influence on Western culture (as we shall see in the conclusion to this study); and it is often difficult to disentangle the influence of the *Phaedrus* from that of the *Symposium*: Oscar Wilde and André Gide, whom I consider in the second part of this chapter, cite both Platonic texts in their own dialogues. But in the modern world the *Phaedrus*, speaking as it does to the questions being asked by philosophy and literary artists in this period, has had a particular influence on literary and other texts. The *Phaedrus*, to be sure, has attracted many admirers and has exerted an influence since it was first written; but it also seems to have spoken with particular eloquence to certain writers of the late nineteenth and twentieth centuries, and it is this specifically modern after-life of the *Phaedrus* that I examine in the second part of this chapter.

Philosophical dialogues *per se* remain an important concern throughout this chapter; but this is a period in which literature and philosophy became more independent of each other than had been the case in earlier periods, and in which both literature and philosophy to some extent abandoned the dialogue form, philosophy in favor of the discursive essay, literature in favor of narrative. For this reason, I also cast a wider literary net in the last portion of this chapter: after discussing several modern dialogues, I also turn my attention to dialogue-inflected novels.

In the *Phaedrus*, as we might now expect, Plato's Socrates promotes a singular truth to be arrived at through the means of dialectical philosophy, and love ideally is that which leads the philosopher to the knowledge of truth. But in this dialogue Socrates also focuses, even more clearly than in the *Symposium*, on the deviations from absolute truth and from this ideal love, deviations that here seem more acceptable to Socrates than they do elsewhere. The route to the singular, self-same truth, here more than in other Platonic dialogues, involves difference and deviation—whether the subject under discussion is the various modes of love or those of discourse.

The three discourses on love that occupy the first part of the *Phaedrus* concern themselves with male–male erotics, but they are also exercises in rhetoric, demonstrations of the persuasive power of discourse. In short, they are models of the rhetoric of seduction: intended as demonstrations of how an older man might discursively pursue the love of a younger man—rather than as actual attempts at "real-life" seduction—they are as much about language as they are about love. They offer lessons in rhetorical persuasion as well as in the nature of love, and these functions must be understood together. Socrates himself conflates rhetoric and erotics quite explicitly in the opening pages of the dialogue. When he asks Phaedrus to recite Lysias' speech, Phaedrus modestly, or disingenuously, claims to be unable to do so. Socrates, however, is certain that Phaedrus has studied the speech until he knows it by heart, and, speaking of his friend and himself in the third person, declares that

> he was going into the country to practise declaiming it. Then he fell in with one who has a passion for listening to discourses [*toi nosounti peri logon*

(τῷ νοσοῦντι περὶ λόγων)]; and when he saw him he was delighted to think he would have someone to share his frenzied enthusiasm [*sugkorybantionta* (συγκορυβαντιῶντα)]; so he asked him to join him on his way. But when the lover of discourses [*ton logon erastou* (τῶν λόγων ἐραστοῦ)] begged him to discourse, he became difficult, pretending he didn't want to, though he meant to do so ultimately, even if he had to force himself on a reluctant listener. So beg him, Phaedrus, to do straightway what he will soon do in any case. (pp. 22–23, 228b–c)[2]

Nosounti suggests a passion (in this case for discourses, *logon*) in the literal sense. It suggests, in fact, the sickness of passion: passion as something suffered or undergone, a powerful outside force, beyond one's control. As we shall see, erotic desire or love is also imagined to be such an uncontrollable passion throughout the *Phaedrus*, especially in the first speech. In the third speech, it is imagined as a divine possession or madness as well, just as the love of discourse is described here with the term *sugkorybantionta*, a "frenzied enthusiasm" again in the literal sense of possession by a deity (like the Corybantic celebrants). Socrates thus unites himself and Phaedrus as sharing a love of discourse, but one that is a sickness in Socrates' case and divine possession in that of Phaedrus. (Placing this passage in the third person also suggests that Socrates and Phaedrus are others as well as themselves, outside or beside themselves in some sense.) Ultimately Socrates places himself in the role of an *erastes*, a lover, again of discourses; but Phaedrus is now imagined as the possessor of that which is desired, who must be flattered and coaxed into yielding it, that is, as an *eromenos*. The language of erotic desire is thus applied throughout this passage to the love of discourse; the two are thoroughly conflated from the outset.

As in the *Lysis* and the *Symposium*, the first encounter between Socrates and his interlocutor—Phaedrus, the sole interlocutor in this dialogue—involves a turning aside, though this is less emphasized here than in the others. Socrates encounters Phaedrus, who is going for a walk outside the walls of Athens after having spent the morning studying a new speech on love with its author, the famous rhetorician and speechmaker Lysias. Socrates, we eventually learn, rarely ventures outside the city, and despite being a native of Athens considers Phaedrus a sort of guide to the beauties of nature that lie outside its walls:

> *Soc.* . . . my dear Phaedrus, you have been the stranger's perfect guide [*hoste arista soi exenagetai* (ὥστε ἄριστά σοι ἐξενάγηται)].
>
> *Ph.* Whereas you, my excellent friend, strike me as the oddest of men. Anyone would take you, as you say, for a stranger being shown the country by a guide [*xenagoumenoi* (ξεναγουμένῳ)] instead of a

> native: never leaving town to cross the frontier nor even, I believe, so much as setting foot outside the walls. (p. 25, 230c–d)

Socrates is a stranger (*xenos* [ξένος]) in his own country, an Athenian who is also not an Athenian, and the emphasis on liminal spaces—the frontier, the city wall, the river Ilissus by which the two friends pause to talk— suggests that Socrates will be venturing into new philosophical as well as geographical territory. In altering his usual routine, Socrates shows himself to be both of and not of Athens, to be literally both an outsider and an insider—to be taking up the space of the deviant or the proximate, in fact. Even as he alters his routine, however, he is also remaining true to his familiar self: what tempts him out of his usual haunts is, as in the *Lysis*, the promise of discourse with a handsome young man on the topic of love— the one topic in which he claims expertise in the *Symposium*, the dialogue in which Phaedrus himself instigates the speeches on love.[3] As Phaedrus says, "the topic is appropriate for your ears, Socrates; for the discussion that engaged us may be said to have concerned love" (p. 22, 227c); and Socrates himself declares that "if you proffer me volumes of speeches I don't doubt you can cart me all round Attica, and anywhere else you please" (p. 25, 230d–e). By following Phaedrus into unfamiliar territory (or leading him: they share the role of leader[4]), Socrates is also returning himself to the familiar, as well as again taking up a deviant position, both outside and within his usual self.[5]

The mythological references that open the *Phaedrus* also contribute to the sense of deviance/proximity that frames the following discourses. The friends' physical location has a divine significance—but not exactly:

> *Ph.* Tell me, Socrates, isn't it somewhere about here [*enthende mentoi pothen* (ἐνθένδε μέντοι ποθὲν)] that they say Boreas seized Oreithuia from the river?
>
> *Soc.* Yes, that is the story.
>
> *Ph.* Was this the actual spot [*enthende* (ἐνθένδε)]? Certainly the water looks charmingly pure and clear; it's just the place for girls to be playing beside the stream.
>
> *Soc.* No, it was about a quarter of a mile lower down . . . (pp. 23–24, 229b–c).

The discourses on love will take place appropriately near the scene of a passionate encounter between a god and a mortal; but there is no strict identification between the location of Socrates and Phaedrus and that of this mythological encounter. It took place only "somewhere about here," a quarter of a mile away, not, it is emphasized, at this "actual spot." Socrates' and Phaedrus' physical location is thus defined at least in part by where they are not, or rather by where they are not-quite: they are not exactly in Athens, though not beyond its frontier, and they are not quite at the shrine to Boreas, which Socrates says occupies the spot in question (p. 24, 229c), though it is "somewhere about here." They are somewhere in between, not exactly in an undefined location but not in one that can be definitively located, either.[6]

The discourses on love spoken in this in-between spot themselves also represent a series of deviations. There are three of them, and each deviates from its predecessor in its pursuit of truth, or at least of persuasion. The first is Lysias' new speech, which Phaedrus has spent the morning studying with its author; it is a rhetorical exercise that purports to demonstrate how a nonlover should persuade a youth to accept his advances: by claiming that a nonlover can provide greater benefits than a lover (pp. 27–30, 230e–234c). Although it takes the form of a spontaneous oral performance, it is in fact deviant because it is written: Phaedrus is carrying a copy of it with him (p. 23, 228d–e). (Socrates also contributes, initially, to this confusion of speech and writing, with his ironic reference to the "volumes" of discourses that might tempt him to go anywhere, cited above—when in fact it is oral conversation that he is really pursuing.) Phaedrus is enthusiastic about his teacher's speech, claiming that "it is impossible for anyone to outdo what he has said with a fuller or more satisfactory oration" (p. 33, 235a).

In the second speech (pp. 38–46, 237b–241c), Socrates takes up this challenge, offering his own example of the rhetorical persuasion of a youth by a nonlover. Typically, however, Socrates refuses to take credit for this performance, suggesting that, like his speech in the *Symposium* that claims merely to quote Diotima, this one, because of his own ignorance, must have "been poured into me, through my ears, as into a vessel, from some external source," though he has forgotten what the source might be: perhaps one of the erotic poets Sappho or Anacreon (p. 33, 235c–d). Socrates thus presents not only a deviation from the doctrine found in Lysias' speech, but a deviation in mode as well, substituting a more aural/oral situation involving memory and repetition for the literate presentation of Lysias' speech. He also presents a self-deviation: he is the speaker actually present, but the words, he claims, are not his.[7]

In the third speech, Socrates repudiates both previous speeches as blasphemous, because of the falsity of their shared doctrine (that a nonlover should be preferred to a lover), and offers instead his own doctrine in praise of love (pp. 56–110, 243e–257b). This speech is more purely oral than either of the others, being represented as a spontaneous, perhaps divinely inspired, discourse by Socrates himself rather than merely the repetition of something he heard elsewhere.

The formal relationship among these speeches should to some extent be familiar from the *Symposium*. As in that dialogue, ideas ultimately shown to be false are initially presented as if they were true; the false discourses are then superseded by a true discourse—which is nevertheless driven by the errors of the preceding ones. Thus, in terms of rhetorical strategy, truth is presented as a deviation from the preceding falsehoods, while in philosophical terms, the falsehoods are deviations from a singular truth. Writing is associated with error and is similarly deviant, while oral speech is associated, even in some sense identical, with truth.

Lysias' speech,[8] read aloud by Phaedrus, first addresses the issue of deviance in love. Commentators have traditionally dismissed this speech, in which a fictitious speaker tries to persuade a youth to accept his erotic advances even though he does not love the youth, as, formally, a "tedious piece of rhetoric . . . a flat, monotonous, repetitive composition"[9] and, doctrinally, as "hedonistic," "deceptive,"[10] "cold,"[11] and even "sordid."[12] Undoubtedly Plato uses Lysias' speech to some extent as a straw man, but the themes of self-deviance and self-sameness in relation to love that are introduced here will continue to influence the two speeches of Socrates, and even the later discussion of writing.

Lysias accepts the traditional structure of ancient Athenian homoerotic relations that we have observed earlier: it is essentially an asymmetrical relationship between an older man who confers various benefits and a youth who bestows erotic favors. Indeed, Lysias tends to reduce this relationship to one of purely economic exchange, and this is one reason he argues that the youth should prefer a nonlover to a lover:

> Lovers [*erastes* (ἐραστὴς)], when their craving is at an end, repent of such benefits as they have conferred: but for the other sort no occasion arises for regretting what has passed; for being free agents under no constraint, they regulate their services by the scale of their means, with an eye to their own personal interest. (p. 27, 231a)

Lovers, that is to say, are constrained by love to perform undisciplined actions, in particular to spend, which they would not perform under ordinary circumstances. Nonlovers, on the other hand, experience no such constraint of passion and are thus free to make disciplined choices according to what they can afford, and therefore, unlike lovers, can have no regrets. This is to suggest that love is a deviation from the self, as Lysias quickly specifies: "Why, the man himself admits that he is not sound, but sick [*homologousin nosein mallon he sophronein* (ὁμολογοῦσιν νοσεῖν μᾶλλον ἢ σωφρονεῖν)];

that he is aware of his folly, but cannot control himself; how then, when he comes to his senses, is he likely to approve of the intentions that he formed in his aberration [*diakeimenoi* (διακείμενοι)]?" (p. 28, 231d). Although *diakeimenoi* suggests the more neutral English translation "such a state" or "that condition" rather than Hackforth's "aberration," Hackforth's term does capture the overall sense of this passage: the lover is a man literally beside himself, not in control. He can see the right thing to do, but is incapable of doing it. He is, in other words, both himself and not himself: erotic love, like the love of discourse cited earlier, is a state of uncontrollable self-deviation. The nonlover, on the other hand, is most crucially "the master of myself [*emautou kraton* (ἐμαυτοῦ κρατῶν)], rather than the victim of love" (p. 29, 233c). *Emautou kraton* suggests a retention of power over the self, the power or discipline that love takes away from the lover: not to love is to be in a state in which one's desires remain in line with one's true self. Unlike the deviant lover, the nonlover remains always self-same, identical to himself. The nonlover's benefits to the youth who yields to him, then, will be unchangeable, whereas those conferred by the lover will be withdrawn once the lover returns to his senses (p. 30, 234a).

The view of love as a powerful outside force that saps the will and ought to be resisted is a traditional one in ancient Greek thought,[13] though the logical position that Lysias tries to derive from it—that youths should bestow their favors instead on nonlovers—is surprising, as Socrates sarcastically suggests after Phaedrus' initial summary of the argument (p. 22, 227c–d). Socrates himself will seize on this concept of love in his own second speech, praising it as a divine possession. His first speech, however, follows that of Lysias in defining love as a state of self-deviation.

As Hackforth suggests, this speech is "extorted" from Socrates by Phaedrus:[14] when Socrates declares that he feels "something welling up within my breast, which makes me feel that I could find something different, and something better to say" (p. 33, 235c) than Lysias' speech, he may be referring to the speech he will eventually make in opposition to Lysias; but Phaedrus assumes that he means he could make the same point as Lysias in a better way, and coaxes him to do so with teasing threats, first of violence ("don't make me use force to open your lips" [p. 35, 236d]), and then of withholding the discursive favors that, as we have seen, they have playfully substituted for erotic ones:

> *Ph.* I swear that unless you deliver your speech . . . I will assuredly never again declaim nor report any other speech by any author whatsoever.
>
> *Soc.* Aha, you rogue! How clever of you to discover the means of compelling a lover of discourse [*philologoi* (φιλολόγῳ)] to do your bidding! (p. 35, 236e)

The upshot is that Socrates must make a speech that deviates from his own beliefs: in the discourse that follows, Socrates, once again, is beside himself, as is suggested by his shame in making such a speech (p. 35, 237a). Because he will be reproducing the effect of Lysias' speech using different arguments, this speech, as well as characterizing love itself as deviance, will also be a deviation from the preceding speech.

Phaedrus and Socrates are both "beside themselves" in another sense throughout the passage leading up to the second speech: each of them suggests that he shares the other's perspective. Socrates, who doesn't approve of Lysias' speech, suggests nevertheless that he has enjoyed it by taking pleasure in Phaedrus' pleasure (p. 32, 234d), while Phaedrus claims to share Socrates' identity: playfully scolding him for his initial reluctance to speak, Phaedrus says "do not deliberately compel me to utter the words 'Don't I know my Socrates? If not, I've forgotten my own identity' " (p. 35, 236c). Again, the friends' participation in these discourses seems to sublimate a closer relationship.

The second speech—Socrates' first—begins in self-deviation: Socrates imagines that its speaker is one of a handsome boy's many lovers (*erastai* [ἐρασταὶ]) (p. 38, 237b). The speech in favor of yielding to a nonlover itself, then, will deviate from the true feelings of the imagined lover. But love itself is here also a state of deviance from the self: as in the speech of Lysias, it is a state of possession in which the self is split. Socrates' first move is to provide a definition of love:

> within each one of us there are two sorts of ruling or guiding principle that we follow: one is an innate desire [*epithumia* ([ἐπιθυμία])] for pleasure, the other an acquired judgment that aims at what is best. Sometimes these internal guides are in accord, sometimes at variance: now one gains the mastery, now the other . . . when desire drags us irrationally towards pleasure, and has come to rule within us, the name given to that rule is wantonness [*hubris* (ὕβρις)]. (pp. 38–39, 237d–238a)

> When irrational desire, pursuing the enjoyment of beauty, has gained the mastery over judgment that prompts to right conduct, and has acquired from other desires, akin to it [*suggenon epithumion* (συγγενῶν ἐπιθυμιῶν)], fresh strength to strain towards bodily beauty, that very strength provides it with its name: it is the strong passion called Love [*eros* (ἔρως)]. (p. 39, 238b–c)

Love, as Hackforth points out, is here not only a category of desire, but also a category of *hubris*,[15] a term implying not only wanton excess, but lewdness and even violence or outrage as well. However, this outrageous violence is not directed outward toward another person, but inward toward the lover's self: love is an irrational desire that overcomes the other aspect of the soul, the judgment that directs the individual toward the good. It prevents the soul's two aspects from acting "in accord" with each other, and substitutes violent overthrow for harmony. Love is even more complex than the simple desire for beauty: only when that desire is reinforced by other desires "akin [*suggenon*] to it"—presumably the desire for erotic possession—does it acquire the violent force necessary for it to be called *eros. Suggenon*, as we have already seen in the *Lysis*, suggests similarity without identity, a kind of family resemblance. But *eros* is the black sheep of this family, the one that allows an already irrational desire to overthrow the rational self completely.

In the opening moves of this speech, then, both love itself and the discourse in which it is being attacked are defined by self-deviance: the defense of the nonlover requires that love be maligned as a loss of self or a division of the self, as it was in Lysias' speech. But it is a lover in disguise as a nonlover who produces this critique of love, and, as Hackforth points out, "we see the lover peeping through the disguise . . . in fact we get a glimpse of the ἐραστής *par excellence*, Socrates himself."[16] In the third speech Socrates will mount a defense of love as another kind of self-deviance, a divine madness or possession, and the way for this defense is already being cleared as Socrates continues this second speech. He has already invoked the Muses for help with it (p. 36, 237a–b), and at 238c he breaks into the fictional, disguised lover's discourse to claim, in his own voice, divine inspiration: "Well, Phaedrus my friend, do you think, as I do, that I am divinely inspired? . . . truly there seems to be a divine presence in this spot, so that you must not be surprised if, as my speech proceeds, I become as one possessed; already my style is not far from dithyrambic" (p. 43, 238c). The style of the discourse itself thus suggests divine possession, as, shortly, will love: once again *eros* and discourse develop in parallel. If in this second speech they are associated with self-division, in the third they will be associated with divine possession.

For the time being, however, this possession is only hinted at; Socrates must now complete the second speech in the voice of the lover disguised as a nonlover. Love, in this critique, is a matter of difference from the love object as well as deviation within the self. The supposed nonlover argues that because the lover is sick, what pleases him is "anything that does not thwart him, whereas anything that is as strong as, or stronger than, himself gives him offence" (p. 43, 238e). He will thus seek out a youth (*paidika* [παιδικὰ]) who is inferior in various ways: one who is physically weaker, but also "the ignorant, the cowardly, the poor speaker, the slow thinker"; indeed, if the beloved is not inferior, the lover in his sickness will cultivate this inferiority (p. 44, 239a). The lover, in short, will seek out difference: love imagined as self-deviation will pursue further deviation in its object of desire. As the speech continues, it is difference that the supposed nonlover emphasizes, especially the age difference normally believed to be an essential component of the ideal Athenian pederasty:

> There's an old saying about 'not matching May with December' [*helika . . . terpein ton helika* (ἥλικα . . . τέρπειν τὸν ἥλικα)] based, I suppose, on the idea that similarity of age tends to similarity of pleasures and consequently makes a couple good friends . . . what pleasure or solace will he have to offer the beloved? How will he save him from experiencing the extremity of discomfort in those long hours at his lover's side, as he looks upon a face which years have robbed of its beauty, together with other consequences which it is unpleasant even to hear mentioned, let alone to have continually to cope with in stark reality. (p. 45, 240c–e)

A more literal translation of *helika terpein ton helika* might be that those in their prime take pleasure in others in their prime,[17] but the point is the same: age differentiation prevents true friendship (*philia*) and leads to a relationship based on the exploitation, rather than the true good, of the youth. What is emphasized throughout the first part of this passage is not age, but difference: the similarity that, according to some of the theories advanced (though ultimately rejected) in the *Lysis*, is the basis of both *philia* and *eros*, is here limited exclusively to *philia*, which is thus advanced as a form of relationality superior to the erotic one. That the difference under discussion is precisely one of age is addressed as the passage continues: the physical debilities of age cannot satisfy youth. Love, based in both self-deviation and difference from the erotic object, must itself be considered a deviation from the presumed ideal of self-sameness and similarity to the other.

The entire speech, then, is opposed to deviation and differentiation; when the lover returns to his senses, "a new authority takes the place within him of the former ruler: love and passion are replaced by wisdom and temperance: he has become a different person" (p. 46, 241a). The youth, having known him only in the previous unhealthy state of self-deviation, will take the return of a proper orientation within the soul as a deviation from the lover he knew: he "demands a return for what he gave in the past . . . as though he were talking to the same person; while the erstwhile lover, who has now acquired wisdom and temperance, cannot for very shame bring himself to declare that he has become a new [*allos* (ἄλλος)] man, nor yet see his way to redeeming the solemn assurances and promises made under the old régime of folly" (p. 46, 241a–b). The continued emphasis is on self-transformation with the return of reason: the lover is not "the same person" but "a new man" (or a different, *allos*, man) who must reject the former beloved along with all his former "folly." What initially appeared as a division within the self, one aspect of the soul dominating the other, now rhetorically becomes a complete self-transformation: it is no longer a question of self-deviation, but of an entirely different self,[18] and the effect of this new differentiation on the beloved is disastrous. Deviation and differentiation lead to ruin; by implication, self-sameness and the *philia* inspired by similarity are conducive to happiness. The friend should be preferred to the lover.

The question of style is raised again as Socrates concludes this second speech, breaking, as he says, into "epic verse" (p. 50, 241e) at 241d in his supposed condemnation of the lover's appetites. Socrates claims to find this poetic sign of possession disturbing: when Phaedrus objects that he has merely condemned the lover without going on to praise the nonlover, Socrates declares that he must truncate the speech in this way in order to avoid further possession: "I've got beyond dithyramb, and am breaking out into epic verse. . . . What do you suppose I shall do if I start extolling the other type? Don't you see that I shall clearly be possessed by those nymphs into whose clutches you deliberately threw me?" (p. 50, 241e). Style itself is a sign of possession and self-deviation, that which Socrates has been condemning in the lover, and Socrates cannot praise the nonlover—who, we must recall, is really a lover in disguise—without risking further loss of self-control. Love, it appears, is as much a matter of deviation from one's own language as it is from one's sense of self.

But the entire second speech has been merely an exercise in sham rhetoric, and Socrates now feels ashamed of it: he can no longer argue against love, nor even against possession: he claims to have recognized his familiar "divine sign," which, here as in the *Apology*, "turns me away from something I am about to do."[19] In this case he must not leave without atoning for the "sin [*hamartema* (ἁμάρτημα)]" (p. 51, 242d) of blasphemy against a god, Eros, committed in his verbal assent to, and extension of, Lysias' vilification of love (pp. 51–52, 242d–243a). "Error" or "failure" might be a more literal translation of *hamartema*, but it is indeed a sinful failure to acknowledge a god. Socrates' third speech will thus acknowledge love as an encounter not only with a human, but also with a divine Other in a fashion reminiscent, for the modern reader, of Buber's theological conceptualization of the meeting. Socrates, however, will find initially that such divine possession leaves little room for dialogue.

Socrates will purify himself with a third, but this time true, "wholesome discourse" (p. 52, 243d), a "palinode" (p. 52, 243b) on love. He already acknowledges himself possessed, like a lover, by Phaedrus, who has "put a spell" on his lips (p. 51, 242e); in the third speech his style will also suggest possession by the god of love himself. (Eros is indeed a god in the *Phaedrus*, not the *daimon* he is in the *Symposium*.[20]) This rapturous, literally enthusiastic style will stand in marked contrast to the calculating rhetorical style of Lysias' speech, which is now forthrightly characterized as "pernicious rubbish" paraded "as though it were good sense because it might deceive a few miserable people and win their applause" (p. 52, 242e–243a). Love, rapturous verbal style, and possession will prove to be inseparable in the third speech, in which the state of being beside oneself will be praised. (That language itself can be the object by which a lover is possessed is suggested by the use of the term *theios* [θεῖός], divine, to describe Phaedrus' devotion to discourse [p. 51, 242a].)

It should be noted that Socrates' divine possession seems to preclude human dialogue at this point: Phaedrus, in fact, is hoping for a discussion of the first two speeches ("Let us wait and discuss what we've heard" [p. 51, 242a]). But Socrates' divine sign suggests that he can do nothing until he has made up for the second speech with a third, retracting it: "Now where is that boy I was talking to? He must listen to me once more, and not rush off to yield to his non-lover before he hears what I have to say" (p. 53, 243e). For the time being, the mode of Socrates' discourse will remain, as in the *Symposium*, oratory rather than dialogue: the god allows no argumentation. Dialogue itself will return to the *Phaedrus* eventually, with the discussion of rhetoric; but even Socrates' third speech will be in some way dialogic. It responds dialogically to Lysias' original proposition that the nonlover is to be preferred to the lover, and thus it also responds to Socrates' own preceding speech in which he extended Lysias' argument. The palinode or recantation therefore records Socrates' carnivalesque dialogue with himself as well as with his rhetorical opponent; it both exemplifies the internal self-division that characterizes love, and, by asserting Socrates' true attitude toward this self-division, corrects it.

As in the *Symposium*, love in Socrates' (or Plato's) doctrine ideally involves the pursuit of the Forms' self-sameness rather than being a matter of difference or deviation: the sight of a beautiful physical object reminds the soul of the ideal beauty of true Being, that is, of the Forms, because the soul is immortal and has beheld true Being before its present incarnation:

> Beauty it was ours to see in all its brightness in those days when, amidst that happy company, we beheld with our eyes that blessed vision . . . whole and unblemished were we that did celebrate it, untouched by the evils that awaited us in days to come; whole and unblemished likewise, free from all alloy, steadfast and blissful were the spectacles upon which we gazed in the

moment of final revelation; pure was the light that shone around us, and pure were we, without taint of that prison-house which now we are encompassed withal, and call a body, fast bound therein as an oyster in its shell. (p. 93, 250b–c)

Different souls "in those days" followed in the trains of different gods, all beholding—with a presumably incorporeal eye—the true Being of the Forms, once again in a Buberian encounter with the divine (". . . justice, its very self, and likewise temperance, and knowledge, not the knowledge that is neighbour to Becoming [*hei genesis prosestin* (ἣ γένεσις πρόσεστιν)] and varies with the various objects to which we commonly ascribe being, but the veritable knowledge of Being [*estin* (ἐστίν)] that veritably is" [p. 78, 247d–e]), and in particular of the Form of Beauty that an example of mere physical beauty will one day recall to the incarnate soul. This Beauty is pure and unalloyed, without beginning (*genesis*); that is to say, it is nothing and includes nothing but itself. The soul, too, was equally pure in those days, untainted by its future admixture with, or imprisonment in, the physical body. The physical reminder should inspire the soul to return to this state of purity and simple self-sameness: love ideally should return the lover to a state of nondivision and indifferentiation similar to that of the ideal Beauty it has beheld. As Hackforth points out, this should be true of the beloved as well as of the lover: "the good of the lover and of the beloved are one and indivisible. . . ."[21]

Understanding itself is thus based on the ideal of unity: "man must needs understand the language of the Forms, passing from a plurality of perceptions to a unity gathered together by reasoning [*logismoi sunairoumenon* (λογισμῷ ξυναιρούμενον)] . . ." (p. 86, 249b–c). But here, as in the *Symposium*, the ascent to unity can be derived only by reasoning from the plurality of sense perceptions. The body, and in particular to physical senses' perception of beauty, is the necessary starting point for the understanding and achievement of unity. The *Phaedrus*, even more than the *Symposium*, devotes the bulk of Socrates' discussion to the deviations and self-divisions involved in this process.

While the soul, for example, is immortal, it is also the "principle of movement (ἀρχὴ κινήσεως) for all bodies,"[22] which in itself suggests change in the midst of permanence: "precisely that is the essence and definition of the soul, to wit self-motion" (p. 63, 245e). This abstract reasoning occurs within a mythological context, and Socrates discusses the soul primarily in the language of myth (a point to which we shall return shortly). He suggest that physical human life is itself a deviation from the ideal state described earlier. The soul, he claims in this dialogue's most famous image, is like

> the union of powers [*symphutoi dynamei* (συμφύτῳ δυνάμει)] in a team of
> winged steeds and their winged charioteer . . . it is a pair of steeds that the
> charioteer controls; moreover one of them is noble and good, and of good
> stock, while the other has the opposite character, and his stock is opposite
> [*enantios* (ἐναντίος)]. Hence the task of our charioteer is difficult and trou-
> blesome . . . when [soul] is perfect and winged it journeys on high and
> controls the whole world; but one that has shed its wings sinks down until
> it can fasten on something solid, and settling there it takes to itself an earthly
> body which seems by reason of the soul's power to move itself. (pp. 69–70,
> 246a–c)

Plato's mythology of the soul has been the occasion of much scholarly
debate; while Hackforth, for example, suggests that the tripartite soul imagined here is the same as that discussed in Book IV of the *Republic*, composed of the "reflective," "spirited," and "appetitive" parts—presumably
the charioteer, the good steed, and the bad steed respectively—he also
points out that Plato's images "are not disguised doctrine but spring from a
non-rational intuition"[23] and that "Plato never attained to a full reconciliation of the various views expressed in the dialogues."[24] In any case, even
before its incarnation, the human soul is a composite: the charioteer must
control both a good steed and one that is opposite (*enantios*) to it. Self-
division is thus built into the basic structure of the human soul itself,
whereas divine souls are unmixed good (p. 69, 246a). Despite the opposition between the two steeds, they are also yoked together in a "union of
powers." *Symphutoi* (Συμφύτῳ) suggests a gathering or commingling: the
steeds are united, yet different, so that the soul itself is defined by self-deviation.
If the earlier speeches assumed that love is a matter of self-difference, this
one suggests that the very nature of every soul is to deviate from itself. A
further deviation occurs when the soul attaches itself to a physical body,
which is likened to a loss of perfection—though this perfection is, as we
have seen, not the perfection of self-sameness.

The process by which a soul loses its wings and is dragged down is the
context in which the immortality of the soul, mentioned above, is discussed. It is due to the "heaviness of the steed of wickedness" that the driver
is pulled down and unable to follow the gods, unless the charioteer has
"schooled him well" (p. 71, 247b). While all souls are "eager to reach the
heights and seek to follow" the gods, "they are not able"; "for all their toil-
ing they are baulked, every one, of the full vision of Being, and departing
therefrom, they feed upon the food of semblance" (p. 79, 248a–b). The
soul's inner self-division thus causes this further deviation from the ideal

through an unspecified "mischance [*syntuchiai* (συντυχία)]" that in turn causes "wrongdoing [*kakias* (κακίας)]" (p. 79, 248c). "Feed upon the food of semblance [*trophei doxastei* (τροφῇ δοξαστῇ)]" at 248b is a particularly interesting turn of phrase. *Doxa*, often translated "opinion," distinguishes this food from the absolute truth of Being. However, Hackforth's "semblance" suggests a relationship between this nourishment and the ideal: this may be understood as a representation of that, and indeed *doxa* is not necessarily false opinion; it may be true even if it does not attain the status of certain knowledge. We may understand it, then, as a deviation from the ideal rather than its opposite. In this condition, appropriately, the philosopher, in his search for true knowledge, most nearly approaches "those things a god's nearness whereunto makes him truly god"; the philosopher's soul alone, then, can "recover her wings" (p. 86, 249c), a recovery that will make the philosopher appear mad to mankind because "he is possessed by a deity" (p. 87, 249d).

It is love's madness that prepares the way for this possession. Various forms of madness are understood throughout this speech as forces external to the self: prophetic madness, for example, is to be distinguished from such forms of prophecy as reading omens because the latter is "a purely human activity of thought belonging to his own intelligence" whereas the former is properly called "manic [*maniken* (μανικὴν)]" rather than "mantic [*mantiken* (μαντικὴν)]" (p. 57, 244c). Madness thus does not belong to the individual's own intelligence, but is a gift from heaven; it is alien, but within, the outside turning up inside, to use Dollimore's terminology in a theological context. Similarly, madness can cure illness (p. 57, 244d–e) and characterizes poetic creation (p. 57, 245a). As Hackforth points out, the *Phaedrus* alone among Plato's works wholeheartedly commends poetic madness: in other dialogues (*Ion, Meno, Apology*) the difference between this sort of madness and true knowledge is condemned, but here Socrates' commendation of this madness "almost goes to the length of saying that the inspired poet is all the better for his lack of knowledge."[25] In this dialogue, in other words, inspired madness' deviation—not only from the self but even from the ideal of knowledge discussed above—is given a positive valuation.[26]

The same is true of the lover's madness. When human souls fall away from the vision of Being and are incarnated, they become various sorts of human beings, which Socrates arranges into a hierarchy according to how much they have perceived of true Being in their preincarnation state. Souls that have seen less may come to dwell in kings, statesmen, athletes, prophets, artists, farmers, demagogues, or tyrants (p. 80, 248d–e); "but the soul that has seen the most of Being shall enter into the human babe that shall grow into a seeker after wisdom or beauty [*philosophou e philokalou* (φιλοσόφου ἢ φιλοκάλου)], a follower of the Muses and a lover [*erotikou* (ἐρωτικοῦ)]" (p. 79, 248d). The lover of beauty, the lover of wisdom, and the erotic lover (*philokalou, philosophou, erotikou*) all occupy the same rung on this hierarchy of souls, and it is the highest: erotic love and philosophy are linked by the pursuit of beauty.

This point is clarified in Socrates' discussion of just how the philosopher's soul comes to regain its wings and to be liberated from the cycle of reincarnation, a discussion reminiscent of Diotima's speech in the *Symposium*. Returning to the theme of divine madness, Socrates declares that

> when he that loves beauty is touched by such madness he is called a lover. Such an one, as soon as he beholds the beauty of this world, is reminded of true Beauty, and his wings begin to grow; then is he fain to lift his wings and fly upward; yet he has not the power, but inasmuch as he gazes upward like a bird, and cares nothing for the world beneath, men charge it upon him that he is demented . . . when these discern some likeness of the things yonder, they are amazed, and no longer masters of themselves, and know not what is come upon them by reason of their perception being dim. (p. 92, 249d–250a)

This passage suggests a shortened version of the "ladder of love" speech in the *Symposium*. Here, too (though without the specific stages and transitions of the process outlined in the *Symposium*), the goal of love is a return to the divine Form of Beauty, which, as we have seen, is characterized by self-sameness. But also as in the *Symposium*, the desire and pursuit of the Form requires the perception of earthly beauty to inspire it. This beauty is not characterized by self-sameness; it is merely a "likeness" of the Form of Beauty, a deviation from it. But this physical deviation is necessary first step in the ascent to the divine unity. In fact, it appears that a certain disunity of the self, a self-difference, is also necessary: the lovers thus possessed are "no longer masters of themselves." What the earlier speeches criticizing love said of it was true, that it is a form of self-division; but the particular self-division of love is now valorized as a necessary step toward reunification.

These points are reinforced in the remainder of this third speech. The value of the erotic experience again depends upon how fully the individual soul experienced the vision of true Being at 251a:

> when one who is fresh from the mystery, and saw much of the vision, beholds a godlike face or bodily form that truly expresses beauty, first there comes upon him a shuddering and a measure of that awe which the vision inspired, and then reverence as at the sight of a god: and but for fear of being

deemed a very madman he would offer sacrifice to his beloved, as to a holy image of deity. (p. 96, 251a)

As in the *Symposium*, earthly beauty—specifically a "boy's beauty [*tou paidos kallos* (τοῦ παιδὸς κάλλος)]" (p. 96, 251c)—is not identical with the Form of Beauty, but serves as a reminder or expression of the latter to the soul who has beheld it clearly. The beloved's body is only an image, but it can be likened to a holy one; it is neither identical with or entirely different from the holy. The likeness, indeed, is close enough to inspire "awe," but only "a measure" of the awe felt before Beauty itself—almost, but not quite, enough to induce worship. This passage also links love to madness, a notion pursued in the passages immediately following.

It should be noted that Socrates is careful to distinguish this holy madness from a merely physical eroticism—whether male–male or male–female. A soul who has not beheld, or does not recall, the vision of Beauty with sufficient clarity looks at a beautiful earthly body "with no reverence, and surrendering to pleasure he essays to go after the fashion of a four-footed beast, and to beget offspring of the flesh; or consorting with wantonness he has no fear nor shame in running after unnatural [*para physin* (παρὰ φύσιν)] pleasure" (p. 96, 251a). Male–male and male–female desire seem equally unenlightened in their physical expression, though only that which occurs between males is deemed "against nature"—a judgment that will shortly be revised. Indeed, the description of the divine, spiritual madness of love that follows is couched in language that demands to be read as physical, even orgasmic: "a strange sweating and fever seizes him: for by reason of the stream [*aporroen* (ἀπορροὴν)] of beauty entering in through his eyes there comes a warmth, whereby his soul's plumage is fostered"; "the stump of the wing swells and hastens to grow from the root over the whole substance of the soul"; the soul "throbs" and feels "a ferment and painful irritation"; the soul "admits a flood of particles flowing" from the boy's beauty; when, after a separation, the soul (imagined as feminine) beholds the beloved, she "lets the flood pour in upon her, releasing the imprisoned waters; then has she refreshment and respite from her stings and sufferings, and at that moment tastes a pleasure that is sweet beyond compare" (pp. 96–97, 251b–e). While it is the divine madness of the soul being described here, the language is entirely physical and sexual: the lover's soul, imagined as feminine, is penetrated with the liquid stream or flood of beauty, causing a sensation of heat, complete with sweating and throbbing, leading to incomparable pleasure. At the same time, the sensation of painful irritation and swelling also suggest male sexual response; the soul may be "she," but it inhabits a male body, and the experience combines the physical sensations of both sexes. Despite the preceding rejection of physical erotic expression, then, Socrates can describe this purely spiritual madness only in the most graphically physical, and specifically orgasmic, terms. This experience, says Socrates, is "what men term love [*erota* (ἔρωτα)]" (p. 97, 252b).[27]

Even within the category of lovers there exists a further hierarchy based on the nature of the god the soul followed before its incarnation: each seeks for a beloved who reminds him of that god, for example, "followers of Zeus seek a beloved who is Zeus-like in soul" (p. 99, 252e). What is striking is the insistence on the fine, but essential, line between similarity and identity among the god, the lover, and the beloved: the lover lives "after the manner of the god in whose company he once was, honouring him and copying [*mimoumenos* (μιμούμενος)] him so far as may be" (p. 99, 252c–d), and "reaching out after him in memory they are possessed by him, and from him they take their ways and manners of life, in so far as a man can partake of a god" (p. 100, 253a). But "all this," adds Socrates, lovers "attribute to the beloved" (p. 100, 253a); "every lover is fain that his beloved should be of a nature like to his own god; and when he has won him, he leads him on to walk in the ways of their god, and after his likeness, patterning [*mimoumenoi* (μιμούμενοι)] himself thereupon and giving counsel and discipline to the boy" (p. 100, 253b). True *eros* is thus a matter of a three-way likeness that can never quite become identity: as Hackforth suggests, divine possession constrains the lover to "keep his gaze fixed upon the god," while "this ὁμοίωσις θεῷ is concurrent with, and indeed hardly to be distinguished from, the love of ἐραστὴς for παιδικά."[28] The lover strives to become a copy or image of the god he follows, and similarly strives to impart the same qualities to the boy he loves. Terms for similarity prevail throughout this passage, especially *mimoumenos* and *mimoumenoi*, which suggest the kind of imitation or *mimesis* that Plato finds so suspicious elsewhere in his dialogues.[29] Here it is an admirable ambition to resemble the gods; but phrases serving as reminders that such a resemblance can only ever be approximate also abound: "so far as may be," "in so far as a man can," and so on. Imitation is also deviation, and human love remains on this level of difference throughout the third speech.

Socrates returns to the image of the charioteer and the team of horses, that is, to the soul's own internal self-division, in the last section of this third speech, though now with specific reference to self-division in regard to *eros*. Lysias' speech claimed the lover lacks self-control; Socrates takes a more complex view, suggesting instead that the lover's internal self-division is precisely a division between such discipline and its absence. The good steed represents this sort of erotic self-control: "Now when the driver

beholds the person of the beloved [*to erotikon omma* (τὸ ἐρωτικὸν ὄμμα)], and causes a sensation of warmth to suffuse the whole soul, he begins to experience a tickling or pricking of desire; and the obedient steed, constrained now as always by modesty, refrains from leaping upon the beloved" (pp. 103–104, 253e–254a). *Omma* suggests not precisely a body or "person," as Hackforth has it, but an object of vision. The charioteer is characterized by desire for beauty perceived with the eye, and the good steed prevents the physical expression of this desire toward the mere physical beauty of the beloved. The opposed steed, on the other hand,

> leaps and dashes on, sorely troubling his companion and his driver, and forcing them to approach the loved one and remind him of the delights of love's commerce [*ton aphrodision kharitos* (τῶν ἀφροδισίων χάριτος)]. For a while they struggle, indignant that he should force them to a monstrous and forbidden act; but at last, finding no end to their evil plight, they yield and agree to do his bidding. And so he drives them on, and now they are quite close and behold the spectacle of the beloved flashing upon them. (p. 104, 254a–b)

Aphrodision kharitos suggests that a specifically physical, erotic pleasure is the goal toward which the bad steed urges the reluctant charioteer; oddly, the one moment of self-agreement in this passage occurs when the driver and the good steed yield to the other one, though they are forced to do so. This is the kind of possession Lysias had in mind: possession by *eros* (or Eros), an overwhelming physical desire forcing the lover to act against himself. But for Socrates, the lover is the follower of another, higher god, Zeus being his usual example, and is possessed by the vision of true Beauty, of which the *eromenos'* beauty is only a reminder. Thus, as the soul's chariot is brought closer and closer to the beloved,

> the driver's memory goes back to that form of Beauty, and he sees her once again enthroned by the side of Temperance [*sophrosunes* (σωφροσύνης)] upon her holy seat; then in awe and reverence he falls upon his back, and therewith is compelled to pull the reins so violently that he brings both steeds down on their haunches, the good one willing and unresistant, but the wanton sore against his will. (p. 104, 254b–c)

This cycle of yielding and resistance to the physical impulse represented by the bad steed continues until the latter becomes obedient to discipline. The eventual goal is this return to self-unity, now through the exercise of precisely that self-control of which Lysias declared the lover to be incapable. This discipline, far from being opposed to divine possession, can come about only because of it: it is only when the charioteer is more forcefully reminded of the true vision of Beauty—not surprisingly accompanied by Temperance or modesty (*sophrosunes*)—that he is able to discipline his physical desires. In some sense this is only a higher form of self-division: the self is unified by the very fact of divine possession, that is, by its adherence to that which stands outside the self. But this sort of chaste self-unity through self-control is Socrates' ideal for human love: as the lover passes this virtue on to the beloved, eventually the latter returns his love, and "his lover is at it were a mirror in which he beholds himself" (p. 105, 255d). Even human love is thus ideally a matter of self-sameness shared between the lover and the beloved; and when the beloved comes to experience the lover's physical desire, the good steed in his own soul provides its own self-discipline (pp. 105–106, 255e–256a). The lovers can now share "the philosophic life," and grow new wings to serve them after death (p. 106, 256b).

The narrative thrust of this myth, then, is toward the disembodied life of the soul in its philosophical pursuit of Beauty and toward self-sameness: the chaste human love between two men makes them into reflections of each other, and encourages the pursuit of union with the Forms as well.[30] The *Phaedrus* thus provides a fine example of the notion of *askēsis*, the creation of a unique and beautiful self through discipline, that has been taken up by such recent historians of philosophy as Foucault, Halperin, and Nehamas, and that was discussed in chapter 2. At this point we need note only that the very concept of *askēsis* requires deviance from self-sameness: some deviant aspect of the self must exist in order to be disciplined.

But Socrates, remarkably, concludes his speech with an emphatic passage on lovers who may not meet this ideal.

> But if they turn to a way of life more ignoble and unphilosophic, yet covetous of honour, then mayhap in a careless hour, or when the wine is flowing, the wanton horses in their two souls will catch them off their guard, bring the pair together, and choosing that part which the multitude account blissful achieve their full desire. And this once done, they continue therein, albeit but rarely, seeing that their minds are not wholly set thereupon. (p. 106, 256c)

As Hackforth points out, since one steed is labeled as evil from the start, "Plato has . . . cut himself off from the conception of a real harmony or equilibrium in the soul."[31] The possibility of self-division remains potent even in the lives of lovers who seem to have achieved philosophical unity. The physical expression of *eros* follows from this ongoing self-division, and exacerbates it: these lovers' minds will not be "wholly set" upon this form of love, but neither can they return to a purely spiritual love. But this physical, self-deviating love, surprisingly, is not exactly condemned:

> Such a pair as this also are dear friends [*philo* (φίλω)], but no so dear as that other pair, one to another, both in the time of their love [*erotos* (ἔρωτος)] and when love is past; for they feel that they have exchanged the most binding pledges, which it were a sin to break by becoming enemies. When death comes they quit the body wingless indeed, yet eager to be winged, and therefore they carry off no mean reward for their lovers' madness: for it is ordained that all such as have taken the first steps on the celestial highway shall no more return to the dark pathways beneath the earth, but shall walk together in a life of shining bliss, and be furnished in due time with like plumage [*homopterous* (ὁμοπτέρους)] the one to the other, because of their love. (p. 106, 256c–d)

The physically erotic relationship described here is a deviation from, and inferior to, the ideally spiritual relationship described earlier: it is less noble and less philosophical, and results in a friendship less dear than the other. Nevertheless, this is no more than a deviation: these lovers are not condemned, and indeed Socrates goes out of his way to make excuses for them. They are instead highly praised and even understood as being rewarded after death because they will have taken the first steps on the ideal path. Indeed, they are allowed a certain leeway from perfect self-discipline precisely because they have embarked on the path of *askēsis*. We may thus find in this deviant love a family resemblance or kinship with the ideal form. Here as in the *Symposium*, the physical expression of love for an individual body is the first step toward the truth, but in the *Phaedrus* Plato allows Socrates to go well beyond the other dialogue's tolerance of the physical: here Socrates suggests that the physical expression of male–male eroticism has the gods' blessing and reward. An aspect of this reward appears to be the ability to remain together after death, and ultimately to be rewarded by being "winged alike (*homopterous*)." While these souls may deviate from the ideal love, in the long run they will not deviate from each other, and can thus achieve their own degree of likeness, if only within their own relationship. *Askēsis*, as we saw in chapter 2, may involve erotic freedom as well as abstention.[32]

Socrates chooses to conclude the main portion of his "true" speech with this lengthy encomium on male–male lovers/friends (*philia* and *eros* seem indistinguishable in this passage) who fulfill their erotic desires physically. All that remains is a summary in favor of the lover as opposed to the nonlover, addressed first to Phaedrus and then to the God of Love (p. 110, 256e–257a). In expressing the hope that Phaedrus has learned to "live for

Love in singleness of purpose with the aid of philosophical discourse"
(p. 110, 257b), Socrates once again—in a move familiar from the dialogues
already discussed—sets himself up as his interlocutor's pedagogue, and thus
to some extent as his *erastes*. This matter will reappear at the end of the
dialogue as a whole.

Socrates also emphasizes that he has now recanted and atoned for his
earlier, false speech, blaming Lysias for it (p. 110, 257b). It should be
noted, however, that in terms of the dialogue's overall structure, here as in
the *Symposium* the false speeches came first, and that the terms set in those
earlier speeches continue to drive the final, true one. In particular, the
notions that the lover is possessed by a divine madness and that he is
divided against himself, crucial to Socrates' true doctrine, are derived from
the preceding speeches. The first two speeches are thus doctrinally deviations from (not opposed to) the truth expressed in the third—and structurally, the true speech is a deviation from the first two. Both love itself and
the doctrine of love being pursued discursively are thus matters of deviance
for Socrates, rather than of identity or opposition. They are also matters
of dialogue, both between Socrates and Lysias, and between Socrates and
himself.

Discourse itself, in fact, is understood as a form of self-deviance, or
possession by an Other, throughout Socrates' speeches. He attributes his
own first speech to Phaedrus both before he begins it, blaming the latter for
having discovered "the means of compelling a lover of discourse to do your
bidding" (p. 35, 236e), and after he has completed it, when introducing his
second, true speech: ". . . whereas the preceding discourse was by Phaedrus,
son of Pythocles, of Myrrinous, that which I shall now pronounce is
by Stesichorus, son of Euphemus, of Himera" (p. 56, 243e–244a). Here
Socrates disclaims responsibility for the second speech as well, as he
becomes more and more possessed. Discourse itself is, like love, a matter of
self-deviation: words both are and are not his own even as he utters them.
In fact, Socrates claims that his words, even in his second, true speech, deviate from the reality they are attempting to capture. Speaking of the soul, he
suggests that "what manner of thing it is would be a long tale to tell; but
what it resembles, that a man might tell in briefer compass: let this therefore be our manner of discourse" (p. 69, 246a).[33] This passage leads directly
into the metaphor of the charioteer and his two horses, the dominant
image for the remainder of the speech. Socrates emphasizes, in other words,
that language itself is only an approximation of reality, a matter of resem-
blances rather than of the Being he tries to describe. Language is akin to
reality or, we might say, a deviation from it. Andrea Wilson Nightingale
suggests that Socrates in his second speech "yields to the discourse of lyric

love poetry in fundamental ways";[34] thus, at the levels both of style and of philosophy, "reason and madness, at a certain level, converge."[35] The poetic style invoked by Socrates throughout his two speeches is a sign of philosophical deviance.

Discourse and love resemble each other, then, and it is therefore natural for the speeches on love to lead into a direct discussion of rhetoric and specifically of speech and writing. As we have seen, Plato is careful to have Socrates link language to *eros* throughout the speeches on love, and even in the first half of the *Phaedrus* the similarities have to do with the relation of each to the self. If love in its different forms can be imagined both as, ideally, self-presence and, in terms of physical human love, self-deviation, the same may be said of writing. In their banter about Lysias' speech, Socrates teasingly suggests that, because Phaedrus is carrying a written copy of the speech, Lysias himself is fully present: ". . . you must first show me what it is that you have in your left hand under your cloak; for I surmise that it is the actual discourse. If that is so, let me assure you of this, that much as I love you I am not altogether inclined to let you practise your oratory on me when Lysias himself is here present" (p. 23, 228d–e). Lysias' writing appears to be identical with Lysias himself, whereas Phaedrus' own attempt to reproduce the written discourse in spoken language would fail to reproduce Lysias himself as faithfully as the written record can. Although Socrates loves Phaedrus, he loves the accuracy provided by his self-presence more. The tone here is teasing and humorous, but it introduces a serious subject—the relationship between language and presence or self-identity—that returns, in more complicated form, in the second half of the dialogue.

Like love, language for Socrates has as its purpose the pursuit and transmission of a truth that is singular and whole; he asks, "does not a good and successful discourse presuppose a knowledge in the mind of the speaker of the truth [*alethes* (ἀληθὲς)] about his subject?" (p. 119, 259e). As love is a matter of educating the beloved about the nature of divine reality, so language is a matter of educating the listener (or reader) about the true nature of its subject. And this can be accomplished only with a knowledge of the individual souls to be persuaded of this truth. Rhetoricians like Lysias who seek persuasion in itself without regard to truth, possess "no art, but a knack that has nothing to do with art" (p. 120, 260e).

Rhetoric, in fact, manipulates similarity and difference with regard to truth, and, in thus pursuing deviations from the truth, is all the more dangerous than an outright opposition.

> *Soc.* . . . Are we misled when the difference between two things is wide, or narrow?

Ph. When it is narrow.

Soc. Well then, if you shift your ground little by little, you are more likely to pass undetected from so-and-so to its opposite than if you do so at one bound.

Ph. Of course.

Soc. It follows that anyone who intends to mislead another, without being misled himself, must discern precisely the degree of resemblance and dissimilarity between this and that.

Rhetoric involves a gradual deviation from the truth rather than the acknowledgment of absolute sameness or difference. The skilled rhetorician must know the truth of his subject matter, but if he is indifferent to this knowledge he may lead his audience through a series of "narrow," erroneous deviations to a conclusion opposite to what he knows to be the truth.

Socrates, on the other hand, proposes a dialectical use of language in which similarity and difference can be marshaled in the service of truth, the complementary methods of collection and division:

> The first is that in which we bring a dispersed plurality under a single form, seeing it all together: the purpose being to define [*orizomenos* (ὁριζόμενος)] so-and-so, and thus to make plain whatever may be chosen as the topic for exposition. For example, take the definition given just now of love: whether it was right or wrong, at all events it was that which enabled our discourse to achieve lucidity and consistency. (p. 132, 265d)

Collection, or as Socrates calls it here, definition or defining, unifies apparently disparate things in a single category that allows clarity and discussion; it is what makes the discourse possible, and, given its emphasis on union and similarity, it is not surprising to find Socrates extolling it as a logical method. It is worth mentioning, however, that *orizomenos* and its cognates also imply a marking-off of boundaries: definition not only brings similar things together, it also marks them off from what is different. Differentiation, or division, in fact, is an even more important aspect of Socrates' dialectical method: once similar things have been collected together, they must also be distinguished. This second aspect is one

> whereby we are enabled to divide into forms, following the objective articulation; . . . take example from our two recent speeches. The single general form which they postulated was irrationality; . . . they conceived of madness as a single objective form existing in human beings: wherefore the first speech divided off a part on the left, and continued to make divisions, never desisting until it discovered one particular part bearing the name of

> "sinister" love. . . . The other speech conducted us to the forms of madness
> which lay on the right-hand side . . . (p. 133, 265e–266a)

As Hackforth points out,[36] and as we have already seen, this is not what
the two speeches in question actually do with regard to madness: Socrates
here offers a reinterpretation of his speeches designed not so much to elu-
cidate them as to illustrate his new dialectical method. In that sense, the
discussion of rhetoric is yet another deviation within the original discussion
of love. More attention is devoted to the explanation of division than to the
preceding discussion of collection, with the result that dialectic itself comes
to seem a matter of differentiation or, indeed, of deviation: this logical
method, or style, entails the understanding of divisions within the same
general category in order to arrive at its essential truth—just as love in the
preceding speech entails the lover's understanding, and control, of his own
internal self-divisions in order to arrive at its ideal form. Love and language,
used and understood correctly, share a common structure.

Socrates once again acknowledges this relationship when he declares
that "I am myself a lover [*erastes* (ἐραστής)] of these divisions and collec-
tions, that I may gain the power to speak and to think; and whenever
I deem another man able to discern an objective unity and plurality, I follow 'in his footsteps where he leadeth as a god' " (p. 134, 266b). Dialectic,
like love, allows a glimpse of the ultimate, divine Being, and, like love, is a
matter of the relations between sameness and difference, unity and plurality. Also like love, dialectic inspires Socrates to a flight of poetry:[37] the shift
in style again signifies the presence of the divine.[38]

In both cases, we must remember, the goal is to transcend deviation and
difference in order to arrive at a singular truth, and it is the traditional
rhetorician's indifference to truth that makes rhetoric a mere knack rather
than an art. Rhetoric, in fact, to be a genuine art would have to involve not
only the knowledge of the truth of its subject-matter, but also the knowledge of the truth of the listener's soul—indeed, of all listeners' souls,
since different types of soul would require different types of persuasion
toward the truth (p. 148, 271c–272b). And these truths are accessible only
through the dialectical method, not through traditional rhetoric itself.[39]
Without them, rhetoric is merely deviation without a goal, and the orator,
as Phaedrus initially suggests, need not "know what is truly good or noble,
but what will be thought so; since it is on the latter, not the former, that
persuasion depends" (p. 119, 260a); if such a method happens upon the
truth, it will do so only by accident, rhetoric in itself being strictly indifferent to truth or falsehood. Dialectic, specifically in its subdivisions of collection and division, is the only corrective to rhetorical deviations from the

truth, especially the truth of such "disputed terms" as "love"—a point that Socrates' own two speeches demonstrates, as Phaedrus points out (p. 127, 263c).

If rhetoric without the support of dialectic deviates from the path to truth, writing—despite Socrates' earlier mocking identification of Lysias' writing with Lysias' himself—is a particular deviation from the true self, as Socrates suggests in the famous myth of Theuth and Ammon. Theuth claims that his invention of writing will improve human memory, but Ammon thinks otherwise:

> If men learn this, it will implant forgetfulness in their souls [*psychais* (ψυχαῖς)]: they will cease to exercise memory because they rely on that which is written, calling things to remembrance no longer from within themselves [*endothen autous* (ἔνδοθεν αὐτούς)], but by means of external marks; what you have discovered is a recipe not for memory [*mnemes* (μνήμης)], but for reminder [*hypomneseos* (ὑπομνήσεως)]. And it is not true wisdom that you offer your disciples, but only its semblance [*doxan* (δόξαν)]; for by telling them of many things without teaching them you will make them seem to know much, while for the most part they know nothing; and as men filled, not with wisdom, but with the conceit of wisdom, they will be a burden to their fellows. (p. 157, 275a–b)

The main distinction here is between the inner self, associated with truth and wisdom, and the external marks of writing, associated with semblance and conceit. Writing offers a form of what appears to be memory, but is in actuality the death of memory, and hence the death of wisdom. In fact, one might go even further: memory is associated here with the true selves, with souls (*psychais*) and an inner (*endothen*) life, while writing in its externality can only diminish the inner self or soul. Writing is the death of memory, knowledge, wisdom, and ultimately of the self.[40] The language of semblance (*doxa*) further implies that writing is so dangerous because it bears a resemblance to memory—it may not be memory, but it is a "reminder [*hypomneseos*]." This is to say that writing, like the physical love described in the earlier speeches, and also like rhetoric unguided by dialectic, is so dangerous not because it opposes truth, but because, bearing a family resemblance, it deviates from truth. Like love, writing is a matter of deviation from the self.

It is also, like physical human love, a deviation from truth:

> And once a thing is put in writing, the composition, whatever it may be, drifts [*kulindeitai* (κυλινδεῖται)] all over the place, getting into the hands not only of those who understand it, but equally of those who have no business

with it; it doesn't know how to address the right people, and not address the wrong. And when it is ill-treated and unfairly abused it always needs its parent to come to its help, being unable to help or defend itself. (p. 158, 275d–e)

Kulindeitai is a passive construction, and some translators translate the phrase as "is bandied about,"[41] but Hackforth's "drifts all over the place" retains the original sense of physically rolling from place to place. This sort of physical dislocation imagines the dissemination of a written text as a spatial deviation from a straight and narrow path similar to the deviation in which Socrates and Phaedrus are engaged, but here this dislocation is given a negative valuation: writing cannot consider its audience (a failing similar to that of the rhetoricians or orators who do not know their auditors' souls), and therefore risks constant misunderstandings that can be corrected only by the father, or author, in person. The model Plato assumes here is one in which the author's true intentions are ideally communicated intact to the audience; writing, because it is detachable from the author's intentions, is inherently subject to deviation from its own truth.

The alternative is spoken language in which both speaker and listener are present, "no dead discourse, but the living speech, to original of which the written discourse may fairly be called a kind of image," as Phaedrus puts it. This kind of discourse "is written in the soul of the learner"; it "can defend itself, and knows to whom it should speak and to whom it should say nothing" (p. 159, 276a). True discourse is thus based neither on writing nor even, as Kenneth M. Sayre points out,[42] on oratory or other univocal uses of language, "the recreation [*paizein* (παίζειν)] that a man finds in words, when he discourses about justice and the other topics you speak of" (p. 160, 276e), as Phaedrus refers to univocal speech. This kind of "recreation" (*paizein*) is comparatively harmless, but Socrates goes on to discuss a better use of language:

> But far more excellent [*kallion* (καλλίων)], I think, is the serious [*spoude* (σπουδή)] treatment of them, which employs the art of dialectic. The dialectician selects a soul of the right type, and in it he plants and sows his words founded on knowledge, words which can defend both themselves and him who planted them, words which instead of remaining barren contain a seed whence new words grow up in new characters; whereby the seed is vouchsafed immortality, and its possessor the fullest measure of blessedness that man can attain unto. (p. 160, 276e–277a)

This dialectical form of discourse is explicitly contrasted with the merely recreational, univocal discourse just praised by Phaedrus; it is "more excellent [*kallion*]" because it is "serious [*spoude*]." And this excellent, serious form of discourse is based on a dialogical and pedagogical model of teacher and student (again suggestive of Buber): the pedagogical dialogue, in which the teacher can defend his discourse directly in the face of a worthy student's response, alone allows the teacher's knowledge to take root in another soul and thus gain immortality.[43]

It is, perhaps, for this reason that speeches give way to dialogue in the last portion of the *Phaedrus*: the text's developing form illustrates Socrates' reorientation of Phaedrus away from rhetoric and oratory and toward participation in dialogue. As we have seen, Phaedrus makes a number of the most important points to be either challenged or developed by Socrates in their discussion of language. The "blessedness" attained in this dialogical relationship is similar, if not identical, to that gained by the ideal lovers of Socrates' second speech, and the pedagogical model represented here is that found in the ideal Platonic version of ancient Athenian pederasty: language in its highest form is the pedagogical dialogue of male lovers.[44] The right use of love cannot be separated from the right use of language.

Discourse thus turns out to operate on the same principles as erotics: writing deviates from the ideal discourse, which is written only metaphorically, "in the soul of the learner" (p. 159, 286a), just as physical eroticism deviates from the ideal desire, or desire for the ideal. And both discourse and erotics are imagined specifically as transformational modes of relationality: Socrates finds writing wanting because it cannot respond to the reader, whereas speech is ideally dialogical in form and effect. In fact, proper rhetoric transforms the soul of the interlocutor (the speaker must have "discernment of the nature of the soul" and "discover the type of speech appropriate to each nature, and order and arrange your discourse accordingly" [p. 161, 277b–c]) just as proper love transforms the beloved, the lover "creating in him the closest possible likeness to the god they worship" (p. 100, 253a). And neither written language nor, as we have seen, physical eroticism is entirely rejected; both have a place in the philosopher's value system, though a subordinate one. Discourse and love, indeed, are two manifestations of the same thing, different but closely related forms of male–male desire.

The *Phaedrus* as a whole, in fact, concludes with the eroticization of philosophical discourse. When Socrates suggests that Phaedrus now teach Lysias the lessons he has learned (p. 165, 278b–d), Phaedrus replies that Socrates too has a friend who might benefit from them: "*Soc.* Then that is what you must tell your friend [*hetairoi* (ἑταίρῳ)]. *Ph.* But what about yourself? What are you going to do? You too have a friend [*hetairon* (ἑταῖρον)] who should not be passed over. *Soc.* What friend? *Ph.* The fair [*ton kalon* (τὸν καλόν)] Isocrates" (p. 166, 278e). The various forms of the masculine noun *hetairos* (unlike the more familiar feminine *hetaira*) suggest companionship or comradeship without any erotic undertone, though Phaedrus' reference to the orator Isocrates as *ton kalon*, "the beautiful," may imply that he is an object of Socrates' erotic/philosophical pursuit. Socrates' message to Isocrates is a prophecy that he will transcend mere rhetoric and eventually become a philosopher (p. 166, 279a): "Well, then, there's the report I convey from the gods of this place to Isocrates my beloved [*emois paidikois* (ἐμοῖς παιδικοῖς)], and there's yours for your beloved Lysias [*sois Lysiai* (σοῖς Λυςίᾳ)]" (p. 166, 279b). Comradeship shifts to love with the reference to Isocrates as the *paidika*, a beloved boy or "darling."[45] The entire discussion of rhetoric, if not the dialogue as a whole, appears in these final passages as a love-letter to Isocrates in which Socrates sets himself up, once again, as the ideal *erastes*, concerned with the education of his beloved. The discussion of rhetoric, then, returns us to the original theme of male–male desire, with a demonstration of their inextricable connection.[46]

And just as the physical expression of male–male erotic desire was found to have its place even in the more ideal, spiritual love that Socrates recommended earlier, so too do the comparatively debased forms of discourse find a place within the his ideal use of language. Writing and rhetoric, while mere recreational deviations from the ideal, are not necessarily evil. The philosopher, suggests Socrates,

> will sow his seed in literary gardens [*grammasi kepous* (γράμμασι κήπους)], I take it, and write when he does write by way of pastime, collecting a store of refreshment both for his own memory, against the day "when age oblivious comes", and for all such as tread in his footsteps; and he will take pleasure in watching the tender plants grow up. (p. 159, 276d)

Phaedrus agrees that this is an excellent pastime (p. 159, 276e), and the reader should presumably agree as well—especially since what he is reading (and the reader is undoubtedly understood as male) is Plato's own written text: both the philosopher himself and future students "who tread in his footsteps" may reap the benefits of these "literary gardens"—"literary" in the sense of "composed of letters (*grammasi*)" or "written." Sayre, drawing on Plato's *Seventh Letter* and *Theaetetus* as well as the *Phaedrus*, has suggested that Plato's dialogues are precisely an attempt to reproduce in the reader the same effect that an oral, face-to-face encounter might produce.[47]

Writing, as a physical deviation from a spiritual ideal, is thus parallel in the realm of discourse to the physical expression of love discussed at the end of Socrates' second speech. Both fail to achieve the ideal form, whether of love or of language, but both may also be of considerable value in themselves. Both are deviant, but also, and simultaneously, valued expressions of the pedagogical impulse that for ancient Athenians defined the ideal of male–male desire. Love between men, expressed physically, finds its image in the act of writing. If Sayre is correct, then, Plato's writing may be understood as establishing an erotic relation between himself and future readers, similar to the one Socrates imagines between himself and Isocrates at the end of the *Phaedrus*: if the lessons of the *Phaedrus* are a love letter to be conveyed to the absent Isocrates, then *Phaedrus* as a text must itself be considered Plato's love letter to his future readers.

Like the *Symposium*, a dialogue with which it has been associated since antiquity, the *Phaedrus* has exerted a profound influence on the history of both philosophy and literature. Plutarch's *Dialogue on Love*, discussed in chapter 2, for example, refers to the *Phaedrus* at least as often as it does to the *Symposium*.[48] And certainly the *Phaedrus*' themes of self-division and of the relationship of love to language are taken up by later authors. As we have seen, discourse is explicitly related to male–male desire by Alan of Lille, for one example, whose dialogue *The Complaint of Nature* makes an argument opposed to Plato's: for Alan, male–male desire cannot be related to proper discourse at all, but disrupts it, as same-sex desire cannot be properly spoken. But in the remainder of this chapter, for the reasons cited earlier, I wish to focus specifically on the *Phaedrus*' afterlife in the modern world, in literary texts that explicitly function as responses of one sort or another to the *Phaedrus* by exploring both this desire–language relationship and the crisis of subjectivity in which the subject deviates from himself.

In the wake of the seventeenth- and eighteenth-century libertines, as well as that of the Enlightenment, the Romantic period, and indeed the nineteenth century generally, witnessed a continued fascination with male–male desire. Under the influence of Winckelmann and Goethe, writers of this period also continued to link it to ancient Greece and specifically to Plato,[49] though such links were less often expressed in dialogue form than they had been in earlier periods.[50] In England, Percy Bysshe Shelley translated the *Symposium* in 1818[51] and appended to it "A Discourse on the Manners of the Antient Greeks Relative to the Subject of Love," an essay in which Shelley's awareness of cultural and historical differences result in a defense of "Greek love" among the ancients, though not among his own contemporaries.[52] But despite this ongoing cultural fascination, sodomy, including the physical expression of male–male desire, not only remained illegal in early nineteenth-century England, but was technically a capital offense.[53] Shelley's accurate translation thus remained unpublished until after his death, when it was printed in a heavily bowdlerized edition.[54]

Otherwise, according to Louis Crompton, "Plato was little read,"[55] and available translations altered the texts so as to disguise their references to male–male eroticism.[56] "Scholars writing on the history of Greek studies have noted the almost total disappearance of Plato from the British educational curriculum in this period and have generally ascribed his eclipse to the new philosophical predominance of Locke."[57]

In the later nineteenth century, however, the sodomy laws were revised: in the "Offense Against the Person Act" of 1861, "the abominable crime of buggery" is punishable by penal servitude rather than death;[58] the later nineteenth century also witnessed the early sexologists' attempts—undoubtedly naïve but nevertheless progressive—to understand same-sex desire scientifically. In Germany, Karl Heinrich Ulrichs was publishing his biological "third-sex" theory of male–male and female–female love beginning in the 1860s, followed by Richard von Krafft-Ebing's *Psychopathia sexualis* in 1886 and eventually Magnus Hirschfeld's *Sappho and Socrates* in 1896, all proposing to one degree or another a medical or psychiatric rather than a moral or religious model of sexuality.[59] In England, "Greek love" also found a defense in various late Victorian cultural critiques, whether in comparisons of European attitudes with those of other cultures, like Sir Richard Burton's "Terminal Essay" to his 1885 translation of *The Thousand Nights and a Night*, or in comparisons of modern and premodern European values, especially ancient Greek, by Edward Carpenter, John Addington Symonds, Walter Pater, and others.[60] And in Victorian Oxford, Plato had become central to the "Greats" curriculum. It was there in the 1860s, under the influence of Benjamin Jowett, that the *Phaedrus* and the *Symposium*, along with Plato's *Republic*, exerted a decisive influence on modern literature and, in the case of the two former dialogues, on the modern world's perception of male–male desire. This influence has been most clearly documented by Linda Dowling in her remarkable book, *Hellenism and Homosexuality in Victorian Oxford*, which traces the process by which university education was secularized, and by which Plato and his main proponent, Jowett, became associated with this secularization.[61] Jowett's students, such as Walter Pater and John Addington Symonds, found in Plato's dialogues a "Socratic eros . . . essential to the survival of liberal England" because "at the highest level of masculine love [in the *Symposium*], men who love men are procreating *ideas* . . . especially that kind of wisdom 'which governs the ordering of society.' "[62] Further, Dowling notes, the perceived civic usefulness of this "Socratic eros" was immediately linked to the potential liberation of erotic bonds between modern men: "it is precisely here that the reformed institutions of Oxford homosociality—that reciprocal network or system of bonds facilitating the interchange of masculine affection, interest, advantage, and obligation—will become in the same moment available to such apologists of male love as Symonds and Pater."[63] What Dowling calls "the counterdiscourse of a legitimate male love"— which we might also term the emerging modern concept of homosexuality— took its late Victorian impetus from Plato's dialogues as understood by Jowett's students.

Oscar Wilde's career gave this counterdiscourse concrete form, both in his life and in his writings. As Dowling suggests,

> the conventions of Greek life—*paiderastia, symposia, dialektike*—would assume the status of lived categories for Wilde, ostentatiously flourished by him on the level of public presentation as a sign of his high Hellenic culture and Oxford credentials, yet simultaneously experienced by him on the level of ordinary existence as elements scarcely more remarkable than air or wine.[64]

We may find signs of the Socratic *askēsis* in this vision of a life stylized into a work of art,[65] though for Wilde, as we shall see, the emphasis is to be placed on the beauty of "sin" itself rather than on a Platonic abstinence from it. It was, however, the Socratic *eros* in its idealized, nonphysical manifestation that Wilde famously called upon in his own defense when he was on trial for sodomy for the first time, in 1895: " 'The love that dare not speak its name' in this century is such a great affection of an elder for a younger man as there was between David and Jonathan, such as Plato made the very basis of his philosophy, and such as you find in the sonnets of Michelangelo and Shakespeare. It is that deep, spiritual affection that is as pure as it is perfect. . . ."[66] Wilde here cites the Biblical friendship of David and Jonathan (from I Samuel) and Renaissance poetry as well as, in a general way, Plato, to outline a form of male–male desire that, he implies, underwrites much of western culture, Judeo-Christian as well as pagan. This idealizing conflation of the two traditions had also been an aspect of the centralization of Plato's place in the university curriculum in the 1860s,[67] and Wilde himself had taken up the subject of both Shakespeare's and Michelangelo's supposed spiritual passions for younger men in "The Portrait of Mr. W. H." (1889).[68]

Wilde appears to have seen himself, and to have been seen, as a Socratic figure. Max Beerbohm wrote that "[i]f he had lived in the days of Socrates, he would surely have been impeached on a charge not only 'of making the worse cause appear the better' . . . but also of 'corrupting the youth.' "[69] Wilde himself compared his fate to Socrates' in a conversation with Frank Harris.[70]

But another famous moment in one of Wilde's trials suggests a more specific, and more physical, Platonic/Socratic influence. Originally, before the two sodomy trials, Wilde himself was suing Lord Alfred Douglas's father, the Marquess of Queensberry, for libel, Queensberry having notoriously addressed his card "To Oscar Wilde posing Somdomite,"[71] referring to Wilde's relationship with his son. Wilde's attorney, anticipating the defense's most potent piece of evidence, read out in court a letter Wilde had written to Douglas in 1893: "My Own Boy, Your sonnet is quite lovely, and it is a marvel that those red rose-leaf lips of yours should have been made no less for music of song than for madness of kisses. Your slim gilt soul walks between passion and poetry. I know Hyacinthus, whom Apollo loved so madly, was you in Greek days. . . ."[72] The salutation, given the following references to ancient Greece, implies the Athenian pederastic ideal. More specifically, the association of love and madness twice in three sentences, including one association of love and madness with the gods of ancient Greece, suggests that the influence of the *Phaedrus*, with its doctrine of love as divine madness or possession, underlies this passage. So does the simultaneous attribution of both love and poetic inspiration to these divinities, recalling the types of divine madness adumbrated at the beginning of Socrates' second speech (244a–245c) as well as Socrates' repeated claims that divine inspiration underlies his own poetic style. For Wilde, his relationship with Douglas was apparently mediated by his Oxford experience of Plato's *Phaedrus*—perhaps not surprisingly, given the *Phaedrus*' comparatively tolerant attitude toward the physical aspect of male–male erotics. And, for both Wilde's and Queensberry's attorneys, as well as for Wilde himself, this relationship was a matter of style: for Wilde's, the letter was not to be understood as evidence of sodomy because "Mr. Wilde is a poet, and the letter is considered by him as a prose sonnet,"[73] whereas for Queensberry's, the style of the letter was itself incriminating:

> "Was that the ordinary way in which you carried on your correspondence?"
> "No. But I have often written to Lord Alfred Douglas, though I never wrote to another young man in the same way."
> "Have you often written letters in the same style as this?"
> "I don't repeat myself in style."[74]

The style, for Queensberry's attorney, is not "ordinary," and suggests, as perhaps it might to a modern reader, a homoerotic relationship between the specific writer and reader of this letter. Wilde is proud of his stylistic abilities and innovations, of his refusal to repeat himself stylistically, and implies that, like Socrates' ideal orator, he chooses a unique style to appeal to each correspondent, or at least to this one. But, as writing, this letter, unlike the speech delivered at the later trial, has gotten out of its "parent's" interpretative control, just as Socrates warned in his discourse on rhetoric. (It had become public in the first place because it had been stolen in an attempt to blackmail Wilde.[75]) The association of Greece and pederasty may have seemed damning enough, but the style of the letter might itself also speak differently to different readers, and what it spoke of might be male–male erotics—or what, by the trial's date, could have been known to some as "homosexuality."[76] As in the *Phaedrus*, a rapturous poetic style is a sign of divine, male–male erotic possession.

Why might a discussion of aesthetics and style in the 1890s be linked to male–male love as described in the *Phaedrus*? Beyond the mere fact that Plato does link style and erotics—perhaps a sufficient cause in itself— a number of recent critics have taken up the question of aestheticism and its relationship to the emergence of a homosexual identity in Wilde's works. Alan Sinfield in particular has suggested that Wilde's writing deployed various elements of one potential homosexual identity, and that the public perception of Wilde himself, after his trials and conviction for sodomy, consolidated these elements into the figure of the modern homosexual:

> Wilde appeared, suddenly but ineluctably, as one who consorted with male prostitutes. Yet he was still the effeminate dandy. So the two figures coalesced. At this point, dandyism forfeited the protection from same-sex imputations that the image of general dissoluteness had afforded. The leisure-class man, not the insignificant molly, was the sodomite. Indeed, as the sexologists were saying, he was a more specific figure than the sodomite—the homosexual.[77]

Among the elements that were about to cohere into a homosexual identity and that Sinfield finds in Wilde's works are thus leisure, effeminacy, decadence, and aestheticism. Among Wilde's writings, Sinfield is concerned primarily with *The Picture of Dorian Gray*: ". . . it is not necessary for Wilde to make any of his characters homosexual. . . . In the nexus of aestheticism, decadence and leisure, as Wilde received it, that is an optional extra. In *Dorian Gray* no one exactly meets the bill—though, as I will argue in a moment, the whole book is pervaded with queerness."[78] I would make a similar argument with regard to "The Critic as Artist" in particular.

The history of this move through ancient Greece, aestheticism, and effeminacy toward the figure of the modern homosexual has also been associated with Walter Pater, a major influence on Wilde's dialogues, especially his famous conclusion to *The Renaissance*. That text all but overtly associates a decadent aestheticism—that is, one in which aesthetics takes precedence over conventional morality—with homosexuality: "While all melts under our feet, we may well grasp at any exquisite passion, or any contribution to knowledge that seems by a lifted horizon to set the spirit free for a moment, or any stirring of the senses, strange dyes, strange colours, and curious odours, or work of the artist's hands, or the face of one's friend."[79] Pater omitted this conclusion from the second edition of *The Renaissance* "as I conceived it might possibly mislead some of those young men into whose hands it might fall."[80] Indeed, according to a recent critic, "[t]he association between 'aestheticism' and homosexuality at the end of the nineteenth century is pervasive."[81] As for effeminacy, according to another critic, in Pater's "aesthetic minoritizing discourse, 'effeminacy' is untied from its moorings in the traditional moral-political ideology of civic masculinity. 'Effeminacy' shifts valence from a negative sign of deficient manhood to a positive sign of perfect masculinity as gender deviance moves into sexual dissidence."[82] And the conduits for this association were precisely such late-Victorian followers of Jowett's Platonism as Pater. As Linda Dowling points out,

> Pater had made a celebrated career out of simultaneously uncovering and reveiling the homoerotic text within the cultural ideal of Victorian liberalism. Driven by scandal and satire at Oxford into a self-protective posture of covert resistance, [he] had had to begin again, in the beautiful, laborious historical fiction of *Marius the Epicurean* (1885), to attempt to vindicate himself and express the case for the cultural power of male love through all the elegant indirections of aesthetic humanism. Yet as this late story and some of his scattered remarks in the collected Oxford lectures known as *Plato and Platonism* (1893) repeatedly suggest, Pater never ceased to realize that the danger to homoerotic Hellenism might in fact come not from the predictably uncomprehending barbarians alone, but also from the Greeks themselves: Socrates' teaching had been corrupted by Alcibiades, his own had been mistaken by Wilde.[83]

Aestheticism and aesthetic, or aestheticist, style, along with effeminacy, thus provide, for the late Victorians, a direct, if hidden, link between Plato and the emerging modern homosexual identity, in particular a link between the Socratic *askēsis* and the stylized aestheticism of late Victorian homosexuality.

The aestheticist style also finds expression in Wilde's dialogues "The Decay of Lying" and "The Critic as Artist," which had been published in 1889 and 1890, respectively, and were both reprinted in his book *Intentions* in 1891. The former draws explicitly on Plato's *Republic*, Book X, for the notion that "[l]ying and poetry are arts—arts, as Plato saw, not unconnected with each other" (p. 218).[84] It also concerns itself with style, and its main speaker, Vivian, enunciates the paradoxical Wildean position that "Life imitates Art far more than Art imitates Life" (p. 239) and that "[t]ruth is entirely and absolutely a matter of style" (p. 227).

For our purposes, however, the most important expression of what we may now term Wilde's "homosexual style" is "The Critic as Artist," for it is in this dialogue—or pair of dialogues, Parts I and II—that Wilde refers most specifically to the *Phaedrus*. The two interlocutors are not a man and an adolescent youth like Socrates and Phaedrus (or Wilde and Douglas, as Wilde saw them), but two men of apparently equal age and leisured status, Gilbert and Ernest, though Gilbert takes the lead as Wilde's spokesman. Over books, drinks, music, dinner, and cigarettes, the two fall into a discussion of the importance of criticism, which Gilbert defends as an art in itself, independent, or nearly so, of the objects it criticizes. (In discussing the highest, most independent form of criticism, Gilbert comes close to defining what we might term "critical theory.") Erotic relations between men are nowhere mentioned in this dialogue, but we would not be wrong, I wish to argue, to find in it coded signs of an erotic relationship between Gilbert and Ernest. I would further argue that the dialogue's references to the *Phaedrus* are one aspect this code, and that Wilde's prose style itself serves a function similar to Socrates' inspired poetic style in indicating the presence of, if not Eros, at least *eros*.[85]

References to the *Phaedrus* may be said to frame the dialogue as a whole and to unite its two parts (which had been published separately in July and September of 1890 before being united in *Intentions*[86]). The first occurs early in Part I, in which Ernest cites Phaedrus in support of his original view that in ancient Greece—"the best days of art"—"there were no art-critics" (p. 245).[87] The viewer of a work of art in those days, he imagines, "wandered, it may be, through the city gates to that nymph-haunted meadow where young Phaedrus bathed his feet, and, lying there on the soft grass, beneath the tall wind-whispering planes and flowering *agnus castus*, began to think of the wonder of beauty, and grew silent with unaccustomed awe" (p. 246). Phaedrus appears here neither in his role as a historical personage nor as a figure in the *Symposium*: "that nymph-haunted meadow where young Phaedrus bathed his feet," as well as such details as the city gates and the flowering *agnus* and plane trees, locate the reference specifically in the *Phaedrus* itself, and even more specifically in its opening pages devoted to setting the scene for a discussion of love. It is Socrates himself who describes the same scene in the *Phaedrus*:

Upon my word, a delightful resting-place, with this tall, spreading plane, and a lovely shade from the high branches of the agnus: now that it's in full flower, it will make the place ever so fragrant. And what a lovely stream under the plane-tree, and how cool to the feet! Judging by the statuettes and images I should say it's consecrated to Achelous and some of the Nymphs. (pp. 24–25, 230b)

Ernest's silent Greek art-appreciator should not be confused with the talk-ative Socrates, especially because Socrates is there not to contemplate the beauty of a statue (as Ernest's imagined Greek is), but rather to hear Phaedrus recite Lysias' speech of seduction—a speech that precisely fails to inspire the awe felt by Ernest's Greek. The latter in his wanderings is imag-ined merely as having happened upon the same spot. In fact, there seems to be no particular reason to bring Phaedrus, or *Phaedrus*, into Wilde's dia-logue at this point, other than to evoke ancient Greece in a general way: even if the critique of rhetoric found in the second half of Plato's dialogue is taken to be art criticism and thus an exemplar of Gilbert's theories, the passage cited here comes instead from the earlier discussion of male–male desire. I would argue that this is exactly why the reference is included: the debate on the relationship between art and criticism is couched in terms that refer in a coded fashion to male–male erotics. The aesthetic theories under discussion thus also refer covertly, but in a manner that would be comprehensible, at least to Wilde's fellow Oxonians, to the practices of male–male desire debated in the *Phaedrus*—if not to an emerging modern homosexual identity. As male–male erotics and rhetoric come to stand in for each other in Plato's dialogue, so male–male erotics and aesthetics come to stand for each other in Wilde's.

This impression is confirmed as Ernest continues his speech in praise of ancient Greece's supposedly nontheoretical practice of art. Imagining a Greek potter at work, he suggests that on the side of his pot "he would write the name of his friend. ΚΑΛΟΣ ΑΛΚΙΒΙΑΔΗΣ or ΚΑΛΟΣ ΧΑΡΜΙΔΗΣ tells us the story of his days" (p. 247). The citations of the most famous and desired male beauties of classical Athens, Alcibiades and Charmides, both of whom are familiar from Platonic dialogues,[88] especially paired with the adjective καλὸς, "beautiful," places this bit of art history too in the context of male–male desire, and now not only aesthetics but the language of friendship as well serve to encode it.[89]

Ernest concludes his discourse with another, less direct reference to the *Phaedrus*, by way of Matthew Arnold. The ancient Greek artist, says Ernest, was not troubled by critical opinions:

By the Ilyssus, says Arnold somewhere, there was no Higginbotham. By the Ilyssus, my dear Gilbert, there were no silly art-congresses, bringing provincialism to the provinces and teaching the mediocrity how to mouth. By the Ilyssus there were no tedious magazines about art, in which the industrious prattle of what they do not understand. On the reed-grown banks of that little stream strutted no ridiculous journalism monopolizing the seat of judgment when it should be apologizing in the dock. The Greeks had no art-critics. (p. 247)

Only the first of these observations is drawn from Matthew Arnold, specifically from his influential 1865 essay entitled "The Function of Criticism as the Present Time." Wilde's dialogue is, in part, a response to this essay as well as to Pater (as Isobel Murray points out[90]), but Wilde's citation of this particular passage is a bit puzzling. It is, for one thing, incorrect. Arnold at this point in his essay is discussing the possibility of taking a critical attitude toward the purveyors of Victorian jingoism, who had recently been declaring the peerlessness of "the old Anglo-Saxon race, so superior to all the world!";[91] Arnold suggests that they might be confronted with a newspaper article, which he quotes, concerning the alleged murder of a child by its mother, a girl named Wragg. Such a critical confrontation, he suggests, might demonstrate "how much that is harsh and ill-favoured there is in this best"[92] race. Not only the sordid circumstances of the murder, but the very name Wragg exemplifies this Anglo-Saxon harshness:

> *Wragg*! If we are to talk of ideal perfection, of "the best in the whole world," has anyone reflected what a touch of grossness in our race, what an original shortcoming in the more delicate spiritual perceptions, is shown by the natural growth amongst us of such hideous names,—Higginbottom, Stiggins, Bugg! In Ionia and Attica they were luckier in this respect than "the best race in the world;" by the Ilissus there was no Wragg, poor thing![93]

Arnold's purpose, then, is to provide an example of how a cultural critique might be deployed against Victorian, and indeed Anglo-Saxon, triumphalism: the English names he cites are used as evidence of an originary, "racial" or ethnic inferiority of spiritual perception among the Anglo-Saxons when compared with presumably more euphonious Greek proper nouns, "Ionia" and "Attica" as well as "Ilissus."

Ernest erroneously substitutes "Higginbotham" for "Wragg," and, though Murray claims that Wilde retains Arnold's sense,[94] in fact Ernest is making virtually the opposite point. Although both use "Higginbotham" or "Higginbottom" as a sign of Anglo-Saxon Philistinism, Ernest is trying to prove that "[t]he Greeks had no art-critics" and by extension the truth of his aesthetic theory that criticism is unnecessary to art, while Arnold's purpose is to encourage cultural criticism. "Higginbotham" for Ernest seems to function in the same way as "silly art-congresses," "tedious magazines about art," and "journalism monopolizing the seat of judgment," that is, as a representative of the Philistine failure of contemporary criticism.

In the context of his essay, Arnold's phrase is not necessarily a reference to the *Phaedrus*: it seems to signify, geographically, ancient Athens in general or even, with "Ionia" and "Attica," ancient Greece as a whole. But by placing it at the end of a speech that began with such a clear evocation of the scene of the *Phaedrus*, including the Ilissus "where young Phaedrus bathed his feet," Wilde reminds us of Plato's dialogue once again, especially in the repetition of "by the Ilyssus." Following as closely as it does upon the imagined inscriptions to "beautiful Alcibiades" and "beautiful Charmides," this passage also serves as yet a further reminder that the topic of that dialogue was male–male love.

The question of Wilde's misquotation of Arnold still remains: why did he, deliberately or not, substitute the name "Higginbotham" for "Wragg" when choosing a name to suggest critical Philistinism? The name "Higginbotham" is to be found nowhere in Wilde's biographies—but a similar name, "Higginson," does turn up, and in a highly charged context. During Wilde's 1882 lecture tour of the United States, some seven or eight years before he would have been working on "The Critic as Artist," Col. T. W. Higginson, a well-respected American critic (remembered now primarily for having discouraged Emily Dickinson from publishing her poems) denounced Wilde together with Walt Whitman—a suggestive pairing[95]—in the *Women's Journal*. In particular, Wilde's poem "Charmides" came under attack for prurience, as did Wilde's poetry generally as an unacceptable alternative to "helping to work out the Irish problem in his own country."[96] Whitman was denounced for "pretending to military experience when he had been only a hospital nurse."[97] In other words, both poets were criticized for failing in arenas traditionally constructed as manly: politics and military service. Though the poem "Charmides" has no homoerotic content, and Higginson directly accused neither Whitman nor Wilde of male–male eroticism, Ellmann nevertheless seems right to consider this and similar episodes as evidence that, to his American audiences, Wilde's "invocations of beauty managed to sound faintly subversive, faintly unhealthy" and that his "unconventional charm was pitted against conventional maleness and resultant suspicion"[98]—presumably suspicion of sodomy, especially given the association of effeminacy and sodomy discussed above. Higginson's article in particular linked Whitman, Wilde, insufficient or suspect manliness, Wilde's aesthetics, and the name "Charmides" in a constellation that should now be familiar: aestheticism, effeminacy, and ancient Greece, with a further, unstated implication of homosexuality. It therefore seems worth considering whether Wilde was, consciously or unconsciously, evoking Higginson in the misquotation of Arnold that follows so closely on the invocation of "beautiful Charmides" in "The Critic as Artist": Higginson's name may help explain why "Higginbotham" might have seemed an appropriate signifier for critical Philistinism, and especially why it makes its appearance as part of the coded system of references in which aesthetics come to stand for male–male erotics. Certainly Wilde had leveled the charge of critical Philistinism at Higginson in 1882: in a letter to a sympathetic American poet, Joaquin Miller, of February 28 of that year, Wilde describes Higginson as "this scribbling anonymuncule in grand old Massachusetts who scrawls and screams so glibly about what he cannot understand."[99] Having consigned Higginson to namelessness in 1882, perhaps Wilde resurrects his name in altered form—one that turns a "son" into a "botham" or, in Arnold's piece, a "bottom"!—in conscious or unconscious revenge for the insinuations of eight years earlier.

Wilde thus hijacks Arnold's critical phrase—and perhaps Higginson's very name—to suggest, once again, that his own discussion of aesthetics also encodes an acknowledgment of male–male erotics. Furthermore, even Arnold, the most distinguished of Victorian critics, merely by virtue of having discussed aesthetic theory, can be read queerly by Wilde, precisely because Wilde continually, through his references to the *Phaedrus*, implies a link between aesthetics and male–male erotics.

Ernest, in devising an aesthetic theory to demonstrate the uselessness of aesthetic theory, and in citing Arnold's defense of criticism in order to attack criticism, places himself in logical difficulties that Gilbert, Wilde's spokesman, is too polite to point out, obvious though they may be to the reader. And Gilbert himself, in arguing his own strong aesthetic theory in favor of criticism, eventually works his way back to the *Phaedrus* in Part II of "The Critic as Artist." Gilbert is answering Ernest's question whether "[t]he true critic will be rational, at any rate, will he not?"

> *Gilbert*: Rational? There are two ways of disliking art, Ernest. One is to dislike it. The other, to like it rationally. For Art, as Plato saw, and not without regret, creates in listener and spectator a form of divine madness. It does not spring from inspiration, but it makes others inspired. Reason is not the faculty to which it appeals. If one loves Art at all, one must love it beyond all other things in the world, and against such love, the reason, if one listened to it, would cry out. There is nothing sane about the worship of beauty . . . (p. 284)

Plato certainly worries about the dangers of imitative art, and poetry in particular, in several dialogues, notably in the *Republic*, Book X; but the reference to "divine madness" echoes the *Phaedrus* in particular, though the aesthetic Gilbert espouses here is hardly that of Plato. As in the letter to Lord Alfred Douglas cited above, Wilde at this point invokes Socrates' discourse on the different varieties of divinely inspired madness at the beginning of his second, true speech (*Phaedrus* 244a–245c). Socrates' third category of *mania* comes from the Muses, and is the type that "seizes a tender, virgin soul and stimulates it to rapt passionate expression, especially in lyric poetry . . . if any man come to the gates of poetry without the madness of the Muses, persuaded that skill alone will make him a good poet, then shall he and his works of sanity with him be brought to naught by the poetry of madness . . ." (p. 57, 245a). But this and the other two categories cited here are for Socrates literally a pretext, merely serving to prepare the way for his ensuing discussion of love, dedicated to proving that "this [erotic] sort of madness is a gift of the gods" (p. 58, 245c). Clearly Gilbert's view that art is not inspired is at odds with that of Socrates; but to some readers, at least, Socrates' connection of poetic inspiration to the madness of male–male desire would also seem to be logically implied by Gilbert's citation of it in this dialogue—just as it would be not merely implied, but explicitly stated, in the letter to Douglas a few years later. Gilbert's rhetorical move from "Art" to "beauty" more generally may provide a similar hint that other beautiful bodies than works of art alone may be under discussion here.

Aestheticism does not appear in this dialogue only as a subject of discussion. It is exemplified in the two friends' verbal styles as well. Oliver Buckton has recently pointed out that even in *De Profundis*, in which he claims to renounce his former appetites, Wilde's rich verbal style still allows him "to surround himself, imaginatively, with the material luxuries now beyond his reach,"[100] and the interlocutors in "The Critic as Artist" also revel in their own sensuous verbal style. Ernest's adaptation of Socrates' description of the "nymph-haunted meadow" is a good example, and Gilbert's speeches provide many more, especially in his descriptions of the poetry of Dante and Baudelaire—and most especially of the passages devoted to sin: "Through the dim purple air fly those who have stained the world with the beauty of their sin, and in the pit of loathsome disease, dropsy-stricken and swollen of body into the semblance of a monstrous lute, lies Adamo di Brescia, the coiner of false coin" (p. 271); "Read the whole book, suffer it to tell even one of its secrets to your soul, and your soul will grow eager to know more, and will feed upon poisonous honey, and seek to repent of strange crimes of which it is guiltless, and to make atonement for terrible pleasures that it has never known" (p. 273).

Ellmann suggests that Wilde's style, specifically in *Intentions*, amounts to a simultaneous concealment and revelation of his own erotic crimes.

Following his introduction to homosexuality, which Ellmann dates to his affair with Robert Ross in 1886, "Wilde was able to think of himself, if he wanted to, as criminal."[101]

> He sensed that his new life was a source of literary effect. . . . He now succeeded in relating his new discoveries about himself to aesthetic theory. His only formal book of criticism, *Intentions*, has the same secret spring as his later plays and stories. . . . occasionally, overtly or covertly, he states that for the artist crime does pay, by instilling itself in his content and affecting his form.[102]

The aesthetic "literary effects" found in Ernest's and particularly in Gilbert's sensuous, decadent verbal style thus spring from the sources of sin and criminality to which they covertly allude in the descriptive passages quoted above. Just as a specific literary style could be understood as itself referring to same-sex desire when Wilde's letter to Douglas was read out in court, so too do Wilde's purple flights—the rapturous aesthetic style of "The Critic as Artist"—serve as a way of encoding male–male erotic desires.

In fact, style expresses and thus represents the truth of individuality: ". . . there is no art where there is no style, and no style where there is no unity, and unity is of the individual" (p. 254). Sin performs a similar function: "By its curiosity, Sin increases the experience of the race. Through its intensified assertion of individualism, it saves us from monotony of type" (p. 257). Criticism is thus "purely subjective, and seeks to reveal its own secret and not the secret of another" (p. 262). Sin produces the individual; the individual is expressed in style; style thus encodes sin, specifically, as we have seen, erotic transgression. Wilde, perhaps one of the men Pater was afraid of corrupting, takes Pater's opposition of aesthetics to conventional morality several steps further.

Jeff Nunokawa has recently made a related observation concerning Wilde's aestheticism in "The Critic as Artist." Citing Gilbert's declaration that "[i]t is through Art, and through Art only . . . that we can shield ourselves from the sordid perils of actual existence," Nunokawa notes that in "proposing art's 'exquisite sterile emotions' as a form of prophylaxis, Wilde both enlists and revises the traditional doctrine of aesthetic disinterestedness" derived from Kant: "while Wilde populates this [aesthetic] region with a species of affect ruled out of court by Kant, he nevertheless upholds the conception of the aesthetic as the zone where the force of that affect is transcended."[103] He adds, however, that "glamorous as he makes it, the spectrum of affective color that Wilde allows the aesthetic subject does not exactly sell itself. His enthusiasm . . . suggests the apostolic determination to convert the unbelieving";[104] in particular, "a specific act of conversion—central to Wilde's life and work: the act of conversion called seduction."[105] Or, as Nunokawa suggests of Lord Henry in *The Picture of Dorian Gray*, "The containment of desire proposed by Lord Henry is a matter of embracing it, an embrace that begins by the act of encircling it within the artful arms of form and ends with the more prosaic act of taking it to bed and thus putting it there."[106]

In "The Critic as Artist," style is also a form of seduction, overtly intellectual but covertly erotic. Gilbert initially suggests that a critical discussion is too impersonal a topic for the two friends' evening entertainment: "You will not ask me to give you a survey of Greek art criticism from Plato to Plotinus. The night is too lovely for that, and the moon, if she heard us, would put more ashes on her face than are there already" (p. 250). The seductive language of the lovely night and the moon make Gilbert sound like an ardent lover, one who would prefer action to theory; indeed, he has already suggested that instead of a critical discussion he might "play to you some mad scarlet thing by Dvořák. The pallid figures on the tapestry are smiling at us, and the heavy eyelids of my bronze Narcissus are folded in sleep. . . . Let us go out into the night. Thought is wonderful, but adventure is more wonderful still" (p. 248). The constellation of madness, Narcissus, and nighttime adventures again imply, without stating, an erotic alternative to critical thought. But, when Ernest (coyly?) insists on conversation instead, Gilbert's criticism itself eventually becomes seductive: "*Gilbert*. . . . The world is made by the singer for the dreamer. *Ernest*. While you talk it seems to me to be so" (p. 259). Critical style too, it appears, can be seductive, as Pater's has seduced Wilde.

Wilde thus frames his dialogue with references to the *Phaedrus*, and takes from Plato also the link between male–male desire and the rapturous, quasi-poetic style in which it is expressed, though for Wilde this style is not inspired, but inspiring—or seductive, as it also is for Socrates. Plato, however, writing in ancient Athens and in accordance with its ethics, represents Socrates' rhetorical male–male seduction as a seduction to philosophy, while for Wilde, writing at the end of the nineteenth century, the seduction is to decadence, aestheticism, and what his period defined as crime or sin.[107] This is also to say that whereas for Plato male–male desire or love was a matter of internal self-deviation, for Wilde it is also a matter of social deviation, of deviance away from cultural and religious norms and thus toward a purer individualism, including, in displaced fashion, erotic individualism or "sexual dissidence" (to use Jonathan Dollimore's phrase): to "deviance" in its modern, and until recently pejorative, erotic sense—suggesting that Pater may have been correct, as Linda Dowling suggests, to perceive a danger in Wilde's appropriation of his, and Socrates', teachings.

Wilde's individualism, however, is not the same thing as a modern self, for Wilde steadfastly refuses any notion of a coherent self-identity. As Dollimore points out, Wilde was reviled not, or not only, for violating conventional morality, but more importantly for attacking "the ideological anchor points for that morality, namely notions of identity as subjective depth. . . . Wilde's transgressive aesthetic subverted the dominant categories of subjectivity which kept desire in subjection, subverted the essentialist categories of identity which kept morality in place."[108] Signs of this refusal of an essential subjective identity are not difficult to find in "The Critic as Artist," and they seem particularly suggestive when contrasted with the Platonic doctrine of self-deviation espoused by Socrates in the *Phaedrus*.

Gilbert suggests, for instance, that the "true critic"

> will never suffer himself to be limited to any settled custom of thought, or stereotyped mode of looking at things. He will realize himself in many forms, and by a thousand different ways, and will ever be curious of new sensations and fresh points of view. Through constant change, and through constant change alone, he will find his true unity. He will not consent to be the slave of his own opinions. For what is mind but motion in the intellectual sphere? The essence of thought, as the essence of life, is growth. You must not be frightened by words, Ernest. What people call insincerity is simply a method by which we can multiply our personalities. (pp. 284–285)

The notion that mind is "motion in the intellectual sphere" may recall Socrates' doctrine at the beginning of his second speech in the *Phaedrus* that "[a]ll soul [*psyche* (ψυχὴ)] is immortal; for that which is ever in motion is immortal" (p. 63, 245c). Socrates uses the soul's, or *psyche*'s motion to prove its immortality, but Gilbert turns motion itself, rather than immortality, into the mind's constitutive characteristic. Wilde is thus able to define the self-deviance described in this passage as a good rather than as the necessary evil that self-deviance appears to be in Socrates' metaphor of the charioteer and his horses. There, one aspect of the self must be repressed, whereas for Wilde (as, by implication, for Pater) desire and morality are to be released from subjection, as Dollimore points out. Wilde's dialogue therefore recalls Plato's only to repudiate it, in this area as in the others noted above. He thus defines himself both as Socrates and as not-Socrates simultaneously, taking up a deviant position with regard to his source and thereby demonstrating the very point about the nature of the self that is under discussion.

Indeed, the very modernity that Wilde espouses in aesthetics may be defined by the way in which it deviates from itself: because the modern world has inherited so much of the past, "it is not our own life that we live, but the lives of the dead"; heredity thus

> can lead us away from surroundings whose beauty is dimmed to us by the mist of familiarity, or whose ignoble ugliness and sordid claims are marring the perfection of our development. It can help us to leave the age in which we were born, and to pass into other ages, and find ourselves not exiled from their air. It can teach us how to escape from our experience, and to realize the experiences of those who are greater than we are. (pp. 276–277)

For Wilde, modern aesthetics is thus precisely an aesthetics of alienation or self-division, of a movement out of self-presence as well as out of the present. The modern is also by definition the not-modern, and therefore deviates from itself. Wilde's aestheticism is in some sense a predecessor of postmodern *bricolage*, the assembly of a style—or a self—unique to its own day out of the styles of the past.[109]

Dialogue itself is the mode in which this deviant self and style can best be expressed, as Gilbert notes at several self-reflexive moments in "The Critic as Artist." As he puts it at the beginning of Part II, "[c]onversation should touch everything, but should concentrate itself on nothing" (p. 267): like internal self-deviance, the give-and-take of conversational dialogue, its wanderings off the narrow path of discourse, are not a temptation ideally to be resisted, as they are for the philosophical Socrates, but rather a good to be actively (or indolently) pursued. Gilbert later reflects at some length on dialogue as a literary technique for which he claims a tradition starting with Plato, one which "can never lose for the thinker its attraction as a mode of expression."

> *Gilbert*: . . . By its means he can both reveal and conceal himself, and give form to every fancy, and reality to every mood. By its means he can exhibit the object from each point of view, and show it to us in the round, as a sculptor shows us things, gaining in this manner all the richness and reality of effect that comes from those side issues that are suddenly suggested by the central idea in its progress, and really illumine the idea more completely, or from those felicitous after-thoughts that give a fuller completeness to the central scheme, and yet convey something of the delicate charm of chance.
> *Ernest*: By its means, too, he can invent an imaginary antagonist, and convert him when he chooses by some absurdly sophistical argument.
> *Gilbert*: Ah! It is so easy to convert others. It is so difficult to convert oneself. To arrive at what one really believes, one must speak through lips different from one's own . . . (p. 283)

Literary dialogues such as "The Critic as Artist" itself are the ideal genre for the critical expression of deviance, in part because they can reproduce the conversational wanderings from the philosophical straight and narrow path to which Gilbert referred earlier: Wilde here comes quite close to Bakhtin's notion of the dialogical, or indeed to Levinas' "proximate." They can also reveal a variety of perspectives on the subject under discussion, as a sculpture allows a variety of perspectives on the subject it depicts—a comparison which suggests that all perspectives so revealed may be equally true (the back of a statue is no truer than its front) or equally necessary to understanding.[110] Since, as Gilbert goes on to point out, truth in "matters of art . . . is one's last mood" (p. 283), one interlocutor may speak the truth as well as another; Ernest in the long run may be as right as Gilbert. But dialogue is also the genre that best expresses deviance from the self: not only can it express "every mood," deviating as they may be, it allows expression through "lips different from one's own." The disagreeing interlocutors thus appear as aspects of the author's own divided self, one that is "so difficult to convert." Ernest may therefore be seduced, but he is not necessarily convinced: "*Gilbert.* Ah! Don't say that you agree with me. When people agree with me I always feel that I must be wrong. *Ernest.* In that case I certainly won't tell you whether I agree with you or not" (p. 292). Agreement leads ironically to self-doubt; here we may be reminded less of the *Phaedrus* or the *Symposium* than of the *Lysis* and other Socratic dialogues in which Socrates deviates endlessly from his own opinions, regardless of the agreement or disagreement of his interlocutors.

Wilde's debt to the *Phaedrus* is thus both direct, in the citation of that dialogue's setting beside the Ilissus, and more devious or covert. The *Phaedrus* provides a model for the association of love and style, as well as, with Plato's other dialogues, a genre that Wilde self-consciously extends. It also provides a model of the deviant self and its deviant style, though one that Wilde embraces while Socrates might prefer to repudiate it. Most importantly, it provides for Wilde and at least some of his readers a language for encoding male–male desire, a language that therefore also plays its part in the emergence of a modern homosexual identity.

A modern homosexual identity, not *the*. Around the same time that Wilde was, in Sinfield's terms, assembling the components of aestheticism, effeminacy, leisure, and a Platonic education that would, after his trials, emerge as one version of homosexuality, others were also possible, for example the "medical model" of gender inversion (the familiar female soul in a male body), Edward Carpenter's Uranianism (homosexuals as an intermediate sex), or "the third sex" proposed by the German sexologists.

English and American writers were proposing yet another version, one that emphasized nature rather than aesthetics, manliness rather than effeminacy, and universality rather than the leisure of an economic minority. T. W. Higginson had associated Whitman with Wilde as examples of insufficient manliness, but for the late-nineteenth and early-twentieth-century apologists of male–male love, Whitman became a sign for this alternative, manly version of homosexuality. They also drew on the Platonic legacy. John Addington Symonds, as we have already seen, looked to Whitman for a model of manly, natural homosexuality, and privately published his famous essay *A Problem in Greek Ethics* in 1883,[111] while Edward Carpenter quoted passages from both the *Symposium* and the *Phaedrus* in his "anthology of friendship" entitled *Ioläus* after Hercules' companion of that name (first published in 1902)—and concluded his anthology with selections from Whitman.[112]

André Gide's dialogue (or series of dialogues) now known as *Corydon* was first issued privately and anonymously under the title *C.R.D.N.* in 1911; this edition consisted of two dialogues and part of a third. The second edition of 1920 was again private and anonymous, but now had its full title *Corydon*, and consisted of "Four Socratic Dialogues and a Preface." The third edition of 1924 was finally offered for sale under the author's name.[113] The text is made up of dialogues that are indeed "Socratic" in a general way: two men, "Corydon" and the narrator, discuss homosexuality, Corydon defending it as natural against the narrator's skepticism. Corydon rather than the first-person narrator is clearly Gide's spokesman, and takes the "Socratic" role of persuading his interlocutor of the truth of his position, though it remains unclear at the end whether or not he has succeeded. Gide also invokes the figure of Whitman at the outset: visiting his friend Corydon, who has been accused of "certain unnatural tendencies" (p. 3; p. 16),[114] he finds, instead of the expected "signs of . . . effeminacy" (p. 4; p. 16), "the portrait of an old man with a long white beard whom I immediately recognized as the American poet Walt Whitman" (p. 4; p. 17). Indeed, the question of Whitman's sexuality as presented in a recent French biography provides the opening gambit in their conversation: Corydon suggests that " 'Whitman can be taken as the typical normal man. Yet Whitman was a pederast [*pédéraste*] . . .' '*Therefore* pederasty [*la pédérastie*] is normal . . . Bravo!' " (p. 5; p. 19).[115] Despite the nameless narrator's sarcastic completion of the syllogism, the Whitmanesque "normality" and naturalness of homosexuality is the dominant theme of the rest of the dialogue; and the use of the Greek-derived term *pédérastie* simultaneously places the discussion in the context of ancient Athenian sexual conventions.

Alan Sheridan has helpfully discussed Gide's terminology for homo-sexuality:

> Because *Corydon* is not a treatise, in which a clear definition of terms might be regarded as essential, but takes the form of a dialogue between two men, there is a natural slipping and sliding of terminology. Gide uses the older term "*uranien*" (uranian) and the newer "*homosexuel*" more or less inter-changeably. By *pédéraste* Gide usually means an adult male lover of adoles-cent boys but, for the French reader, this term, too, was synonymous with "homosexual," being its current, colloquial equivalent.[116]

Gide placed himself in the category of *pédéraste*,[117] and thus in the Athenian tradition of *paiderastia*, which for him carried none of the impli-cations of effeminacy or androgyny of the "Uranians" or of the third sex posited by such German sexologists as Hirschfeld; despite his use of *uranien*, Gide insists throughout the four *Corydon* dialogues that such androgyny or effeminacy is not an aspect of the healthy and normal "Greek love" that Corydon defends.[118] Whitman and ancient Athens are thus both evoked as contexts for the manly homosexuality to be considered normal.

Nevertheless, the third context in which Gide places his dialogue is that of Oscar Wilde's trials.[119] The third edition includes as an appendix Gide's response to a book by François Porché entitled *The Love that Dare Not Speak Its Name* (p. 129; p. 191), a phrase drawn from Lord Alfred Douglas' poem "Two Loves" and made famous at Wilde's first trial when the poem was read aloud in court[120] and Wilde made his stirring defense of "a great affection of an elder for a younger man," quoted above. The friendship between Wilde and Gide has been well documented,[121] and Gide was in fact writing his memoir of Wilde at the same time that he was composing *Corydon*.[122] It is therefore not surprising to find that *Corydon* itself also refers to Wilde in its opening pages: Corydon, in fact, is quick to dissoci-ate himself from Wilde—not because of the accusations of homosexuality, but because of Wilde's refusal to admit to them directly:

> "It's true that the cause lacks martyrs."
>   "Let's not use such high-sounding words."
>   "I'm using the words that are needed. We've had Wilde and Krupp and Eulenberg and Macdonald . . ."
>   "And they're not enough for you?"
>   "Oh, victims! As many victims as you like—but not martyrs. They all denied—they always will deny." (p. 8; p. 22)

Corydon admits that he too might deny if he were to be "dragged into court by a Queensberry" (p. 8; p. 23), and Gide himself might be subjected to a similar critique: not only did he hesitate to publish *Corydon* at all, he also provided the narrative "I" with a conventional homophobic ideology, distancing himself from Corydon's arguments even though he espoused them.[123] We may also understand this exchange as a reference to Wilde's use of an indeterminate or coded style to discuss sexuality. Unlike Wilde, Corydon insists on writing a direct *Defense of Pederasty*, the book whose argument will be adumbrated in the ensuing dialogues. What Wilde denied in his famous speech, of course, was the physical aspect of his relations with Douglas, and among other things it is precisely the physical attractions of homosexuality that Gide, through Corydon, will be defending: the second dialogue, indeed, draws on natural history to explain it (though the explanation remains steadfastly on an abstract scientific plane rather than providing any concrete examples of male–male erotics).

But Gide also distances himself from the entire construction of homosexuality associated with Wilde and described by Sinfield, the effeminate homosexuality whose signs the narrator sought for in vain in Corydon's apartment. Gide was both inspired and frightened by Wilde's style of homosexuality, finding in him the seductive figure we have discovered in "The Critic as Artist": "Wilde represented for Gide a sort of Mephistopheles to his Faust: the tempter's power of attraction was undeniable. . . . Gide described Wilde as 'always trying to insinuate inside you the *authorization of evil.*' "[124] In a letter to his mother written after meeting Wilde and Lord Alfred Douglas in North Africa, Gide described Douglas as having been corrupted by Wilde to the point that he is capable of "doing anything under the pretext of aestheticism."[125] Instead of that Wildean homosexuality, effeminate and aesthetic, Corydon is concerned with that of the "virile" (p. 19; p. 37) "normal pederasts" (p. 18; p. 36). He understands, indeed, that homosexuality can be variously manifested, but Gide's note to his preface makes it clear that he is not interested in inversion or in Hirschfeld's theory of a third sex, but rather in what he calls "Greek love": "Even granting that Hirschfeld's theory accounts for these cases, his 'third sex' argument certainly cannot explain what we habitually call 'Greek love: pederasty [*l'amour grec: la pédérastie*]—in which effeminacy is neither here nor there" (p. xx; pp. 9–10). As Corydon puts it, "my book will deal with healthy uranism [*uranisme*] or, as you just put it yourself, with *normal pederasty* [*la pédérastie normale* (emphasis in text)]." And furthermore, "[t]he only thing in the world I concede as not natural is a work of art. Everything else, like it or not, belongs to the natural order" (p. 20; p. 38; emphasis in text). Homosexuality is thus separated from the aesthetic as it is from the effeminate, and Gide's own style in *Corydon* emphasizes the difference: particularly in the second dialogue, with its twenty-five footnotes citing contemporary scientific treatises, Gide adopts a sober, objective, quasi-scientific style at odds with Wilde's purple flights. "Healthy homosexuality" is thus severed from the decadent, effeminate aestheticism of Wilde and his circle as it is also severed from what Corydon regards as their timidity in the face of martyrdom. And this separation is a matter of style as well as morality.

It is still, however, deviant: recounting the story of a young man who fell in love with him before he recognized his own homosexuality, Corydon declares that he could have cured the young man "[b]y convincing him that the deviation of his instinct [*la déviation de son instinct*] was quite natural" (p. 17; p. 34). Homosexuality is here a deviation, but one that remains within the boundaries of the natural. The lengthy second dialogue, in fact, turns to natural history in order to prove that homosexuality is no less, and possibly more, natural than heterosexuality, which is here understood as a cultural construction propped up by law, religion, the fashion system, and so on: he concludes the second dialogue by posing the question

> If, despite the almost constant superabundance of the male element, nature requires so many expedients and adjuvants in order to ensure the perpetuation of the race, will we be surprised to learn that just as many constraints of just as many kinds are necessary in order to deter the human species from its tendency toward that behavior you have declared "abnormal"; and that so many arguments, examples, invitations, encouragements, of so many kinds, are required to maintain human heterosexuality at the desired coefficient? (p. 71; pp. 110–111)

Corydon produces here the same kind of cultural critique that we encountered in the Italian humanist and French Enlightenment defenders of sodomy, whether Rocco or Sade. Those writers were responding primarily to the *Symposium*, and that text is invoked at several points in *Corydon*'s third and fourth dialogues (see, for instance, p. 94; p. 142).

If Corydon has defended homosexuality in its physical, or at least scientific, aspect in the second dialogue, in the third and fourth he draws on Plato to defend its spiritual aspect. Indeed, Gide places himself in that same *Symposium*-neoplatonic tradition not only by direct citation of the *Symposium*, but also by claiming Plato's Athens and Renaissance Florence as two periods of cultural efflorescence in which homosexuality also flourished. Thus Corydon follows up the narrator's complaint about the alleged "singular corruption of Greek morals" with a reference to Renaissance Florence: "Or Florentine morals. Remarkable, isn't it, how each great renaissance or artistic exuberance is always and in whatever country it occurs accompanied by a great outburst of uranism [*d'uranisme*]" (p. 87; p. 133). It is thus only the Wildean, decadent aesthetic that Gide wishes to dissociate from homosexuality; periods of healthy art are also periods of the healthy expression of homosexuality. Wilde's influence is repudiated, as are the medical or psychiatric models of homosexuality, inversion and uranianism, in favor of the "healthy" tradition of Plato and Renaissance Florence.

Although the *Phaedrus* is nowhere named explicitly in *Corydon*, it is nevertheless present in Gide's work as part of the historical context for what Gide calls normal homosexuality. Its influence first appears in Corydon's discussion, in the fourth dialogue, of the Sacred Band of Thebes, the battalion of lovers described by Plutarch (in the *Life of Pelopidas*) in terms reminiscent of the "army of lovers" imagined by Phaedrus in his speech in the *Symposium* 178e–179b. Corydon praises the Sacred band in Platonic terms: ". . . it is likely that this troop was named the 'sacred battalion' for the same reason that prompted Plato to define a lover as a friend in whom one feels something divine" (p. 114; p. 169). While the description of the Sacred Band may remind us of the *Symposium*, the direct reference to Plato also returns us to the *Phaedrus*, specifically to Socrates' explanation of human love in his second speech: when a soul "who is fresh from the mystery, and saw much of the vision, beholds a godlike face or bodily form that truly expresses beauty, first there comes upon him a shuddering and a measure of awe which the vision inspired, and then reverence as at the sight of a god" (p. 96, 251a). The Platonic love that is understood as divine madness or possession thus underlies Gide's historical perspective on modern homosexuality as it also underlies Wilde's: Gide may refuse the Wildean construction of homosexuality, but his own version draws on the same source, though differently interpreted. Corydon returns to the *Phaedrus'* notion of the lover as inspired rather than inspiring, a characterization that Wilde's description of the artist reversed, as we have seen: Gide thus reverses Wilde's reversal, or deviates from Wilde's deviation, in reaffirming the Platonic doctrine of possession. If Wilde's encoded homosexuality is seductive, Gide's is protective (and thus, perhaps, has less need of encryption), as Corydon suggests in another reference to the *Phaedrus*—one, in fact, that brings Gide's dialogue to its conclusion:

So long as he remains this *molliter juvenis*, as Pliny calls him, more desirable and desired than desiring, if some older man should fall in love with him, I believe, as was believed long ago in that civilization of which you consent to admire only the shell—I believe that nothing can be better for him than a lover of his own sex. I believe that such a lover will jealously watch over him, protect him, and himself exalted, purified by this love, will guide him toward those radiant heights which are not to be reached without love. (p. 125; p. 185)

Once again Corydon cites ancient Athenian views of male–male desire as authorizing his own, and indirectly refers to the *Phaedrus* and specifically to Socrates' discussion, in his second speech, of the lover's treatment of the beloved: the lover, Gide claims, will be exalted by his love and will simultaneously lead the beloved to otherwise unattainable heights, just as Socrates' ideal lover leads his beloved "to walk in the ways of their god, and after his likeness, patterning himself thereupon and giving counsel and discipline to the boy" (p. 100, 253b). Gide again reverses Wilde's vision of Plato, preferring the protective and spiritual Socrates to the more clearly seductive one we encounter elsewhere (for example in the *Lysis*). As he suggests in what we may now understand as another allusion to the *Phaedrus*, "[w]hether lust is homo- or hetero-sexual, virtue consists in mastering it" (p. 119; p. 176), a hint at the *Phaedrus'* doctrine of the divided self as well as a return to a more conventional view of the Socratic *askēsis* than we encountered in Wilde's dialogues.

In the passage cited above, Corydon also complains that the narrator admires ancient Greek civilization only for it shell—its culture—rather than for the form of desire that, Gide suggests, inspired it. "Do you refuse to understand that there exists a direct relation between the flower and the plant which bears it, between the essential quality of its sap and its behavior and its economy?" (pp. 106–107; p. 158). Gide is making an extreme suggestion here, that male–male desire is the basis of all of ancient Greek culture. It is a claim that Wilde made as well, in the speech in which he declared that Plato made such desires the basis of his philosophy—a speech to which we have already seen Gide allude. While Gide separates himself from Wilde on many essential points, here, in perhaps his most radical claim, he follows him: Gide thus remains in some sense within Wilde's tradition as well as Plato's, even as he insists on his deviations from it.

The nature of the two writers' different modes of deviation from orthodoxy has been well outlined by Jonathan Dollimore: ". . . the very categories of identity which, through transgression, Wilde subjects to inversion and displacement, Gide reconstitutes for a different transgressive aesthetic, or as it might now more suitably be called, in contradistinction to Wilde, a transgressive ethic. . . ."[126] Despite the hint of a divided self noted above, Gide's deviance is much less a deviation from self-identity than is Wilde's, or even Plato's: the healthy homosexual appears here as one who deviates not from himself, but from artificial sociocultural strictures. If homosexuality is a deviation for Gide, it is, as we have seen, merely a statistical deviation within normative boundaries—when nature rather than culture determines the norm. It is perhaps too easy to find in this view a kind of essentialism, as Dollimore does in referring to Gide's "essentialist ethic" that remained simultaneously divergent from and proximate to the ethics of his Catholic past.[127] For Gide, at least in *Corydon*, homosexuality may be a matter of natural identity, but it is not necessarily a matter of any *essential* identity, as Corydon suggests in a remarkable passage:

> I do maintain that, in most cases, the appetite which awakens in the youth is not of any very specific urgency; that he experiences pleasure in whatever form it is offered, no matter by which sex, and that he owes his habits more to outside influences than to the promptings of desire; or, if you prefer, I say that it is rare for desire to make itself specific of its own accord and without the support of experience. (p. 99; p. 149)

By placing himself in the Athenian tradition, Gide also accepts the possibility that homosexuality may not necessarily be a psychologically deep-seated identity: this passage presents the adolescent boy as an unanchored subject-in-process (to adopt Julia Kristeva's term[128]), subjected precisely to a variety of cultural and ideological pressures, rather than as a fixed identity, homosexual or heterosexual.[129] To naturalize homosexuality is not, for Gide, to essentialize it, because in passages like this he de-essentializes nature itself as drifting among the possibilities offered by homosexuality and heterosexuality. This view seems to reflect Gide's understanding of ancient Athenian eroticism, including as it did both possibilities. Sheridan also finds that it characterized Gide's own homosexual experiences, which Gide himself understood as Socratic, for instance in his relationship with Marc Allégret: "In true Socratic fashion, Gide was teaching his young lover how to use his body as well as his mind. Again, Socratically, and in the spirit of *Corydon*, this was not, in any final or exclusive sense, a homosexual initiation. It was made clear that, at some future date, Gide would initiate the young man into heterosexuality—a promise that Marc did not forget."[130] I would suggest instead that, in *Corydon* at least, the body is dealt with separately (in the second dialogue) from the mind or spirit, and that the latter is what Gide associates with Socrates and Plato, in part by means of the *Phaedrus*.[131]

As I suggested at the beginning of this chapter, several twentieth-century fictional narratives also place themselves in the *Phaedrus* tradition, and I would like to consider them briefly even though, strictly speaking, they do not belong to the dialogue genre. The dialogue and the novel are difficult genres to separate; indeed, for Bakhtin the novel is the dialogic genre *par excellence*.[132]

The genres of novel and dialogue clearly overlap in the works of some of the authors we have already considered: for example, we have already seen, in chapter two, that Sade's novels, especially *Justine*, seem more genuinely dialogical than *La Philosophie dans le boudoir*.[133] Diderot, too, was particularly fond of the dialogue genre, and his fictional works might be ranged along a scale from those in which narrative predominates (for example, *La Religieuse*) through the more dialogic (*Les Bijoux indiscrets*) to the almost purely non-narrative and fully dialogical (*Le Neveu de Rameau*). His most ambitious fiction, *Jacques le fataliste*, fuses the two genres, alternating between passages of narration and set dialogues between Jacques and his master. Indeed, this novel/dialogue places itself at a tangent to the Platonic tradition of male–male desire, though not specifically in the *Phaedrus* tradition: Diderot imagines the servant Jacques as a Socratic philosopher,[134] and the various forms of male–male homosociality thematized throughout also threaten Jacques with the role of catamite.[135] The dialogic novel has links to the Platonic tradition similar to those of the dialogue genre proper.

Similarly, Gary Schmidgall points out that "several chapters in *Dorian Gray* are fashioned as Socratic dialogues."[136] In particular, the second chapter of *Dorian Gray*, in which Lord Henry first exerts his seductive influence over Dorian, echoes Wilde's own Socratic dialogues, and the novel as a whole evinces a similar concern with such Platonic themes as the divided self, the beloved as divine, and the *askēsis* by which life is disciplined into an art.[137] Unlike Wilde's dialogues, however, *Dorian Gray* does not specifically echo the *Phaedrus*.

However, around the same time that Gide published the first, anonymous edition of *C.R.D.N.* (1911), Thomas Mann was working on his famous tale of homosexual desire *Der Tod in Venedig*, which was originally published in 1912, and at every turn this novella cites not only the Platonic tradition, but the *Phaedrus* in particular.[138] Questions of style and rhetoric are among the most important of Mann's concerns; its writer-protagonist Aschenbach is known for the classicism of his literary style:

> in later years his style dispensed with forthright audacities, with subtle new nuances; he transformed himself into the exemplary established author, the polished traditionalist, conservative, formal, even formulaic [*Formelle, selbst Formelhafte*]; and, as the story about Louis XIV goes, the aging man banished all vulgar words from his vocabulary. It was then that the Board of Education included selected pages from his works in compulsory primary-school readers. (p. 10; pp. 15–16)[139]

Aschenbach's is an instructional style, suitable for school textbooks and thus far removed from the rapturous poetic style that Socrates invoked to discuss love in the *Phaedrus* or from Wilde's purple aestheticism—though possibly closer to the communicative rhetoric recommended in the second half of Plato's dialogue or to Gide's quasi-scientific style, intended to instruct their audiences. Some of Aschenbach's works also take the form of Socratic dialogues (p. 9; p. 15). This rigorous, highly formal style reflects the *askēsis* of Aschenbach's own rigorous self-discipline: deriving his creativity from his artistic, Bohemian mother, he disciplines it with the "sober official conscientiousness" derived from his German father's family; the union of the two "produced an artist" (p. 6; p. 11). Aschenbach is thus a man internally at odds with himself, like the soul in *Phaedrus*: one aspect of his personality must be kept in check by the other as the charioteer must drive the bad horse to work harmoniously with the good. And yet for Aschenbach, his "darker, more ardent impulses" (p. 6; p. 11) are not bad; they too make his art possible. And even Aschenbach's concern with form and formality itself poses a danger: ". . . does not form possess a double face [*zweierlei Gesicht*]? Is it not moral and amoral at the same time—moral inasmuch as it is the result and expression of discipline, but amoral and even immoral to the extent that by nature it contains within itself an indifference to morality . . . ?" (p. 10; p. 15). The very discipline or *askēsis* with which Aschenbach creates his life and work is itself divided, double, *zweierlei*, marked by difference.

It is these multiple internal self-deviations that bring Aschenbach, famously, both to Venice and to his fatal desire for the boy Tadzio, in the familiar pattern of what Robert Aldrich calls northern intellectuals' "homosexual fantasy" of southern Europe, a fantasy apparently experienced by Mann himself as well as his hero.[140] Aschenbach is initially attracted to Tadzio because of the boy's classical beauty of form, resembling "Greek statues of the noblest period" (p. 20; p. 25), and thus consonant with Aschenbach's own classical *askēsis*. But this devotion to an abstract, formal beauty brings him at last to a physical passion in which his attempts at *askēsis* are abandoned.

The story of Aschenbach's loss of self-control is indicated both stylistically and through references to the *Phaedrus*, as well as in the narrative itself. Stylistically, Aschenbach's desire for the south is represented with dream-images of excess and danger: his initial impulse to travel comes as "a delusion of the senses" in which he imagines that "between the knotty, tubular stalks of the bamboo thicket he saw the eyes of a crouching tiger sparkle—and he felt his heart pounding with fright and a puzzling desire" (p. 3; p. 9). Near the end of the story, the final indication of Aschenbach's loss of self-control with regard to his erotic desire for Tadzio is another such stylistically extravagant fantasy, this one an explicitly ithyphallic and Dionysian dream of revelry:

> The obscene wooden symbol, gigantic, was unveiled and uplifted: then they howled their watchword with even less restraint. Foam on their lips, they raged, stimulated one another with lascivious gestures and groping hands, laughing and moaning; they poked the goads into one another's flesh and licked the blood from their limbs. But the dreamer was now with them, one of them [*in ihnen*], a slave of the foreign god. (p. 56; p. 60)

Aschenbach's imagined or desired participation in the worship of Dionysus links homosexual desire not only to stylistic extravagance, but also to "the stranger, the enemy of the sedate and dignified intellect" as well as to disease, "sores and a rampant sickness" (p. 56; p. 60). We are far from Gide's healthy homosexual here: the linkage of male–male desire and illness suggests the medical model of homosexuality, one of the several competing models circulating through German sexology around the turn of the century, as we have seen.[141] The connection with Nietzsche's influential division of ancient Greek culture between its Apollonian and Dionysian aspects in *The Birth of Tragedy* (1872) is also crucial:[142] homosexuality here undermines Aschenbach's Apollonian *askēsis* and brings him to its opposite, imagined as an utter dissolution of the self.

The dream's explicit Bacchism may also remind us of Plato's *Symposium*, in which, as we have seen, Alcibiades interrupts Socrates' discourse of *askēsis* with his own Dionysian revelry. Indeed, Mann cites several of the works that I have placed in the *Symposium* tradition as well: when Aschenbach, in the early stages of his infatuation, observes Tadzio's friend Jaschu kissing the boy, he casts himself as the Socrates of Xenophon's *Symposium*, jokingly warning Critobolus: " 'I advise you, however, Critobolus,' he thought, smiling, 'go traveling for a year! For you will need at least that much time to recover' " (p. 26; p. 31). Mann also refers to Plutarch's *Erotikos* (the *Dialogue on Love*) at several points.[143]

But it is the *Phaedrus* that Mann uses to chart Aschenbach's dissolution most explicitly. Aschenbach, in counterpoint to his uncontrollable sensual fantasies, also engages in more classical daydreams, specifically imagining his own Socratic additions—presumably directed at Tadzio—to the dialogue between Socrates and Phaedrus, in "that place of sacred shade filled with the fragrance of the agnus-castus bush blossoms, adorned with votive images and pious offerings in honor of the nymphs and Achelous," complete with the Ilissus and the "chirping cicadas," where "amid the compliments and witty sallies of his courtship, Socrates instructed Phaedrus about desire and virtue" (pp. 36–37; p. 41). Mann emphasizes the seductiveness of Socrates, but in this first revision of the dialogue he also emphasizes that beauty—such as the beauty of his young interlocutor—must be only a means to an end: " '. . . beauty . . . is the only form of intellectuality [*des Geistigen*] which we perceive with, and can tolerate with, our senses.' '. . . beauty is the path taken by the man of feeling to attain the intellectual [*zum Geiste*]—only the path, only the means, young Phaedrus' " (p. 37; p. 42). *Geist* implies spirit or soul as well as mind or intellect, and the theory here is derived from the *Symposium's* doctrine of the ladder of love. But Aschenbach imagines this doctrine as an aspect of the "crafty wooer's" seduction (p. 37; p. 42): for his purposes, the *Phaedrus*, in which Socrates speaks in the person of a lover possessed by the gods as Aschenbach himself is possessed by the divine vision of Tadzio,[144] provides a more useful setting for the doctrine of eros. Already the notion of an idealized, spiritual erotics is compromised by physical desire—as indeed it may be in the *Phaedrus* itself.

The second daydream of the *Phaedrus* leads Aschenbach more directly to the brink of "the abyss" by an unexpected route:

> . . . education of the people and of youth by means of art is a risky enterprise that ought to be prohibited. For, how could a man be suitable as an educator when he is born with an incorrigible natural penchant for the abyss? We may deny the abyss and acquire dignity but, no matter how we try, it attracts us. Thus, we may perhaps renounce knowledge, which is a dissolvent; for knowledge, Phaedrus, has no dignity or severity; it knows, understands and forgives, without self-discipline or form; it sympathizes with the abyss, it *is* the abyss. Therefore we decidedly reject it, and henceforth our only concern will be for beauty—that is, for simplicity [*Einfachheit*], greatness, a different kind of severity, the "new naïveté," and form. But form and naïveté, Phaedrus, lead to intoxication and desire, they may even lead a noble man to horrifying crimes of the passions [*Gefühlsfrevel*], which his own beautiful severity rejects as being detestable; they lead to the abyss, they, too, lead to the abyss. They lead us poets there, I say, for we are unable to soar upward, we are only able to commit extravagances. (p. 60; p. 64)

The very formalism with which Aschenbach has disciplined his "ardent" creativity, and which attracted him to Tadzio in the first place, is here found to be merely another route to the abyss of unbridled physical passion: it is difficult not to find in this passage a reminiscence to Socrates' acknowledgment that even male lovers who have undertaken the path of *askēsis* may be led into physical eroticism, though the medical model of homosexuality within which Mann and Aschenbach are operating precludes the indulgence with which Socrates treats such lovers: rather than being furnished with similar plumage, as Socrates' imagined lovers are, Aschenbach's poet-lovers are "unable to soar upwards," but can only commit the kind of "extravagance" we have observed in the style of the novella itself. Artists may imagine that a devotion to form leads to simplicity, or singleness—*Einfachheit*—but Aschenbach's fantasies suggest that it leads instead to dissolution, precisely because of the amorality of form that the narrator noted in the opening pages of *Death in Venice*.[145] Not merely crimes of passion, *Gefühlsfrevel* also suggests emotional blasphemies, and thus opposition to the spirituality Aschenbach believed he was pursuing in pursuing Tadzio. Homosexual passion, indeed, is understood here as a deviation from the Platonic ideal—but a deviation that, at least for the artist, is implied in the ideal itself.

For Mann the internally deviating self described at the beginning, then, cannot be disciplined with *askēsis* because *askēsis* itself, the transformation of the self into art by the imposition of form, is inherently amoral. The deviant elements of the personality, rather than being harmonized, or even multiplying the possibilities of selfhood as they do for Wilde, simply fall apart into a terrifying fragmentation. Mann appears to reject Wilde's aestheticism without finding a satisfactory alternative for the literary artist: it is difficult to imagine finding Gide's healthy homosexual in the world of *Death in Venice*.

It is worth noting, too, that Mann's novella—unlike *Justine* or *Jacques le fataliste* or *The Picture of Dorian Gray*—turns the dialogue inward in a fashion that might be disallowed by Bakhtin or Buber. Aschenbach's dialogues take place entirely within his own head, and the sense of self-division and psychological crack-up that ensues is therefore all the more powerful. Interior dialogue thus becomes the sign of an unresolved self-deviance derived from, but unlike, the deviation resolved through *askēsis* found in Plato's metaphor of the charioteer.[146]

Also, shortly before World War I, and just after Gide and Mann composed *Corydon* and *Death in Venice*, respectively, E. M. Forster was working on his own homosexual novel, *Maurice*, which was written in 1913–1914, though not published until 1971, after Forster's death.[147] Like these other works, Forster's refers both to the *Symposium* and to the *Phaedrus*. Although Maurice and his friends are Cambridge rather than Oxford men, their understanding of homosexuality too is mediated by the *Symposium*: when Maurice admits his love for Clive Durham, who has suggested he read it, he does so by referring to Plato's dialogue: "I mean the *Symposium*, like the ancient Greeks" (p. 64).[148] Clive insists on the ideal Socratic *askēsis* of chastity, as Maurice recalls after their love affair has ended: "It had been understood between them that their love, though including the body, should not gratify it, and the understanding had proceeded—no words were used—from Clive" (p. 151).

For Clive, indeed, homosexuality is merely a phase, but Maurice discovers himself to be exclusively homosexual, and is eventually described in Dionysian terms that link him, like Aschenbach, with the unruly Alcibiades rather than with Socrates: "He found that his head was all yellow with evening primrose pollen. 'Oh, don't brush it off. I like it on your black hair. Mr. Borenius, is he not quite bacchanalian?' " (p. 188); ". . . how the tangle of flowers and fruit wreathed his brain!" (p. 191). For Forster (and, as we shall see, for Mary Renault), male–male desire is less a matter of verbal style than of lifestyle: Maurice and Clive, like Corydon (and, in his futile attempt, like Aschenbach) repudiate the effeminate, aesthetic style, here represented by another college friend, Risley; the Apollonian Clive thus recalls "that Maurice had once lifted him out of aestheticism into the sun and wind of love" (p. 163), while the "bacchanalian" Maurice himself accepts the universal condemnation of Wildean homosexuality, briefly classifying himself as "an unspeakable of the Oscar Wilde sort" (p. 159). The various medical models of homosexuality are also found to be inadequate, in Dr. Barry's and the hypnotist's failures to provide Maurice with realistic alternatives. But Maurice also eventually repudiates Clive's idealized Platonic chastity[149] in pursuing his affair with Clive's gamekeeper Alec and thus outlawing himself from polite society: according to his "Terminal Note," Forster composed, and later eliminated, a coda to the novel in which Maurice's sister, years later, finds her brother and Alec as "two woodcutters" (p. 254). Style of life rather than of language thus characterizes homosexual love for Forster, a style of life and love apparently inspired by Edward Carpenter and his lover George Merrill ("Terminal Note," p. 249).[150]

The "hellenic" Clive's own homosexual phase is mediated by the *Phaedrus*: "Never would he forget his emotion at first reading the *Phaedrus*. He saw there his malady described exquisitely, calmly, as a passion which we can direct, like any other, towards good or bad. Here was no invitation to licence" (p. 70). In a charming scene, Forster even transmutes the *Phaedrus*' central metaphor of the chariot with its two horses into Maurice's unruly motorbike with a sidecar in which Clive rides (pp. 75–78): "the machine took on a life of its own, in which they met and realized the unity preached by Plato" (p. 80). And indeed the love affair, as long as it lasts, suggests precisely this Platonic harmony, expressed stylistically: in a scene structured like a Platonic dialogue, with Clive instructing the unscholarly

Maurice, "their love scene drew out, having the inestimable gain of a new language. No tradition overawed the boys. No convention settled what was poetic, what absurd. . . . Something of exquisite beauty arose in the mind of each at last, something unforgettable and eternal . . ." (p. 93). The language here, reminiscent of the *Phaedrus*' mental images of immortality, links Plato's dialogue with both homosexuality and Clive's chaste erotic style.

Once their affair is over, however, with Clive's newfound heterosexuality and marriage, Maurice's own internal harmony breaks down, especially as he is drawn away from the ideal Platonic chastity and toward physical passion. Even with Clive, Maurice finds that the "stories of Harmodius and Aristogeiton, of Phaedrus, of the Theban Band were well enough for those whose hearts were empty, but no substitute for life"; rather than following Clive's idealistic hellenism, Maurice, in Forster's resignification of the *Phaedrus*' ideal love relationship, finds that the "desire for union was too strong to admit resentment" and found himself "going his own way towards light, in hope that the beloved would follow" (p. 111). The "light" in this case is not Plato's god-image, but a physical consummation that Clive refuses. After the breakup, Maurice tries to practice Clive's form of *askēsis*, "proving on how little the soul could exist" (p. 143), and experiences dreams of physical passion that "tried to disintegrate him" (p. 135)—like Aschenbach—and in fact seems to be headed for a mental crisis expressed as internal self-division and dialogue, especially after his first, ambiguous encounters with Alec at Clive's estate, Penge: "Since coming to Penge he seemed a bundle of voices, not Maurice, and now he could almost hear them quarrelling inside him" (p. 176). This internal self-deviance is introduced as a conflict between bodily desire and spiritual *askēsis* ("[b]y pleasuring the body Maurice . . . had confirmed his spirit in its perversion" [p. 214]), but it is quickly deconstructed as class conflict, between Maurice's conventional, upper-middle-class-bound self and the desire to step outside class, and hence society, in his relations with the gamekeeper Alec:

> "But I must belong to my class, that's fixed," he persisted.
> "Very well," said his old self. "Now go home, and tomorrow morning mind you catch the 8.36 up to the office, for your holiday is over, remember, and mind you never turn your head, as I may, towards Sherwood."
> "I'm not a poet, I'm not that kind of an ass—" . . .
> "The life of the earth, Maurice? Don't you belong to that?"
> "Well, what do you call the 'life of the earth'—it ought to be the same as my daily life—the same as society. One ought to be built on the other, as Clive once said."
> "Quite so. Most unfortunate, that facts pay no attention to Clive." (p. 215)

Male–male desire here is both a question of deviance from the social norm, as it was for Gide's *Corydon*, and one of deviation in status between the two male lovers: within their overall sex and gender similarity, there is also an essential class difference (the same is true of the middle-class Maurice's earlier relations with the aristocratic Clive): for Forster, difference within sameness, or deviance, is an essential component of male–male desire. Class is only one such difference: Maurice is also briefly tempted by the age difference between himself and his mother's young guest, the boy Dickie (pp. 146–149).[151] But class is Forster's overriding concern in the final pages of *Maurice*, and it is the class difference as well as the sex and gender sameness between himself and Alec that is socially deviant in their relationship, for Alec as well as for Maurice: Alec can initially conceive of this relationship with a higher-status man only in terms of blackmail until he is able to admit to his own feelings for Maurice. Even then, as Maurice tells him,

> ". . . you're still trying hard to hurt me in my mind."
> "Why did you go and say you love me?"
> "Why do you call me Maurice?"
> "Oh, let's give over talking. Here—" and he held out his hand. Maurice took it, and they knew at that moment the greatest triumph ordinary man can win. (p. 226)

Maurice's fruitless, Aschenbachian internal dialogue left him embedded in class difference; but sexuality, which now includes a genuine, other-directed dialogue across class boundaries, is understood as that which can liberate the lovers from their social embeddedness and allow the achievement of unity. Maurice recognizes that they must live as outlaws, "outside class, without relations or money; they must work and stick to each other till death" (p. 239); homosexuality is thus, at least implicitly, understood both as natural, in its "greenwood" aspect[152] (confirmed in the abortive woodcutter coda), and as a political act of resistance to the unnatural pre–World War I British class system.[153] (This is also how the real-life example of Edward Carpenter's relationship with George Merrill might be understood.) Ultimately, *Maurice* seeks ideally to eliminate difference socially and politically as the *Phaedrus* sought ideally to eliminate it spiritually, though again like the *Phaedrus* it recognizes the elusiveness of its goal and the pleasures that deviance might allow in the meantime.

Mary Renault's 1953 novel *The Charioteer* draws its title from the same Platonic metaphor that Forster draws from the *Phaedrus*:[154]

> "Each of the gods has a pair of divine white horses, but the soul only has one. The other" (he smiled to himself; he always remembered this part best)

"is black and scruffy, with a thick neck, a flat face, hairy fetlocks, gray blood-shot eyes, and shaggy ears. He's hard of hearing, thick-skinned, and given to bolting whenever he sees something he wants. So the two beasts rarely see eye to eye, but the charioteer has to keep them on the road together . . ." (p. 108)[155]

If Mann imagined homosexual passion as deviant from, yet implied by, the Platonic ideal, Renault reinterprets Plato's metaphor to suggest that the modern "queer's" allegiance to—or, better, resignification of—the Platonic ideal may include physical passion even as it deviates, not only from what we might term heteronormativity, but from the effeminate, Wildean homosexual "scene" itself. A tattered schoolroom copy of the *Phaedrus* cir-culates among the novel's three main homosexual characters in wartime England and serves as the primary image of a homosexual tradition that, if not exactly healthy in Gide's sense (for the novel's hero Laurie it represents at best "one's limitations" [p. 273]), nevertheless constructs homosexuality as manly rather than effeminate and repudiates the bitchy, drama-queen—Wildean—stereotype represented by many of the novel's minor characters. While postmodern queer readers may find Laurie's stiff-upper-lip stoicism about his "limitations" insufferable, especially his noble self-renunciation in refusing to reveal the naïve Andrew's own unsuspected homosexuality to him, it's also important to note that the novel's entire narrative thrust suggests that Laurie's idealism, including his devotion to the *Phaedrus*, may be misplaced and merely immature. He can't protect Andrew from self-knowledge, and the adult relationship with the third major character, Ralph, that Laurie eventually pursues is physically as well as emotionally satisfying.

Alan Sinfield's recent analysis of *The Charioteer* suggests some of the ways in which the Platonic tradition allows Renault's characters to deviate from the already deviant "Wildean" homosexual norm: "Laurie comes upon an effeminate milieu, but cannot locate himself there. . . . The alter-native, manly ideal is borrowed from Plato's *Phaedrus*."[156] The image of the charioteer and his horses thus initially figures for Renault an *askēsis* in which the effeminate aspect of homosexuality must be repudiated in favor of a manly Greek ideal: "The manly task, as the novel projects it, is to reject that part of oneself; a masculine homosexuality is the only kind that can be admirable, but it is imagined as the heroic repudiation of the effete, effem-inate norm."[157] Even deviant sexuality has its "norm" by 1953, and invok-ing the *Phaedrus* allows Renault's characters to deviate from it. Sinfield suggests that Renault follows popular understandings of the psychoanalyt-ical interpretation of homosexuality, offering "Freudian scenarios" (absent father, overprotective mother) to explain her characters' preferences and "applying the invert/pervert schema (the former are innately homosexual, the latter have been got at)."[158] But the novel is queerer than that in its understanding of the multifarious ways in which homosexuality might be constructed: Laurie recognizes that for the ancient Greeks male–male desire did not preclude heterosexual marriage and reproduction (p. 217) and finds himself attracted to a woman, Nurse Adrian, as well as to Ralph and Andrew, while Alec, a sympathetic, even wise, minor character, offers what we might now see as a sociobiological interpretation: "I think that probably we're all part of nature's remedy for a state of gross overpopulation" (p. 216). At least one scene, in fact, is constructed as a Platonic dialogue among these characters, one whose topic is homosexuality itself (pp. 215–218).[159] Renault's adaptation of the dialogue genre, indeed, is what allows the queer reading of the novel I am proposing here, a reading in which Laurie's single-minded manliness is to be understood as only one, and not necessarily the best, version of homosexuality among the several being dialogically introduced and, in Bakhtinian mode, debated.

For example, the very abjected effeminate queerness repudiated throughout the novel is also simultaneously recognized as an aspect even of the masculine homosexuals Laurie and Ralph, as Sinfield points out: Laurie's own bitchy effeminacy reveals itself in the very responses with which he repudiates those traits in another character.[160] In fact, Laurie's manly relationship with Ralph begins with an effeminate "send-up" when Ralph recognizes him during the heroic circumstances of the evacuation from Dunkirk: " 'Sorry, dearie. Some other time' " (p. 35), a scene to which the novel returns repeatedly. Sinfield suggests that for Renault this effeminacy is only what must be repudiated in the manly homosexual's *askēsis*[161] (though he does not use that term), but the novel's conclusion suggests otherwise: Laurie gives up his immature, stoical idealism (as well as the "Platonic," that is, anerotic friendship with Andrew) in favor of a physically erotic, adult relationship with Ralph, the very character who, despite his manliness, has also and simultaneously been marked with effeminacy by Laurie himself. Renault returns to the *Phaedrus* and the metaphor of the charioteer to make this point:

> Staying each his hunger on what pasture the place affords them, neither the white horse nor the black reproaches his fellow for drawing their master out of the way. They are far, both of them, from home, and lonely, and lengthened by their strife the way has been hard. Now their heads droop side by side till their long manes mingle; and when the voice of the charioteer falls silent they are reconciled for a night in sleep. (p. 380)

This conclusion might remind us of Socrates' own self-deviance in the *Phaedrus'* ultimately indulgent view of physical eroticism between men.

For Renault, the two horses figure the two homosexual lovers, Ralph and Laurie themselves, as well as the conflicting aspects of the soul. This resignification of Plato is reinforced by a further deviance or reinterpretation: the horses/lovers, in their erotic reconciliation (staying their hunger and sleeping together), are acknowledged to have drawn the charioteer off the straight and narrow Platonic path that Laurie tried to follow, but this deviation, unlike that in the *Phaedrus*, is now entirely without reproach. If the "bad" horse formerly represented the tendencies toward effeminacy that the manly homosexual must repudiate, as Sinfield suggests, here the lovers seem reconciled to all aspects of their souls. The Platonic idealism of the *Phaedrus* is what *The Charioteer* ultimately repudiates; only in deviating from it does the homosexual soul reduce, if not eliminate, its own self-deviation.

We might consider one further modern novel as a coda to this chapter on the *Phaedrus* tradition, Robert M. Pirsig's fictional/philosophical extravaganza of 1974, *Zen and the Art of Motorcycle Maintenance: An Inquiry into Values*. This book concerns a man whose philosophical pursuit of "Quality" formerly drove him to madness; following his treatment for mental illness, which has almost completely eliminated this former personality, the narrator now, in the novel's present, is narrating what he remembers of that pursuit while on a motorcycle trip with his son, who is himself showing signs of incipient mental illness. The narrator has named his former self "Phaedrus" because of the identification of the Platonic character of that name with rhetoric: for the narrator, the ancient Greek split between rhetoric and logic is the source of the subject/object division that has plagued Western thought ever since, and he therefore identifies his former self with the rhetoricians.

The novel's philosophical speculations are far removed from the our concerns here, but its presentation of a divided self is also derived from the *Phaedrus* and may serve as a useful reminder that all male–male desire need not be erotic: in *Zen and the Art of Motorcycle Maintenance*, a man's desire for his son's love is linked to his desire for reunification with himself. At issue here, perhaps, is the question of kinship discussed in chapter 1 rather than that of erotic desire, which plays no part at all in this novel.

The narrator's former self, "Phaedrus," is frightening because of his associations with mental illness: "Evil spirit. Insane. From a world without life or death" (p. 65).[162] But this supposedly evil spirit is also the object of the narrator's pursuit, as he and his son Chris motorcycle through the landscape of his own past, specifically the mountains where "Phaedrus" thought out his philosophical discoveries and the town of Bozeman, Montana, where he was an English instructor, and as the narrator's own thoughts retrace the genesis of the ideas that drove "Phaedrus" insane by taking him outside the Western paradigm of normal thought:

> I don't know his whole story. No one ever will, except Phaedrus himself, and he can no longer speak. But from his writings and from what others have said and from fragments of my own recall it should be possible to piece together some kind of approximation of what he was talking about. Since the basic ideas for this Chautauqua were taken from him there will be no real deviation, only an enlargement that may make the Chautauqua more understandable than if it were presented in a purely abstract way. The purpose of the enlargement is not to argue for him, certainly not to praise him. The purpose is to bury him—forever. (p. 69)

The narrator's intentions seem paradoxical from the first: he intends to "bury" or exorcise the ghost of "Phaedrus," the remnants of his former personality, but he intends to do so by recreating the thought processes that led to "Phaedrus' " destruction. Although he intends to bury "Phaedrus," what he actually does is recreate him. And even in this early passage the narrator is clearly longing for self-unity: although he suggests at first that what he recreates will only be an "approximation" of "Phaedrus," he immediately revises himself and declares that there will be no "real deviation." Self-deviance is precisely the problem that must be overcome in *Zen and the Art of Motorcycle Maintenance*, reluctant though the narrator may also be to reunite with his supposedly insane former self.

The term the narrator uses for his philosophical discourse is important for our purposes here as well: "Chautauquas," as he defines them, are "an old-time series of popular talks intended to edify and entertain, improve the mind and bring culture and enlightenment to the ears and thoughts of the hearer" (p. 7). A Chautauqua is precisely not a dialogue whether in Bakhtin's, Buber's, Levinas', or Dollimore's sense, but a one-way lecture delivered by someone more enlightened for the edification of those less so: it seems the perfect mode of discourse for someone determined not to tolerate deviation.

The reunification of the self does take place over the course of the novel, but not in the way the narrator expects: as he recreates "Phaedrus' " intellectual journey, "Phaedrus" himself becomes more and more real, appearing first in the narrator's dreams and then in his relationship with Chris, signaled in the 1999 edition by a typographical shift: " '**Everything is all right now, Chris.**' That's not my voice" (p. 418). In the final pages, "Phaedrus" rather than the narrator becomes the single, unified personality, and is able to establish a relationship with Chris, which the narrator has failed to do:

> "Were you really insane?"
> Why should he ask that?
> "*No!*"
> Astonishment hits. But Chris's eyes sparkle.
> "I knew it," he says. (p. 419)

As Phaedrus remarks, "It has all come together" (p. 419): the two aspects of the narrator's self have not exactly been unified; instead, the former self, "Phaedrus," has driven out or exorcised or buried the original narrator, who disappears for good at this point.[163] "Phaedrus," the "real" self, has triumphed, and in doing so initiates a Buberian dialogue/encounter with Chris rather than lecturing him as the narrator lectured the reader in his Chautauquas. The undivided self is what makes the new father–son dialogue possible: as "Phaedrus" tells himself, "For God's sake relieve him of his burden! Be one person again!" (p. 421). Ironically, the reunification of the self allows for the possibility of deviance in love: "Phaedrus" can tolerate and even encourage Chris' deviating opinions as the narrator, anxiously pursuing self-sameness without ever finding it, could not:

> It's so hot I feel like leaving this helmet off. I remember that in this state
>   they're not required. I fasten it around one of the cables.
> "Put mine there too," Chris says.
> "You need it for safety."
> "You're not wearing yours."
> "All right," I agree, and stow his too. . . .
> When the helmets are off you can talk in a conversational voice. After all
>   these days! (pp. 421–422).

Conversation—which is to say, deviance and friendly, even loving, Bakhtinian disagreement, rather than the hectoring Chautauqua favored by the narrator, is now possible because the narrator's anxiety about himself and his son has disappeared with the old narrator himself.[164] Male–male love, once again, is a matter of style. In *Zen and the Art of Motorcycle Maintenance*, love between a man and a boy is father–son love rather than that between *erastes* and *eromenos*. But as in Plato's *Phaedrus*, an ideal self-identity, once achieved, can tolerate deviation in love.

Conclusion: Deviant Erotics from Plato to the Postmodern ↫

As I was thinking about the conclusion to this book, while my partner and I were visiting my sister in Puerto Rico in the summer of 2003, the U.S. Supreme Court had just struck down *Bowers v. Hardwick*—the 1986 decision that had enabled individual states to continue to criminalize, and to prosecute people for engaging in, "sodomy," even when their laws singled out homosexual sodomy alone. The Supreme Court's 2003 decision in *Lawrence et al. v. Texas* also struck down all remaining state antisodomy laws, including that of the state in which my partner and I reside, Louisiana. Already that summer, on June 17, 2003, Canada had become the first North American country to legalize same-sex marriage, when Prime Minister Jean Chrétien announced that his government would not appeal an Ontario court's decision that equal marriage rights had to be granted to same-sex couples in that province immediately. In fact, one reason we chose to vacation in Puerto Rico that year was to invite my sister to the wedding we were planning in Toronto, which, with luck, will have taken place by the time this book is published. As erotic activity between members of the same sex gains increasing social acceptance and legal recognition, the notion that it is "deviant" may eventually come to be of merely historical interest, rather than the grinding force for daily oppression, repression, depression, and suppression that my partner and I, like other gay men and lesbians, have found it to be all our lives.

However, my fantasized future has, to put it mildly, not yet arrived. As I was writing about E. M. Forster's pessimistic assessment, in the "Terminal Note" to *Maurice*, of the possibilities for positive change in British laws regulating sexuality in 1960, President George W. Bush, in a press conference forty-three years later, was hinting that he might support a Constitutional amendment limiting marriage to one man and one woman.[1] And the next day, the very day that I again sat down at the computer to begin the actual writing of this conclusion—July 31, 2003—the Vatican released a document approved by Pope John Paul II and issued under his orders, "Considerations Regarding Proposals to Give Legal Recognition to Unions Between Homosexual Persons," which stated, according to the *New York Times*, that "legal recognition for gay and lesbian couples would amount to 'approval of deviant behavior, with the consequence of making it a model in present-day society.' "[2] The Vatican document also deems support for such recognition "immoral" because "homosexual acts go against the natural moral law,"[3] and on the same basis opposes the adoption of children by lesbian and gay couples. The Vatican's move is applauded in a letter to the editor in this morning's local newspaper: one Ronald Johnson writes that although he "rarely agree[s] with the Catholic Church," "its 'war on gay marriage' gets a thumbs up from me."[4] The language (at least) of antigay violence, even holy war or Crusade, now (or still) finds its justification in the Vatican's pronouncements.

Such formulations and pronouncements will seem wearisomely familiar to readers of this book, as they are to all who identify themselves as lesbians and gay men: homosexual = unnatural = deviant = immoral = to be suppressed. And despite the recent North American advances in gay rights mentioned above, the legal, religious, and social ramifications of this formula still retain their oppressive force, as the president gears up to write us out of the Constitution, as the pope writes us out of the Kingdom of God, and as our fellow citizens declare war.

It is in this all too immediate context that the merely historical may regain some of its urgency. History, as I hope this book has shown, can help us resignify one of the key terms in the formula of oppression, deviance, and, in doing so, may help us resignify the entire equation as well. For while a church may believe that it speaks an eternal truth good for all times, and while a government with imperial ambitions may believe that its own values are transcultural—good for all people—history is considerably queerer. It is true that male–male desire has been understood as deviant in one sense or another in all the texts I have examined; however, this form of deviance has itself been valued differently in each: its links to law, religion, nature, and morality shift with historical and cultural currents, and the current views of popes and presidents represent no more than one such shift, oppressive though it presently is. Queer intellectual history allows us to claim the deviant as our kin, just as, according to the *Lysis*, we claim one another: as that which can be both ourselves and not-ourselves at once.

For classical Athens, indeed, male–male desire and its physical expression—within the rather strict limits described in chapter 1—were inscribed within the behavioral norm even to the extent of standing in for all forms of erotic desire; and male–male desire, at least, is (as Wilde claimed) foundational for Plato's understanding of the philosophical life in his early and middle-period dialogues. Its physical expression, however, is already understood as deviant in Plato's works: genital contact between men is a deviation from the ideally spiritual love of the Forms, which ultimately excludes desire altogether. But for Plato, this deviance is not abjected as it often is in later constructions of male–male desire; instead, physical desire is understood as essential to the pursuit of spiritual love. In the *Symposium*, the ascent of Diotima's ladder of love never leaves behind the desire for bodies (presumptively male), while the *Phaedrus* explicitly excuses this deviant physicality as it occurs between male partners who have started on the path of *askēsis* together. The physical expression of male–male desire is thus for Plato, through his middle period, a necessary form of deviance— deviance not from a social norm, but from an ideal.

The male–male erotic relationship itself is also, for the early- and middle-period Plato, defined by deviance rather than by identity or opposition, sameness or difference: the least unsatisfactory definition of *philia* for Socrates in the *Lysis* involves kinship, or difference within sameness, and it is this particular definition that, at least temporarily, points his interlocutors toward a pedagogical/erotic *erastes*/*eromenos* relationship. The deviant remains central to the understanding of *eros* in both the *Symposium* (especially in the speeches preceding and following Socrates') and in the *Phaedrus*, in which the lover, the beloved, and the god may resemble one another (or, to use Levinas' terms, exist in proximity to one another) without ever achieving identity, even as human life itself deviates from the divine. Love here is also, crucially, a matter of self-deviance, as the soul's conflicting impulses can be brought into harmony only through *askēsis*. While the ultimate goal may be self-sameness, it is deviance that leads to it.

The exploration of deviance finds its complementary form in the dialogue, itself an expression of deviance. The structure of both the *Symposium* and the *Phaedrus*, in which the true Socratic doctrine is expressed only in a speech that follows other, faulty speeches, and which therefore is able to draw on them, demonstrates this point perfectly: because Socrates' interlocutors are heard first, the true speech is structurally deviant from them— not opposed to them, because in both cases it is driven by the terms they have already established, but merely deviating in a manner that Kristeva might deem carnivalesque. And because the final speeches are in each case understood as true, the preceding speeches are themselves doctrinally deviant. (And in the *Symposium*, giving Alcibiades the last word suggests yet another deviant truth). In the *Lysis*, Socrates' own unending internal deviations from his own doctrines mirror the deviant kinship of male–male desire, as do the physical wanderings that frame all three dialogues. For Xenophon, the dialogue form can suggest a flirtatious male–male eroticism at odds with the doctrine of self-sameness that favors love of the mind over love of the body in all its difference.

The Greco-Roman period itself deviates from the normativization of male–male desire in classical Athens. The revaluation of marriage evident in the dialogues of Plutarch and Pseudo-Lucian simultaneously suggests, not necessarily a rejection, but a revaluation of male–male erotics as well. Specifically, the emergence of the physical Alcibiades rather than the spiritual Socrates as a figure for this form of *eros* complements a new devaluation of male–male desire itself, whether in Pseudo-Lucian's ambiguity or in Plutarch's suggestion that male–male desire may now be understood not only as deviant, but also as abject, a negative valuation reflected in the irreducible difference between the philosophical positions his characters take in their irascible debates.

It is not surprising, then, that Cicero's refusal of male–male erotics is couched in a dialogue form that eschews dialogue. The *Tusculan Disputations* rejects male–male erotics in a way that suggests a specific rebuke to the *Lysis*, while *Laelius: On Friendship* eliminates all discussion of the topic, just as it eliminates the possibility of desire in friendship. In doing so, Cicero also eliminates the delicate Platonic balance of sameness and difference that I have been calling "deviance" for a ruthless self-sameness in friendship, in which the friend is simply—imperialistically—assimilated to the self. The elimination of genuine dialogism must logically follow, as no deviant opinions, whether from others or within the self, are allowed to question Cicero's monologic doctrines.

The Christian Middle Ages draw on both Ciceronian Stoicism and the Bible to create another monologic, and condemnatory, understanding of male–male erotics. But even from within this tradition, writers like Aelred of Rievaulx are also able to reintroduce desire as a factor in relations between men, precisely because these relations also participate in the Christian's desire for God. The reintroduction of desire also reintroduces difference: the self-identity that for Cicero constituted friendship becomes for Aelred a self-deviation that can never achieve perfect unity short of heaven. Equality in friendship for Aelred thus becomes a matter of trying out different hierarchical, and even gender, roles. And for Aelred as for Plato, even carnal relationships, marked by such deviations, can serve as an introduction to spiritual friendship. As it was for Plato, dialogue is for Aelred the form that best complements his doctrine of friendship: for Aelred the performative nature of male–male relations requires multiple, even carnivalesque, voices.

The monologic Christian doctrine in which male–male desire must be rejected as deviant from the Biblical and sacramental norm remains powerful in Italian humanist thought of the early modern era, and is clearly expressed in such Christian neoplatonic dialogues as Ficino's commentary on the *Symposium* and Castiglione's *Book of the Courtier*. Their deliberate misrepresentations of Plato tend to eliminate, excoriate, or trivialize male–male erotics as they attempt to reorient Platonic philosophy. Christian Neo-Platonism thus also tends to eliminate carnivalesque or Bakhtinian dialogue itself, not only in Ficino's undifferentiated speeches but even in Castiglione's lively text: the expression of the Christian neoplatonic doctrine of love monologically silences all discussion.

The same is not true of those humanist thinkers more heavily influenced by Aristotle. Tullia d'Aragona, for example, imagines a lively discussion of male–male desire. Less committed to the neoplatonic ideal of unity and more interested in the irreducible differences that define human life on earth, Tullia can find a place for deviant erotics in her philosophical system. While such thinkers, still Christian, may not allow male–male desire into the mainstream, her Bakhtinian commitment to multiple perspectives carves out a space for it precisely as (a nonabject) deviant. The same commitment to exploring multiple points of view also returns the genuinely dialogical to the dialogue genre in Tullia's work.

A more radical understanding of deviance is evident in the libertine dialogues of the sixteenth, seventeenth, and eighteenth centuries. The scientific revolution allows for a more skeptical cultural critique than was possible in the earlier period, and this tool is wielded against Christianity itself—and indeed against all monological models of truth—by such writers as Vignali, Rocco, Diderot, and Sade. All four use cultural critique to reclaim the deviant for nature, and suggest that at least some form of male–male desire, if not male–male desire itself, is inscribed within the natural: it is deviant only as defined by artificial human laws, themselves erected for political ends. Sade goes so far as to make phallic similarity itself the natural norm in all human relations, including the erotic—a move that leads in his case to a solipsistic dead end that is also the end of the dialogical.

The scientific revolution, continuing into the nineteenth century and beyond, also played its role in the development of sexology, including the various competing theories medicalizing and psychologizing what now came to be called "homosexuality" even as religious and civil law continued to stigmatize it; in most such formulations homosexuality remained deviant, however it was explained. Late nineteenth- and twentieth-century writers thus had several competing discourses of homosexual deviance upon which they might draw. Wilde chose to encode it as "sin" and "criminality," though at the same time radically resignifying and revaluing those discourses with another, that of aestheticism. Even more radically, he also resignified Plato in order to call the self-identical subject into question, and dialogue proved to be the ideal genre for the expression of such self-deviance.

Gide chose another available discourse of homosexuality, repudiating both Wilde and Wilde's resignification of Plato as well as the medical models of homosexuality. For Gide, homosexuality is deviant only statistically, and—in line with the *Symposium* tradition of cultural critique—only when judged by social conventions rather than nature. In strictly natural, even natural-historical, terms, homosexuality is healthy. But in naturalizing homosexuality, Gide also rejects the notion of any homosexual identity, de-essentializing nature itself, and once again the oscillations of the homo-sexual subject-in-process are reflected in the oscillations of dialogue.

Twentieth-century novelists who draw on the Platonic dialogue, from Mann to Pirsig, emphasize the *Phaedrus'* internal self-deviations. Represented as internal dialogue, this self-deviance may result in a com-plete breakdown of the self: drawing on the medical model of homosexual-ity as disease, Mann finds that deviance from the Platonic ideal is, at least for the creative artist, built into the ideal itself. But this self-deviance may also be resolved through the acceptance of the physicality of homosexuality along with its social deviance, as Forster for this purpose resignifies Plato once again. Forster also varies the traditional notion of difference within the homosexual relationship itself, finding in class difference a replacement for the more traditional age difference emphasized by Mann. Indeed, for most of the writers considered here, the homosexual relationship is defined by deviance within the relationship itself: sex-sameness is varied by age or class differences. For Renault, the important deviance may be one of gender identity, as her hero gives up his naïve Platonism in favor of an adult sexuality that accepts several deviant ways of being homosexual.

Male–male desire, then, is always understood as involving deviance, both deviance from a cultural ideal and deviance between male–male lovers themselves. However, the modern insistence that deviance is identical with immorality is far from being a necessary corollary. The recent controversies over gay rights suggest that the postmodern period may be one in which deviance is resignified yet again. Two recent texts hint at the directions such resignification may be taking, as well as the roles that dialogue—and Plato himself—may play in this ongoing process.

Hedwig and the Angry Inch, a rock musical by John Cameron Mitchell (book) and Stephen Trask (music and lyrics), opened off-Broadway to rave reviews on Valentine's Day, 1998; it was an immediate hit, and was eventually published and turned into a well-received film.[5] While plays and films technically fall outside the scope of this study, as evidence of the continued influence of Plato's dialogues on postmodern considerations of sex- and gender- (as well as political) deviance, *Hedwig* could scarcely be bettered. It tells the story of a young German man, Hansel, who is born into the Berlin bifurcated by the Wall, seduced by an American corporal, and left neither male nor female—now "Hedwig"—after a botched sex-change operation that he undergoes at the corporal's behest (hence the titular "angry inch"). Abandoned by the corporal, Hedwig eventually becomes an unsuccessful singer and tells the audience this story in a performance interspersed with songs. Meanwhile, another lover, Tommy Gnosis, who has become a star using Hedwig's songs, is performing across the street; the two are united at the end, as "projected male and female faces merge into a single one" (p. 79).

Hedwig's life is defined by Aristophanes' speech in the *Symposium*, "a bedtime story that mother once whispered to me in the dark and later retracted" (p. 25), the subject of one of her songs entitled "The Origin of Love" (pp. 26–31), during which the complementary male and female faces are first projected: originally,

> Folks roamed the earth
> Like big rolling kegs.
> They had two sets of arms.
> They had two sets of legs.
> They had two faces peering
> Out of one giant head
> So they could watch all around them
> As they talked; while they read.
> And they never knew nothing of love.
> It was before the origin of love. (p. 26)

The original humans, in Hedwig's understanding of the Platonic myth, had no experience of love because, in their fully unified state, they had nothing to desire. In her song, Hedwig continues recounting the familiar story, supplementing and universalizing it with other myths of origin, Norse (p. 27), Hindu, and Egyptian (p. 30), as well as with evolutionary theory (p. 27). Love—specifically Hedwig's love for Tommy Gnosis—results from the violent bifurcation of this originary unity:

> Last time I saw you
> We had just split in two.

You were looking at me.
I was looking at you.
You had a way so familiar,
But I could not recognize,
Cause you had blood on your face;
I had blood in my eyes.
But I could swear by your expression
That the pain down in your soul
Was the same as the one down in mine.
That's the pain,
Cuts a straight line
Down through the heart;
We called it love.
So we wrapped our arms around each other,
Trying to shove ourselves back together.
We were making love,
Making love. (pp. 30–31)

As in much Platonic theory, desire results from a lack, and the Platonic myth provides a satisfying description of erotic longing—but also of a longing for political unification, and for the unification of the self. (It's worth noting that Aristophanes' speech, clearly to be understood as deficient in the *Symposium* itself, is here taken as the true definition of love, while Socrates'/Diotima's speech, for Plato the true one, is ignored;[6] this preference for Aristophanes' speech is characteristic of modern popular culture.) Having heard Aristophanes' story, Hansel/Hedwig realizes that it will define her/his future course:

It is clear that I must find my other half. But is it a he or a she? . . . What does this person look like? Identical to me? Or somehow complementary? Does my other half have what I don't? Did he get the looks, the luck, the love? Were we really separated forcibly or did he just run off with the good stuff? Or did I? Will this person embarrass me? And what about sex? Is that how we put ourselves back together again? . . . can two people actually become one again? And if we're driving on the Autobahn when it happens, can we still use the diamond lane? (pp. 31–32)

The pointed joke about the German Autobahn reminds the audience that Hedwig's situation is political as well as sexual, and the questions about sex that it is erotic; but most of Hedwig's questions concern her/his own identity. Hedwig's stage manager and current lover, Yitzhak, sardonically holds up a mirror in answer to Hedwig's questions.

For Hedwig herself embodies an answer: neither male nor female—or both male and female—s/he may be understood either as a tragically divided figure, or as an embodiment of unity. S/he is, in fact, like the Berlin Wall: "Don't you know me? I'm the new Berlin Wall. Try and tear me down!" (p. 14). The challenge, here and in the following song "Tear Me Down" (pp. 14–18), is also a plea:

> Listen
> There ain't much of a difference
> between a bridge and a wall
> Without me right in the middle, babe
> you would be nothing at all. (pp. 15–18)

The wall can be a point of crossing as well as a barrier, and Hedwig a site of unity as well as self-division ("East and West / Slavery and Freedom / Man and Woman / Top and Bottom" [p. 15], as Yitzhak sings). The merging or reunion of personae that concludes the play thus merely confirms the potential for unity that the in-between character has embodied from the beginning. This potential is not confined to Hedwig: Yitzhak, a male character performed by a woman, Miriam Shor, in the original production and in the film, also becomes an in-between figure at the end as Hedwig (performed by John Cameron Mitchell himself), according to the stage directions, cross-dresses him: "(She holds the wig out to YITZHAK. With a sigh, YITZHAK takes it and begins to put it on HEDWIG's head. HEDWIG stops him. YITZHAK hesitates, then places the wig on his own head)" (p. 75). Hedwig hands over her/his identifying "wig" in a gesture that encourages universal participation in his/her own in-betweenness.[7]

Hedwig and the Angry Inch suggests that postmodernity may make the very concept of "male–male desire" obsolete, as it dispenses with anatomical sex itself as a meaningful category. Eve Kosofsky Sedgwick, perhaps the most influential figure in the establishment of Queer Theory as a mode of cultural inquiry, reinforces this impression in a dialogical text published the year after *Hedwig* made its debut, *A Dialogue on Love*.[8] A journal of Sedgwick's therapy sessions, undertaken after a breast-cancer diagnosis, with Dr. Shannon Van Wey, whose own notes on their sessions (typographically distinguished with small capitals) provide the dialogical counterpoint to Sedgwick's observations, *A Dialogue on Love* acknowledges a debt to Plato's dialogues in a journal entry in which Sedgwick, or Eve as she is named in the journal, considers various genres for "writing of Shannon and me": she rejects the case history and the novel, but acknowledges that

"I've thought about Platonic dialogues—that's getting closer," though finally settling on the Japanese form of haibun: prose narrative interspersed with haiku, typically used for travel narratives, the haiku in this case also distinguished typographically (p. 194). While "haibun" provides an accurate generic term for the portions of the book that Eve composes herself, the title, *A Dialogue on Love*, harks back to Plato and specifically to the dialogues I have been considering in this book, and the overall structure, in which Eve's haibun alternates with Shannon's notes—the latter occupying more and more space as the text continues—is more dialogical than the classic, reflective Japanese haibun. It is, in fact, even Buberian in its record of encounters with the other.

Eve's central concern, as it emerges over the course of her therapy, is one she shares with Hedwig: the boundaries of the self. The construction of a self is understood as *askēsis*: according to Shannon, "THE YOU I SEE WHEN I LOOK AT YOU, SITTING THERE ON THE COUCH SO NICELY, IS THE PRODUCT OF AN ARDUOUS AND ALMOST ENDLESS LABOR. . . . THE PERSON I KNOW IS SOMEONE WHO'S BEEN TORTUOUSLY POLISHED . . ." (p. 32). So is the project of therapy, a remaking of the self: Shannon thinks about "HOW I WANT YOU TO *TURN OUT* DIFFERENT"—and Eve is "a bit surprised he'll admit to keeping a list of how he wants me different" (p. 60; emphasis in text).

Remaking the self is initially understood as the problem to be solved in therapy: "If I can fit the pieces of this self back together at all, I don't want them to be the way they were" (p. 7). Eve feels, indeed, that she lacks any identity at all because of her particular family situation,

> as if "middle child"
> were like an identity—
> or the lack of one,

since it seemed the very essence of middle-childness to identify with everyone *but* myself. (p. 36; emphasis in text)

Shannon agrees: "SHE COMES INTO THESE YEARS WITHOUT A SECURE GRASP ON WHO HER SELF IS" (p. 77), a problem related to her sexuality ("ESTRANGEMENT FROM FEELINGS OF SEXUALITY" [p. 90]) as well as to the family romance involving both her mother's ambiguous sexuality and her relationship with her sister (pp. 134–135). Shannon's notes cite Eve's own sense of failure as a self: "I'VE RUINED MY BODY OR IT'S RUINED ME, NOTHING IS GOING TO WORK. I REFUSE OR FAIL GENDER CATEGORIES" (p. 193).

But as the text continues, the emphasis of the therapeutic *askēsis* shifts away from fixing to embracing Eve's lack of self-identity. Shannon is the first to suggest that a viable self need not include rigid self-identity:

> he wants me to have
> a more continuous sense
> of moving through time.

"Less spastic" is his gracious description. "To see yourself being more of the same person."

> Not identical,
> not grappled tight to myself,
> just floating onward. (p. 60)

Eve herself comes to value the self that is not self-identity, especially in love:

> . . . So
> the point could only
>
> lie in valuing
> all the transformations and
> transitivities
>
> in all directions
> *for* their difference, trans-i-ness,
> and their skilled nature. (p. 114)

"Also, think how inefficient it is, this way of keeping one's own self consolidated and comforted" (p. 140). Eve in fact eventually has trouble reconciling this unconsolidated self with writing her first-person journal entries, especially as she becomes interested in the craft of weaving, as Shannon notes:

> RESISTANCE TO GOING BACK TO THE *DIALOGUE ON LOVE* IS THAT PRODUCTION OF THE FIRST PERSON IS BOTH LABOR INTENSIVE AND FELT TO BE CONSTRAINING, THAT THERE WERE EMOTIONAL REGISTERS THAT WEREN'T AVAILABLE WHILE GENERATING FIRST PERSON. A TEXTURE BOOK WOULDN'T NEED TO HAVE A FIRST PERSON AT ALL, ANY MORE THAN WEAVING ITSELF DOES. (p. 207)

Tibetan Buddhism, especially as expressed in *The Tibetan Book of the Dead*, like weaving, provides an alternative manner for imagining the self: "THE MODELS USED ARE INTERSUBJECTIVE (E.G., TEACHER/STUDENT) BUT NONDUAL. BUT E: 'NONDUALISM IS MOTHER'S MILK TO ME' " (p. 215).[9] "Mother's milk"—the family romance centering on Eve's abject love for her mother—is now the source of pleasure rather than anxiety about the unconsolidated self.

An aspect of this unconsolidated self—perhaps the aspect that allows this pleasure in it—is Eve's queer self-identification with gay men, one that joyfully blurs the very boundaries of gender identity that at other times she considers her failure. As she tells Shannon near the outset of their therapy, she is proudest of "having a life where work and love are impossible to tell apart. Most of my academic work is about gay men, so it might seem strange that I would say that—not being a man, not even, I don't think, being gay. . . . one true thing about me is that my love is *with* gay men" (p. 23; emphasis in text). In this carefully worded observation Eve identifies herself neither as gay nor as not-gay, but identifies her "love" with both gayness and maleness: here as in *Hedwig* (which lacks the careful qualifications Eve provides here), binary distinctions like male/female and gay/straight come to seem terribly crude term and concepts for the categorization of selves.[10] From her mother's first explanation of homosexuality, Eve understands gayness as a mode of resistance to rigid sex/gender relations, as Shannon's notes suggest:

> THERE COULD BE SOMETHING OTHER THAN THE TRADITIONAL HETERO RELATIONS, AND MEN WHO MIGHT HAVE AN INTEREST IN WOMEN OTHER THAN THE TRADITIONAL ONE. WHAT STRIKES ME MOST HERE IS EARLY ABILITY TO TURN A SITUATION OF PROHIBITION AND RIGID EITHER/OR INTO A NEW INTEREST THAT IS ELASTIC, PRODUCTIVE, EXCITING FOR E'S VIEW OF WORLD. (p. 75)

Rigid prohibition, the cultural policing of sex/gender roles and relations, becomes through gayness a mode of production and creativity that helps Eve understand her own unconsolidated self. This is especially true in her relation to her family because gayness provides a model of affiliation not based on blood ties, "[n]ot structured around blood and law" (p. 130). In fact, her relation to gayness eventually provides a model for understanding her own anomalous place within her family:

> imagine somebody who expends extortionate amounts of energy trying to convince the members of some group (not a particularly high-status group, in fact a clannish, defensive, stigmatized, but proud, and above all an interesting group) that she, too, is to be accepted as—and in fact, truly is—a member of this group. A kid, a Kosofsky—or later, gay. But each time it's in the face of some inherent, in fact obvious absurdity about the claim. (p. 154)

To be accepted as "truly" gay is a goal of Eve's self-fashioning *askēsis* (the desire for an interesting life) comparable to acceptance by her family.[11] But this identification is also, and simultaneously, understood as obviously absurd. It is neither an identification nor a disidentification with her family or with gay men, but precisely the absurd situation between the two that drives the self Eve is constantly creating. As Shannon notes, "SHE FEELS SHE HAS ALWAYS BEEN THE WRONG PERSON TO DO THINGS SHE HAS DONE PROFESSIONALLY AND HAS SOME INVESTMENT IN MAKING THAT WORK, OR IN DEMONSTRATING THE INTEREST OF THAT BORDER-CROSSING POSITION" (p. 179). The carnivalesque, border-crossing position is the position Eve takes up not only professionally, but as a self; or, she takes it up professionally because of the investment she has made in it as a self.

Eve and Shannon are also able to take up such a position in their own relationship within the project of therapy; after initial frustration with what she perceives as his lack of intelligence, countered by her own pedagogical impulse to make him smarter, they eventually reach "a tectonic shift in what I've presumed were the fixed zones of permission and prohibition" (p. 94)—another moment of border crossing, this time in an individual relationship rather than in identification with a group. Thus,

> The space of Shannon is both myself and not.
>
> > The place where talking
> > to someone else is also
> > talking to myself.
>
> I've never experienced this interlocution before. (p. 115)

It is the unconsolidated self that, like gay men, crosses outside the zones of prohibition. The therapeutic "interlocution" is here the model, as identification with gayness is elsewhere in the book, and the therapeutic project becomes mutual ["Shannon's avowal of my functioning as something of a transformational object for him as he also does for me" (p. 167)]. As Eve observes when she sees Shannon's notes, "THE NOTES ARE TOLD MOSTLY FROM MY POINT OF VIEW" (p. 200)—a point illustrated by this note itself, as it is in several cited above.[12] This crossing of the boundaries of the self is ultimately a source of love: having accidentally kicked some pine mulch onto the sidewalk while running an errand before one of their sessions, Eve observes Shannon replacing it, "a time-lapse graphic that lets Shannon occupy the place where I was, encountering my ghost without recognition, unmaking my mistake—me, turning back, seeing it. And I love that his care for me was not care for *me*" (p. 219; emphasis in text). Eve and Shannon occupy the same space, though at different moments, and share a relation with the displaced pine mulch, though not the same relation. His care for her—unmaking her mistake—is impersonal, and the very impersonality of his care and their connection in this incident is what produces

Eve's love. As Deborah P. Britzman has suggested, "[i]f we are to work our identifications and not our points of view, if the resources that the other offers are what allows one and the other's reparative urges to deepen, then *A Dialogue on Love* is one place to learn this again."[13]

The therapeutic "interlocution" that signals the pleasurable border crossing between selves is also expressed as dialogue, both the dialogues recorded in Eve's narratives and Shannon's notes and the dialogue between the narratives and the notes themselves, which do not always agree, as in the differing accounts of the same incident given on pp. 118–119. Early on, Eve feels that Shannon's sloppiness leaves her "all alone (it feels that way) with way too much responsibility. How, in such loose-knit colloquy, to find a place for my desire? Or anger?" (p. 43). But the looseness of the colloquy soon comes to be understood as a desirable quality of their dialogue:

> And yet our absolutely alien mental flows
>
> > Debouch so freely
> > into the room where we meet!
> > A promise to me. (p. 56)

Eve comes to see their therapy sessions as a shared, dialogical creation,

> > giddily welcoming
> > speculation of
> >
> > what words may arise
> > and at what instant they may,
> > bubbling, between us. (p. 184)

Postmodern dialogue points one direction toward the future I fantasized at the beginning of this conclusion: it arises in the space in between, the space occupied by Hedwig, by Eve, by the queer—no longer necessarily to be defined as male.

Notes ⤳

INTRODUCTION

1. C. P. Cavafy, "In a Town of Osroini," 1917, in his *Collected Poems*, trans. Edmund Keeley and Philip Sherrard, ed. George Savidis (Princeton, NJ: Princeton University Press, 1975), p. 66. The Greek text appears in Cavafy's *Ta Poiemata*, ed. G. P. Savidis, 2 vols. (Athens: Ikaros, 1963, repr. 1997), vol. 1, p. 80.

2. Plato, *Charmides*, trans. Rosamond Kent Sprague, in his *Complete Works*, ed. John M. Cooper (Indianapolis: Hackett, 1997), pp. 640–663, at p. 641, 154a.

3. Ibid., p. 641, 154d. *Sophrosune* is translated variously as "prudence," "temperance," "wisdom"; it suggests "a well-developed consciousness of oneself and one's legitimate duties in relation to others (where it will involve self-restraint and showing due respect) and in relation to one's own ambitions, social standing, and the relevant expectations as regards one's own behavior": John M. Cooper, headnote to *Charmides*, in Plato, *Complete Works*, p. 639. See also Matthias Vorwerk, "Plato on Virtue: Definitions of *sophrosune* in Plato's *Charmides* and in Plotinus' *Enneads* 1.2 (19)," *American Journal of Philology* 122 (2001): 29–47.

4. C. P. Cavafy, "In a Town of Osroene," in *Complete Poems*, trans. Rae Dalven (New York: Harcourt Brace, 1976), p. 68; "In a Town of Osroini," in *Before Time Could Change Them: The Complete Poems of Constantine P. Cavafy*, trans. Theoharis C. Theoharis (New York: Harcourt, 2001), p. 61. The Greek term is "*to erotiko tou prosopo* [τὸ ἐρωτικό του πρόσωπο]."

5. Plato, *Charmides*, p. 642, 155d.

6. See Savidis' note on this poem in Cavafy, *Collected Poems*, p. 216.

7. David Greenberg, *The Construction of Homosexuality* (Chicago: University of Chicago Press, 1988). For another major work of historical synthesis, see Byrne Fone, *Homophobia: A History* (New York: Metropolitan, 2000).

8. Scholarly work on Plato's use of the dialogue form is voluminous. For some useful guidance, see Michael C. Stokes, *Plato's Socratic Conversations: Drama and Dialectic in Three Dialogues* (New Haven: Yale University Press, 1983), especially the bibliographical survey, pp. 1–3; Kent F. Moors, "Plato's Use of Dialogue," *Classical World* 72 (1978): 77–93; Kenneth M. Sayre, *Plato's Literary Gardens: How to Read a Platonic Dialogue* (Notre Dame: Notre Dame University Press, 1995); and the essays collected in *Platonic Writings, Platonic Readings*, ed.

Charles L. Griswold (New York: Routledge, 1988), especially Rosemary Desjardins, "Why Dialogues? Plato's Serious Play," pp. 110–125. Also informative is David Sedley's lecture "The Dramatis Personae of Plato's *Phaedo*," in *Philosophical Dialogues: Plato, Hume, Wittgenstein*, ed. Timothy Smiley (Oxford: Oxford University Press/British Academy, 1995), pp. 3–26; Francisco J. Gonzalez, "Introduction: The Need for a Reexamination of Plato's Dialectic," in his *Dialectic and Dialogue: Plato's Practice of Philosophical Inquiry* (Evanston: Northwestern University Press, 1998), pp. 1–16.

9. I am not the first to consider these three Platonic dialogues as a group: see *Lysis, Phaedrus, and Symposium: Plato on Homosexuality*, trans. Benjamin Jowett, ed. Eugene O'Connor (Amherst, NY: Prometheus, 1991).

10. See the discussion below.

11. Jonathan Dollimore, *Sexual Dissidence: Augustine to Wilde, Freud to Foucault* (Oxford: Clarendon, 1991), p. 15.

12. See Dylan Evans, *An Introductory Dictionary of Lacanian Psychoanalysis* (New York: Routledge, 1996), pp. 58–59.

13. Jeffrey Jerome Cohen, *Of Giants: Sex, Monsters, and the Middle Ages*, Medieval Cultures 17 (Minneapolis: University of Minnesota Press, 1999), p. 180.

14. Dollimore, *Sexual Dissidence*, p. 21.

15. "Their Beginning," trans. Rae Dalven, in *Complete Poems*, p. 109. In Theoharis' version, it is in their "lawless pleasure" that "the lines of power" originate: "Their Origin," p. 118.

16. See the discussion in chapter 2.

17. Dollimore, *Sexual Dissidence*, p. 33.

18. Roger Scruton, *Sexual Desire: A Philosophical Investigation* (London: Weidenfeld and Nicolson, 1986), pp. 283, 305–311. Elisabeth Young-Bruehl turns the accusation of narcissism back against the accusers, defining "narcissistic" homophobia as intolerance for "the idea that their exist people who are not like them": Elisabeth Young-Bruehl, *The Anatomy of Prejudices* (Cambridge, MA: Harvard University Press, 1996), p. 33. She also understands homophobia as the desire to preserve sameness, p. 36.

19. Steven Bruhm, *Reflecting Narcissus: A Queer Aesthetic* (Minneapolis: University of Minnesota Press, 2001) reads the myth of Narcissus as a figure for male–male desire that does not represent a fear of otherness but is rather "continually destroying the political safety promised by sameness," p. 178.

20. Cf. David Halperin, "How to Do the History of Homosexuality," in his *How to Do the History of Homosexuality* (Chicago: University of Chicago Press, 2002), pp. 104–137, especially his discussion of the category "paederasty," pp. 113–117. Halperin rightly distinguishes between the tradition of pederasty and those of male–male friendship (pp. 117–121), of inversion (pp. 121–130), and of modern homosexuality (pp. 130–134), but for my purposes here it is more important to point out that deviance—an interplay of sameness and difference—is an essential component of the relationships that fall into most, if not all, of these categories, as the remainder of this book suggests.

21. Mixail Bakhtin, "Discourse Typology in Prose," trans. Richard Balthazar and I. R. Titunik, in *Readings in Russian Poetics: Formalist and Structuralist Views*, ed. Ladislav Matejka and Krystyna Pomorska (Ann Arbor: University of Michigan Press, 1978), pp. 176–198, at p. 176. This essay first appeared in the original version of Bakhtin's *Problems of Dostoevsky's Poetics: Problemy tvorchestva Dostoevskogo* (Leningrad: Priboj, 1929), pp. 105–135. A somewhat different version of this essay appears in the revised version of 1963 as a portion of ch. 5, "Discourse in Dostoevsky": see *Problems of Dostoevsky's Poetics*, ed. and trans. Caryl Emerson (Minneapolis: University of Minnesota Press, 1984), pp. 185–203.

22. Ibid., p. 189.

23. Julia Kristeva, "Word, Dialogue, and Novel" (1969), in her *Desire in Language: A Semiotic Approach to Literature and Art*, ed. Leon S. Roudiez, trans. Thomas Gora, Alice Jardine, and Leon S. Roudiez (New York: Columbia University Press, 1980), pp. 64–91, at p. 81. For Bakhtin's own comments on Socrates and the Socratic dialogue, see M. M. Bakhtin, "Epic and Novel: Toward a Methodology for the Study of the Novel," in *The Dialogic Imagination*, ed. Michael Holquist, trans. Caryl Emerson and Michael Holquist (Austin: University of Texas Press, 1981), pp. 3–40, at pp. 24–26, and his *Rabelais and His World*, trans. Hélène Iswolsky (Bloomington, IN: Indiana University Press, 1984), pp. 121, 168–169, 286. But cf. Julia Annas, "Many Voices: Dialogue and Development in Plato," in her *Platonic Ethics, Old and New* (Ithaca, NY: Cornell University Press, 1999), pp. 9–30, which argues that the polyphonic quality of Plato's dialogues masks a unitary ethical doctrine.

24. Martin Buber, *I and Thou*, 2nd ed., trans. Walter Kaufmann (New York: Scribner's, 1970), p. 133.

25. Ibid., p. 53.

26. Ibid., p. 150.

27. Ibid., p. 151.

28. "[I]n truth language does not reside in man but man stands in language and speaks out of it," ibid., p. 89.

29. Ibid., pp. 115–116.

30. On dialogue with the self, see ibid., p. 152.

31. Ibid., p. 151.

32. Ibid., p. 182.

33. Emmanuel Levinas, "Martin Buber's Thought and Contemporary Judaism," in *Outside the Subject*, trans. Michael B. Smith (Stanford: Stanford University Press, 1993), pp. 4–19, at p. 10. See also ibid. "Apropos of Buber: Some Notes," in pp. 40–48.

34. Ibid., "Martin Buber, Gabriel Marcel, and Philosophy," pp. 20–39, at p. 21.

35. As is evident throughout *Problems of Dostoevsky's Poetics*. In the passage from "Epic and Novel" cited above, "Bakhtin comes very close to naming Socrates as the first novelist" (Michael Holquist, "Introduction" to *The Dialogic Imagination*, pp. xv–xxxiv, at p. xxxii).

36. Michel Foucault, *The History of Sexuality, Volume I: An Introduction*, trans. Robert Hurley (New York: Vintage, 1980), especially pp. 17–49.

37. Eve Kosofsky Sedgwick, "Paranoid Reading and Reparative Reading; or, You're So Paranoid, You Probably Think This Introduction Is about You," in *Novel Gazing: Queer Readings in Fiction*, ed. Eve Kosofsky Sedgwick (Durham, NC: Duke University Press, 1997), pp. 1–37, at pp. 2–3. The revised version of this essay, "Paranoid Reading and Reparative Reading, or, You're So Paranoid, You Probably Think This Essay is about You," in Sedgwick's *Touching Feeling: Affect, Pedogogy, Performativity* (Durham, NC: Duke University Press, 2003), pp. 123–151, omits this passage.

1   EROTICS OF FRIENDSHIP: FROM PLATO'S *LYSIS* TO AELRED OF RIEVAULX

1. For Cicero's Greek influences, see the Introduction to *Laelius de Amicitia*, in Cicero, *De Senectute, De Amicitia, De Divinatione*, ed. and trans. William Armistead Falconer, Loeb Classical Library 154 (Cambridge, MA: Harvard University Press, 1923), p. 106, and the Introduction to Cicero, *Laelius: On Friendship*, in *Cicero: On the Good Life*, trans. Michael Grant (Harmondsworth: Penguin, 1971), pp. 13–20.

2. David Konstan, *Friendship in the Classical World* (Cambridge, Eng.: Cambridge University Press, 1997), p. 53; this entire chapter, pp. 53–92, is helpful in this context, and see also *Aspects of Friendship in the Greco-Roman World, Journal of Roman Archaeology* Supplementary Series 43 (Portsmouth, RI, 2001); Lynette G. Mitchell, "Friends and Enemies in Athenian Politics," *Greece and Rome*, second series 43 (1996): 11–30. Alfons Fürst, "Freundschaft als Tugend: Über den Verlust der Wirklichkeit im antiken Freundschaftsbegriff," *Gymnasium* 104 (1997): 413–433 traces what he sees as a decline in the classical understanding of friendship (judged from a modern point of view).

3. Konstan, *Friendship*, p. 73. On the social functions of friendship in Athenian democracy, see Konstan's "Reciprocity and Friendship," in *Reciprocity in Ancient Greece*, ed. Christopher Gill, Norman Postlethwaite, and Richard Seaford (Oxford: Oxford University Press, 1998), pp. 270–301.

4. Plato's dialogues cannot be dated precisely; the early manuscripts of his works arrange them thematically in groups of four, not chronologically. Most scholars believe that those dialogues, like the *Lysis*, that remain close to the historical Socrates' methods, must for that reason be dated to the early stage of Plato's career, while the development of Plato's own philosophical doctrines, first using Socrates as his spokesman and then diminishing or eliminating Socrates' role, occurs later. For the complexities of this relationship, see Daniel W. Graham, "Socrates and Plato," *Phronesis* 37 (1992): 141–165; Charles H. Kahn, "Did Plato Write Socratic Dialogs?," *Classical Quarterly* 31 (1981): 305–320. On chronology, see Holger Thesleff, "Platonic Chronology," *Phronesis* 34 (1989): 1–26.

5. See David Bolotin, *Plato's Dialogue on Friendship: An Interpretation of the* Lysis, *with a New Translation* (Ithaca, NY: Cornell University Press, 1979), p. 53, n. 1.

6. Citations of Bolotin's translation by page number and Stephanus number appear in the text. Citations of the Greek text follow Plato, *Lysis*, in *Platonis Opera*, vol. 3, ed. John Burnet (Oxford: Oxford University Press, 1903).

7. But cf. Christopher Planeaux, "Socrates, an Unreliable Narrator? The Dramatic Setting of he *Lysis,*" *Classical Philology* 96 (2001): 5–13, which claims that "Socrates maneuvered himself for the express purpose of encountering Hippothales' new love interest," p. 64.

8. Compare Socrates' earlier assertion that the argument is making him dizzy (Bolotin, *Plato's Dialogue on Friendship*, p. 39, 216c).

9. Catherine Pickstock, "The Problem of Reported Speech: Friendship and Philosophy in Plato's *Lysis* and *Symposium,*" *Telos* 123 (Spring 2002): 35–65, suggests that, despite the apparent philosophical aporia, the undefinable concept of friendship is concretely depicted in the friendly relations of the frame story.

10. Bolotin's commentary suggests that the reader is meant to understand that the most complete friendship is friendship to oneself: *Plato's Dialogue on Friendship*, see pp. 191–193.

11. See K. J. Dover, *Greek Homosexuality*, 2nd ed. (Cambridge, MA: Harvard University Press, 1989), p. 16, for his use of this terminology. Dover's has been the most influential treatment of this topic, and many later scholars have adopted his usage; Greek writers use other terms as well as these.

12. Daniel H. Garrison, *Sexual Culture in Ancient Greece* (Norman: University of Oklahoma Press, 2000), p. 157. Dover's book is in some ways an extended and nuanced description of this same phenomenon. Dover, p. 204, revises his earlier opinions that intercrural, rather than anal, sex was the real-life (as opposed to the represented) norm and that the *eromenos* was assumed (again in reality rather than representation) not to experience sexual pleasure. My concern here, however, is with Plato's nonstandard representation and idealization of erotic experience. For a recent history of the phenomenon of institutionalized pederasty throughout ancient Greece, see William Armstrong Percy III, *Pederasty and Pedagogy in Archaic Greece* (Urbana and Chicago: University of Illinois Press, 1996). On the construction and regulation of male–male desire in ancient Greece, see especially (amidst the ever-expanding literature), in addition to Dover and Garrison, John J. Winkler's classic essay "Laying Down the Law: The Oversight of Men's Sexual Behavior in Classical Athens," in *Before Sexuality: The Construction of Erotic Experience in the Ancient Greek World*, ed. David M. Halperin, John J. Winkler, and Froma I. Zeitlin (Princeton: Princeton University Press, 1990), pp. 171–209 (also in Winkler's *The Constraints of Desire: The Anthropology of Sex and Gender in Ancient Greece* [New York: Routledge, 1990], pp. 45–70); H. A. Shapiro, "Eros in Love: Pederasty and Pornography in Greece," in *Pornography and Representation in Greece and Rome*, ed. Amy Richlin (New York: Oxford University Press, 1992), pp. 53–72; and the influential work of David M. Halperin, e.g., "Sex Before

Sexuality: Pederasty, Politics, and Power in Classical Athens," in *Hidden From History: Reclaiming the Gay and Lesbian Past*, ed. Martin Bauml Duberman, Martha Vicinus, and George Chauncey, Jr. (New York: NAL, 1989), pp. 37–53; as well as the essays collected in his *One Hundred Years of Homosexuality and Other Essays on Greek Love* (New York: Routledge, 1990). See also the exchange between David Cohen, "Law, Society and Homosexuality in Classical Athens," *Past and Present* 117 (November 1987): 3–21, and Clifford Hindley's essay of the same title, *Past and Present* 133 (November 1991): 167–183. More recently, see James Davidson, *Courtesans and Fishcakes: The Consuming Passions of Classical Athens* (New York: St. Martin's, 1997), pp. 73–108; Bruce S. Thornton, *Eros: The Myth of Ancient Greek Sexuality* (Boulder, CO: Westview, 1997), pp. 193–212; and Halperin, "Appendix: Questions of Evidence," in his *How to Do the History of Homosexuality* (Chicago: University of Chicago Press, 2002), pp. 138–154. The syntheses in David F. Greenberg, *The Construction of Homosexuality* (Chicago: University of Chicago Press, 1988), pp. 141–151, 202–205, and Byrne Fone, *Homophobia: A History* (New York: Metropolitan, 2000), pp. 17–43 are also helpful. Documentary evidence is conveniently collected in *Homosexuality in Greece and Rome: A Sourcebook of Basic Documents*, ed. Thomas K. Hubbard (Berkeley: University of California Press, 2003), pp. 21–307. On the distinction between the "privileged society's" and more popular perceptions of male–male desire, see T. K. Hubbard, "Popular Perceptions of Elite Homosexuality in Classical Athens," *Arion* 6.1 (Spring–Summer 1998): 48–78.

13. Other influential scholars who, following the lead of Michel Foucault, insist on the power relations inherent in these practices, include Dover, Halperin, and Winkler.

14. A. W. Nightingale, "Plato and Praise: Plato's Critique of Encomiastic Discourse in the *Lysis* and *Symposium*," *Classical Quarterly* 43.i (1993): 112–130; see especially pp. 114–116.

15. Bolotin, *Plato's Dialogue on Friendship*, pp. 104–105; quotation on p. 104.

16. Ibid. Bolotin's translation distinguishes between *eros* and *philia* by using the terms "love passionately" and "love [as a friend]."

17. Bolotin, *Plato's Dialogue on Friendship*, pp. 184–185.

18. Compare Halperin, "Appendix," on this point. On desire and "one's own," see David K. Glidden, "The *Lysis* on Loving One's Own," *Classical Quarterly* 21 (1981): 39–59.

19. As Bolotin points out, *Plato's Dialogue on Friendship*, p. 185.

20. Bolotin points out that "[t]he Greek word for "favorite" is itself a plural form, and the choice between singular and plural must depend upon the context" (*Plato's Dialogue on Friendship*, p. 61, n. 84). Given Hippothales' pleasure, and his single-minded pursuit of Lysis, it would perhaps be more appropriate to use the singular form here. The word in question is *paidikon* (παιδικῶν). His use of "[both]" indicates the dual number.

21. See, for example, the *Laws* 841d: the Athenian's ideal "standards of sexual conduct" include one forbidding men to "sow sterile seed in males in defiance of

nature" (trans. Trevor J. Saunders, in Plato, *Complete Works*, ed. John M. Cooper (Indianapolis: Hackett, 1997), pp. 1318–1616, at p. 1502). As always, the use of the dialogue form makes it impossible to decide Plato's own views with absolute certainty, but most scholars identify the Athenian's views with the author's.

22. Dover, *Greek Homosexuality*, p. 12. Plato may well have been understood in the ancient world as having experienced erotic desire for members of his own sex; Diogenes Laertius, for instance, reports on his passionate attachment [the term is *eronta* (ἔρωντα)] to several young men in *Lives of the Eminent Philosophers*, ed. and trans. R. D. Hicks, 2 vols., Loeb Classical Library 184–185 (Cambridge, MA: Harvard University Press, 1972), III.29–32, vol. 1, pp. 302–307. Diogenes Laertius, writing several centuries after Plato, is not a particularly reliable witness about Plato's life, but his quotations from others do indicate that a number of ancient Greek writers perceived Plato as subject to male–male desire.

23. Dover, *Greek Homosexuality*, p. 12.

24. Bolotin, *Plato's Dialogue on Friendship*, p. 186.

25. Dover, *Greek Homosexuality*, p. 140.

26. Francisco J. Gonzalez, "Socrates on Loving One's Own: A Traditional Concept of Φιλία Radically Transformed," *Classical Philology* 95 (2000), pp. 279–298, also links these two portions of the dialogue by the repeated use of τὸ οἰκεῖον.

27. Bolotin, *Plato's Dialogue on Friendship*, p. 120.

28. Ibid.

29. Socrates claims that it is Hesiod who uses this terminology. Cf. Hesiod, *Works and Days*, ed. Friedrich Solmsen (Oxford: Oxford University Press, 1970), l. 25 ff.; trans. Dorothea Wender, in *Hesiod and Theognis* (Harmondsworth: Penguin, 1973), pp. 59–86, at pp. 59–60.

30. For a clarification of the philosophical issues, see Naomi Reshotko, "The Good, the Bad, and the Neither Good nor Bad in Plato's *Lysis*," *Southern Journal of Philosophy* 38.3 (2000): 251–262.

31. Ἀφαιρετός is derived form the verb ἀφαιρέω, "to take from, take away from a person" (Liddell and Scott, *An Intermediate Greek-English Lexicon* [Oxford: Clarendon, 1889, repr. 1997], s.v. ἀφαιρέω).

32. See also Samuel Scolnicov, "Friends and Friendship in Plato: Some Remarks on the *Lysis*," *Scripta Classica Israelica* 12 (1993): 67–74.

33. But cf. Gonzalez, "Socrates on Loving One's Own," who suggests that Socrates establishes a new form of kinship with the boys and that this kinship is the true solution to the dialogue's problems.

34. Bolotin, *Plato's Dialogue on Friendship*, p. 193.

35. Ibid., pp. 194–195.

36. Ibid., p. 180.

37. In his *Dialogue and Dialectic: Eight Hermeneutical Studies on Plato*, trans. P. Christopher Smith (New Haven: Yale University Press, 1980), pp. 1–20. The essay was originally published in 1972. See also Maria Joó, "The Concept of *Philia* in Plato's Dialogue Lysis," *Acta antiqua Academiae Scientiarum Hungaricae* 40 (2000): 195–204.

38. Gadamer, "Logos and Ergon in Plato's Lysis," p. 9. Other critics who find that the *Lysis* does resolve its apparent aporia in one way or another include Pickstock; Reshotko; Joó; and James Haden, "Friendship in Plato's *Lysis*," *Review of Metaphysics* 37 (1983): 327–356; Beatriz Bossi, "Is the *Lysis* Really Aporetic?," in *Plato:* Euthydemus, Lysis, Charmides: *Proceedings of the V Symposium Platonicum,* ed. Thomas M. Robinson and Luc Brisson (Sankt Augustin: Academia Verlag, 2000): 172–179; Don Adams, "A Socratic Theory of Friendship," *International Philosophical Quarterly* 35 (1995): 269–282.

39. Gadamer, "Logos and Ergon in Plato's *Lysis*," p. 19.

40. Ibid.

41. Ibid., pp. 8–9.

42. Ibid., pp. 13–14.

43. Ibid., p. 20.

44. See Jacques Derrida, "Freud and the Scene of Writing," in his *Writing and Difference,* trans. Alan Bass (Chicago: University of Chicago Press, 1978), pp. 196–231.

45. Martin Buber, *I and Thou,* 2nd ed., trans. Walter Kauffman (New York: Scribner's, 1970), p. 178.

46. See Plato's *Apology* for the charges brought against Socrates.

47. On the importance of the interlocutors in the *Lysis,* see James Leslie Siebach and Mark Wrathall, "Socratic Elenchus in Plato's *Lysis*," in *Plato:* Euthydemus, Lysis, Charmides, pp. 194–203.

48. See Pierre Grimal, "Caractères généraux du dialogue romain, de Lucilius à Cicéron," *L'information littéraire* 7 (1955): 192–198; M. Levine, "Cicero and the Literary Dialogue," *The Classical Journal* 53 (1958): 146–151; Michel Ruch, *Le préambule dans les oeuvres philosophiques de Cicéron: essai sur la genèse et l'art du dialogue* (Paris: Les Belles Lettres, 1958).

49. Cicero (Marcus Tullius), *Tusculan Disputations,* ed. and trans. J. E. King, 2nd ed., Loeb Classical Library 18 (Cambridge, MA: Harvard University Press, 1945). Citations of this edition and translation by page, book, chapter, and subdivision numbers appear in the text.

50. Ibid., p. 410, n. 2.

51. Ibid., p. 406, n. 1.

52. Cicero's view finds recent support from Percy, *Pederasty and Pedagogy,* who also links the origins of institutionalized pederasty in Greece with exercising naked (e.g., pp. 114–116). Cf. Myles McDonnell, "The Introduction of Athletic Nudity: Thucydides, Plato, and the Vases," *Journal of Hellenic Studies* 111 (1991): 182–193.

53. Craig A. Williams, *Roman Homosexuality: Ideologies of Masculinity in Classical Antiquity* (Oxford: Oxford University Press, 1999), p. 63. Williams cites Cornelius Nepos as another author who declares that such "Greek" practices are considered dishonorable among Romans, ibid. Williams' book as a whole provides an essential corrective to this view.

54. John R. Clarke, *Looking at Lovemaking: Constructions of Sexuality in Roman Art, 100 B.C.–A.D. 250* (Berkeley: University of California Press, 1998), p. 78.

Clarke's more recent, popular book *Roman Sex: 100 B.C.–A.D. 250* (New York: Harry N. Abrams, 2003) adds the qualification that "[t]he Roman elite man must not have sex with another freeborn male—boy or adult," pp. 88–90—a qualification that begs the question of power relations. The Roman–Greek difference in this area may have been less striking in reality than in its artistic representations.

55. Williams, *Roman Homosexuality*, pp. 245–252, addresses the controversial issue of same-sex marriage in ancient Rome, and concludes both that "Romans did participate in formal wedding ceremonies in which one male was married to another" and that "such marriages were anomalous in view of the fundamental nature of *matrimonium*, a hierarchical institution that was aimed at creating legitimate offspring as well as a route for the transmission of property (*patrimonium*) and that required the participation of a woman as subordinate partner" (p. 252). Cicero's antipathy to Mark Antony was expressed in an accusation that Antony had in his early life been married to Curio (in Cicero's *Second Philippic*, quoted by Williams, p. 245), an accusation that also expresses his antipathy to male–male marriage—hence his refusal to allow legal status to such relations in the *Disputations*.

56. Ibid., p. 241.

57. Marilyn B. Skinner, "Introduction: *Quod multo fit aliter in Graecia*," in *Roman Sexualities*, ed. Judith P. Hallett and Marilyn B. Skinner (Princeton, NJ: Princeton University Press, 1997), pp. 3–25, at p. 11. On *stuprum*, see also Elaine Fantham, "*Stuprum*: Public Attitudes and Penalties for Sexual Offenses in Republican Rome," *Échos du monde classique* 35 (1991): 267–291; Amy Richlin, "Not Before Homosexuality: The Materiality of the *Cinaedus* and the Roman Law against Love Between Men," *Journal of the History of Sexuality* 3.4 (1993): 523–573; Williams, *Roman Homosexuality*, pp. 96–124. On the "cult of virility," see Paul Veyne, "L'Homosexualité à Rome," *Communications* 35 (1982): 26–33; Eva Cantarella, *Bisexuality in the Ancient World*, trans. C. Ó. Cuilleanáin (New Haven: Yale University Press, 1992), p. 218. More recently, see Emma Dench, "Austerity, Excess, Success, and Failure in Hellenistic and Early Imperial Italy," in *Parchments of Gender: Deciphering the Bodies of Antiquity*, ed. Emma Wyke (Oxford: Clarendon, 1998), pp. 121–146; Erik Gunderson, "Discovering the Body in Roman Oratory," in *Parchments of Gender*, pp. 169–189; and Williams, *Roman Homosexuality*, pp. 125–224. For a typology of Roman attitudes, see Holt N. Parker, "The Teratogenic Grid," in *Roman Sexualities*, pp. 47–65. The syntheses in Greenberg, *Construction of Homosexuality*, pp. 152–163, and Fone, *Homophobia*, pp. 44–59, are also helpful. Documentary evidence is collected in *Homosexuality in Greece and Rome*, ed. Hubbard, pp. 308–532.

58. Alan E. Douglas, "Form and Content in the *Tusculan Disputations*," in *Cicero the Philosopher: Twelve Papers*, ed. J. G. F. Powell (Oxford: Oxford University Press, 1995), pp. 197–218, provides a more positive assessment of the *Tusculans'* nondialogical form.

59. It is worth noting that Cicero himself was thought by some Roman writers to have participated in an erotic relationship with his slave/secretary Tiro: see Williams, *Roman Homosexuality*, pp. 243–244.

60. Cicero, *Laelius: On Friendship*, in *Cicero: On the Good Life*, pp. 175–227. Citations of this translation, by page, chapter, and subdivision numbers appear in the text. Latin citations are drawn from Falconer's edition.

61. Eleanor Winsor Leach, "Absence and Desire in Cicero's *De amicitia*," *Classical World* 87.2 (1993–1994): 3–20 does find an erotic undertone in the desire for what is absent, as well as in Cicero's political desires.

62. Ellen Oliensis, "The Erotics of *amicitia*: Readings in Tibullus, Propertius, and Horace," in *Roman Sexualities*, pp. 151–171, at p. 155.

63. Konstan, *Friendship,* p. 131. See also Thomas N. Habinek, "Towards a History of Friendly Advice: The Politics of Candor in Cicero's *de Amicitia*," *Apeiron* 23 (1990): 165–185.

64. Cf., e.g., pp. 208–209, xvii.62–63 and pp. 223–224, xxvi.98.

65. Lewis and Short, *A Latin Dictionary*, rev. ed. (Oxford: Oxford University Press, 1979), s.v. "traho."

66. On the relationship of one's personal and political status in the early imperial period, see Michel Foucault, *The Care of the Self: The History of Sexuality*, vol. 3, trans. Robert Hurley (1986; New York: Vintage, 1988), pp. 81–104. Earlier, according to Foucault—and relevant to our consideration of Cicero—"[s]elf-mastery had implied a close connection between the superiority one exercised over oneself, the authority one exercised in the context of the household, and the power one exercised in the field of an agonistic society," p. 94. See also Benjamin Fiore, S. J., "The Theory and Practice of Friendship in Cicero," in *Greco-Roman Perspectives on Friendship*, ed. John T. Fitzgerald (Atlanta: Scholars' Press, 1997), pp. 59–76. Sandra Citroni Marchetti, *Amicizia e potere nelle lettere di Cicerone e nelle Elegie Ovidiane dell'Esilio* (Florence: Università degli Studi, 2000) provides a more recent and specific analysis of the relationship between friendship and power in the changing political climate, as expressed in Cicero's letters. On hierarchies of friendship in Cicero's period, see Richard Saller, "Patronage and Friendship in early Imperial Rome: Drawing the Distinction," in *Patronage in Ancient Society*, ed. Andrew Wallace-Hadrill (London: Routledge, 1989), pp. 49–62; Mario Attilio Levi, "Da *clientela* ad *amicitia*," *Epigrafia e territorio* 3 (1994): 375–381; John Nichols, "*Hospitium* and Political Friendship in the Late Republic," in *Aspects of Friendship*, pp. 99–108.

67. But compare Carl P. E. Springer, "Fannius and Scaevola in Cicero's *De amicitia*," *Studies in Latin Literature and Roman History* 7 (1994): 267–278 for a suggestion that the friction between these two interlocutors, and therefore their personalities as well, are better developed than is usually supposed.

68. Williams, *Roman Homosexuality*, pp. 231–244, suggests that Cicero's views on the "unnaturalness" of male–male erotics were not mainstream in ancient Rome.

69. See Grant's Introduction, Cicero, p. 34.

70. Aelred of Rievaulx, *Spiritual Friendship*, trans. Mary Eugenia Laker SSND, Cistercian Fathers Series 5 (Kalamazoo, MI: Cistercian Publications, 1974). Citations of this translation by page number appear in the text (a number of obvious misprints have been silently corrected), followed by chapter and

subdivision citations of the Latin edition: Aelred of Rievaulx, *De spiritali amicitia*, in *Aelredi Rievallensis opera omnia*, ed. A. Hoste and H. Talbot, Corpus Christianorum 1 (Turnhout: Brepols, 1971), pp. 287–350. A helpful reading of the prologue is James McEvoy, "Notes on the Prologue to Saint Aelred of Rievaulx's *De Spirituali amicitia*, with a Translation," *Traditio* 37 (1981): 396–411. For a general description of Aelred's theory of friendship, see Adele M. Fiske, *Friends and Friendship in the Monastic Tradition* (Cuernavaca: CIDOC, 1970), ch. 18 (pp. 18/1–18/49).

71. John Boswell, *Christianity, Social Tolerance, and Homosexuality: Gay People in Western Europe from the Beginning of the Christian Era to the Fourteenth Century* (Chicago: University of Chicago Press, 1980), p. 222. See also Kenneth C. Russell, "Aelred: The Gay Abbot of Rievaulx," *Studia Mystica* 5 (1982): 51–64.

72. The standard study of Aelred, Aelred Squire's *Aelred of Rievaulx: A Study* (Kalamazoo: Cistercian Publications, 1969), has little to offer on the subject of Aelred's sexuality. More useful for my purposes is Brian Patrick McGuire, *Brother and Lover: Aelred of Rievaulx* (New York: Crossroad, 1994), which offers a sensible assessment of Aelred's erotic desires and behaviors, concluding both that Aelred, while a courtier at the court of King David of Scotland, probably had at least one passionate (and in Aelred's view, sinful) erotic attachment to another man, pp. 48–50, and that throughout his life his primary emotional attachments were with other men, pp. 105–118, 142, though in the monastery "he could transfer his sexual energies in this area to a calmer desire for companionship," p. 113. For a full consideration of the evidence, see McGuire's essay "Sexual Awareness and Identity in Aelred of Rievaulx," *American Benedictine Review* 45 (1994): 184–226.

73. For the chronology, see Douglas Roby's introduction to Laker's translation, p. 10.

74. Mark D. Jordan, *The Invention of Sodomy in Christian Theology* (Chicago: University of Chicago Press, 1997), especially pp. 29–91; Elizabeth Keiser, *Courtly Desire and Medieval Homophobia: The Legitimation of Sexual Pleasure in* Cleanness *and its Contexts* (New Haven: Yale University Press, 1997), especially pp. 71–92. The attempts at regulating same-sex erotics described in these texts may be best understood in the context of the larger medieval attempt to regulate all forms of sexuality: see Pierre J. Payer, *The Bridling of Desire: Views of Sex in the Later Middle Ages* (Toronto: University of Toronto Press, 1993). On the construction and regulation of male–male desire in the Middle Ages, see also the relevant sections of James Brundage's exhaustive study *Law, Sex, and Christian Society in Medieval Europe* (Chicago: University of Chicago Press, 1987); Michael Goodich, *The Unmentionable Vice: Homosexuality in the Later Medieval Period* (Santa Barbara, CA [?]: Dorset, 1979); Allen J. Frantzen, *Before the Closet: From* Beowulf *to* Angels in America (Chicago: University of Chicago Press, 1998); C. Stephen Jaeger, *Ennobling Love: In Search of a Lost Sensibility* (Philadelphia: University of Pennsylvania Press, 1999); and the essays collected in *Constructing Medieval Sexuality*, ed. Karma Lochrie, Peggy McCracken, and James A. Schultz (Minneapolis: University of Minnesota Press, 1997) and in *Queering the Middle Ages*, ed. Glenn Burger and

Steven F. Kruger (Minneapolis: University of Minnesota Press, 2001); the syntheses of Greenberg, *Construction of Homosexuality*, pp. 242–298, and Fone, *Homophobia*, pp. 111–175, are also helpful.

75. Aelred's sermons are particularly harsh in their condemnation of sodomy: see McGuire's discussion of this point, *Brother*, pp. 100–101.

76. See Jordan, *Invention*, pp. 92–113; Keiser, *Courtly*, p. 236, nn. 19–20. See also the discussion of this topic in Robert S. Sturges, *Chaucer's Pardoner and Gender Theory: Bodies of Discourse* (New York: St. Martin's Press, 2000), pp. 47–59.

77. Cf. p. 78, II.36 ("friendship cannot exist among the wicked") and pp. 93–94, III.10 ("friendship can exist only among the good").

78. Introduction, p. 30. McGuire, *Brother*, takes this Walter to be identical with Aelred's medieval biographer/hagiographer Walter Daniel, p. 105.

79. On Aelred as a Christian adaptor of Cicero, see Amédée Hallier, "God Is Friendship: The Key to Aelred of Rievaulx's Christian Humanism," *American Benedictine Review* 18 (1967): 393–420; Letterio Mauro, "L'Amicitia come compimento di umanià nel *De spiritali amicitia* di Aelredo di Rievaulx," *Rivista di filosofia neo-scolastica* 66 (1974): 89–103; Charles Dumont, "L'Amitié spirituelle d'Aelred de Rievaulx," *Revue générale* 134.10 (October, 1999): 67–73.

80. See, for example, St. Bernard of Clairvaux's series of sermons *On the Song of Songs*, trans. Kilian Walsh OCSO, 4 vols., Cistercian Fathers series 4, 7, 31, 40 (Kalamazoo: Cistercian Publications, Inc., 1971–1980), especially sermons 2–8, vol. 1, pp. 8–52. On Aelred's homoerotic, or at least physical, attachment to the body of Christ (especially as mediated by the Song of Songs), see McGuire, *Brother*, pp. 35–38, 141.

81. Yannick Carré, *Le Baiser sur la bouche au Moyen Age: Rites, symboles, mentalités, à travers les textes et les images, XIe–XVe siècles* (Paris: Le Léopard d'Or, 1992), finds that the late medieval kiss typically unites the carnal with the spiritual ("réalise l'union du charnel et du spirituel"), p. 325. Carré briefly discusses the kiss in Aelred's *Spiritual Friendship*, but places his emphasis on the metaphorical nature of Aelred's spiritual kiss, p. 130, n. 6.

82. On carnal friendships "as a point of departure for deeper bonds" in Book III, see also McGuire, *Brother*, p. 106. McGuire also points out Aelred's similarity to Plato in this regard, speculating that a line of influence might be traced from Plato through St. Augustine to Aelred, p. 148.

83. Note, however, that Aelred elsewhere insists that the abbot alone rules the monastery; see ibid., *Brother*, p. 56, for discussion on this point.

84. McGuire, *Brother*, points out that Aelred's choir monks at Rievaulx, as at other Cistercian monasteries, would have been the sons of the Norman aristocracy, pp. 48, 55, and that his description of the bonds of friendship is reminiscent of feudal loyalty, p. 109, but he also points out that these aristocrats "had given up position and pretension. . . . In a world wild about hierarchy and rights, Rievaulx was a different kind of human society in which pride and propriety gave way to love and equality," p. 55.

85. Since the friends referred to in these conversations all remain nameless, it is possible that Aelred is actually discussing two different friends in these two

passages. The point is not really essential: the exchange of roles between superior and inferior is still taking place in general terms. However, the verbal parallels between the two passages do strongly suggest that the same friend is under discussion in both.

86. This is only a claim about general tendencies, and is not intended to deny agency or authority in certain cases to those who were gendered feminine. See Joan Cadden, *Meanings of Sex Difference in the Middle Ages: Medicine, Science, and Culture* (Cambridge, Eng.: Cambridge University Press, 1993), pp. 167–227. For a nuanced view of these issues in Aelred's period, see the essays collected in David Townsend and Andrew Taylor, eds., *The Tongue of the Fathers: Gender and Ideology in Twelfth-Century Latin Literature* (Philadelphia: University of Pennsylvania Press, 1998), especially the editors' introduction, pp. 1–13, as well as the works of Carolyn Walker Bynum, especially, in this regard, *Jesus as Mother: Studies in the Spirituality of the High Middle Ages* (Berkeley: University of California Press, 1982). Bynum specifically discusses Aelred's appropriation of the image of Jesus as mother, pp. 122–124, and points out that Aelred's medieval biographer/hagiographer, Walter Daniel, records Aelred's understanding of himself as a mother to his monks, p. 124. See also McGuire, *Brother*, on this point, pp. 96, 123, and cf. Marsha Dutton, "Christ Our Mother: Aelred's Iconography for Contemplative Union," in *Goad and Nail*, ed. E. Rozanne Elder, Studies in Medieval Cistercian History 10 (Kalamazoo: Cistercian Publications, 1985), 21–45.

87. McGuire, *Brother*, on the other hand, finds that real as opposed to metaphorical women have little place in Aelred's thought, pp. 27–38; cf. Bynum *Jesus as Mother*, pp. 143–146.

88. On the positive fruits of friendship, see also p. 71, II.9; on false friendship as the forbidden fruit of Genesis, see p. 79, II.40.

89. The sexual potential of Adam and Eve before the Fall was widely discussed by twelfth-century and later medieval theologians. While some dissented, most agreed that that Adam and Eve were differentiated by gender for the purpose of sexual intercourse at the divine behest of Genesis 1:28. In the twelfth century, Peter Lombard's influential *Books of Sentences* cited St. Augustine's opinion that there would have been sexual intercourse in Paradise, though without desire: "they would have used the genital organs without any itching of the flesh." For a full discussion of these issues, see Payer, *Bridling*, pp. 18–41. Payer cites the passage from Peter Lombard, *Sentences* 2.20.1.3, on pp. 24–25.

90. On friendship as Paradise in the monastic tradition, see Fiske, *Friends*, chapter 19 (pp. 19/1–19/23).

91. On sex/gender differentiation in Paradise, see Payer, *Bridling*, pp. 20–24.

92. For theologians of Aelred's period, marriage was first instituted between Adam and Eve, in Paradise before the Fall. See Payer, *Bridling*, p. 18, and the theological opinions he cites, p. 199, n. 1. Most usefully, Payer provides the Latin text and an English translation of Gratian's *Decretum* on this point, pp. 185–186. McGuire suggests that Aelred had little interest in the institution of marriage, but Katherine M. TePas, "Spiritual Friendship in Aelred of Rievaulx and

Mutual Sanctification in Marriage," *Cistercian Studies Quarterly* 27 (1992): 63–76, 153–165, takes a more positive view. See also Brian Bethune, "Personality and Spirituality: Aelred of Rievaulx and Human Relationships," *Cistercian Studies* 20 (1985): 98–112.

93. Aelred of Rievaulx, *The Mirror of Charity*, trans. Elizabeth Connor, OCSO, Cistercian Fathers series 17 (Kalamazoo, MI: Cistercian Publications, 1990), p. 299. The Latin text can be found in Hoste and Talbot, eds., *De speculo caritatis* in *Aelredi Rievallensis Opera omnia*, p. 159, III.39.110.

94. Boswell, *Christianity*, p. 226, n. 57.

95. Ibid., p. 225.

96. On the dialogical relationship of Walter and Gratian, see also McGuire, *Brother*, p. 107.

97. See Aelred, *Spiritual Friendship*, p. 81, II.48; p. 87, II.72; p. 91, III.1.

98. McGuire, *Brother*, p. 136. For a discussion of Aelred's followers Thomas of Frakaham and Peter of Blois, see McGuire's *Friendship and Community: The Monastic Experience, 350–1250* (Kalamazoo: Cistercian Publications, 1988), pp. 341–352. For parallel Latin texts of these and other epitomes, see *Abbreviationes de Spiritali Amicitia*, in Hoste and Talbot's edition of Aelred's works, I: 352–634. Even the brief epitome entitled *Dialogus inter Aelredum et discipulum* (pp. 497–623) reduces Aelred's several contentious interlocutors to a single, anonymous, uncharacterized disciple, and the dialogue itself to a Ciceronian exchange dominated by the single voice of "Aelred."

99. McGuire, *Friendship and Community*, p. 342.

2   SPIRITUAL EROTICS: FROM PLATO'S *SYMPOSIUM* TO SADE'S *LA PHILOSOPHIE DANS LE BOUDOIR*

1. On friendship, see Michel de Montaigne, "De l'amitié," in *Essais*, ed. Maurice Rat, 2 vols. (Paris: Garnier, 1962), 1, pp. 197–212. Montaigne's low opinion of the Platonic dialogue form can be found in "Des livres," 2, pp. 447–462, at p. 455.

2. R. E. Allen, Preface, in Plato, *The Symposium*, translated with comment by R. E. Allen (New Haven, CT: Yale University Press, 1991), p. vii.

3. Other editors, translators, and commentators who attempt this task in English, besides Allen, include R. G. Bury, *The Symposium of Plato*, 2nd ed. (Cambridge, Eng.: W. Heffer and Sons, Ltd., 1973); Stanley Rosen, *Plato's Symposium* (1968; repr. South Bend, IN: St. Augustine's Press, 1999); Kenneth Dover, *Plato: Symposium* (Cambridge: Cambridge University Press, 1980); William S. Cobb, *The* Symposium *and the* Phaedrus: *Plato's Erotic Dialogues* (Albany: State University of New York Press, 1993), pp. 61–84.

4. On the dramatic frame, see Peter H. von Blanckenhagen, "Stage and Actors in Plato's *Symposium*," *Greek, Roman and Byzantine Studies* 33 (1992): 51–68. On Plato's treatment of the institution of the symposium in his other dialogues, see Manuela Tecusan, "*Logos sympotikos*: Patterns of the Irrational in Philosophical

Drinking: Plato Outside the *Symposium*," in *Sympotica*, ed. Oswyn Murray (Oxford: Clarendon, 1990), pp. 238–260.

5. See chapter 1, n. 4. Dover dates the *Symposium* to 384–379 B.C., p. 10.

6. English quotations of the *Symposium* are from Allen's translation, cited by page and Stephanus numbers; Greek citations follow Dover's edition. On the question of eros and immortality, see M. Dyson, "Immortality and Procreation in Plato's *Symposium*," *Antichthon* 20 (1986): 59–72.

7. William A. Johnson, "Dramatic Frame and Philosophical Idea in Plato," *American Journal of Philology* 119 (1998): 577–598, expresses the opposite view of the *Symposium* (pp. 581–583): he claims that the indirection of the narrative frame suggests a distance between the written dialogue and philosophical discourse, as well as a distance between the perceptible and the ideal worlds; while this may be true of the other speeches, it is demonstrably not true of Diotima's.

8. See the examples given below.

9. See my discussion of *Hedwig and the Angry Inch* in the conclusion to this volume.

10. Allen, *Symposium*, pp. 7–8. For a fuller consideration of eros as primarily a destructive natural force in need of discipline and control, see Bruce Thornton, *Eros: The Myth of Ancient Greek Sexuality* (Boulder, CO: Westview Press, 1997).

11. See Bury, *Symposium of Plato*, p. xxv, and Rosen, *Plato's Symposium*, pp. 56–59, for example. Cobb, *Symposium and Phaedrus*, p. 64, finds Phaedrus' speech naïve and conventional. Dover, *Plato: Symposium*, pp. 89–95, is more sympathetic.

12. Allen, *Symposium*, p. 16.

13. See Dover, *Plato: Symposium*, pp. 100–109.

14. On the significance of Aristophanes' hiccups, see Allen, *Symposium*, pp. 20 ff.; Rosen, *Plato's Symposium*, pp. 90–91 and 120; Cobb, *Symposium and Phaedrus*, p. 66.

15. Cf. Rosen on likeness and unlikeness in this speech, *Plato's Symposium*, pp. 101–107.

16. See David Konstan and Elisabeth Young-Bruehl, "Eryximachus' Speech in the *Symposium*," *Apeiron* 16 (1982): 40–46, for a consideration of the speech's comments on similarity and difference in the context of contemporary medical opinion.

17. For example, Bury, *Symposium of Plato*, p. xxxv; Allen, *Symposium*, suggests that Agathon's peroration "can sing without saying anything," p. 39; Rosen, *Plato's Symposium*, finds Agathon's speech positively pernicious in its emphasis on "corporeal Eros," p. 196. Dover, *Plato: Symposium*, is again more sympathetic, p. 123.

18. Allen, *Symposium*, p. 40.

19. See, for example, concerning the earlier speeches' influence on the later ones, Robert Nola, "On Some Neglected Minor Speakers in Plato's *Symposium*: Phaedrus and Pausanias," *Prudentia* 22 (1990): 54–73.

20. Paul W. Ludwig, "Politics and Eros in Aristophanes' Speech: 'Symposium' 191E–192A and the Comedies," *American Journal of Philology* 117 (1996): 537–562 also gives a positive valuation to Aristophanes' speech, suggesting the reason why "Plato wrote for Aristophanes the most affecting speech in the

dialogue: so that the majority of us would eschew restless striving in favor of settling down with someone whom eros tells us is our other half," p. 561.

21. Allen, *Symposium*, p. 153, n. 239.

22. See David Halperin's essay "Why Is Diotima a Woman?" in his *One Hundred Years of Homosexuality and Other Essays on Greek Love* (New York: 1990), pp. 113–151, for an influential discussion of these issues; see also Andrea Nye, "Irigaray and Diotima at Plato's Symposium," in *Feminist Interpretations of Plato*, ed. Nancy Tuana (University Park, PA: Pennsylvania State University, 1994), pp. 197–215. But for readings that attempt to recuperate Diotima's speech for feminism, cf. Miglena Nikolchina, "The Feminine Erotic and the Paternal Legacy: Revisiting Plato's *Symposium*," *Paragraph* 16 (1993): 239–260, which argues that Diotima's speech remains feminine; and see Luce Irigaray, "Sorcerer Love: A Reading of Plato's *Symposium*, Diotima's Speech," trans. Eleanor H. Kuykendall, in *Feminist Interpretations of Plato*, pp. 181–195; Barbara Freeman, "Irigaray at the Symposium: Speaking Otherwise," *Oxford Literary Review* 8 (1986): 170–177.

23. Michel Foucault, *The Use of Pleasure: The History of Sexuality*, vol. 2, trans. Robert Hurley (New York: Pantheon, 1985), pp. 72–77, at p. 77. See also Alexander Nehamas, *The Art of Living: Socratic Reflections from Plato to Foucault* (Berkeley: University of California Press, 1998).

24. Foucault, *Use*, p. 97. See also David Halperin's discussion of this passage, among others, in his *Saint Foucault: Towards a Gay Hagiography* (Oxford: Oxford University Press, 1995), pp. 107–111.

25. For example, Plato, *Symposium*, trans. Alexander Nehamas and Paul Woodruff (Indianapolis: Hackett, 1989), p. 57, n. 90.

26. Xenophon, *Memorabilia* I.3.8–13, in Xenophon, *Memorabilia, Oeconomicus, Symposium, Apology*, ed. and trans. E. C. Marchant and O. J. Todd, Loeb Classical Library 168 (Cambridge, MA: Harvard University Press, 1923), pp. 48–51.

27. Allen, (*Symposium*, p. 156, n. 249) notes that this comparison is also a direct reference to the earlier speech of Aristophanes, 191a and 192b–d— Aristophanes' speech continues to haunt Socrates' as it continues to haunt later discussions of the *Symposium*. See also the classic critique of Platonic love by Gregory Vlastos, "The Individual as an Object of Love in Plato," in his *Platonic Studies* (Princeton: Princeton University Press, 1973, repr. 1981), pp. 3–42, and the critique of Vlastos by Donald Levy, "The Definition of Love in Plato's *Symposium*," *Journal of the History of Ideas* 40 (1979): 285–291.

28. Cf. Ludwig C. H. Chen, "Knowledge and Beauty in Plato's *Symposium*," *Classical Quarterly* 33 (1983): 66–74, which suggests that the detachment of the soul from the body need not be as radical here as in other middle-period dialogues such as the *Phaedo*.

29. Halperin, "Why Is Diotima a Woman?" See also Dover, *Plato: Symposium*, pp. 136–137. On the exclusion of women in the *Symposium*, see Page DuBois, *Sappho Is Burning* (Chicago: University of Chicago Press, 1995), pp. 77–97.

30. On heterogeneity and homogeneity in Diotima's speech, see Martha C. Nussbaum, "Plato on Commensurability and Desire," in her *Love's*

Knowledge: Essays on Philosophy and Literature (Oxford: Oxford University Press, 1990), pp. 106–124, at pp. 114–117.

31. As Allen points out (*Symposium*, p. 164, n. 264). See Liddell and Scott, *An Intermediate Greek-English Lexicon* (Oxford: Clarendon, 1889, repr. 1997) s.v. βακχεία. Cf. Rosen, *Plato's Symposium*, pp. 283–290; Cobb, Symposium *and* Phaedrus, pp. 81–82. Daniel E. Anderson, *The Masks of Dionysos: A Commentary on Plato's* Symposium (Albany: State University of New York Press, 1993) reads the entire dialogue from this Dionysian perspective. See also David Sider, "Plato's *Symposium* as Dionysian Festival," *Quaderni urbinati di cultura classica* 33 (1980): 41–56.

32. Radcliffe G. Edmonds III, "Socrates the Beautiful," *Transactions and Proceedings of the American Philological Association* 130 (2000): 261–285 explores the *erastes/eromenos* role reversals, suggesting that Socrates and Alcibiades both take both roles reciprocally.

33. Foucault, *Use*, p. 20. Cf. Dover, *Plato: Symposium*, pp. 164–165. Nehamas, *Art*, finds an ironic ambiguity in Socrates' refusal of Alcibiades, pp. 59–63. Martha C. Nussbaum's reading in "The Speech of Alcibiades: A Reading of Plato's 'Symposium,'" *Philosophy and Literature* 3 (1979): 131–172 is similar to mine: "We see now that philosophy is not fully human; but we are terrified of our humanity and what it leads to," p. 168; see also Dominic Scott, "Socrates and Alcibiades in the *Symposium*," *Hermathena* 168 (2000): 25–37. (A critique of Nussbaum may be found in A. W. Price, "Martha Nussbaum's *Symposium*," *Ancient Philosophy* 11 (1991): 285–299.) Also critical of Socrates' avowed erotics is C. D. C. Reeve, "Telling the Truth About Love," *Proceedings of the Boston Area Colloquium in Ancient Philosophy* 8 (1994 for 1992): 89–114. On the reader's identification with Alcibiades, see also Elizabeth Belfiore, "Dialectic with the Reader in Plato's *Symposium*," *Maia* 36 (1984): 137–149. More critical of Alcibiadean erotics are Gary Alan Scott and William A. Welton, "An Overlooked Motive in Alcibiades' *Symposium* Speech," *Interpretation* 24 (1996–1997): 67–84, which explores its political consequences; see also Seth L. Schein, "Alcibiades and the Politics of Misguided Love in Plato's *Symposium*," *ΘΠ* 3 (1974): 158–167.

34. Cf. J. L. Penwill, "Men in Love: Aspects of Plato's *Symposium*," *Ramus* 7 (1978): 143–175, which suggests that Socrates detaches his love from human experience and that it allows no fruitful relationship with human beauty, a reading I would dispute.

35. See essays cited by Halperin, "Why Is Diotima a Woman?" on this point.

36. See Allen's critique of other viewpoints, *Symposium*, pp. 99–102; but cf. Dover, *Plato: Symposium*, pp. 137–138.

37. On the date of Xenophon's *Symposium* in relation to Plato's, see K. J. Dover, "The Date of Plato's *Symposium*," *Phronesis* 10 (1965): 2–20.

38. See n. 26 of this chapter. For Xenophon's claim that his dialogues provide a true, eye-witness picture of Socrates, see *Symposium* I.1, in the Marchant and Todd edition, to which subsequent Greek citations of Xenophon will refer.

39. Xenophon, *The Dinner-Party*, trans. Hugh Tredennick, rev. Robin Waterfield, in Xenophon, *Conversations of Socrates*, trans. Hugh Tredennick and Robin

Waterfield, ed. Robin Waterfield (Harmondsworth: Penguin, 1990). Citations of this translation by page and subdivision appear in the text; Greek citations follow Xenophon, *Memorabilia, Oeconomicus, Symposium, Apology*, ed. O. J. Todd, Loeb Classical Library 168 (Cambridge, MA: Harvard University Press, 1923).

40. See Thornton, *Eros*.

41. On the tone of this text, see Bernhard Huss, "The Dancing Sokrates and the Laughing Xenophon, or the Other 'Symposium,'" *American Journal of Philology* 120 (1999): 381–409.

42. But note the importance of the male–female difference in terms of the mind–body split at VIII.29, discussed above.

43. On this point, see Clifford Hindley, "Xenophon on Male Love," *Classical Quarterly* 49 (1999): 74–99.

44. See, for example, Halperin, "Why Is Diotima a Woman?," pp. 129–137.

45. Michel Foucault, *The Care of the Self: The History of Sexuality*, vol. 3, trans. Robert Hurley (New York: Random House, 1986).

46. Plutarch, *The Dialogue on Love*, ed. and trans. W. C. Helmbold, in Plutarch, *Moralia*, vol. IX, ed. and trans. Edwin L. Minar, Jr., F. H. Sandbach, and W. C. Helmbold, Loeb Classical Library 425 (Cambridge, MA: Harvard University Press, 1961), pp. 306–344. Citations of this edition and translation by page and subdivision numbers will appear in the text. *Affairs of the Heart*, in *Lucian*, vol. VIII, ed. and trans. M. D. MacLeod, Loeb Classical Library 32 (Cambridge, MA: Harvard University Press, 1967), pp. 150–235. Citations of this edition and translation by page and subdivision numbers will appear in the text.

47. Foucault, *Care of the Self*, p. 227.

48. Ibid., p. 199; Foucault is referring specifically to Plutarch's dialogue at this point.

49. Foucault, *Care of the Self*, p. 149. For the earlier stages of these developments, see also Michel Foucault, *Use*.

50. The following discussion is indebted throughout to Foucault, *Care of the Self*, pp. 193–227.

51. Ibid., p. 202.

52. It might be added that this development also requires a male concept of female desire somewhat removed from the classical Greek stereotype of sexually insatiable women "conditioned by their physical nature, which aims at procreation and needs to fulfill itself by drawing off substance from men" (Halperin, "Why Is Diotima a Woman?," pp. 129–130).

53. Foucault, *Care of the Self*, p. 209.

54. Ibid., p. 210.

55. Ibid., p. 227.

56. Ibid.

57. Several such poems are printed and discussed by John Boswell in his *Christianity, Social Tolerance, and Homosexuality: Gay People in Western Europe from the Beginning of the Christian Era to the Fourteenth Century* (Chicago: University of Chicago Press, 1980), pp. 254–261, 381–398. Boswell understands them as evidence of a flourishing medieval "homosexual" subculture, though they ultimately tend to favor male–female love over male–male.

58. Alan of Lille, *Plaint of Nature*, trans. James J. Sheridan, Mediaeval Sources in Translation 26 (Toronto: University of Toronto Press, 1980), Metre 1, pp. 67–68. Latin citations are drawn from "Alan of Lille, *De Planctu naturae*," ed. Nikolaus Häring, *Studi Medievali* 19 (1978): 797–879, *metrum primum*, ll.15–20, p. 806. On the medieval sexual/grammatical metaphor, see John A. Alford, "The Medieval Grammatical Metaphor: A Survey of Its Use in the Middle Ages," *Speculum* 57 (1982): 728–760, and Jan Ziolkowski, *Alan of Lille's Grammar of Sex: The Meaning of Grammar to a Twelfth-Century Intellectual*, Speculum Anniversary Monographs 10 (Cambridge, MA: The Medieval Academy of America, 1985). Boswell discusses Alan of Lille in the context of medieval views of male–male desire, pp. 310–311. More recent readings of Alan of Lille in this context include Alexandre Leupin, "The Hermaphrodite: Alan of Lille's *De planctu Naturae*," in his *Barbarolexis: Medieval Writing and Sexuality*, trans. Kate M. Cooper (Cambridge, MA: Harvard University Press, 1989), pp. 59–78; Leonard Barkan, *Transuming Passion: Ganymede and the Erotics of Humanism* (Stanford: Stanford University Press, 1991), pp. 50–53; Elizabeth Pittenger, "Explicit Ink," in *Premodern Sexualities*, ed. Louise Fradenburg and Carla Freccero (New York: Routledge, 1996), pp. 223–242; Mark D. Jordan, *The Invention of Sodomy in Christian Theology* (Chicago: University of Chicago Press, 1997), pp. 61–91; and Elizabeth B. Keiser, *Courtly Desire and Medieval Homophobia: The Legitimation of Sexual Pleasure in* Cleanness *and Its Contexts* (New Haven: Yale University Press, 1997), pp. 74–86.

59. Alan of Lille, *Plaint of Nature*, Metre 1, p. 72; *De Planctu naturae, metrum primum*, ll.59–60, p. 808.

60. Sheridan's introduction to his translation of the *Complaint*, pp. 1–31, is helpful on the somewhat obscure details of Alan's biography.

61. Keiser's book is particularly acute on the perception of male–male erotics as a violation of divine authority.

62. Jordan's book is the best source of information on the development of these attitudes in the Middle Ages.

63. Virginia Cox, *The Renaissance Dialogue: Literary Dialogue in its Social and Political Contexts, Castiglione to Galileo* (Cambridge, Eng.: Cambridge University Press, 1992), pp. 2–4. She finds a contemporary statement of this distinction in Sforza Pallavicino, *Trattato dello stile e del dialogo* (Rome: 1662) (Cox, p. 115, n. 12). See also David Simpson's helpful essay "Hume's Intimate Voices and the Method of Dialogue," *Texas Studies in Literature and Language* 21, no.1 (1979): 68–72, which Cox cites as well. Cox also suggests that the "dialogical" model becomes more important in the less authoritative, more insistently questioning, French Enlightenment, pp. 3–4. On early modern theories of dialogue, see also Donald Gilman, "Theories of Dialogue," in *The Dialogue in Early Modern France, 1547–1630: Art and Argument*, ed. Colette H. Winn (Washington, D.C.: Catholic University of America Press, 1993), pp. 7–76.

64. Jon R. Snyder, *Writing the Scene of Speaking: Theories of Dialogue in the Late Italian Renaissance* (Stanford: Stanford University Press, 1989), p. 213. This

development is traced throughout Snyder's book; see also Cox's latter chapters, pp. 61–113. On Sperone Speroni's theorization of the "open" dialogue as a genre, see Olga Zorzi Pugliese, "Sperone Speroni and the Labyrinthine Discourse of Renaissance Dialogue," in *Imagining Culture: Essays in Early Modern History and Literature*, ed. Jonathan Hart (New York: Garland, 1996), pp. 57–72. On the Renaissance dialogue conceived as primarily heuristic, see Marta Spranzi Zuber, "Dialogue as a 'Road to Truth': a Renaissance View," in *Dialoganalyse, VI: Referate der 6. Arbeitsagung, Prag 1996*, ed. Svetla Cmejrková et al. (Tübingen: Niemeyer, 1998), pp. 85–90.

65. Cox, *Renaissance*, pp. 26–27.

66. Ibid., p. 13.

67. "It is scarcely decorous for a philosopher—still less a statesman—to be seen wandering aimlessly up riverbanks, discoursing of love with a beardless youth," ibid., p. 16. Cox is paraphrasing Carlo Sigonio's astonishment at the setting of Plato's *Phaedrus* in *De dialogo liber* (1562). The *Phaedrus* and its setting will be discussed in chapter 3. Cox does discuss a third tradition, modeled on the dialogues of Lucian, that provide a comic counterpoint to the sober Ciceronian model, that of the *poligrafi*, pp. 17–19.

68. A more complete survey of the Ficino's process of composing and publishing the *Commentary* may be found in Sears Jayne's Introduction to Marsilio Ficino, *Commentary on Plato's Symposium on Love*, trans. Sears Jayne, 2nd. rev. ed. (Dallas: Spring Publications, Inc., 1985), pp. 3–4. Quotations from this translation will be cited by speech, chapter, and page numbers in the text, followed by page citations of the Latin edition: Marsile Ficin, *Commentaire sur le Banquet de Platon*, ed. Raymond Marcel (Paris: Les Belles Lettres, 1956). A new five-volume edition and English translation of Marsilio Ficino, *Platonic Theology*, ed. James Hankins with William Bowen, trans. Michael J. B. Allen with John Warden, I Tatti Renaissance Library (Cambridge, MA: Harvard University Press, 2001–) is currently being published.

69. On the construction and regulation of male–male desire in early modern Italy, see the books by Michael Rocke and Guido Ruggiero cited below, n. 88 of this chapter; see also James M. Saslow, "Homosexuality in the Renaissance: Behavior, Identity, and Artistic Expression," in *Hidden From History: Reclaiming the Gay and Lesbian Past*, ed. Martin Bauml Duberman, Martha Vicinus, and George Chauncey, Jr. (New York: NAL, 1989), pp. 90–105, as well as the syntheses in David F. Greenberg, *The Construction of Homosexuality* (Chicago: University of Chicago Press, 1988), pp. 305–310, and in Byrne Fone, *Homophobia: A History* (New York: Metropolitan, 2000), pp. 193–200; for specifically Platonic and neoplatonic influences, see Barkan; James M. Saslow, *Ganymede in the Renaissance: Homosexuality in Art and Society* (New Haven: Yale University Press, 1986); Giovanni Dall'Orto, " 'Socratic Love' as a disguise for Same-Sex Love in the Italian Renaissance," in *The Pursuit of Sodomy: Male Homosexuality in Renaissance and Enlightenment Europe*, ed. Kent Gerard and Gert Hekma (New York: Harrington Park Press, 1989), pp. 33–65.

70. Jayne, Introduction, *Commentary*, p. 3.

71. Paul Richard Blum, "Methoden und Motive der Platointerpretation bei Marsilio Ficino," in *Acta Conventus Neo-Latini Sanctandreani: Proceedings of the Fifth International Congress of Neo-Latin Studies*, ed. I. D. McFarlane (Binghamton, NY: Medieval and Renaissance Texts and Studies, 1986), pp. 119–126, explores the relationship between Plato's and Ficino's texts, concluding that Ficino derived his interpretation—whether right or wrong—directly from the *Symposium*. See also Raffaele Riccio, "Per un'analisi del *Simposio* Platonica e el *Convito* o ver' *Dialogo d'amore* di M. Ficino," *Rivista di estetica* 34–35.47 (1994–1995): 17–35. Laura Westra, "Love and Beauty in Ficino and Plotinus," in *Ficino and Renaissance Neoplatonism*, ed. Konrad Eisenbichler and Olga Zorzi Pugliese (Toronto: Dovehouse, 1986), pp. 175–187 shows how the Christian distrust of the body influenced Ficino's doctrine of love.

72. Jayne, Introduction, *Commentary*, p. 7.

73. Ibid. See also Paul Oskar Kristeller, *The Philosophy of Marsilio Ficino* (Gloucester, MA: Peter Smith, 1964), pp. 276–288.

74. See Ficino, *Commentary*, VI.10, p. 129; pp. 222–223; and VII.8–12, pp. 164–168; pp. 252–256.

75. Compare Ficino, *Commentary*, V.3, pp. 87–88; pp. 182–183.

76. See, for example, Ficino, *Commentary*, II.8, pp. 56–57; pp. 157–158; III.2, p. 65; p. 162; V.4, p. 90; p. 185. On love as the resolution of difference, see Bertrand Schefer, "L'Amour des opposés: Remarques sur Marsile Ficin et Domenico Ghirlandaio," *Revue des études Italiennes* 44.1–2 (January–June, 1998): 97–105.

77. But note that male bodies are able to "ensnare" one another with particular ease, precisely "since they are more like men than women are," VII.9, p. 165; p. 253.

78. For other examples of "virtuous" male–male desire inspired by masculine beauty, see I.2, p. 36; p. 137 (Socrates and Phaedrus); II.8, p. 55; p. 156; IV.1, p. 72; p. 167 (the commentary on Aristophanes' myth—but note that the desires discussed there are quickly allegorized, that is to say, decorporealized, in IV.2); V.5, p. 91; p. 187; VI.14, p. 135; p. 229 (the commentary on Diotima's two types of love); VII.4, p. 161; pp. 248–249; VII.8, p. 165; pp. 252–253.

79. Reginald Hyatte, "The 'Visual Spirits' and Body-Soul Mediation: Socratic Love in Marsilio Ficino's *De amore*," *Rinascimento* 33 (1993): 213–222 argues convincingly that one of the difficulties in Ficino's approach is that "his strategy for representing the . . . operations of sublime male-to-male Socratic love is to illustrate in detail what it is not—homosexual lust and love-madness," p. 213.

80. See Plato's *Laws* 636b–d, 836b–838c, 841d.

81. Ficino, *Commentary*, I.1, pp. 35–36; pp. 136–137.

82. Leone Ebreo [Jehudah Abarbanel], *Dialoghi d'amore*, ed. Santino Caramella (Bari: Laterza, 1929); *The Philosophy of Love*, trans. F. Friedeberg-Siely and Jean H. Barnes (London: Soncino, 1937); Pietro Bembo, *Gli Asolani*, ed. Giorgio Dilemmi (Florence: Presso l'Accademia della Crusca, 1991); *Gli Asolani*, trans. Rudolf B. Gottfried (Bloomington, IN: Indiana University Press, 1954); Baldesar

Castiglione, *Il libro del Cortegiano*, ed. Walter Barberis (Turin: Einaudi, 1998); Baldesar Castiglione, *The Book of the Courtier: The Singleton Translation*, trans. Charles S. Singleton, ed. Edgar Mayhew, ed. Daniel Javitch (New York: W. W. Norton, 2002); Sperone Speroni, *Dialogo d'amore*, in *Trattatisti del Cinquecento* ed. Mario Pozzi (Milan and Naples: Ricciardi, 1978) I, pp. 511–563. Ebreo does not mention male–male desire even as a possibility, while Speroni, following Ficino, allows only a purely spiritual or intellectual love between men. On Speroni's dialogues, see Francesco Bruni, "Sperone Speroni e l'Accademia degli Infiammati," *Filologia e letteratura* 13 (1967): 24–71. Like Leone Ebreo, Bembo assumes a male–female model of love.

83. Leone Ebreo insists on the sensual aspect of love particularly in the first of the dialogues, "D'amore e desiderio," that comprise the *Dialoghi d'amore*: see pp. 48–56; *Philosophy of Love*, pp. 52–62. Bembo, too, devotes the early portions of *Gli Asolani* (Books I and II) to earthly love, but turns to a neoplatonic, spiritual model in Book III. See also the exchange between Tullia and Molza on the subject of sensual love in Speroni's *Dialogo d'amore*, pp. 529–534. On spiritual love in Ficino and Bembo, see Giulio Vallese, "La filosofia dell'amore nel Rinascimento: Dal Ficino al Bembo," *Le Parole e le idee* 6 (1964): 15–30.

84. Barkan, *Transuming Passion*, pp. 67–68, citing Ariosto, *The Satires of Ludovico Ariosto*, trans. Peter Desa Wiggins (Athens, OH: Ohio University Press, 1976), 6.31–33.

85. Barkan, *Transuming Passion*, p. 68.

86. See also Saslow, *Ganymede in the Renaissance*.

87. Gian Paolo Lomazzo, *Il libro dei sogni*, in his *Scritti sulle arti*, ed. Roberto Paolo Ciardi, 2 vols. (Florence: Marchi & Bertolli, 1973), vol. 1, pp. 1–240; Antonio Vignali, *La cazzaria*, ed. Pasquale Stoppelli (Rome: Edizioni dell'Elephante, 1984); *La Cazzaria: The Book of the Prick*, ed. and trans. Ian Frederick Moulton (New York: Routledge, 2003); Tullia d'Aragona, *Dialogo della infinità d'amore*, in *Trattati d'amore del Cinquecento*, ed. Giuseppe Zonta (1912; repr. Bari: Laterza, 1975), pp. 185–248; Antonio Rocco, *L'Alcibiade fanciullo a scola*, ed. Laura Coci (Rome: Salerno Editrice, 1988). The most famous, or infamous, erotic dialogues of the Italian Renaissance, Pietro Aretino's *Ragionamenti* (1534–1536), fall outside the scope of the present study, as they belong to a Boccaccian (and, in Cox's terms, Lucianic) rather than a Platonic tradition and, like the dialogues of Ficino's followers, all but ignore male–male desire. See Pietro Aretino, *Sei giornate*, ed. Giovanni Aquilecchia (Bari: Laterza, 1969); *Aretino's Dialogues*, trans. Raymond Rosenthal (New York: Stein and Day, 1971, repr. New York: Ballantine, 1973).

88. For the age differentials in Florence, see Michael Rocke, *Forbidden Friendships: Homosexuality and Male Culture in Renaissance Florence* (Oxford: Oxford University Press, 1996), pp. 113–117; for Venice, see Guido Ruggiero, *The Boundaries of Eros: Sex Crime and Sexuality in Renaissance Venice* (Oxford: Oxford University Press, 1985), pp. 123–124.

89. On Florentine class relations in male–male desire, see Rocke, *Forbidden Friendships*, pp. 134–147; for Venice, see Ruggiero's entire chapter on sodomy, *Boundaries*, pp. 109–145.

90. On the regulation of sodomy in Florence, see Rocke, *Forbidden Friendships*, pp. 19–84, 227–235. For Venice, see Ruggiero's chapter, pp. 109–145.

91. Rocke, p. 191. This entire chapter, pp. 148–191, is highly instructive.

92. Castiglione, *Book of the Courtier: The Singleton Translation*. Citations of this translation by book, chapter, and page numbers appear in the text, followed by page citations of Barberis' Italian edition.

93. On the use of the term *kinaidos* to police male erotic behavior in ancient Athenian society, see John J. Winkler, "Laying Down the Law: The Oversight of Men's Sexual behavior in Classical Athens," in his *The Constraints of Desire: The Anthropology of Sex and Gender in Ancient Greece* (New York: Routledge, 1990), pp. 45–70. For a recent discussion of *kinaidos* and the related concept *katapugon*, see James N. Davidson, *Courtesans and Fishcakes: The Consuming Passions of Classical Athens* (New York: St. Martin's Press, 1997), pp. 167–182. On the Roman *cinaedus*, see Williams, *Roman Homosexuality* pp. 175–178; John R. Clarke, *Looking at Lovemaking: Constructions of Sexuality in Roman Art, 100 B.C.–A.D. 250* (Berkeley: University of California Press, 2001), pp. 84–85, 234–235. All these discussions make it clear that Singleton's translation of *cinaedus* as "satyrs" (Castiglione, p. 116, n. 6) is excessively coy.

94. There are a number of studies of the jokes in *The Book of the Courtier*; most interesting for our purposes is Robert Grudin, "Renaissance Laughter: The Jests in Castiglione's *Il Cortegiano*," *Neophilologus* 58 (1974): 199–204, which argues that the jokes are a way of dealing with the moral depravity of contemporary Italy. If Grudin is correct, sodomy may thus be understood as an aspect of that depravity. Cf. on joking as a form of social control more generally Giuseppe Falvo, "The Art of 'Facezie' in Castiglione's *Cortegiano*," in *Interpreting the Italian Renaissance: Literary Perspectives*, ed. Antonio Toscano (Stony Brook, NY: Forum Italicum, 1991), pp. 127–137; Robert S. Dombroski, "A Note on Jokes and their Relation to the Perfect Courtier," *Italiana* 9 (2000): 132–137.

95. On Castiglione's debt to Bembo, see Piero Floriani, *Bembo e Castiglione: Studi sul classicismo del Cinquecento* (Rome: Bulzoni, 1976), pp. 169–186. On Bembo's "closed" dialogue form, see Olga Zorzi Pugliese, "Bembo and the 'Dialogic' Path of Love," in *Italiana 1988: Selected Papers from the Proceedings of the Fifth Annual Conference of the American Association of Teachers of Italian, November 18–20, 1988, Monterey, California*, ed. Albert N. Mancini, Paolo A. Giordano, and Anthony J. Tamburri (River Forest, IL: Rosary College, 1990), pp. 109–119.

96. But cf. Cinzia di Giulio, "La mimesi dell'amore nel *Cortegiano*," *Romance Notes* 36 (1996): 253–260, which argues that Castiglione's vision of love is more realistic and corporeal than is usually believed.

97. On this multivoiced dialogism of *The Book of the Courtier*, see Roland Galle, "Dialogform und Menschenbild in Castigliones *Il libro del Cortegiano*," *Neohelicon* 17.1 (1990): 233–251; Silke Segler-Messner, "Der Dialog als Raum spielerischer Selbstentfaltung: Baldessar Castiglione, Stefano Guazzo, Moderata Fonte," in *Spielwelten: Performanz und Inszenierunng in der Renaissance*,

ed. Klaus W. Hempfer and Helmut Pfeiffer (Stuttgart: Franz Steiner, 2002), pp. 47–66, at pp. 50–55.

98. But cf. Lawrence Lipking, "The Dialectic of *Il Cortegiano*," *PMLA* 81 (1966): 355–362, for an argument that the text remains dialogical throughout because of its "unresolved reciprocation between ideas and life," p. 362.

99. On Tullia d'Aragona's potentially disruptive presence in Speroni's dialogue, see Robert Buranello, "*Figura meretricis*: Tullia d'Aragona in Sperone Speroni's *Dialogo d'amore*," *Spunti e Ricerche* 15 (2000): 53–68. On her own dialogical relationship to these earlier dialogues, especially in terms of the addition of an explicitly feminine voice to them, see Janet Smarr, "A Dialogue of Dialogues: Tullia d'Aragona and Sperone Speroni," *Modern Language Notes* 113 (1998): 204–212; Ann Rosalind Jones, "Enabling Sites and Gender Difference: Reading City Women with Men," *Women's Studies* 19.2 (1991): 239–249.

100. See Rinaldina Russell's Introduction to Tullia d'Aragona, *Dialogue on the Infinity of Love*, ed. and trans. Rinaldina Russell and Bruce Merry (Chicago: University of Chicago Press, 1997), pp. 21–42, at p. 31. Citations of this translation by page number appear in the text, followed by page citations of Zonta's Italian edition.

101. Russell, pp. 90–91, n. 57, points out a similarity with Leone Ebreo's doctrine.

102. See p. 110 of Russell's and Merry's translation, and Russell's n. 81, as well as p. 57, n. 8. The source for this information is Umberto Pirotti, *Benedetto Varchi e la cultura del suo tempo* (Florence: Olschki, 1971), pp. 14–15, 28–29, but this entire section of Pirotti's book, pp. 1–63, is of interest.

103. See Russell's and Merry's translation, *Dialogue*, p. 96, n. 66, which cites Pirotti, pp. 47–53.

104. She also asks why this form of love excludes women, asserting that women too possess the necessary "intellectual soul" (p. 97; p. 229), and is pleased to hear Varchi agree with her: see Smarr, "A Dialogue," on this point.

105. See *La Cazzaria*, trans. Moulton, pp. 125–164. For an analysis of the allegory, see Paula Findlen, "Humanism, Politics, and Pornography in Renaissance Italy," in *The Invention of Pornography: Obscenity and the Origins of Modernity, 1500–1800*, ed. Lynn Hunt (New York: Zone, 1993), pp. 49–108, at pp. 86–94; Ian Frederick Moulton, "Bawdy Politic: Renaissance Republicanism and the Discourse of Pricks," in *Opening the Borders: Inclusivity and Early Modern Studies, Essays in Honor of James V. Mirollo*, ed. Peter C. Herman (Newark, DE: University of Delaware Press, 1999), pp. 255–242. See also Moulton's introduction to his translation of *La Cazzaria*, pp. 1–70.

106. On Bernardino, see Rocke, *Forbidden Friendships*, pp. 36–44.

107. On this group see, in addition to Moulton's texts, Lolita Petracchi Constantini, *L'Accademia degli Intronati di Siena e una sua commedia* (Siena: Editrice d'Arte "La Diana," 1928).

108. *La Cazzaria*, trans. Moulton. Citations of this translation by page numbers will appear in the text, followed by page citations of Stoppelli's Italian edition.

109. See *Gli Asolani*, Book II.

110. Thomas Laqueur, *Making Sex: Body and Gender From the Greeks to Freud* (Cambridge, MA: Harvard University Press, 1990).

111. While there is no equivalent study of the specifically Sienese regulation of sodomy, Ruggiero's study of Venice and especially Rocke's study of Florence, another Tuscan city-state, may be consulted as representative.

112. See the Introduction to this book.

113. Lomazzo, *Il Libro*, p. 104; trans. in Rocke, *Forbidden Friendships*, p. 255, n. 4.

114. Rocke, *Forbidden Friendships*, p. 149. Rocke translates Lomazzo's defense of *l'amore masculino* as "a work of virtue" (in a phrase spoken by Leonardo), p. 148, and insists that this term "refers explicitly to sexual relations between men . . . not to sanitized, neo-Platonic 'friendship,' " p. 300, n. 1. On this term see also Joseph Cady, " 'Masculine Love,' Renaissance Writing, and the 'New Invention' of Homosexuality," *Journal of Homosexuality* 23 (1992): 9–40. On Leonardo (and Salai), see Saslow, *Ganymede in the Renaissance*, pp. 85–90, 127, 197–199.

115. Rocke, *Forbidden Friendships*, p. 94, gives 1630 as an approximate date of composition; Maria Dimitrakis, in her Preface to a recent revision of the anonymous nineteenth-century French translation, dates the publication to 1651: Antonio Rocco, *Pour convaincre Alcibiade* (Paris: NiL, 1999), p. 7.

116. English translations from *L'Alcibiade fanciullo a scola* are my own, based on Coci's Italian edition; I have consulted the anonymous nineteenth-century French translation cited in n. 74. Page citations of Coci's edition appear in the text.

117. On Venetian laws concerning sodomy, see Ruggiero, *Boundaries*, pp. 109–145. On medieval Christian (and other possible) interpretations of the story of Sodom and Gomorrah, see Boswell, *Christianity*, pp. 92–98; Jordan, *Invention*, 30–36; Keiser, *Courtly Desire*, pp. 49–50.

118. See Jayne, *Commentary*, Introduction, pp. 17–18.

119. On Alcibiades' own desirable androgyny, see pp. 39, 41.

120. See Joan Cadden, *Meanings of Sex Difference in the Middle Ages: Medicine, Science, and Culture* (Cambridge, Eng.: Cambridge University Press, 1993), pp. 214–218.

121. See, for example, the English Restoration play attributed to Lord Rochester, entitled *The Farce of Sodom, or the Quintessence of Debauchery*, in *Rochester: Complete Poems and Plays*, ed. Paddy Lyons (London: J. M. Dent, 1993), pp. 125–154.

122. Louis Althusser, "Ideology and Ideological State Apparatuses: Notes Towards an Investigation," in his *Lenin and Philosophy and Other Essays*, trans. Ben Brewster (New York: Monthly Review Press, 1971, repr. 1991), pp. 85–126.

123. Gramsci's observations on ideology can be found throughout his *Prison Notebooks*; for one useful formulation, see Antonio Gramsci, "Cultural topics. Ideological Material," in his *Prison Notebooks*, vol. 2, ed. and trans. Joseph A. Buttigieg (New York: Columbia University Press, 1996), Notebook 4, §49, pp. 52–53.

124. For a Lacanian deconstruction of Filotimo's speech on Sodom, see Armando Maggi, "The discourse of Sodom in a Seventeenth-Century Venetian Text," in

Reclaiming the Sacred: The Bible in Gay and Lesbian Culture, ed. Raymond-Jean Frontain, 2nd ed. (New York: Haworth, 1997), pp. 41–60.

125. On the rhetorical aspect of Rocco's dialogue, see Philippe-Joseph Salazar, "Sex and Rhetoric: An Assessment of Rocco's *Alcibiade*," *Studi d'italianistica nell'Africa australe* 12.2 (1999): 5–19.

126. On the reception and afterlife of Rocco's book, see Wolfram Setz, "Anonio Roccos *Der Schüler Alkibiades*: Ein Buch und seine Leser," *Forum Homosexualität und Literatur* 40 (2002): 99–110.

127. Denis Diderot, "Rameau's Nephew", in *Rameau's Nephew and D'Alembert's Dream*, trans. Leonard Tancock (Harmondsworth: Penguin, 1966), pp. 33–130. Citations of this translation by page number appear in the text, followed by page citations of the French edition: *Le Neveu de Rameau* in Diderot, *Oeuvres romanesques*, ed. Henri Bénac (Paris: Garnier, 1962), pp. 395–492.

128. For an interesting overview of Plato's influence on Diderot, see Mihály Szívós, "Le rôle des motifs socratiques et platoniciens dans la structure et la genèse du *Neveu de Rameau* de Diderot," *Recherches sur Diderot et sur l'Encyclopédie* 20 (1996): 39–55. See also David Lee, "Diderot's *Le Neveu de Rameau*: A Socratic Dialogue," *Publications of the Missouri Philological Association* 10 (1985): 13–20.

129. Jane Rush, "Diderot, Socrate, et l'esthétique de la farce dans *Le Neveu de Rameau*," *Eighteenth-Century Fiction* 6 (1993): 47–64 reaches a similar conclusion.

130. See Diderot, *Neveu*, pp. 98–105, pp. 83–84; pp. 464–470, pp. 448–449. Michael Prince, *Philosophical Dialogue in the British Enlightenment: Theology, Aesthetics and the Novel* (Cambridge, Eng.: Cambridge University Press, 1996) focuses on England, but Prince's observations on the eighteenth century's varying appropriations of Socrates and the Platonic tradition, pp. 163–189, is helpful nonetheless. Specifically on Diderot's use of the dialogue form, see also H. R. Jauss, "*Le Neveu de Rameau*: Dialogue et dialectique; ou: Diderot lecteur de Socrate et Hegel lecteur de Diderot," *Revue de Métaphysique et de Morale* 89 (1984): 145–181; Pierre Hartmann, "Remarques sur les procédés et la fonction du dialogue dans *Le neveu de Rameau*," *L'Information littéraire* 44.2 (March–April, 1992): 29–31; Anthony Wall, "Bakhtine et Diderot: à propos du *Neveu de Rameau*," *Recherches sur Diderot et sur l'Encyclopédie* 17 (1994): 83–106. James E. Fowler, " 'Je m'entretiens avec moi-même': Self versus Other in *Le Neveu de Rameau*," *Dalhousie French Studies* 42 (Spring, 1998): 77–87 traces the theme of sameness and difference in Diderot's dialogue that we have observed elsewhere in the Platonic tradition.

131. On Enlightenment materialism and same-sex desire, especially with reference to this series of dialogues, see also Donald Morton's comments in *The Material Queer: A LesBiGay Cultural Studies Reader*, ed. Donald Morton (Boulder, CO: Westview, 1996), p. 56.

132. Denis Diderot, *Sequel to the Conversation*, in Denis Diderot, *Rameau's Nephew and D'Alembert's Dream*, trans. Leonard Tancock (Harmondsworth: Penguin, 1966), pp. 225–233. Citations of this translation by page number will appear

in the text, followed by page citations of the French edition: Diderot, *Le Rêve de d'Alembert* in his *Oeuvres complètes*, vol. 17, ed. Jean Varloot et al. (Paris: Hermann, 1987), pp. 89–207.

133. Théodore Tarczylo, "Moral Values in 'La suite de l'entretien,'" trans. James Coke and Michael Murray, *Eighteenth-Century Life* 9 (1985): 43–60, finds a less positive valuation of male–male desire in Diderot, but cites no real evidence for this view.

134. On the complexities of Sade's vision of nature, see Timo Airaksinen, *The Philosophy of the Marquis de Sade* (New York: Routledge, 1991, repr. 1995), pp. 45–66. Marcel Hénaff, *Sade: The Invention of the Libertine Body*, trans. Xavier Callahan (Minneapolis: University of Minnesota Press, 1999), suggests, however, that for Sade the concept of "nature" is merely a "screen," pp. 130–131.

135. Margaret C. Jacob, "The Materialist World of Pornography," in *The Invention of Pornography: Obscenity and the Origins of Modernity, 1500–1800*, ed. Lynn Hunt (New York: Zone, 1996), pp. 157–202, at 157. See also Lynn Hunt, "Pornography and the French Revolution," in *The Invention of Pornography*, pp. 301–339; on Sade specifically, pp. 330–332.

136. Jacob, "Pornography," p. 163. On the complexities of Sade's appropriation of materialist discourse, see Caroline Warman, "The Jewels of Virtue: Sade's Claim to the Legacy of Materialism," *Paragraph* 23.1 (March, 2000): 87–97.

137. Jacob, "Pornography," p. 164.

138. Ibid., p. 177.

139. Ibid., p. 164.

140. *La Nouvelle Justine, ou les Malheurs de la Vertu, suivie de l'Histoire de Juliette, sa soeur* (Paris: 1797); Marquis de Sade, *Juliette*, trans. Austryn Wainhouse (New York: Grove, 1968).

141. Marquis de Sade, *Philosophy in the Bedroom*, in *Justine, Philosophy in the Bedroom, Eugénie de Franval and Other Writings*, trans. Richard Seaver and Austryn Wainhouse (New York: Grove, 1965). Citations of his translation by page number appear in the text, followed by page citations of the Pléiade French edition: *La Philosophie dans le boudoir*, in Sade, *Oeuvres*, vol. 3, ed. Michel Delon (Paris: Gallimard, 1998), pp. 1–178.

The question of Sade's value for women has generated a voluminous critical literature. Certain feminist critics, such as Angela Carter, find in Sade a subversive possibility for women's sexual liberation, though even Carter suggests that both the passive Justine and the active Juliette "are women whose identities have been defined exclusively by men": Angela Carter, *The Sadeian Woman and the Ideology of Pornography: An Exercise in Cultural History* (1979; rpt. Harmondsworth: Penguin, 2001), p. 77. See also Hénaff, who understands *La Philosophie dans le boudoir* as an assault on the "monogamous family system," based on male power and the confinement of female sexuality, *Sade*, pp. 272–273 (and compare Carter, *Sadeian Woman*, pp. 118–133); Robert L. Mazzola, "Sade's Woman: Essential Pornogony and Virtual Embodiment," in *Gender Reconstructions: Pornography and Perversions in Literature and Culture* (Aldershot, Eng.: Ashgate, 2002), pp. 108–124; Sabine

Wilke, "The Sexual Woman and her struggle for Sexuality: Cruel Women in Sade, Sacher-Masoch, and Treut," *Women in German Yearbook* 14 (1999): 245–260; Jane Gallop, "Sade, Mothers, and Other Women," in *Sade and the Narrative of Transgression*, ed. David B. Allison, Mark S. Roberts, and Allen S. Weiss (Cambridge, Eng.: Cambridge University Press, 1995), pp. 122–141. Cautionary notes regarding Sade's value to feminism are sounded by Kristin Roodenburg, "Sade and Feminism," *Restant* 21 (1993): 259–271; "Beat Me! Beat Me!: Feminists and Sade," *ENclitic* 11.4 (1989): 62–72. For a feminist reading of *La Philosophie dans le boudoir* specifically, see Jane Gallop, *The Daughter's Seduction: Feminism and Psychoanalysis* (Ithaca, NY: Cornell University Press, 1982), pp. 82–91; Gallop's observations take the form of a commentary on two further texts: Luce Irigaray, " 'Frenchwomen, Stop Trying,' " in her *This Sex Which is Not One* (1977), trans. Catherine Porter with Caroline Burke (Ithaca, NY: Cornell University Press, 1985), pp. 198–204, and Jacques Lacan, "Kant avec Sade" (1963), repr. in his *Écrits* [1966; repr. as *Écrits*, 2 vols. (Paris: Éditions du Seuil, 1971)], vol. 2, pp. 119–148. Most critics assume, as I do, that Dolmancé is Sade's spokesman; see, for example, Simone de Beauvoir's classic essay "Must We Burn Sade?," trans. Annette Michelson, in Marquis de Sade, *The 120 Days of Sodom and Other Writings*, compiled and trans. Austryn Wainhouse and Richard Seaver (New York: Grove, 1966), pp. 3–64, at pp. 10–11, and more recently, Neil Schaeffer, *The Marquis de Sade: A Life* (1999; rpt. Cambridge, MA: Harvard University Press, 2000), pp. 455–461.

142. Writing of Dolmancé's relationship with this female disciples, Carter suggests that "since he is good enough to class them with the masters, they, too, will be permitted to tyrannise as much as they please," p. 143. Roland Barthes, *Sade, Fourier, Loyola*, trans. Richard Miller (Baltimore: Johns Hopkins University Press, 1976), notes that "Sade's adventures . . . take place in a real world contemporary with the time of Sade's youth," and that Sade uses contemporary class relationships "not as an image to be portrayed, but as a *model to be reproduced*" (pp. 130–131; emphasis in text). On Barthes' engagement with Sade, see Philippe Roger, "Traitement de faveur (Barthes lecteur de Sade)," *Nottingham French Studies* 36.1 (Spring 1997): 34–44; Bertrand du Chambon, "Un Eros masculin," *(Pre)Publications* 91 (November 1984): 20–25. Hénaff sees Sade's works as a disruption of the class system, pp. 7–8.

143. The scientific/naturalistic/libertine views of sodomy were, of course, contrary to the officially sanctioned legal views. On the shifting constructions and methods of regulating of male–male desire in eighteenth-century France, see the work of Michel Rey, e.g., "Parisian Homosexuals Create a Lifestyle, 1700–1750: The Police Archives," *Eighteenth-Century Life* n.s. 9 (1985): 179–191; "Police and Sodomy in Eighteenth-Century Paris: From Sin to Disorder," 1982, trans. Kent Gerard and Gert Hekma in *The Pursuit of Sodomy: Male Homosexuality in Renaissance and Enlightenment Europe*, ed. Kent Gerard and Gert Hekma (New York: Harrington Park Press, 1989), pp. 129–146, as well as Jacob Stockinger, "Homosexuality and the French

Enlightenment," in *Homosexualities and French Literature: Cultural Contexts/Critical Texts*, ed. George Stambolian and Elaine Marks (Ithaca, NY: Cornell University Press, 1979), pp. 161–185; D. A. Coward, "Attitudes to Homosexuality in Eighteenth-Century France," *Journal of European Studies* 10 (1980): 231–255. See also the synthesis in Greenberg, pp. 318–320. Specifically on the Platonic influence, see Gert Hekma, "Sodomites, Platonic Lovers, Contrary Lovers: The Backgrounds of the Modern Homosexual," in *The Pursuit of Sodomy*, pp. 433–455, at pp. 435–445. It should also be noted that post-Revolutionary France led the way in the decriminalization of sodomy in 1791.

144. Barthes, *Sade, Fourier, Loyola*, p. 30. See also Hénaff, *Sade*, pp. 129–130.

145. See Schaeffer, *Marquis de Sade*, pp. 126–130, for an account of the entire Marseilles incident, and p. 139 for its legal consequences. See also Laurence L. Bongie, *Sade: A Biographical Essay* (Chicago: University of Chicago Press, 1998), pp. 129–138, for a less sympathetic account, and pp. 81–83 for Sade's earlier "homosexual" experiences.

146. "Sade felt himself to be feminine, and he resented the fact that women were not the males he really desired," "Must we Burn Sade?," p. 25.

147. Schaeffer, *Marguis de Sade*, p. 135. On the question of Sade's "bisexuality," see also Donald E. Hall, "Graphic Sexuality and the Erasure of a Polymorphous Perversity," in *RePresenting Bisexualities: Subjects and Cultures of Fluid Desire*, ed. Donald E. Hall and Maria Pramaggiore (New York: New York University Press, 1996), pp. 99–123.

148. For Ganymede's function as a sign of male–male desire in the Middle Ages, see Boswell, pp. 243–266, 381–389; for the later period, see Barkan, *Transuming passion*; Saslow, *Ganymede in the Renaissance*. In the fifth dialogue, Dolmancé also compares Mme. de Saint-Ange's own ass to Ganymede's (p. 271; p. 87). On the libertine's use of the woman as if she were a boy, see Barthes, *Sade, Fourier, Loyola*, p. 124: "only Woman offers the choice of two sites of intromission: in choosing one over the other *in the area of the same body*, the libertine produces and assumes a meaning, that of transgression. The boy, because his body provides the libertine with no opportunity for stating the paradigm of sites (he offers but one), is less *forbidden* than Woman: thus, systematically, he is less interesting" (emphasis in text). On male libertine eroticism as primarily "homosexual," see Irigaray, "Frenchwomen," Gallop, *Seduction*.

149. Carter, *Sadeian Woman*, p. 116. William F. Edmiston, "Shifting Ground: Sade, Same-Sex Desire, and the One-, Two-, and Three-Sex Models," in *Illicit Sex: Identity Politics in Early Modern Culture*, ed. Thomas DiPiero and Pat Gill (Athens, GA: University of Georgia Press, 1997), pp. 143–160, argues that Sade understands same-sex desire both as a "taste" and as an identity.

150. On Sade's understanding of female biology, see for example Airaksinen, *Philosophy of Sade*, pp. 74–78.

151. Thomas Laqueur, *Making Sex: Body and Gender from the Greeks to Freud* (Cambridge, MA: Harvard University Press, 1990), p. 149.

152. The 1795 French edition included such illustrations; for an example, see Hunt, "Pornography and the French Revolution," p. 318, fig. 9.2. The Pléiade edition also includes them.

153. Schaeffer, *Marquis de Sade*, p. 458.

154. Ibid., p. 459.

155. William F. Edmiston, "Nature, Sodomy, and Semantics in Sade's *La Philosophie dans le boudoir*," *Studies in Eighteenth-Century Culture* 24 (1995): 121–136 argues that "Nature" is for Sade so multivalent that it fails as a moral category, and goes so far as to suggest that Sade may be intentionally parodying the naturalist position.

156. Sade explores the incest theme in several other works, including both *Justine* and *Juliette*, and most notably in the novella *Eugénie de Franval* [(Paris: 1788); included in *Justine, Philosophy in the Bedroom, and Other Writings*, pp. 375–445], which foreshadows *La Philosophie dans le boudoir* in several important respects, notably in its narrative concerning the libertine education of a girl named Eugénie, in which a libertine father is pitted against a conventionally moralistic mother, who is eventually murdered. The novella's sympathies, however, at least ostensibly lie with the forces of conventional morality, while the later dialogue obviously celebrates libertinism.

157. Schaeffer, *Marquis de Sade*, p. 11; cf. Carter, *Sadeian Woman*, pp. 137–150, for a fascinating reading of Sade's solipsism.

158. Barthes, *Sade, Fourier, Loyola*, p. 165.

159. For Sade's own extensive masturbatory practices, see Schaeffer, *Marquis de Sade*, especially pp. 131–133, 253–254, 292–293, and 297–299. These practices must, of course, be understood in the context of Sade's lengthy imprisonments throughout his adult life. Douglas B. Saylor's psychoanalytical reading of Sade in his *The Sadomasochistic Homotext: Readings in Sade, Balzac, and Proust* (New York: Peter Lang, 1993), pp. 39–63, suggests that "Sade himself aspires to the role of the Father," p. 59.

160. *Dialogue entre un prêtre et un moribond* (Paris: 1782); *Dialogue Between a Priest and a Dying Man*, in *Justine, Philosophy in the Bedroom, and Other Writings*, pp. 165–175.

161. Albert W. Levi, "Philosophy as Literature: the Dialogue," *Philosophy and Rhetoric* 9, no. 1 (1976): 1–20, at p. 11.

162. Compare the Chevalier's earlier attempt to argue against Dolmancé's principles, *Philosophy*, pp. 340–342 (pp. 154–156): again his objections are overcome as soon as they are stated, and within three pages Eugénie declares Dolmancé to be unambiguously the winner of the "debate" (p. 342; p. 156).

163. Barthes, *Sade, Fourier, Loyola*, p. 31.

164. Cf. Barthes' remarks on "libertine solitude," p. 16, and Georges Bataille's essay on "De Sade's Sovereign Man," in his *Erotism: Death and Sensuality*, trans. Mary Dalwood (San Francisco: City Lights, 1986), pp. 164–176. Lucienne Frappier-Mazur, *Writing the Orgy: Power and Parody in Sade* (Philadelphia: University of Pennsylvania Press, 1996), suggests that for Sade the orgy scene itself eliminates difference in favor of orgiastic indistinction, pp. 11–57.

165. Gilles Deleuze, *Sacher-Masoch: An Interpretation* (London: Faber, 1971), p. 18. My attention was drawn to this passage by Glenn Burger, *Chaucer's Queer Nation* (Minneapolis: University of Minnesota Press, 2003), p. 26. Cf. Barthes' contention that "erotic energy is renewed" in the pause for such a dissertation in Sade's other works, p. 146.

166. Cf. Barthes: "the agent is not he who has power or pleasure, but he who controls the direction of the scene and the sentence," p. 31. Henri Blanc, "Sur le statut du dialogue dans l'oeuvre de Sade," *Dix-Huitième Siècle* 4 (1972): 301–314 also understands *La Philosophie dans le boudoir* as essentially monological; and cf. Béatrice Didier, "Sade et le dialogue philosophique," *Cahiers de l'Association Internationale des Etudes Françaises* 24 (1972): 59–74. See also Claude Lefort, "Sade: The Boudoir and the City," *South Atlantic Quarterly* 95 (1996): 1009–1028, which argues that the Sadeian impulse to corruption is by definition not solipsistic, whereas Scott Carpenter, "Sade and the Problem of Closure: Keeping Philosophy in the Bedroom," *Neophilologus* 75 (1991): 519–528 argues that this drive to contamination is contained by an equally powerful drive for closure.

167. As Barthes points out, Augustin the gardener is excluded from the reading of the "revolutionary" pamphlet, p. 159; see also Bongie, pp. 226–227. Marcel Hénaff gives the treatise a more straightforward political reading, pp. 250–251, but see also Hénaff's later essay, "Naked Terror: Political Violence, Libertine Violence," *SubStance* 27.2 (1998): 5–32, which links Sade's revolutionary rhetoric to his solipsism. On Sade's debt to contemporary revolutionary politics and pamphleteering, see Maurice Blanchot, "Français, encore un effort," *Nouvelle revue française* 13 (154) (1965): 600–618; Michel Delon, "L'Invention Sadienne et les pamphlets révolutionnaires," in *Le Travail des lumières: pour Georges Benrekessa*, ed. Caroline Jacot Grapa et al. (Paris: Champion, 2002), pp. 557–568.

168. Michel Foucault, *The History of Sexuality*, Vol. I: *An Introduction*, trans. Robert Hurley (New York: Vintage, 1980), p. 149. My attention was drawn to this and the following quotation by James Miller, *The Passion of Michel Foucault* (New York: Simon and Schuster, 1993), p. 244.

169. Foucault, *History*, p. 157.

170. On the emergence of a modern homosexual identity in the Enlightenment period, see Randolph Trumbach's work, especially his influential essay "The Birth of the Queen: Sodomy and the emergence of Gender Equality in Modern Culture, 1660–1750," in *Hidden From History*, pp. 129–140 and, more recently, his book *Sex and the Gender Revolution*, Vol. 1: *Homosexuality and the Third Gender in Enlightenment London* (Chicago: University of Chicago Press, 1998).

3   EROTIC STYLE: FROM PLATO'S *PHAEDRUS* TO THE MODERN NOVEL

1. On the modern homosexual identity, see the work of Randolph Trumbach cited at the end of chapter 2.

2. *Plato's Phaedrus*, trans. R. Hackforth (Cambridge, Eng.: Cambridge University Press, 1952). Page and Stephanus numbers from this translation will be cited in the text. Greek citations follow Plato, *Phaedrus*, in *Platonis Opera*, vol. 2, ed. John Burnet (Oxford: Oxford University Press, 1901).

3. On the relationship between the two dialogues, see John D. Moore, "The Relation Between Plato's *Symposium* and *Phaedrus*," in *Patterns in Plato's Thought: Papers Arising out of the 1971 West Coast Greek Philosophy Conference*, ed. J. M. E. Moravçsik (Dordrecht: Reidel, 1973), pp. 52–71. On Phaedrus himself, see Martha C. Nussbaum, " 'This story isn't true': madness, reason, and recantation in the *Phaedrus*," in her *The Fragility of Goodness: Luck and Ethics in Greek Tragedy and Philosophy* (Cambridge, Eng.: Cambridge University Press, 1986), pp. 200–233, at p. 212.

4. Socrates took the lead at *Phaedrus*, p. 22, 227c.

5. Ibid. Perhaps even Socrates' confession a bit later that "I can't as yet 'know myself' " (p. 24, 230a) might suggest that he regards himself as other, an object of inquiry as well as an inquiring subject.

6. On the prologue's scene-setting for the following three speeches, see Anne Lebeck, "The Central Myth of Plato's *Phaedrus*," *Greek, Roman and Byzantine Studies* 13 (1972): 267–290, at pp. 280–283.

7. This passage has given rise to much comment. Many critics believe, given Plato's harsh treatment of poetry elsewhere, that his comments on poetic inspiration must be ironic: see C. J. Rowe, *Plato's* Phaedrus (Warminster: Aris and Phillips, 1986), p. 151; Charles L. Griswold, Jr., *Self-Knowledge in Plato's* Phaedrus (New Haven: Yale University Press, 1986), p. 53; Andrea Wilson Nightingale, *Genres in Dialogue: Plato and the Construct of Philosophy* (Cambridge, Eng.: Cambridge University Press, 1995), pp. 135–238; Page DuBois, *Sappho Is Burning* (Chicago: University of Chicago Press, 1995), p. 85. But Helene Foley, " 'The Mother of the Argument': *Eros* and the Body in Sappho and Plato's *Phaedrus*," in *Parchments of Gender: Deciphering the Body in Antiquity*, ed. Maria Wyke (Oxford: Clarendon, 1998), points out that the similar poetic inspiration for Socrates' second speech is taken seriously, pp. 45–49.

8. It is uncertain whether this speech is to be attributed to the real Lysias or should be considered simply as Plato's imitation of Lysias' style. See Siegmar Doepp, "Der Verfasser des Erotikos in Platons *Phaedrus*," *Glotta* 61 (1983): 15–29.

9. *Phaedrus*, trans. Hackforth, p. 31; see also Josef Pieper, *Love and Inspiration: A Study of Plato's* Phaedrus, trans. Richard and Clara Winston (London: Faber and Faber, 1964), pp. 19–20, and, more recently, *The* Symposium *and the* Phaedrus: *Plato's Erotic Dialogues*, ed. and trans. William S. Cobb (Albany: State University of New York Press, 1993), p. 144.

10. G. R. F. Ferrari, *Listening to the Cicadas: A Study of Plato's* Phaedrus (Cambridge, Eng.: Cambridge University Press, 1987), pp. 93, 95.

11. *Phaedrus*, trans. Hackforth, p. 31.

12. A. E. Taylor, *Plato: The Man and His Work*, cited by Hackforth, *Phaedrus*, p. 31. For a more positive assessment of the speech's skill, see C. J. Rowe's commentary in *Plato:* Phaedrus (Warminster: Aris and Phillips, 1986), pp. 143–145.

13. See Bruce Thornton, *Eros: The Myth of Ancient Greek Sexuality* (Boulder, CO: Westview Press, 1997).

14. Hackforth, *Phaedrus*, p. 37. For negative judgments of this speech, see Ferrari, *Listening*, pp. 105–110; Cobb, Symposium *and* Phaedrus, pp. 145–146. Pieper, *Love*, pp. 33–34, reads it ironically.

15. Hackforth, *Phaedrus*, p. 40.

16. Ibid.

17. Or "people who are one age enjoy those of the same age": see Cobb, Symposium *and* Phaedrus, p. 98.

18. But cf. Hackforth, who claims that "[t]he reformed lover has, as we say, 'come to his senses,' but no more than that" (*Phaedrus*, p. 48). The repeated emphasis on his "difference" contradicts this view.

19. Plato, *Apology*, trans. G. M. A. Grube, in Plato, *Complete Works*, ed. John M. Cooper (Indianapolis: Hackett, 1997), pp. 18–36, at p. 29, 31d. For the view that the second speech is entirely repudiated in the third, see Malcolm Brown and James Coulter, "The Middle Speech of Plato's *Phaedrus*," *Journal of the History of Philosophy* 9 (1971): 405–423.

20. On this point, see Hackforth, *Phaedrus*, pp. 54–55. Pieper emphasizes the religious language of the third speech, *Love*, pp. 39–41.

21. Hackforth *Phaedrus*, p. 94.

22. Ibid., p. 63. Cf. Dougal Blyth, "The Ever-Moving Soul in Plato's *Phaedrus*," *American Journal of Philology* 118 (1997): 185–217.

23. Hackforth, *Phaedrus*, p. 72.

24. Ibid., p. 75.

25. Ibid., p. 61.

26. Nussbaum, "This story," understands the *Phaedrus* as a whole as a disavowal of many of the views expressed in his other middle-period dialogues, pp. 202–203. See also Albert Cook, "Dialectic, Irony, and Myth in Plato's *Phaedrus*," *American Journal of Philology* 106 (1985): 427–441.

27. On this passage, see also Ferrari, *Listening*, pp. 153–159; Gregory Vlastos, "The Individual as an Object of Love in Plato," in his *Platonic Studies* (Princeton: Princeton University Press, 1973, repr. 1981), pp. 3–42, at pp. 38–42; Nussbaum, "This story," pp. 217–222; Foley, "Mother," pp. 46–47.

28. Hackforth, *Phaedrus*, pp. 101–102.

29. See Plato, *Republic*, trans. G. M. A. Grube, rev. C. D. C. Reeve, in Plato, *Complete Works*, ed. John M. Cooper (Indianapolis: Hackett, 1997), pp. 971–1223, at 391e–400e, pp. 1029–1038.

30. For another view of this passage, see G. R. F. Ferrari, "The Struggle in the Soul: *Phaedrus* 253c7–255a1," *Ancient Philosophy* 5 (1985): 1–10.

31. Hackforth, *Phaedrus*, p. 108.

32. Foley suggests that "the kind of lifelong, reciprocal, more egalitarian, and far less hierarchical relation formed between two specific individuals for the mutual pursuit of philosophy in *Phaedrus* implicitly marks a radical withdrawal from the social and political world that produced the standard homoerotic relation" and is inspired by Socrates' invocation of Sappho, "Mother," p. 69. See

also Ferrari, *Listening*, pp. 175–184; David M. Halperin, "Plato and Erotic Reciprocity," *Classical Antiquity* 5 (1986): 60–80; but cf. Paul W. Gooch, "Has Plato Changed Socrates' Heart in *Phaedrus*?," in *Understanding the Phaedrus: Proceedings of the II Symposium Platonicum*, ed. Livio Rossetti (Sankt Augustin: Academia Verlag, 1992), pp. 309–312, for the view that while Plato's theory of love may have changed, his depiction of Socrates has not. Casey Charles, "A Horse is a Horse: Love and Sex in Plato's *Phaedrus*," *Literature and Psychology* 38.3 (1992): 47–70 is a Lacanian reading emphasizing this passage. On the love of individuals, see Vlastos, "Individual" Martha C. Nussbaum, "Love and the Individual: Romantic Rightness and Platonic Aspiration," in her *Love's Knowledge: Essays on Philosophy and Literature* (Oxford: Oxford University Press, 1990), pp. 314–334; Gerasimos Santas, "Passionate Platonic Love in the *Phaedrus*," *Ancient Philosophy* 2 (1982): 105–114.

33. See also *Phaedrus*, 265b–c.

34. Nightingale, *Genres in Dialogue*, p. 159.

35. Ibid., p. 161; and see Foley, "Mother," pp. 47–48, which also cites Nightingale, *Genres in Dialogue*; Ferrari, *Cicadas*, p. 118; Nussbaum, "This story"; and on the relationship of erotic to philosophical desire, cf. Anne Lebeck, "The Central Myth of Plato's *Phaedrus*," *Greek, Roman, and Byzantine Studies* 13 (1972): 267–290; Robert Switzer, "The Topology of Madness: Philosophic Seduction in Plato's *Phaedrus*," *Alif* 14 (1994): 6–36; Marian Demos, "Stesichorus' Palinode in the *Phaedrus*," *Classical World* 90.4 (April, 1997): 235–249. Page du Bois, "Phallocentrism and its Subversion in Plato's *Phaedrus*," *Arethusa* 18 (1985): 91–103 makes a similar argument for the relationship of philosophy and eros in the *Phaedrus*, and extends it to suggest that this dialogue also liberates "the reader to a paradoxical sense of the fluidity of sexual boundaries," p. 91.

36. Hackforth, *Phaedrus*, pp. 133–134, n. 1.

37. Hackforth suggests that the quotation is an adaptation of *Odyssey* V, 193, *Phaedrus*, p. 134, n. 3.

38. See Claud A. Thompson, "Rhetorical Madness: An Ideal in the *Phaedrus*," *Quarterly Journal of Speech* 55 (1969): 358–363.

39. See Christopher Gill, "Dogmatic Dialogue in *Phaedrus* 276–7," in *Understanding the Phaedrus*, pp. 156–172.

40. Jacques Derrida, "Plato's Pharmacy," in his *Dissemination*, trans. Barbara Johnson (Chicago: University of Chicago Press, 1981), pp. 61–171 famously deconstructs this Platonic problematic of writing.

41. See Cobb's translation (Symposium *and* Phaedrus), for example.

42. Kenneth M. Sayre, *Plato's Literary Garden: How to Read a Platonic Dialogue* (Notre Dame, IN: Notre Dame University Press, 1995), p. xiv, suggests that this point is made at 276d, but it seems clearer at 276e.

43. Hackforth, *Phaedrus*, contrasts "the conversing (διαλέγεσθαι) of Socrates with those willing to join him in the quest for truth" with "the contentious wrangling (ἐπίγειν) of men like Euthydemus and Dionysodorus" (p. 135). On the political implications of this view, see Charles L. Griswold, "The Politics of

Self-Knowledge: Liberal Variations on the *Phaedrus*," in *Understanding the Phaedrus*, pp. 173–190.

44. On this point, see also Hackforth, *Phaedrus*, pp. 163–164.

45. As Cobb properly translates it (Symposium *and* Phaedrus), p. 136. The degree of irony in Socrates' praise of Isocrates is matter of debate; for a review of the issues, see G. J. de Vries, "Isocrates in the *Phaedrus*: A Reply," *Mnemosyne* 24 (1971): 387–390.

46. Hans Wagner, "Über eine spezielle Art platonistische Dialogkomposition (*Sophistes* und *Phaedrus*)," *Archiv für Geschichte der Philosophie* 66 (1984): 1–10 argues that the rhetorical theme serves as a clarification of the erotic one. For an argument basing the dialogue's unity on its verisimilitude rather than on its philosophy, see Malcolm Heath, "The Unity of Plato's *Phaedrus*," *Oxford Studies in Ancient Philosophy* 7 (1989): 151–173; see also the subsequent exchange between Heath and Christopher Rowe in the same issue, pp. 175–191.

47. Sayre, *Plato's Literary Gardens*, pp. 1–32, especially pp. 27–32.

48. See Plutarch, *Dialogue on Love*, pp. 306–307 (749a), 312–313 (749f), 322–323 (751d–e), 326–327 (752c), 362–363 (758d), 364–365 (758f), 388–389 (762e), 396–397 (764a), 400–401 (764e), 402–403 (765a–b), 410–411 (766b).

49. For expressions of male–male desire in this period's literature, see, for example, the texts usefully collected in Chris White, ed., *Nineteenth-Century Writings on Homosexuality: A Sourcebook* (New York: Routledge, 1999); Louis Crompton, *Byron and Greek Love: Homophobia in 19th-Century England* (Berkeley, CA: University of California Press, 1985); Andrew Elfenbein, *Romantic Genius: The Prehistory of a Homosexual Role* (New York: Columbia University Press, 1999); and the essays collected in Alice A. Kuzniar, ed. *Outing Goethe and His Age* (Stanford, CA: Stanford University Press, 1996). Several essays in the latter volume address the connection drawn between Plato and male–male desire in late-eighteenth and early nineteenth-century German literature: see Kuzniar's Introduction, pp. 1–32, especially pp. 7–8; Martha B. Helfer, " 'Confessions of an Improper Man': Friedrich Schlegel's *Lucinde*," pp. 174–193; Catriona MacLeod, "The 'Third Sex' in an Age of Difference: Androgyny and Homosexuality in Winckelmann, Friedrich Schlegel, and Kleist," pp. 194–214. On Winckelmann, see also Dennis M. Sweet, "The Personal, the Political, and the Aesthetic: Johann Joachim Winckelmann's German Enlightenment Life," in *The Pursuit of Sodomy: Male Homosexuality in Renaissance and Enlightenment Europe*, ed. Kent Gerard and Gert Hekma (New York: Harrington Park Press, 1989), pp. 147–162. None of the texts discussed take the dialogue form.

50. Michael S. Macovski, *Dialogue and Literature: Apostrophe, Auditors, and the Collapse of Romantic Discourse* (Oxford: Oxford University Press, 1994), finds that Romantic poetry appropriates "dialogism" in Bakhtin's sense rather than the dialogue form itself.

51. Plato, *The Banquet*, trans. Percy Bysshe Shelley (Provincetown, MA: Pagan Press, 2001).

52. Ibid., pp. 12–21. Crompton, *Byron*, pp. 284–299, provides a helpful discussion of this essay.

53. See the relevant portions of the "Offenses Against the Person Act" of 1828 and of Edward E. Deacon's 1831 *Digest of the Criminal Law of England*, quoted in White, ed., *Nineteenth-Century Writings*, pp. 27–28.

54. Crompton, *Byron*, pp. 298–299.

55. Ibid., p. 89.

56. Ibid., pp. 89–91.

57. Ibid., p. 285.

58. Quoted in White, ed., *Nineteenth-Century Writings*, p. 44.

59. On Ulrichs, see Hubert C. Kennedy, *Ulrichs: The Life and Work of Karl Heinrich Ulrichs, Pioneer of the Modern Gay Movement* (Boston: Alyson, 1988); on Krafft-Ebing, Harry Oosterhuis, *Step-Children of Nature: Krafft-Ebing, Psychiatry, and the Making of Sexual Identity* (Chicago: University of Chicago Press, 2000); on Hirschfeld, Charlotte Wolff, *Magnus Hirschfeld: A Portrait of a Pioneer in Sexology* (London: Quartet, 1986). White, ed., *Nineteenth-Century Writings*, conveniently collects relevant texts from English sexologists Havelock Ellis, John Addington Symonds, Xavier Mayne, and so on, pp. 66–115, and see Jeffrey Weeks, *Coming Out: Homosexual Politics in Britain from the Nineteenth Century to the Present* (London: Quartet, 1977).

60. White provides a selection of the most influential defenses, *Nineteenth-Century Writings*, pp. 116–235. See especially John Addington Symonds, *A Problem in Greek Ethics* (London: 1883). On the construction and regulation of male–male desire in late nineteenth- and early twentieth-century England, see also Jeffrey Weeks, "Inverts, Perverts, and Mary-Annes: Male Prostitution and the Regulation of Homosexuality in the Nineteenth and Early Twentieth Centuries," in *Hidden From History*, pp. 195–211; Christopher Craft, *Another Kind of Love: Male Homosexual Desire in English Discourse, 1850–1920* (Berkeley: University of California Press, 1994); Jonathan Ned Katz, *The Invention of Heterosexuality* (New York: Dutton, 1995); Francis Mark Mondimore, *A Natural History of Homosexuality* (Baltimore: Johns Hopkins University Press, 1996), pp. 21–95. The syntheses in Greenberg, *Construction of Homosexuality*, pp. 347–433, and Fone, *Homophobia*, pp. 271–315 and 355–394, are also helpful.

61. Linda Dowling, *Hellenism and Homosexuality in Victorian Oxford* (Ithaca, NY: Cornell University Press, 1994), chs. 2 and 3, pp. 32–103.

62. Ibid., p. 80 (emphasis in text), quoting Plato, *Symposium* 209a, in *The Collected Dialogues including the Letters*, ed. Edith Hamilton and Huntington Cairns (Princeton: Princeton University Press, 1961), p. 560.

63. Dowling, *Hellenism*, p. 81.

64. Ibid., p. 124.

65. Nehamas, *Art*, draws this connection in passing, p. 6; see also Halperin, *Saint Foucault*, pp. 73–74.

66. H. Montgomery Hyde, *The Trials of Oscar Wilde*, 2nd ed. (1962), repr. New York: Dover, 1973, p. 201.

67. See Dowling, *Hellenism*, pp. 77–78, on W. E. Gladstone's 1865 address to the students of Edinburgh University on this topic.

68. In Richard Ellmann, ed. *The Artist as Critic: Critical Writings of Oscar Wilde* (1969; rpt. Chicago: University of Chicago Press, 1982), pp. 152–220. This narrative as a whole is concerned with Shakespeare's sonnets; the passage on Michelangelo, with its direct reference to the idealized male–male desire of Plato's *Symposium*, appears on pp. 184–185.

69. Max Beerbohm, letter in *Anglo-American Times*, March 25, 1893, in his *Letters to Reggie Turner*, ed. Rupert Hart-Davies (1964), quoted in Gary Schmidgall, *The Stranger Wilde: Interpreting Oscar* (New York: Dutton, 1994), p. 251.

70. Schmidgall, *The Stranger*, p. 251, citing Frank Harris, *Contemporary Portraits* (1915). Schmidgall develops the comparison with Socrates throughout his book, pp. 29, 177, 251, 313.

71. Richard Ellmann, *Oscar Wilde* (New York: Knopf, 1988), p. 438.

72. I quote the text of this letter from Rupert Hart-Davies, ed., *The Letters of Oscar Wilde* (New York: Harcourt, 1962), p. 326. It is quoted in the context of the trial, in slightly different form, in Hyde, *Trials*, p. 101.

73. Hyde, *Trials*, p. 101.

74. Ibid., p. 116.

75. See Hart-Davies' note to this letter in *Letters*, p. 326, n. 1.

76. See Katz, *Invention*; David M. Halperin, "One Hundred Years of Homosexuality," in his *One Hundred Years of Homosexuality and Other Essays on Greek Love* (New York: Routledge; 1990), pp. 15–40.

77. Alan Sinfield, *The Wilde Century: Effeminacy, Oscar Wilde and the Queer Moment* (New York: Columbia University Press, 1994), p. 122. On Wilde and effeminacy, see also Joseph Bristow, *Effeminate England: Homoerotic Writing after 1885* (New York: Columbia University Press, 1995), pp. 16–54.

78. Sinfield, *Wilde Century*, p. 100.

79. Walter Pater, "Conclusion" to *The Renaissance* (1888), repr. in White, *Nineteenth-Century Writings*, pp. 183–186, at p. 185.

80. Ibid., in White, *Nineteenth-Century Writings*, p. 234, n. 87. Like Wilde, Pater associates himself here with Socrates, the paradigmatic corrupter of youth.

81. Robert Sulcer, "Ten Percent: Poetry and Pathology," in *Victorian Sexual Dissidence*, ed. Richard Dellamora (Chicago: University of Chicago Press, 1999), pp. 235–252, at p. 252, n. 14. Sulcer explicitly connects this association with Wilde.

82. Thaïs E. Morgan, "Victorian Effeminacies," in *Victorian Sexual Dissidence*, pp. 109–125, at p. 118.

83. Dowling, *Hellenism*, p. 140.

84. "The Decay of Lying: An Observation," in Oscar Wilde, *The Major Works*, ed. Isobel Murray, Oxford World's Classics (Oxford: Oxford University Press, 1989), pp. 215–239. Citations of this edition by page numbers will continue to appear in the text. Cf. the *Republic* 379a–391e, pp. 1017–1029. "The Decay of Lying" also refers to Plato on pp. 234 and 238.

85. On the indeterminacy of Wilde's language with regard to sexuality, see also William A. Cohen, "Indeterminate Wilde," in his *Sex Scandal: The Private Parts of Victorian Fiction* (Durham, NC: Duke University Press, 1996), pp. 191–236.

86. See Murray's note, *Major Works*, p. 598.

87. "The Critic as Artist," in *Major Works*, pp. 241–297. Citations of this edition by page numbers will continue to appear in the text.

88. On Alcibiades' role in Plato's *Symposium*, see chapter 2. Two further classical Greek dialogues, probably not by Plato but sometimes attributed to him, are also known by the title *Alcibiades*: see *Alcibiades*, trans. D. S. Hutchinson, and *Second Alcibiades*, trans. Anthony Kenny, in Plato, *Complete Works*, ed. John M. Cooper (Indianapolis: Hackett, 1997), pp. 557–595 and 596–608. Both dialogues suggest a love relationship of some sort between Alcibiades and Socrates. Charmides appears in Plato's dialogue named for him: see *Charmides*, trans. Rosamond Kent Sprague, in *Complete Works*, pp. 639–663.

89. Murray translates καλὸς as "beautiful," *Major Works*, p. 601 n. "Noble" is also a possible translation of καλὸς and the one preferred in *The Works of Oscar Wilde*, ed. G. F. Maine (London: Collins, 1948), pp. 953, n. 1 and 954, n. 1. But on the sort of pottery inscription that presumably inspired this passage, see K. J. Dover, *Greek Homosexuality*, 2nd ed. (Cambridge, MA: Harvard University Press, 1989), pp. 114–122. Dover stipulates that καλὸς when, as here, applied to persons, always means "beautiful," and means "noble" only when applied to ideas or institutions, pp. 15–16. On friendship as an aspect of the late Victorian homoerotic code, see the discussion of Edward Carpenter, below, as well as the passage from Pater's *Renaissance* cited above.

90. The original title of "The Critic as Artist" in its periodical publication ("The True Function and Value of Criticism") was an echo of Arnold's title: see Oscar Wilde, *Major Works*, p. 598.

91. Matthew Arnold, "The Function of Criticism at the Present Time," in his *Essays in Criticism* (London: Macmillan, 1865), pp. 1–41, at p. 22.

92. Ibid., p. 23.

93. Ibid.; emphasis in text.

94. Oscar Wilde, *Major Works*, p. 601.

95. On the contemporary perception of male–male eroticism in Whitman's poetry, see, for example, John Addington Symonds' famous 1890 letter to Whitman, inquiring whether the latter's "Calamus" poems might be understood as referring to "those semi-sexual emotions and actions which no doubt do occur between men[.]" In White, *Nineteenth-Century Writings*, pp. 211–213, at p. 211.

96. Ellmann, *Oscar Wilde*, p. 183. The entire episode is recounted on pp. 183–184. Higginson's attack appeared in the February 4, 1882, issue of *Woman's Journal*. Julia Ward Howe, author of "The Battle Hymn of the Republic," came to Wilde's defense in a letter to the Boston *Evening Transcript*, February 15, 1882.

97. Ellmann, *Oscar Wilde*, p. 183.

98. Ibid.

99. In Hart-Davis, ed., *Letters*, pp. 97–99, at p. 98.

100. Oliver Buckton, " 'Desire Without Limit': Dissident Confession in Oscar Wilde's *De Profundis*," in *Victorian Sexual Dissidence*, pp. 171–87, at p. 174.
101. Richard Ellmann, "Introduction" to *The Artist as Critic*, pp. xviii–xix.
102. Ibid., pp. xix–xx.
103. Jeff Nunokawa, *Tame Passions of Wilde: The Styles of Manageable Desire* (Princeton: Princeton University Press, 2003), p. 117, citing "The Critic as Artist," in Ellmann, ed., *The Artist as Critic*, pp. 273–274.
104. Ibid., p. 118.
105. Ibid., p. 119.
106. Ibid., p. 6.
107. See also Eva Thienpont, " 'To Play Gracefully With Ideas': Oscar Wilde's Personal Platonism in Poetics," *The Wildean* 20 (2000): 37–48.
108. Jonathan Dollimore, *Sexual Dissidence: Augustine to Wilde, Freud to Foucault* (Oxford: Clarendon Press, 1991), p. 68.
109. On Wilde as one of the inventors of modernity, as well as the sign of an abjected homosexuality, see Philip Hoare, *Oscar Wilde's Last Stand: Decadence, Conspiracy, and the Most Outrageous Trial of the Century* (New York: Arcade, 1997).
110. For another discussion of the dialogue genre in these terms by Wilde, see his review entitled "A Chinese Sage [Confucius]" (1890), in Ellmann, ed., *The Artist as Critic*, pp. 221–228, at p. 227. Edward A. Watson, "Wilde's Iconoclastic Classicism: 'The Critic as Artist,' " *English Literature in Transition (1880–1920)* 27 (1984): 225–235 links Wilde's dialogism to Plato's.
111. See White, *Nineteenth-Century Writings*, pp. 165–173.
112. Edward Carpenter, ed., *Iolāus: An Anthology of Friendship* (London: Sonnenschein, 1902; 2nd ed. 1906; 3rd ed. 1915; repr. 1917; repr. New York: Pagan Press, 1982). Selections from Plato can be found on pp. 43–53, selections from Whitman on pp. 188–192. Both Symonds and Carpenter also published studies of Whitman: John Addington Symonds, *Walt Whitman: A Study* (London: John C. Nimmo, 1893); Edward Carpenter, *Days With Walt Whitman* (London: George Allen, 1906). A useful selection of Carpenter's writings is Edward Carpenter, *Selected Writings*, Vol. 1: *Sex* (London: GMP, 1984). For American constructions of homosexuality at the turn of the century, see George Chauncey, *Gay New York: Gender, Urban Culture, and the Making of the Gay Male World, 1890–1940* (New York: Basic Books, 1994).
113. See Richard Howard, "Translator's note" to André Gide, *Corydon*, trans. Richard Howard (Urbana: University of Illinois Press, p. xv), and Alan Sheridan, *André Gide: A Life in the Present* (Cambridge, MA: Harvard University Press, 1999), pp. 248–249, 373.
114. Quotations from Howard's translation will be cited by page number in the text, followed by page citations of the French text: André Gide, *Corydon* (Paris: NRF/Gallimard, 1928, repr. 1947).
115. On contemporary French appropriations of Whitman, see Martin Kanes, "Whitman, Gide, and Bazalgette: An International Encounter," *Comparative Literature* 14 (1962): 341–355.

116. Sheridan, *André Gide*, p. 378.

117. Ibid., p. 376.

118. See Daniel Moutote, "*Corydon* en 1918," *Bulletin des amis d'André Gide* 16 (78–79) (April–July, 1988): 9–24. Gide aligned himself with Freud rather than with any of the earlier sexologists: see, for example, Sheridan, *André Gide*, p. 353. On Freud and the shifting models of homosexuality at the turn of the century, see Henry Abelove, "Freud, Male Homosexuality, and the Americans," in *The Lesbian and Gay Studies Reader*, ed. Henry Abelove, Michèle Aina Barale, and David M. Halperin (New York: Routledge, 1993), pp. 381–393; Sandor L. Gilman, "Sigmund Freud and the Sexologists: A Second Reading," in *Reading Freud's Reading*, ed. Sander L. Gilman et al. (New York: New York University Press, 1994), pp. 47–76. On the construction and regulation of homosexuality in twentieth-century France, see *Homosexuality in Modern France*, ed. Jeffrey Merrick and Bryant T. Ragan, Jr. (Oxford: Oxford University Press, 1996).

119. Michael Lucey, *Gide's Bent: Sexuality, Politics, Writing* (Oxford: Oxford University Press, 1995), also places *Corydon* in the context of the dialogue genre (see p. 70), and specifically in the context of Wilde's two dialogues (p. 81, n. 23); he also finds a sexual tension between the two interlocutors comparable to that which I find between the speakers in "The Critic as Artist" (pp. 90–91).

120. The text of the poem read in court can be found in Hyde, *The Trials*, p. 200.

121. Especially in Jonathan Fryer, *André and Oscar: The Literary Friendship of André Gide and Oscar Wilde* (New York: St. Martin's, 1997); but see also Alan Sheridan, *André Gide: A Life in the Present* (Cambridge, MA: Harvard University Press, 1999), especially pp. 75–77 and 116–120; and Colm Tóibín, "Oscar Wilde: Love in a Dark Time," in his *Love in a Dark Time and Other Explorations of Gay Lives and Literature* (New York: Scribner, 2001), pp. 37–85. For analyses of the two writers' views on sexuality, see also Dollimore, pp. 3–18, and Lucey, *Gide's Bent*, especially pp. 8–13.

122. Fryer, *André and Oscar*, pp. 229–31.

123. On the ironies of Gide's use of the dialogue form in this way, see Lucey, *Gide's Bent*, p. 77; Christine Ligier, "Discours de l'autre et discours du moi: l'ironie gidienne dans *Si le grain ne meurt* et *Corydon*," *Revue des lettres modernes* 1362–1370 (1998): 257–265. *Corydon* is discussed at pp. 262–265. On the very real concerns that caused Gide's hesitation to publish *Corydon*, see Sheridan, *André Gide*, pp. 237, 319, 376.

124. Sheridan, *André Gide*, p. 76.

125. André Gide, *Correspondance avec sa mère 1880–1896* (Paris: Gallimard, 1988), pp. 587–588, quoted in Sheridan, *André Gide*, p. 116.

126. Dollimore, *Dissidence*, p. 18. Lucille Cairns, "Gide's *Corydon*: The Politics of Sexuality and Sexual Politics," *Modern Language Review* 91 (1996): 582–596 condemns Gide's apparent conservatism with regard to effeminacy and to women.

127. Dollimore, *Dissidence*, p. 18.

128. See Julia Kristeva, "From One Identity to an Other," in her *Desire in Language: A Semiotic Approach to Literature and Art*, ed. Leon S. Roudiez, trans. Thomas Gora, Alice Jardine, and Leon S. Roudiez (New York: Columbia University Press, 1980), pp. 124–147, at p. 135.

129. Lucey, *Gide's Bent*, makes a similar point, though he finds that Gide himself possesses only a "half-conscious knowledge that pushes toward a realization that gender systems never really allow for clean distinctions and that there is no nonideological, no 'natural' way to read back to sex or instinct after having been trained in gender" (p. 94).

130. Sheridan, *André Gide*, pp. 303–304. Gide was in fact, like Wilde, regarded by some of his contemporaries as a Socratic figure: see ibid., pp. 626–627.

131. On this paradox, see Patrick Pollard, "L'Idéal de *Corydon*," *La Revue des lettres modernes* 1033–1038 (série André Gide 9) (1991): 61–82, which argues that the tension between the natural ideal of pleasure and the Platonic ideal of self-restraint remains unresolved in *Corydon*.

132. See, for example, M. M. Bakhtin, "Epic and Novel: Toward a Methodology for the Study of the Novel," in his *The Dialogic Imagination*, ed. Michael Holquist, trans. Caryl Emerson and Michael Holquist (Austin: University of Texas Press, 1981), pp. 3–40.

133. And Samuel R. Delany's brilliant erotic novel of 1973, *Equinox*, in its turn echoes Sade's dialogue when the characters interrupt elaborate orgy scenes with philosophical speeches, just as Dolmancé does in *La Philosophie dans le boudoir*. See Samuel R. Delany, *Equinox* (1973; repr. New York, Rhinoceros, 1994), pp. 118–122 and 145–148.

134. "Well, Socrates did what you've just done. . . . Jacques, you're a sort of philosopher, admit it." Denis Diderot, *Jacques the Fatalist and His Master*, trans. Michael Henry (Harmondsworth: Penguin, 1986), p. 80; cf. *Jacques le fataliste et son maître* in Denis Diderot, *Oeuvres romanesques*, ed. Henri Bénac (Paris: Garnier, 1962), pp. 493–780, at p. 563.

135. "Do you take me for my Captain's mistress?" *Jacques the Fatalist*, p. 60; *Jacques le fataliste*, p. 539.

136. Schmidgall, The Stranger, p. 29.

137. See *The Portrait of Dorian Gray* in Wilde, *Major Works*, ed. Murray, pp. 47–214, at pp. 59–71 (ch. 2), 153–154 (self-division), 132–133 and 164–165 (beloved as divine), 128–130 (life as art).

138. See George Bridges, "The Problem of Pederastic Love in Thomas Mann's *Death in Venice* and Plato's *Phaedrus*," *Selecta: Journal of the Pacific Northwest Council on Foreign Languages* 7 (1986): 39–46.

139. Thomas Mann, *Death in Venice*, trans. Stanley Applebaum (New York: Dover, 1995). Citations of this translation by page number will appear in the text. I prefer this recent translation as more complete and accurate than the more familiar version by H. T. Lowe-Porter. German citations follow Thomas Mann, *Der Tod in Venedig*, in his *Der Tod in Venedig und andere Erzählungen* (Frankfurt am Main: Fischer, 1954), pp. 7–66, by page number.

140. Robert Aldrich, *The Seduction of the Mediterranean: Writing, Art and Homosexual Fantasy* (New York: Routledge, 1993); *Death in Venice*—Mann's novella, Visconti's film, and Britten's opera—is discussed on pp. 1–12, and provides a keynote for the entire study. On Mann's "homosexuality," see Robert Tobin, "The Life and Work of Thomas Mann: A Gay Perspective," in Thomas Mann, *Death in Venice*, ed. Naomi Ritter (New York: Bedford, 1998), pp. 225–244. On the experience that inspired the novella, see Katia Mann, *Meine ungeschriebenen Memoiren*, ed. Elisabeth Plessen and Michael Mann (Frankfurt am Main: Fischer, 1974); she identifies the youth who inspired Mann as the young Polish aristocrat Wladislaw Moes, pp. 70–72. Gilbert Adair, *The Real Tadzio: Thomas Mann's "Death in Venice" and the Boy who Inspired It* (New York: Carroll and Graf, 2003) reviews the evidence. See also Doris Alexander, *Creating Literature Out of Life: The Making of Four Masterpieces* (University Park, PA: Pennsylvania State University Press, 1996), pp. 7–21. On Mann's view of his own homosexuality, see Colm Tóibín, "Thomas Mann: Exit Pursued by Biographers," in his *Love in a Dark Time*, pp. 111–130.

141. On the medical aspects of the novella, see Laura Otis, "The Tigers of Wrath: Mann's *Death in Venice* as Myth and Medicine," in *Teaching Literature and Medicine*, ed. Anne Hunsaker Hawkins and Marilyn Chandler McEntyre (New York: MLA, 2000), pp. 243–251.

142. Eve Kosofsky Sedgwick, "Some Binarisms (II): Wilde, Nietzsche, and the Sentimental Relations of the Male Body," in her *Epistemology of the Closet* (Berkeley: University of California Press, 1990), pp. 131–181, links Nietzsche to Wilde, decadence, and male–male desire.

143. See the commentary appended to Applebaum's translation, *Death in Venice*, pp. 72–73.

144. Aschenbach imagines Tadzio as a god-figure at several points, for instance as Eros (*Death in Venice*, p. 23; p. 28).

145. On the relationship of form to erotic abjection, see Edward S. Brinkley, "Fear of Form: Thomas Mann's *Der Tod in Venedig*," *Monatshefte* 91.1 (1999): 2–27.

146. A recent comic reimagining of *Death in Venice*, Gilbert Adair's novel *Love and Death on Long Island* (New York: Grove, 1990), goes even further and eschews dialogue altogether; it might be seen as an antidialogue in its self-conscious exclusion of any voice other than that of the narrator.

147. A doctor who fails to cure Maurice of his homosexuality suggests at one point that he might try living abroad, "in some country that has adopted the Code Napoléon," for example France or Italy (p. 211), and Forster feared that the harsher laws of England would never change: see also his "Terminal Note," p. 255.

148. E. M. Forster, *Maurice* (New York: Norton, 1971). Page numbers of this edition will be cited in the text.

149. On Forster's rejection of Plato, see Debrah Raschke, "Breaking the Engagement with Philosophy: Re-Envisioning Hetero/Homo Relations in

Maurice," in *Queer Forster*, ed. Robert K. Martin and George Piggford (Chicago: University of Chicago Press, 1997), pp. 151–165.

150. See Robert K. Martin, "Edward Carpenter and the Double Structure of *Maurice*," *Journal of Homosexuality* 8 (1983): 35–46. John Fletcher, "Forster's Self-Erasure: *Maurice* and the Scene of Masculine Love," in *Sexual Sameness: Textual Differences in Lesbian and Gay Writing*, ed. Joseph Bristow (New York: Routledge: 1992), pp. 64–90 situates *Maurice* in its turn-of-the-century intellectual context, including both Carpenter and Symonds.

151. Tariq Rahman, "E. M. Forster and the Break Away from the Ephebophobic Literary Tradition," *Etudes Anglaises* 40 (1987): 267–278 argues that same-age and different-age desire are equally natural in Forster's scheme.

152. On the novel's homosexual-pastoral aspect, see Anne Hartree, " 'A Passion that Few English Minds Have Admitted': Homosexuality and Englishness in E. M. Forster's *Maurice*," *Paragraph* 19 (1996): 127–138; Ira Bruce Nadel, "Moments in the Greenwood: *Maurice* in Context," in *E. M. Forster: Centenary Revaluations*, ed. Judith Scherer and Robert K. Martin (Toronto: University of Toronto Press, 1982), pp. 177–190.

153. See Byrne R. S. Fone, *A Road to Stonewall: Male Homosexuality and Homophobia in English and American Literature, 1750–1969* (New York: Twayne, 1995), p. 173; Matthew Curr, "Recuperating E. M. Forster's *Maurice*," *Modern Language Quarterly* 62 (2001): 53–69; Jon Harned, "Becoming Gay in E. M. Forster's *Maurice*," *Papers on Language and Literature* 29 (1993): 49–66.

154. See Bernard F. Dick, *The Hellenism of Mary Renault* (Carbondale, IL: Southern Illinois University Press, 1972), pp. 30–37, on Renault's symbolic use of the *Phaedrus* in *The Charioteer*; my reading differs from Dick's substantially. And cf. David Sweetman, *Mary Renault: A Biography* (New York: Harcourt Brace, 1993), pp. 143–144.

155. Mary Renault, *The Charioteer* (1953; repr. New York: Pantheon, 1959). Quotations from this edition, cited by page number, will appear in the text.

156. Sinfield, *The Wilde Century*, p. 143. The passage that Sinfield quotes to illustrate this point, in which Renault in turn quotes Plato, is, however, drawn not from the *Phaedrus* but from Phaedrus' speech on the army of lovers in the *Symposium*. Sinfield's point is nevertheless correct; everywhere else in the novel, it is the *Phaedrus* that provides its characters with the manly alternative to an abjected effeminacy.

157. Ibid., p. 144.

158. Ibid., pp. 144–145.

159. Concerning the novel's multiple perspectives on homosexuality, see Caroline Zilboorg, *The Masks of Mary Renault* (Columbia, MO: University of Missouri Press, 2001), pp. 112–115.

160. Sinfield, *The Wilde Century*, p. 145.

161. Ibid.

162. Robert M. Pirsig, *Zen and the Art of Motorcycle Maintenance: An Inquiry Into Values*. Twenty-fifth Anniversary Edition (New York: HarperCollins/Perennial,

1999). Quotations from this edition, which makes some crucial typographical changes from the 1974 edition, will be cited by page number in the text.

163. Beverly Gross, " 'A Mind Divided Against Itself': Madness in *Zen and the Art of Motorcycle Maintenance*," *Journal of Narrative Technique* 14 (1984): 201–213 argues that the process of self-unification involves the "integration" of the Phaedrus personality, p. 213.

164. Geoffrey Galt Harpham, "Rhetoric and the Madness of Philosophy in Plato and Pirsig," *Contemporary Literature* 29 (1988): 64–81 suggests that what the original Phaedrus himself could not abide in Socrates was "his tolerance of dialogism," p. 80.

CONCLUSION: DEVIANT EROTICS FROM PLATO TO THE POSTMODERN

1. Because the so-called "Defense of Marriage Act" had already been signed into law by President Clinton, many observers understood President Bush's remarks on the possibility of further legislation enshrining this definition as supportive of a Constitutional amendment. For a representative example, see Cynthia Tucker's syndicated column: "Leave the Constitution Alone," *The Times-Picayune* (New Orleans), August 9, 2003, B-7. Eventually the President's support for such an amendment became explicit.

2. Frank Bruni, "Vatican Exhorts Legislators to Reject Same-Sex Unions," *The New York Times*, August 1, 2003, A1, A14, at A14, quoting "Considerations."

3. Ibid., A1.

4. Ronald Johnson, "Church right on gay marriage," *The Times-Picayune* (New Orleans), August 1, 2003, B-6. Another letter on the same topic, on the other hand, declares that "[t]olerating the Vatican's pronouncements feels to me more like tolerating the perpetuation of ignorance." Sarah Edell, "Love is love," ibid.

5. John Cameron Mitchell and Stephen Trask, *Hedwig and the Angry Inch* (Woodstock, NY: Overlook, 2000); page numbers of this edition will be cited in the text. *Hedwig and the Angry Inch*, written by John Cameron Mitchell and Stephen Trask, directed by John Cameron Mitchell (New Line Cinema/Killer Films, 2001), New Line Platinum Series DVD N5401, 2001.

6. The published version of *Hedwig* reprints Aristophanes' speech—but nothing else from the *Symposium*—in Jowett's translation, as an appendix, pp. 81–85. Holly M. Sypniewski, "The Nature of Love is *Hedwig and the Angry Inch* and Plato's *Symposium*," a paper delivered at the 2004 South Central Modern Language Association Convention in New Orleans (October 30, 2004), finds allusions to other speeches in the *Symposium* to be as important in *Hedwig* as its citation of Aristophanes.

7. For an intelligent theorization of the transsexual as neither female nor male, see Kate Bornstein, *Gender Outlaw* (New York: Vintage, 1995). Bornstein is also the coauthor, with Caitlin Sullivan, of *Nearly Roadkill* (New York: Serpent's Tail/High Risk, 1996), a highly dialogical e-mail novel about the transsexual possibilities of cyberspace.

8. Eve Kosofsky Sedgwick, *A Dialogue on Love* (Boston: Beacon, 1999); page numbers of this edition will be cited in the text.

9. Both Sedgwick's weaving and her interest in Buddhism have been the object of recent critical discussion: see Stephen M. Barber and David L. Clark, "Queer Moments: The Performative Temporalities of Eve Kosofsky Sedgwick," the introduction to *Regarding Sedgwick: Essays on Queer Culture and Critical Theory*, ed. Stephen M. Barber and David L. Clark (New York: Routledge, 2002), pp. 1–53, at pp. 5, 45. See also Barber's and Clark's interview with Sedgwick, "This Piercing Bouquet: An Interview with Eve Kosofsky Sedgwick," in *Regarding Sedgwick*, pp. 243–262, at pp. 250, 258–259, 261, and, on weaving and Buddhism in relation to *A Dialogue on Love*, Nancy K. Miller, "Reviewing Eve," in *Regarding Sedgwick*, pp. 217–225.

10. This is, of course, a foundational principle of Queer Theory, the mode of inquiry that Sedgwick herself was largely responsible for creating. See her masterly book *Epistemology of the Closet* (Berkeley: University of California Press, 1990), especially the chapters entitled "Some Binarisms (I)," and "Some Binarisms (II)," pp. 91–181.

11. Miller, "Reviewing," suggests that Sedgwick wishes to "transform, as she comes to see in therapy, the childhood drama of loneliness and isolation into a passionate project of community," p. 219.

12. Miller, "Reviweing," notes Shannon's "increased presence on the page in the last chapters," p. 220.

13. Deborah P. Britzman, "Theory Kindergarten," in *Regarding Sedgwick*, pp. 121–142, at p. 137. Compare Barber's and Clark's characterization of *A Dialogue on Love*, and Sedgwick's agreement, in "This Piercing Bouquet," p. 258.

Index

Names are indexed here in their most common modern English spellings. Titles of primary sources are indexed under the names of their respective authors. Complete bibliographical information for all works cited will be found in the first endnote for that work (in the case of primary sources) or author (in the case of secondary sources).